GOOD
HOUSEKEEPING
Home Freezer
Cook Book

GOOD HOUSEKEEPING
Home Freezer
Cook Book

compiled by
GOOD HOUSEKEEPING
INSTITUTE

E BURY PRESS
LONDON

Published in Great Britain
by Ebury Press
Chestergate House, Vauxhall Bridge Road,
London SW1V 1HF

First impression 1972
Second impression 1972
Third impression 1973
Fourth impression 1973
Fifth impression 1973
Sixth impression 1974
Seventh impression 1974
Eighth impression 1975
Ninth impression 1976
Tenth impression 1977

ISBN 0 85223 019 2

Photographs by Rex Bamber and Kenneth Swain

Filmset and printed in Great Britain by
BAS Printers Ltd, Wallop, Hampshire
and bound by
Webb, Son & Co Ltd, London and Ferndale

Contents

Colour Plates

Foreword

The experts at Good Housekeeping Institute spent many months investigating all aspects of home freezing, to find out how to make the best and most economical use of a freezer. We cooked, froze and thawed until we were sure we could present you with a collection of interesting, mouth-watering, yet practical recipes, together with everything you need to know about home freezing.

After using freezers for everyday cooking and party menus, for emergency meals and for many other situations, we really can't think of anyone a freezer isn't meant for. If you've already got yours, you won't need convincing. If you haven't, *get* one—and you'll soon be wondering how you survived until now without it.

Margaret Coombes, Good Housekeeping Institute's Cookery Editor, assisted by Diana Stabbins and Sallie Glaister, is responsible for the cookery expertise in this book. Shirley Green wrote the text.

If we haven't answered the one thing you want to know about home freezing —write to us at Good Housekeeping Institute, Chestergate House, Vauxhall Bridge Road, London SW1V 1HF.

Carol Macartney
Director

Why Home Freezing?

Why home freezing? Ask any busy mum. She'll tell you how she does the shopping in one fell fortnightly swoop, forgetting those almost daily super-market treks with the kids practically swinging from the shelves and trying to grab everything in sight. Ask any children, and they'll tell you how smashing it is to have ice cream on tap, favourite cakes and puddings at the ready, and a mother who's actually got time to play with them. Ask any working-wife. She'll tell you how marvellous it is to have a lunch-hour, instead of racing round the shops like a lunatic and staggering home with a bursting carrier bag. What's more, she'll tell you how she cooks in one grand weekly slam, so she can spend the evenings with her husband instead of vanishing to the kitchen the minute she gets in, and only re-appearing for meals and bed-times. Ask any wife who does a lot of business entertaining. She'll tell you worrying's a thing of the past, because she can be sure the meal's a success by cooking it in advance—and if her husband rings up with an 'Er . . . I forgot to tell you, but the boss is coming to dinner tonight', she can 'sweetly' rattle off a few sumptuous menus for him to choose from. Ask anyone who's budgeting hard—and that probably means all of us. She'll tell you how she saves up to one-third on ordinary retail prices by buying in bulk, and can snap up every 'bargain offer' as soon as she spots it.

Ask anyone you like—but be prepared for embarrassingly effusive answers. Phrases like 'My freezer's changed my whole life', or 'If I could only take one thing with me I'd take the freezer' really will trip off their tongues like something from a TV commercial. But unlike a TV commercial, they'll trip off with total conviction. Freezers aren't just for farmers' wives, battling with gluts of plums and bumper runner-bean crops, or hardy Amazons hacking at meat carcases with fearsome-looking cleavers. And they aren't just for people trying to save time and money, either. They're for anyone who's an erratic cook, long-ing to beat cake-mixtures and roll pastry when the mood takes her, but treat-ing the whole thing as a dreary chore when it doesn't. They're for anyone who dreads being caught on the hop, whether by an unexpected illness or an un-expected guest. They're for anyone who can't get used to cooking miserably small quantities once the children have left home, but can't get used to plodding through the left-overs, either. They're for anyone who lives at the end of an isolated country lane, and knows how monotonous corned beef and baked beans can get after a few days of being snowed up. Above all, they're for anyone who cares about the *quality* of her food. When you freeze anything you can catch it at its peak of freshness—and it will come out every bit as fresh as the day it went in.

Golden Rules For Freezing

Whatever kind of food you're dealing with, these general notes apply. For detailed instructions, please turn to the appropriate section—see Contents page and Index.

1. Always start with good-quality foods and freeze them at peak freshness. Food can only come out of the freezer as good as you put it in.
2. Keep handling to a minimum and make sure everything is scrupulously clean. Freezing doesn't kill bacteria and germs.
3. Pay special attention to packaging and sealing. Exposure to air and moisture damage frozen foods.
4. Cool food rapidly if it's been cooked or blanched; never put anything hot—or even warm—into your freezer.
5. Freeze as quickly as possible, and in small quantities.
6. Freeze in the coldest part of the freezer, and don't pack the food to be frozen too closely together—spread it out until it is frozen.
7. Transfer newly added items to the main part of the cabinet once they've been frozen.
8. Remember to return the switch from "accelerated" to "normal" once newly added foods have been frozen, i.e., after about 24 hours.
9. Maintain a steady storage temperature of -18°C (0°F), and don't do anything that will cause temperatures within the freezer to keep fluctuating.
10. Label and date food so that you can ensure a good rotation of stock. Ideally, keep a record and tick off items as you eat them, then you can tell at a glance which supplies are getting low.
11. Defrost the freezer at a time when stocks are low, and if possible on a cold day
12. Be prepared for emergencies. Make sure you know what steps to take in case of a breakdown or power cut.

When you're Freezing Cooked Foods

1. When preparing a dish for the freezer, keep a light hand with the seasoning.
2. Use shallow rather than deep dishes
3. As already directed above, cool everything as rapidly as possible, and freeze at once.
4. To ensure best results, don't keep cooked dishes in the freezer for more than two months, unless otherwise stated.

SPECIAL WARNING: Remember, polythene bags or film must always be removed before food is re-heated.

PART 1

Cooking for the Freezer

In this section you will find all our freezer recipes, and menus incorporating the recipes. If you want to look up a point about packaging or any other matter of technique or background information, turn to Part 2. The choice of freezers and a description of the way they work are covered in Part 3.

1. Family Meals

Here we offer a handful of Breakfast Ideas, followed by menus to cope with a variety of family situations. To help you pick out the one that will meet your needs, we give a list of the menus, with the freezer recipes starred.

Just for Two

Grapefruit Segments in Syrup*
Veal in Sherry Sauce*
Parsley Rice
Orange and Chicory Salad
Caramel Custard* with Cream

Beef Balls* in Tomato Sauce*
Creamed Potatoes
Sliced Green Beans*
Cheese Board   Celery Sticks

Cheese Pudding*
Tomato and Onion Salad
French Dressing*
Raspberry Mousse*

Egg Mayonnaise
Pork Chops with Pineapple and Pepper Sauce*
Broccoli Spears
Duchesse Potatoes*
Lemon Sorbet*

Put Your Feet Up

Fresh Grapefruit Halves
Individual Steak and Kidney Puddings*
Creamed Potatoes
Glazed Carrots   Green Peas*
Cherry Chocolate Log*

Melon and Ginger Cocktail*
Chicken Hash*   Rice with Pimiento
Tomato and Chive Salad
Coffee Cream Ring*

Haddock and Mushroom Flan*
Haricots Verts*
Sweet Corn with Pimiento*
Apple Cheesecake*

Oeufs à la Maison*
Grilled Pork Chops*
Buttered Celery with
Carrots and Peas
Minted New Potatoes
Chocolate Pear Upside-Down Pudding*

Chilled Orange Juice*
Beef El Dorado*
Spring Greens   Sauté Potatoes
Pear and Lemon Crumble*
Pouring Custard or Cream

Easy Weekends

Cream of Carrot Soup*
Hot Sausage Flan*
Baked Jacket Potatoes
Tomato and Cucumber Salad
Iced Zabaione*

Lancashire Hot-pot*
Wedges of Savoy Cabbage
Glazed Carrot Slices
Choco-Liqueur*

Grilled Grapefruit Cups
Cheese-crusted Beef Roll*
Tomato Garnish   Leaf Spinach
Apple Fool*   Sponge Fingers

Florida Cocktail
Chicken Paprika*   Fluffy Rice*
Courgettes with Parsley Butter
Lemon Crumb Pie*

Melon Balls or Wedges
Chicken Chablis*
Parsleyed New Potatoes
Broad Beans
Apple Dumplings*
with Clotted Cream

Holiday Time

Cream of Mushroom Soup*
Ham Roll-ups*   Cheese Sauce*
Whole Baked Tomatoes
Baby Sprouts   Potato Crisps
Coffee Crunch Flan*

Cream of Vegetable Soup*   Bread Sticks
Cheesy Haddock Roll*
Potato Nests*   Buttered Peas*
Apple Snow*   Sponge Fingers

Cream of Celery Soup*   Croûtons*
Sweet-sour Gammon*
Casseroled Rice
Green Salad   French Dressing*
Strawberries and Cream*

Cream of Avocado Soup* with Croûtons*
Beef with Horseradish*
Rice with Paprika
Baked Tomato Halves
Buttered Spinach
Lattice Almond Sponge*   Custard*

Husband on His Own

Kidneys in Red Wine*
Creamed Potatoes
Tossed Green Salad
Whole Peaches in Syrup*

Grapefruit Juice*
Upside-down Beef and Potato Pie*
Buttered Savoy Cabbage
Individual Caramel Custards*
with Pouring Cream

Grapefruit Juice*
Barbecued Spare Ribs*
Casseroled Rice
Dressed Chicory
Iced Strawberry Mousse*

Out All Day

Chilled Minted Tomato Juice
Cornish Pasties*
Chunky Green Beans with Butter
Cornish Ice Cream
Hot Chocolate Sauce*

Veal and Leek Pie*
Glazed Vegetables
Fruit and Nut Ice Cream Sundae*

Broccoli Soup*
Lamb Parcels with Fruit Sauce*
Duchesse Potatoes*
Green Beans or Young Whole Carrots
Chocolate Eclairs*

Cream of Carrot Soup* Bread Sticks
Liver Balls en Casserole*
Duchesse Potatoes*
Green Beans*
Cinnamon-Apple Pie*

Lamb and Aubergine Casserole*
Jacket Potatoes
Cauliflower Florets
Apple Crumble*   Pouring Custard

BREAKFAST IDEAS

If you're bleary-eyed and bungling first thing in the morning, freeze several breakfasts later in the day, when you're feeling more human. Then you'll manage a smile over *tomorrow's* breakfast table.

Prune and orange compote

(*see picture opposite*)

1 lb. dried prunes
6 large oranges
4 oz. caster sugar
3 level tbsps. golden syrup
juice of 1 lemon
2 tbsps. apricot brandy

Serves 4–6

TO MAKE: Place the washed prunes in a large saucepan, cover with water and bring to the boil. Reduce the heat and simmer for about 20 min., until the prunes are really tender; drain. Peel and segment the oranges, removing all traces of pith, and reserving the juice. Make up the juice with water to $\frac{3}{4}$ pt., put into a saucepan and add the sugar, syrup and lemon juice. Stir until the sugar has dissolved, then boil rapidly until the syrup is reduced by half. Remove from the heat and allow to get cold before adding the apricot brandy. Pour over the fruit.

TO PACK AND FREEZE: Use two 4-portion ($1\frac{1}{4}$ pt.) size shallow foil containers. Leave uncovered until solid. Cover with a lid or double foil, seal and label.

TO USE: Thaw overnight in the refrigerator. Serve in individual dishes.

Fresh grapefruit in sugar syrup

6 large grapefruit
1 lb. caster or granulated sugar

Serves 8–10

TO MAKE: Peel and segment the grapefruit over a bowl to retain the juice; remove all trace of pith and membrane. Drain the juice from the fruit and make up to 1 pt. with water. Place the liquid in a large saucepan with the sugar and stir over a low heat until dissolved; bring to the boil, stirring. Remove from the heat and allow to get cold.

TO PACK AND FREEZE: Divide the grapefruit segments into 2 portions and place each in a polythene bag lining a rigid square container. Add just enough cold syrup to cover the fruit. Freeze uncovered until solid; seal and label.

TO USE: Remove the fruit from the freezer the night before it is required and thaw by placing in a bowl in the refrigerator. (You can turn it into a tangy appetiser by serving it with a little finely chopped stem ginger.)

Breakfast juices

TOMATO
Peel 4 lb. ripe tomatoes, then purée in an electric blender or use a juicer. Afterwards put the purée through a fine nylon or hair sieve. The yield should be approx. $2\frac{1}{4}$ pts. thick tomato juice.

TO PACK: Pour into waxed containers or pre-formed polythene bags. Seal and label.

TO FREEZE: Freeze until solid.

TO USE: Thaw, unopened, in the refrigerator for about 16 hr., or at a warm room temperature for about 5 hr.

GRAPEFRUIT
Squeeze the juice from 4 average-size grapefruit—it should be about $1\frac{1}{4}$ pts. Freeze as above, unsweetened. Thaw as above.

ORANGE
Squeeze the juice from 6 average-size juicy oranges—about $1\frac{1}{2}$ pts. Freeze unsweetened, as above; thaw as above.

Note: Fruit juices are best packed in $\frac{1}{2}$-pt. quantities, to reduce the thawing time.

Kedgeree

(*see picture on right*)

1 lb. smoked haddock fillet
6 oz. long-grain rice, freshly cooked
4 oz. butter
3 hard-boiled eggs—shelled and chopped
2 level tbsps. chopped parsley
$\frac{1}{8}$ level tsp. cayenne pepper
$\frac{1}{4}$ level tsp. salt

Serves 8

TO MAKE: Gently poach the haddock in boiling water for 7–10 min. until the flesh is tender. Drain, skin and flake the fish. Combine the fluffy rice, fish, 1 oz. butter, chopped hard-boiled egg, parsley and seasonings together. Allow to cool.

TO PACK AND FREEZE: Divide the kedgeree into two. Dot the base of 2 4-portion-size (1$\frac{1}{4}$-pt.) foil freezer dishes with the remaining butter. Spoon the kedgeree over, seal and label. Freeze in the usual way.

TO USE: Loosen the coverings but leave in position. Heat through in the oven at 400°F (mark 6) for about 45 min., forking through occasionally. Pile onto a hot serving dish and garnish with parsley sprigs or lemon wedges.

Muesli

(*see picture above*)

8 oz. seedless raisins
4 oz. rolled oats
2 oz. hazelnuts, roasted and chopped
1 oz. nibbed almonds
1 lb. crisp eating apples
juice of 1 lemon
4 level tbsps. clear honey

Serves 8

TO MAKE: Put the raisins, oats and nuts in a bowl and mix thoroughly. Peel and core the apples; place in cold water with the lemon juice. Roughly dice into pieces of manageable size, and blanch in boiling water for 1 min., then rapidly cool and dry. Add the honey to

Kedgeree with Muesli (*left*) *and Prune and orange compote*

the oats, etc., then, using the fingertips, rub in as for pastry. Add the apples and blend all together.

TO PACK: Divide the mixture into the number of servings required and pack each portion in a polythene bag. Seal and label.

TO FREEZE: Freeze until solid.

TO USE: Thaw in the sealed bag overnight in the refrigerator. Turn the muesli into serving dishes, and spoon some top of the milk or single cream over the top.

Waffles

6 oz. plain flour
$\frac{1}{8}$ level tsp. salt
3 level tsps. baking powder
1 oz. vanilla caster sugar
2 eggs, separated
$\frac{1}{2}$ pt. milk
2 oz. butter, melted

Makes 6 whole waffles

TO MAKE: Sift the flour, salt and baking powder into a basin. Stir in the sugar. Make a well in the centre and add the egg yolks.

Alternately add the milk and the melted butter, beating until a smooth batter is obtained. Lastly, whip the egg whites very stiffly and fold in lightly. Pour a little of the batter into a heated and lightly greased waffle iron, cook for 3–4 min., take out and leave to cool. Repeat with rest of mixture.

TO PACK: When cold, freeze in polythene bags. Seal and label.

TO FREEZE: Freeze until solid.

TO USE: Remove the frozen waffles from the package, lay on a baking sheet, cover with foil and 'refresh' in the oven at 375°F (mark 5) for about 10 min. Serve with clear honey, maple syrup or softened butter.

Date muffins

7 oz. plain flour
1 level tsp. salt
6 level tsps. baking powder
4 oz. wheatgerm
1 pt. less 6 tbsps. milk
3 oz. blended white vegetable fat
3 oz. caster sugar
2 eggs, beaten
8 oz. stoned dates, chopped

Makes 24

TO MAKE: Grease muffin pans or deep-sided bun tins. Sift together the flour, salt and baking powder. Soak the wheatgerm in milk for 5 min. Cream the fat and sugar together, add the eggs and stir until blended. Stir in the wheatgerm and dates. Add the flour, stirring until just mixed—no longer. Fill the muffin pans two-thirds full. Bake at 400°F (mark 6) for about 25 min., until well risen and spongy to the touch. Cool on a wire rack.

TO PACK: Pack in groups as required, using polythene bags. Seal and label.

TO FREEZE: Freeze until solid.

TO USE: Remove from the bag, place on baking trays, cover with foil and 'refresh' in the oven at 375°F (mark 5) for about 30 min. Serve warm, split and generously buttered.

Wholemeal baps

1 level tbsp. brown sugar
$\frac{3}{4}$ pt. warm water (110°F)
1 level tbsp. dried yeast
1 level tsp. salt
1 tbsp. vegetable oil
1 lb. 8 oz. Allinson's 100% wholewheat
  stoneground flour

Makes 12

TO MAKE: Dissolve 1 level tsp. of the measured sugar in $\frac{1}{4}$ pt. of the measured water. Sprinkle the yeast on top, whisk, and leave in a warm place for 15 min., until frothy. Dissolve the rest of the sugar and the salt in $\frac{1}{2}$ pt. of water. Add the oil and stir into the flour, together with yeast mixture. Mix thoroughly to a smooth dough, turn onto a floured surface and knead for 5 min. Place the dough inside an oiled polythene bag and leave in a warm place for 20 min., until doubled in size. Re-knead the dough for a further 5 min. Divide into 12 pieces and knead each piece into a ball. Roll each ball into a flat round. Dust the tops with flour, place on greased baking trays, cover with greased polythene and leave to prove for 15 min., until again doubled in size. Remove the polythene. Pre-heat the oven to 475°F (mark 9). Reduce to 425°F (mark 7) and bake the baps for about 10 min. Cool on a wire rack covered by a tea towel.

TO PACK: Place the freshly baked but cold baps in polythene bags, seal and label.

TO FREEZE: Freeze until firm. Store for up to 4 weeks.

TO USE: Put the frozen baps on a baking sheet, cover with foil and 'refresh' in the oven at 450°F (mark 8) for about 15 min., or leave at room temperature for about $1\frac{1}{2}$ hr.

Tête-à-têtes become far more intimate if you sit down to dinner cool and collected instead of hot and flustered from last-minute panics. A freezer may look unromantic—but it's a good way of keeping romance in a marriage.

Menu for two

Grapefruit segments in syrup
Veal in sherry sauce   *Parsley rice*   *Orange and chicory salad*
Caramel custard with cream

THE PLAN

The recipe for the grapefruit is on page 14. Allow it to thaw out overnight in the refrigerator. For the caramel custard see page 51; serve it warm, with pouring cream. The main course (recipe here) is cooked from frozen, and needs 35–40 min. at 375°F (mark 5). Place 4 oz. long-grain rice in a small casserole, pour over it ½ pt. boiling water, add some salt, cover, and cook alongside the veal for about 40 min. To serve, add a knob of butter, some chopped parsley and freshly milled black pepper. The frozen caramel custard is served warm, with pouring cream.

Veal in sherry sauce

2 medium-sized escalopes of veal
1 egg, beaten
2 oz. breadcrumbs
3 oz. butter
½ a small red pepper
½ a small green pepper
½ pt. pouring white sauce
3 tbsps. dry sherry
freshly milled pepper

TO MAKE: Coat the veal in beaten egg and then in breadcrumbs. Melt 2 oz. butter and fry the veal until golden-brown and evenly coloured. Drain and place in a rigid foil dish. Add the remaining butter to the frying pan. Seed the peppers, slice roughly and fry for a few min., spoon them over the meat. Heat the white sauce until boiling; boil for 1–2 min., but remove from the heat before adding the sherry. Blend fully, and add some freshly milled pepper.

TO PACK: Put the escalopes and the sauce into separate containers, overwrap, cover, label and seal.

TO FREEZE: Freeze rapidly until solid.

TO USE: Remove the wrappings. The escalopes are re-heated from frozen: place on a baking sheet, cover, and bake at 375°F (mark 5) for 35–40 min. Meanwhile re-heat the sauce in a double boiler, thinning it with a little milk if necessary. Garnish the escalopes with parsley and lemon wedges.

Menu for two

Beef balls in tomato sauce   *Creamed potatoes*   *Sliced green beans*
Cheeseboard celery sticks

THE PLAN

Thaw ½ pt. sauce as directed. Add 2 portions (10) beef balls and heat through for 20 min. in a lidded flameproof casserole on top of the cooker. Meanwhile prepare 1 lb. potatoes for cooking and creaming, and cook a small pkt. of frozen beans as directed; drain, and add a knob of butter and a squeeze of lemon juice.

If to hand, add a few toasted flaked almonds to the green beans.

Beef balls in sauce

1 lb. fresh lean mince
¼ lb. onions, peeled and chopped
½ a clove of garlic, peeled (optional)
½ level tsp. mixed dried herbs
salt and freshly ground black pepper
2 level tbsps. plain flour
2 tbsps. oil
tomato, curry or cheese sauce (see pages 44, 125 and 129)

4 servings, packed in 1- or 2-portion units

TO MAKE: In a large bowl combine the beef,

onion, crushed garlic, herbs and seasoning. Shape into about 24 small balls. Toss in flour and fry until sealed in hot oil. Drain and cool.

TO PACK: Group in small units to make 1 or 2 portions each. Pack in foil parcels, plastic containers or small foil containers. Cover with a lid and overwrap. Seal and label.

TO FREEZE: Freeze rapidly until solid.

TO USE: Thaw only the amount of sauce required (¼–½ pt. for 1–2 servings, or 1 pt. for 4 servings). Use an easy-clean saucepan over a very low heat; when the sauce is liquid, add the frozen meat balls and continue to simmer, covered, for about 20 min. Stir occasionally.

Menu for two

Cheese pudding   Tomato and onion salad   French dressing
Raspberry mousse

THE PLAN

The cheese pudding cooks from frozen in about 1 hr. Prepared individually, the raspberry mousses take 1–2 hr. at room temperature to thaw. Meanwhile peel ½ lb. tomatoes and 1 small onion; roughly slice the tomatoes and very finely slice the onion. Arrange overlapping each other on a flat plate; just before serving add French dressing to moisten.

Cheese pudding

4 slices of white bread (4 oz.)
1 oz. butter
2 eggs, beaten
½ pt. milk
½ level tsp. salt
freshly ground black pepper
2 oz. mature Cheddar cheese, grated

TO MAKE: Cut the bread into squares and place in a 7 in. by 3½ in. greased foil dish. Melt the butter and spoon it over. Mix the eggs and milk together with a fork, season well and spoon over the bread; press the bread well into the custard, and sprinkle the top with cheese.

TO PACK AND FREEZE: Place on a baking

sheet (uncovered) to give support whilst taking it to the freezer. Leave in the freezer until firm, then cover the foil container with a lid or foil. Seal and label.

TO USE: Remove the lid, return the dish to a baking sheet and cook from frozen at 375°F (mark 5) for about 1 hr., until golden and well risen. Serve at once.

Raspberry mousse

(*see colour picture facing page 97*)

1 raspberry jelly tablet
boiling water
8 oz. frozen raspberries, thawed
1 small can of evaporated milk, chilled
1 tbsp. Kirsch (optional)

Serves 4 (i.e. two 2-portion packs)

TO MAKE: Place the jelly in a measure and make up to ½ pt. with water. Stir to dissolve the jelly and leave until beginning to set. Sieve the raspberries. Whisk the evaporated milk until really thick and creamy. Whisk the fruit purée into the setting jelly and continue to whisk until frothy. Fold in the evaporated milk until even blended; add the Kirsch. Divide between 4 individual containers suitable for unmoulding on thawing (or use a larger container—about 2 pt. capacity—see the colour picture). Leave in the refrigerator to set.

TO PACK AND FREEZE: Overwrap in foil and a polythene bag. Seal, label and freeze.

TO USE: Unmould in the frozen state, taking 2 small packs. If you use a large pack, slice whilst semi-frozen. Thaw at room temperature for 1–2 hr. (About 3 hr. for the large 2-pt. size.) Decorate with whipped cream, whole raspberries or glacé cherries, crystallised violets, grated chocolate or angelica.

Menu for two

Egg mayonnaise

Pork chops with pineapple and pepper sauce   Broccoli spears Duchesse potatoes

Lemon sorbet

THE PLAN

Check that you have sufficient duchesse potatoes in the freezer (see page 49 Bulk Cooking). Alternatively, use a pkt. of commercially frozen potato croquettes. The lemon sorbet recipe is on page 91, or you can use a bought one.

Whilst the pork dish is re-heating in the oven from frozen—375°F (mark 5) for about 1¼ hr.—prepare the egg mayonnaise. Hardboil 2 eggs and when cold, cut in half lengthwise. Place each egg, flat surface downwards, on a small plate. Combine 4 level tbsps. thick mayonnaise with 2 tbsps. top of the milk and use to coat the eggs. Garnish with sliced stuffed olives and cress, when available. Chill lightly before serving. Take the duchesse potatoes out of the freezer and re-heat.

Pork chops in pineapple and pepper sauce

2 fresh pork chops, trimmed
½ oz. butter
1 oz. sugar
1 clove of garlic, peeled and sliced
¼ oz. cornflour
¼ level tsp. dried rosemary
¼ pt. water
an 8-oz. can of pineapple slices
1 tbsp. lemon juice
½ green pepper, seeded and chopped

Brown the pork in the melted butter, with a little of the sugar and the garlic; remove from the pan. Discard garlic, then add the rest of the sugar, the cornflour and rosemary to the pan drippings. Stir well, and add the water gradually, along with the juice from the pineapple and the lemon juice. Bring to the boil and add the green pepper and 1 pineapple ring, cut into pieces.

TO PACK: Line a shallow small casserole with foil and place in it 2 pineapple rings; put a chop on each, then place a second ring on top of each chop. Pour the sauce over.

TO FREEZE: Put into the freezer until firm, then remove from the casserole, wrap foil round and overwrap in a polythene bag. Seal, label and return the packs to the freezer.

TO USE: Remove wrapping and return chops to casserole. Cover and cook from frozen at 375°F (mark 5) for about 1¼ hr. Spoon the sauce over the meat during the re-heating.

PUT YOUR FEET UP

A few family menus that take the minimum of effort; keep them in reserve, to bring out when you don't feel like too much cooking.

Menu for four

Fresh grapefruit halves

Individual steak and kidney puddings   Creamed potatoes
Glazed carrots   Peas

Cherry chocolate log

THE PLAN

If fresh grapefruit are not available, you can use frozen grapefruit in syrup (see page 14). Steak and kidney puddings will take about 2 hr. to re-heat from frozen. For the vegetables allow 1 lb. carrots, slice, cook, then add butter and some fresh or frozen chopped parsley; cream 1½ lb. cooked old potatoes and garnish with frozen snipped chives; cook 8 oz. frozen peas.

The cherries in syrup (see page 216) needed for the sweet take 3 hr. to defrost.

Individual steak and kidney puddings

(*see picture opposite*)

1 lb. lean stewing steak
½ lb. lambs' kidneys
1 onion
salt and pepper
a bouquet garni
6 oz. self raising flour
3 oz. shredded suet

TO MAKE: Cut the steak into ½-in. cubes. Skin and core the kidney and chop finely. Peel and chop the onion. Add the meat to a casserole with the onion, ½ pt. of water, some seasoning and the bouquet garni. Cook in the oven at 325°F (mark 3) for 1½ hr., until tender. Allow to cool. Meanwhile mix the flour and suet in a bowl and add sufficient water to bind to a soft dough. Divide the mixture into 4 and have ready 4 foil basins of 16 fl. oz. capacity. Roll out two-thirds of each portion of dough to fit a basin; roll out the remaining

one-third for a lid. Fill the lined basins with stewed meat and liquor; top with the moistened pastry lids. Any surplus liquor can be frozen separately and re-heated as gravy.

TO PACK AND FREEZE: Freeze uncovered until firm. Cover with pleated greaseproof and foil, securing these round the edges, over-wrap in polythene film, seal and label. Freeze rapidly until solid.

TO USE: Cook from frozen in a steamer. Steam the required number of puddings for about 2 hr.; top up the steamer regularly with boiling water. Turn puddings out, and serve with more hot beef gravy (previously frozen and re-heated).

Cherry chocolate log

8 oz. frozen cherries in syrup (see page 216)
17 fl. oz. of Cornish vanilla ice cream
2 oz. plain chocolate
1 level tbsp. golden syrup
1 oz. butter

Put the frozen cherries in the refrigerator to thaw for about 3 hr. Place the ice cream on a serving plate and return it to the freezer. Before serving, melt the chocolate in a basin over hot water, add the syrup and butter and blend until the butter has melted. Arrange the cherries over the ice cream block, and either serve the chocolate sauce separately, or fill a paper icing bag with a little of the sauce, snip off the tip with scissors and drizzle sauce over the fruit. Pour the remaining sauce into a sauce-boat and serve separately.

Menu for four

Melon and ginger cocktail
Chicken hash   Rice with pimiento
Tomato and chive salad
Coffee cream ring

THE PLAN

Remember to thaw the melon and ginger cocktail well in advance—this will take about 3 hr. at room temperature. Start cooking the meal about 1 hr. before it is required. Set the oven at 400°F (mark 6) and refresh the split choux ring for about 5 min.; cool on a wire rack. Increase the oven temperature to 450°F (mark 8) and re-heat the hash from frozen for about 40 min., until bubbling hot. Oven-casserole the rice for 15 min. below the chicken hash and fork in some sautéed pimiento just before serving.

Melon and ginger cocktail

1 honeydew melon (2½ lb.)
2 oz. caster sugar
¼ level tsp. ground ginger
juice and rind of 1 lemon

TO MAKE: Cut the melon in half, discard the seeds and, using a melon ball cutter, scoop out as many balls as practical. Place in con-

Individual Steak and kidney pudding

tainers suitable for freezing. In a saucepan heat the melon juice, made up to ¼ pt. with water; add the sugar, ginger, lemon juice and rind. Bring to the boil, stirring. Strain, and when cold add enough to cover melon balls.

TO PACK: Cover the container, seal, over-wrap and label.

TO FREEZE: Freeze until solid.

TO USE: Partially thaw the melon by leaving it at room temperature, but serve it still chilled. Spoon a little chopped stem ginger over it.

Chicken or turkey hash

1 lb. cooked chicken or turkey flesh
¾ pt. chicken or turkey stock
1 lb. firm tomatoes
1 lb. lean streaky bacon, rinded
4 oz. onion, peeled and chopped
2 level tbsps. flour
1 tbsp. Worcestershire sauce
salt and freshly ground black pepper

TO MAKE: Remove the chicken or turkey flesh from the bones and keep in a cool place while you make stock from the bones. Dice the chicken flesh finely. Skin and seed the tomatoes and add the trimmings to the stock. Finely dice the bacon and fry in a pan until crisp and brown; remove, add the onion and cook until tender. Stir in the flour and cook for a few min. Strain off ¾ pt. stock, stir into the roux and bubble for 1–2 min., stirring. Add the Worcestershire sauce and the meats. Roughly dice the tomato flesh, then stir into the chicken and bacon. Season to taste (but be cautious, as the bacon might be salty).

TO PACK: Turn the mixture into a family-size rectangular foil container (3½ pt. capacity) and allow to cool. Cover, seal and label.

TO FREEZE: Freeze rapidly until solid.

TO USE: Heat from frozen, uncovered, at 450°F (mark 8) for about 40 min. Fork the hash through half-way through the re-heating. Add freshly chopped parsley in a line down the centre just before serving.

Note: This mixture may also be used as a pie filling, in pasties or to stuff pancakes.

Coffee cream ring

1 baked choux ring (see page 50)
2 oz. butter
2 oz. soft dark brown sugar
2 oz. mixed nuts, roughly chopped
½ pt. double cream
1 tbsp. coffee essence

Split the choux ring in half, place on a baking sheet and 'refresh' at 400°F (mark 6) for about 5 min. Cool on a wire rack. In a small saucepan, melt the butter and sugar together; boil for 1–2 min. and stir in the nuts; drizzle the mixture over the top choux half. Whip the cream until it holds its shape, add the coffee essence and spoon inside the lower half of the choux ring. Top with the nut-encrusted ring.

Menu for six

Haddock and mushroom flan   Haricots verts
Sweet corn with pimiento
Apple cheesecake

THE PLAN

Take the apple cheesecake (*see page* 53) from the freezer and thaw it overnight in the refrigerator, along with the flan. Allow about 30 min. for the flan to re-heat. Follow the packet directions for vegetables, adding a good knob of butter before serving. Decorate the cheesecake with ¼ pt. double cream, whipped, and with a red-skinned apple, sliced and dipped in lemon juice.

Haddock and mushroom flan

6 oz. shortcrust pastry
1 lb. smoked haddock, rinsed
rind and juice of 1 lemon
1 bay leaf
3 oz. butter
½ lb. button mushrooms
3 level tbsps. flour
½ pt. fish stock
1 level tbsp. chopped chives
seasoning

TO MAKE: Roll out the pastry and use to line a 9-in. plain flan ring. Lightly prick the base and bake blind at 400°F (mark 6) for about 20–25 min. Place the haddock fillets in a small roasting pan and just cover with water. Add a sliver of lemon rind and the bay leaf, and gently poach until the fish is quite cooked—about 10 min. Drain off the fish stock (keeping it for the sauce). Remove the fish skin, bones, etc., and roughly flake the fish into a bowl. Gently melt 2 oz. butter in a saucepan; quickly sauté the mushrooms, but don't over-cook. Remove from the heat and combine with the fish. Melt the remaining fat in the pan and blend in the flour. Measure off ½ pt. fish stock and gradually add to the roux until fully incorporated. Bring slowly to the boil, cook for 2–3 min. and remove from the heat; allow to cool. Combine the fish and mushrooms with the cooled sauce and add the chopped chives, lemon juice and seasoning to taste. Fill the flan case.

TO PACK: Place the cold flan on a tin foil plate. Loosely cover to freeze.

TO FREEZE: Freeze rapidly until firm. When solid place in a polythene bag, label and seal.

TO THAW: Loosen the wrappings and leave covered in the refrigerator overnight, or thaw at room temperature for 3–4 hr.

TO COOK: Re-heat, covered, at 375°F (mark 5) for about 30 min. Garnish with parsley and lemon wedges.

Menu for four

Oeufs à la maison Crusty French bread
Grilled pork chops Buttered celery and carrots with peas
Minted new potatoes
Chocolate pear upside-down pudding Pouring custard

THE PLAN

Take the chops from the freezer and put them to thaw in the refrigerator overnight. The pudding cooks from frozen, taking about $1\frac{3}{4}$ hr. at 350°F (mark 4), so calculate the starting time from this. Oeufs à la maison go into the oven at the same temperature as the pudding, for about 1 hr. The vegetables require last-minute cooking from frozen. Don't forget that French bread stores well in a freezer for about 1 week; to 'refresh' it, wrap in foil and pop it into the oven at 400°F (mark 6) for about 30 min. from frozen.

Oeufs à la maison

a 4-oz. pkt. of frozen peas
1 medium-size onion
4 tomatoes
$\frac{1}{8}$ level tsp. garlic salt
salt
freshly ground black pepper
3 large eggs
$\frac{1}{2}$ pt. milk
parsley

TO MAKE: Cook the peas according to the pkt. directions. Peel and finely chop the onion. Peel and chop the tomatoes. Add the onion to the peas 2 min. before the end of cooking time; drain. Divide the peas, onion and tomatoes between 4 individual heatproof dishes. Season with the salts and pepper. Whisk the eggs and milk in a bowl with a fork, then strain over the vegetables.

TO FREEZE AND PACK: Place the containers on a baking sheet and freeze rapidly, un-covered, until firm. Overwrap in polythene bags, seal and label.

TO USE: Remove from the polythene bags. Place the dishes in a container with $\frac{1}{4}$–$\frac{1}{2}$ in. water and cook in the oven at 350°F (mark 4)

for about 50 min.–1 hr., until set. Garnish with chopped parsley.

Grilled pork chops

Thaw 4 pork chops overnight in the refrigerator.

TO COOK: Place on a grill rack, brush with melted butter and gently grill for about 7 min. on both sides—the time depends on the size and thickness of chops.

VEGETABLES

Take a $\frac{1}{2}$-lb. celery and a $\frac{1}{2}$-lb. carrot pack (*see page 213*), add 4 oz. frozen peas and cook in boiling salted water for 5–7 min., until tender. Drain well and add a knob of butter.

Chocolate pear upside-down pudding

4 tbsps. warmed golden syrup
2 oz. soft brown sugar
a 15-oz. can of pear halves
2 oz. glacé cherries
4 oz. butter or margarine
4 oz. caster sugar
2 eggs, beaten
5 oz. self-raising flour
1 oz. cocoa
2–3 tbsps. pear juice or milk

Serves 4–6

TO MAKE: Grease a 9 in. by 9 in. square foil container. Spread the golden syrup over the base of the container and sprinkle the sugar on top. Drain the pears and cut in half again lengthwise. Arrange in the base of the container with the cherries. Cream together the fat and caster sugar until pale and fluffy. Add the beaten egg a little at a time, beating well after each addition. Fold in the flour, sifted with the cocoa, and add some pear juice or milk to give a dropping consistency; spread on top of the pears.

TO FREEZE AND PACK: Freeze uncovered till firm. Cover, seal, label; return to freezer.

TO USE: Discard the lid and lightly cover with foil. Bake from frozen at 350°F (mark 4) for about 1½–2 hr. Test with a skewer. Invert the pudding upside-down on a serving plate. Serve with hot custard.

Menu for four

Chilled orange juice
Beef el dorado   Spring greens   Sauté potatoes
Pear and lemon crumble

THE PLAN

Here the main dish and the dessert are cooked from frozen; start the meal 1½ hr. before it is required. Remove the lid of the foil container holding the beef, re-cover with foil and re-heat at 350°F (mark 4) for about 1½ hr. The crumble takes about 45 min. alongside the beef. Allow 1½ lb. fresh greens. For the sauté potatoes, peel and slice 1½ lb. potatoes; lightly cover the base of a frying-pan with 1 oz. butter and oil; heat before adding the potatoes, then quickly fry on both sides until golden-brown; drain and sprinkle with salt. The orange juice starter is either home-produced (see page 14, Breakfast Juices), or commercially frozen, and diluted as directed.

Beef el dorado

2 small onions, peeled
4 young carrots, pared
3 level tbsps. oil
1 lb. lean chuck steak
seasoned flour
½ pt. light ale
½ level tbsp. black treacle
3 oz. sultanas
seasoning

TO MAKE: Thickly slice the onions. Pare the carrots and cut into thin rings. Heat the oil and fry the onions and carrots for about 2 min.; remove from pan. Cut the steak into cubes, toss in seasoned flour and fry until it is coloured. Return the vegetables to pan. Pour in the light ale, bring to the boil and add the treacle and sultanas. Place in an oven-proof dish, cover and cook at 325°F (mark 3) for 1½ hr. Check seasoning. Cool quickly.

TO PACK: Spoon into a rigid foil container. Cover with lid, and label.

TO FREEZE: Freeze rapidly until solid.

TO USE: Remove the lid and cover loosely with foil. Re-heat in the oven from frozen at 350°F (mark 4) for about 1½ hr., until bubbling. Serve with natural yoghurt, sprinkled with chopped parsley.

Pear and lemon crumble

1½ lb. cooking pears, peeled and cored
2 tbsps. golden syrup
grated rind of ½ a lemon
3 oz. butter or margarine
6 oz. plain flour
2 oz. Demerara sugar

TO MAKE: Blanch the pears in boiling water for 2 min.; cool quickly. Drain well before cutting into thin slices and placing in a dish. Drool the syrup over and sprinkle with lemon rind. Rub the fat into the flour until of a fine breadcrumb consistency. Add the sugar and blend thoroughly before spooning over the fruit; press down lightly.

TO PACK: Make in a foil container, or for a short-term stay, use an ovenproof serving dish.

TO FREEZE: Freeze uncovered until solid. Cover with lid or foil, then wrap in polythene. Seal, label and return to the freezer.

TO USE: Cook uncovered from frozen at 350°F (mark 4) for about 45 min. Serve with lightly whipped double cream or thick pouring cream, or custard, to which a little chopped stem ginger has been added.

Organise yourself a five-day week like the rest of the world's workers, so you can relax at weekends with the best of them.

Menu for four

Cream of carrot soup

Hot sausage flan   Baked jacket potatoes   Tomato and cucumber salad

Iced zabaione

THE PLAN

The sausage flan should be taken out of the freezer and put in the refrigerator 3½ hr. before it is required. If it is to be served hot, allow a further 30 min. to re-heat it in the oven at 350°F (mark 4). Start the potatoes cooking before the flan, then reduce the heat. You'll find the preparation of carrot soup in the section 'So good to freeze' (page 137). Take the iced zabaione straight from the freezer, and serve with biscuits.

Hot sausage flan

6 oz. shortcrust pastry (6 oz. flour, etc.)
1 medium-size onion
½ a green pepper
4 oz. back bacon rashers
1 level tbsp. oil
1 lb. skinless sausages
1 egg
¼ pt. milk
¼ level tsp. salt
freshly ground black pepper

TO MAKE: Roll out the pastry and use to line a 7-in. loose-bottomed French fluted flan tin. Roll out the trimmings and cut into long strips with a pastry wheel. Peel and finely chop the onion. Seed and chop the pepper. Rind and scissor-snip the bacon. In a frying-pan lightly fry the sausages; keep on one side. In the same pan add the oil and gently fry the onion, pepper and bacon until cooked through. Turn the mixture into the pastry case. Arrange the sausages on the onion mixture like the spokes of a wheel. In a bowl whisk the egg and milk together, add season-ing and strain into the flan case; decorate with pastry strips. Bake at 375°F (mark 5) for about 45 min., until the custard is set. Remove the flan ring and allow flan to cool. Carefully ease away the metal base.

TO PACK AND FREEZE: Place the flan on a flat foil plate or other rigid base. Freeze until firm, then over-wrap in a polythene bag, plastic film or foil. Seal, label and return the flan to the freezer.

TO USE: To serve hot, unwrap and allow to thaw at room temperature for about 3½ hr., then re-heat, lightly covered, at 350°F (mark 4) for about 30 min. To serve cold, thaw, then cover, and place in the oven at 400°F (mark 6) for 10–15 min., to 'refresh' the pastry. Cool, and garnish with parsley sprigs.

Iced zabaione

4 eggs yolks
4 oz. caster sugar
6 fl. oz. Marsala

Beat the egg yolks to a pale cream and mix in the sugar and Marsala. Cook in a double sauce-pan until the custard coats the back of the spoon. Pour the custard into 4 individual ramekin dishes and cool.

TO FREEZE AND PACK: Freeze until firm. Wrap in foil and overwrap in a polythene bag.

TO SERVE: Remove the wrappings and serve straight from the freezer, accompanied by crisp wafer or boudoir biscuits.

Menu for four

Lancashire hot-pot   Wedges of savoy cabbage   Glazed carrot slices
Choco-liqueur

THE PLAN

About 1¾ hr. before the meat course is required, take the hot-pot from the freezer, unwrap and put straight into the oven, set at 375°F (mark 5). At the same time put the dessert into the refrigerator, topped with crumbled chocolate flake or coarsely grated chocolate. Cook the vegetables in the usual way.

Lancashire hot-pot

8 middle neck chops
2 lambs' kidneys (optional)
½ lb. onions, peeled and sliced
1 lb. potatoes, peeled and sliced
salt and pepper
½ pt. stock
1 oz. lard

TO MAKE: Remove any excess fat from the chops and place them in a casserole. Skin, core and dice the kidneys. Add with the onion to the casserole, then top with potatoes. Season well and pour on the stock. Brush the top of the potatoes with melted lard and cook for 1 hr. Cover and allow to cool.

TO PACK: Either make and freeze in a casserole dish, or use a foil container, depending on how it is to be served.

TO FREEZE: Cover, overwrap, seal and label.

TO USE: Remove wrappings, cover and place dish on a baking sheet. Cook in the oven at 375°F (mark 5) for about 1¼ hr., or until bubbling hot.

Choco-liqueur

6 oz. plain chocolate
3 eggs, separated
1 level tbsp. coffee essence
2 tbsps. Tia Maria

TO MAKE: Melt the chocolate in a bowl over a pan of hot water. Beat the egg yolks into the melted chocolate, with the coffee and liqueur. Whisk the egg whites until stiff and fold evenly into the chocolate mixture. Pour into a 6-in. soufflé dish (2 pt. capacity), or divide between 4 individual soufflé dishes.

TO FREEZE AND PACK: Freeze uncovered until firm. Overwrap in foil, seal and label. Return to the freezer.

TO USE: Remove from freezer, loosen wrappings. Leave in the refrigerator for about 1 hr., to thaw fully. Serve topped with crumbled chocolate flake or coarsely grated chocolate.

Menu for six

Grilled grapefruit cups
Cheese-crusted beef roll   Tomato garnish   Leaf spinach
Apple fool   Sponge fingers

THE PLAN

Thaw the beef roll and the apple purée overnight in the refrigerator. Loosen the polythene bags and leave wrapped in foil—start cooking 2½ hr. before the meal. Make up the apple fool early in the day and refrigerate. For the grapefruit allow ½ per person. Sprinkle each half with 2 level tsps. Demerara sugar, add a little chopped mint and grill until the sugar starts to melt, then serve at once. For the garnish to the beef roll place 6 firm tomatoes on a baking sheet and remove a thin slice from the rounded end of each. In a pan melt 1 oz. butter, add 6 firm mushrooms, with their stems, and sauté for 1–2 min. Invert a mushroom on each tomato, pour the pan juices over and season. Cook in the oven at 325°F (mark 3) for 25–30 min. until the tomatoes are soft.

Cheese-crusted beef roll

(*see picture on right*)

8 oz. self-raising flour
4 oz. shredded suet
4 oz. Cheddar cheese, finely grated
salt and pepper
cold water to mix

For the Filling
4 oz. onion
1 lb. lean minced beef
1 level tsp. dried marjoram
1 oz. fresh white breadcrumbs
salt and freshly ground black pepper
1 egg

TO MAKE: Mix together in a bowl the flour, suet, cheese and seasoning. Add enough cold water to mix to a soft but manageable dough. Knead lightly on a floured board and roll into a rectangle about 12 in. by 10 in. Peel and chop the onion and put in a bowl with the beef, marjoram, breadcrumbs, salt and pepper. Mix well, add the egg and again mix well. Spread over the rectangle of pastry to within 1 in. of one long edge, and brush the pastry edge with water. Carefully roll up.

TO PACK: Wrap loosely in oiled kitchen foil, making a concertina fold. Seal the edges well.

TO FREEZE: Freeze quickly until firm, then place in a polythene bag or film for extra protection. Seal, label and return to the freezer.

TO USE: Thaw overnight in a refrigerator. Remove the polythene bag and loosely over-wrap with more foil. Place the foil-wrapped roll in a roasting tin with $\frac{1}{4}$ in. water. Bake in the centre of the oven at 325°F (mark 3) for 2 hr. About 45 min. before the end of the

Cheese-crusted beef roll

cooking time, pour the water from the baking tray, loosen the foil and cook uncovered for the remaining time, to crisp the suetcrust. Serve with gravy or tomato sauce.

Apple fool

1 level tbsp. cornflour
1 egg
$\frac{1}{2}$ pt. milk
1 oz. caster sugar
1 pt. frozen apple purée, thawed
$\frac{1}{4}$ pt. double cream, whipped
1 red-skinned eating apple
lemon juice

TO MAKE: Combine the cornflour with the egg to give a smooth cream. Gradually add the milk, a little at a time, until fully blended. Fold in the sugar. Pour into a pan and gently heat, stirring continuously. Bring to the boil and cook for 1–2 min. Remove from the heat, beating well. Allow to cool before adding the apple purée. Divide between 6 sundae glasses and chill before topping with a whirl of piped whipped cream. Thinly slice the eating apple, leaving the skin on, cut in half and then in half again, to make fans; dip these fans in lemon juice and place on the cream.

Menu for four

Florida cocktail

Chicken paprika   Fluffy rice   Courgettes with parsley butter

Lemon crumb pie

THE PLAN

Leave frozen grapefruit—the equivalent of 3 whole fruit—to thaw at room temperature for 4–5 hr., or overnight in the refrigerator (see page 14 for freezing directions). Lemon crumb pie needs to thaw for 2¼ hr. at room temperature before the meringue topping is added and the pie is put in the oven for about 15 min. Start preparing the meal about 1½ hr. before serving. Chicken paprika re-heats from frozen at 375°F (mark 5) for 1¼ hr. before the soured cream is added. 'Refresh' the frozen cooked rice, or start from scratch. Buy 1½ lb. courgettes, trim, slice thickly and blanch in salted water for 5 min. Drain thoroughly, and finish by sautéing in butter, with parsley and milled black pepper. To finish the cocktail, fold through the grapefruit the segments from 2 large fresh oranges. Serve in glasses, with fresh mint sprigs or cocktail cherries.

Chicken paprika

a 3-lb. fresh (unfrozen) oven-ready chicken
2 oz. seasoned flour
1 lb. onions
6 oz. butter
1 level tsp. paprika
3 level tsps. tomato paste
¾ pt. chicken stock
salt and freshly milled pepper

TO MAKE: Joint the chicken into small serving-sized pieces. Coat in seasoned flour. Peel and slice the onions, fry in half the butter until golden and keep on one side. Add the rest of the butter to the pan and fry the chicken until evenly browned. Return the onions to the pan, then add the paprika and tomato paste. Sprinkle the remainder of the seasoned flour over and stir well. Gradually add the chicken stock, bring to the boil, adjust the seasoning and turn the mixture into a casserole, if a flameproof casserole has

not been used in the initial cooking. Cover and cook in the oven at 325°F (mark 3) for 1 hr. Cool rapidly.

TO PACK: Turn the chicken paprika into a party-size shallow foil container, or use a foil-lined 4½-pt. casserole.

TO FREEZE: Cover with a lid and freeze until solid. Treat casserole as on page 205. Seal and label.

TO USE: Re-heat from frozen, lightly covered, in the oven at 375°F (mark 5) for about 1¼ hr., until bubbling hot. Remove from oven. Blend in ½ pt. soured cream, adjust seasonings and re-heat, uncovered, for a further 10–15 min. Garnish with chopped parsley.

Lemon crumb pie

8 oz. gingernut biscuits
4 oz. unsalted butter
3 level tbsps. cornflour
¼ pt. water
juice and grated rind of 2 lemons
4 oz. sugar
2 eggs, separated

Serves 4–6

TO MAKE: Crush the biscuits to give a fine crumb. Melt the butter and mix with the biscuit crumbs. Press the crumb mixture into an 8½-in. loose-bottomed French fluted flan ring to line the base and sides. Chill until firm. Blend the cornflour with the water in a saucepan, add the lemon juice and rind and bring slowly to the boil, stirring, until the mixture thickens and clears, then add the sugar. Remove from the heat, beat in the egg yolks and return to the heat for a further 1–2 min. Pour into the crumb crust and leave until cold. Remove the flan ring from around the biscuits.

TO PACK: Place the pie on a baking sheet and freeze until firm; wrap in foil. Pack egg whites separately in a rigid plastic container.

TO FREEZE: Label and freeze.

TO USE: Leave the egg whites to thaw in the container for about $2\frac{1}{4}$ hr. at room temperature, together with the lemon pie; whisk the egg whites stiffly. Whisk in 2 oz. caster sugar and re-whisk until stiff again. Fold in another 2 oz. sugar. Pile or pipe the meringue on top of the lemon filling. Decorate with a few glacé cherries and some angelica leaves. Replace flan ring. Place the pie on a baking sheet and bake in the centre of the oven at 400°F (mark 6) for 5–7 min., to brown the meringue. Reduce the heat to 300°F (mark 2) and cook for a further 10 min. Remove from the oven, leave in the metal case until cool, remove the tin and serve the pie with cream.

Menu for four

Melon balls or wedges
Chicken Chablis Parsleyed new potatoes Broad beans
Apple dumplings Clotted cream

THE PLAN

No thawing time is required for this menu.

Start cooking 2 hr. before the meal. The Chicken Chablis takes $1\frac{3}{4}$ hr. and the apple dumplings 1 hr., both at 375°F (mark 5). When new potatoes are not available, serve casseroled potatoes cooked alongside the apple dumplings—par-cook thickly sliced old potatoes for 5 min., drain and layer with thinly sliced onion; add enough stock to come halfway up, season and cover.

Chicken Chablis

(*see picture on right*)

1 lb. cooked roast chicken meat
1 oz. butter
1 oz. flour
$\frac{3}{4}$ pt. milk
$\frac{1}{4}$ pt. dry Chablis
5 oz. grated cheese
1 level tbsp. chopped parsley
salt and freshly milled pepper
$\frac{3}{4}$ lb. tomatoes, peeled

TO MAKE: Cut the carved chicken meat into long, narrow strips. Melt the butter, stir in the flour and cook for a few min. Add the milk gradually, beating well, bring to the boil, stirring, and cook gently for 2–3 min. Remove from the heat; add the wine, 3 oz. of the cheese and the parsley, blending thoroughly. Adjust the seasoning.

TO PACK: Turn the chicken into a rigid foil container and pour the sauce over. Cover with alternate rows of sliced skinned tomatoes and cheese. Cover with a lid, seal and label.

TO FREEZE: Freeze rapidly until solid.

TO USE: Loosen wrapping. Re-heat from frozen, covered, at 375°F (mark 5) for 1 hr., until thawed. Remove the covering and cook for a further $\frac{3}{4}$ hr. Garnish with parsley. Serve grated cheese as an accompaniment.

Chicken Chablis with parsleyed new potatoes, broad beans and grated cheese

Apple dumplings

8 oz. shortcrust pastry (8 oz. flour, etc.)
4 even-sized cooking apples
2–3 oz. granulated sugar

TO MAKE: Divide the pastry into four portions and roll out each piece into a round 8–10 in. across. Peel and core the apples, place one on each round and fill the centre with some of the sugar. Moisten edges of pastry with water, gather the edges to the top, pressing well to seal them together, and turn over. If liked, decorate with leaves cut from any leftover pastry, or trimmings.

TO PACK: Place on a baking sheet, uncovered, and freeze until firm. Remove from baking sheet, wrap singly in double foil or polythene bags, seal, label and freeze.

TO USE: Unwrap, place on a baking sheet, with foil cupped around to support the dumpling and to catch any apple juice that may run out. Bake in the centre of the oven, uncovered, at 375°F (mark 5) for about 1–1½ hr. Just before the end of the cooking, brush pastry with a little milk and sprinkle with Demerara sugar.

HOLIDAY TIME

Make the school holidays bearable by breaking the back of the cooking before they start. You should be able to keep your cool with a freezer—even if your kids have invited *all* their best friends to stay.

Menu for six

Cream of mushroom soup

Ham roll-ups   *Cheese sauce*   *Whole baked tomatoes*
Baby sprouts   *Potato crisps*
Coffee crunch flan

Coffee crunch flan

THE PLAN

The ham roll-ups and the coffee crunch flan need to be thawed in the refrigerator overnight. Make up ¾ pt. of coating cheese sauce to serve with the roll-ups. Cook the tomatoes alongside the ham. Towards the end of the cooking time, refresh the crisps if necessary —also in the oven. Re-heat 2 pt. of frozen soup (see page 139) in a double boiler, or use an easy-clean pan over a low heat, whisk in ¼ pt. single cream or top of milk, but don't boil. Garnish with thinly sliced and sautéed mushroom.

Ham roll-ups

6 oz. long-grain rice
salt
1 small green pepper
1 small red pepper
freshly ground black pepper
6 thick slices of cooked ham

For the French Dressing
6 tbsps. oil
2–3 tbsps. vinegar
1½ level tsps. French mustard
½ oz. finely chopped onion
1 clove of garlic, peeled and crushed
1 level tsp. caster sugar
¼ level tsp. salt
freshly milled pepper

TO MAKE: Cook the rice in fast-boiling salted water. Seed and very finely slice the peppers; add them to the rice for the last 2–3 min. Strain the rice into a sieve, rinse under a cold tap and allow to drain fully. Make up the French dressing by shaking all ingredients together in a small screw-top jar, or use an electric blender. Thoroughly blend the dressing through the rice. Lay the slices of ham out on a flat surface. Use the rice to fill the ham slices, roll up and secure.

TO PACK: Pack closely together in a rigid container, side by side, in a single layer. Any remaining rice filling may be placed neatly either side of the roll-ups.

TO FREEZE: Lightly cover with greaseproof paper. Freeze until firm before sealing with a lid or overwrapping.

TO USE: Thaw overnight in refrigerator. Leave the rolls in foil dish and cook at 325°F (mark 3) for about 45 min. When heated, place on a serving dish. Pour part of the cheese sauce down the centre and place the remainder in a sauce-boat. Garnish with parsley.

Coffee crunch flan

(*see picture opposite*)

2 egg yolks
¼ pt. strong coffee
2 oz. caster sugar
⅛ level tsp. salt
1½ level tsps. gelatine
1½ tbsps. water
2 tbsps. coffee liqueur
2 egg whites
a 7½-in. digestive biscuit crust flan

TO MAKE: Make a custard with the egg yolks and strong coffee and cook slowly in a double pan; add the sugar and salt. Dissolve the gelatine in the water and add to the hot custard mixture. Allow to cool before adding the liqueur. Beat the egg whites until stiff. When the custard is nearly setting, fold in the egg whites. Pour into the biscuit crumb case and chill well before removing the flan from the tin.

TO PACK AND FREEZE: Put on a baking sheet lined with non-stick paper. When frozen, remove onto a foil plate. Cover the top with non-stick paper and slip it into a polythene bag; seal, label and return to freezer.

TO USE: Thaw, covered, in the refrigerator overnight. Decorate with ½ pt. double cream, whipped. Melt 2 oz. plain chocolate, fill a paper piping bag, snip off the tip and drizzle the chocolate over the cream to form a 'zebra' pattern.

Menu for six

Cream of vegetable soup   Breadsticks
Cheesy haddock roll   Potato nests   Buttered peas
Apple snow   Sponge fingers

THE PLAN

Take both the haddock roll and apple purée (for apple snow) out of the freezer overnight and thaw in the refrigerator. Prepare apple snow about 1 hr. before the meal, followed by the haddock roll. The recipe for preparing, freezing and re-heating duchesse potatoes is on page 49—allow about 1½ lb. potatoes, etc., and pipe into 'nests' instead of whirls. Cook ½ lb. frozen peas for filling the nests. You will need 2 pt. of soup—see page 140; during the re-heating add 2 tbsps. lemon juice; enrich the soup with ¼ pt. single cream, but don't reboil. Garnish with fresh or frozen chopped parsley.

Cheesy haddock roll

(see picture opposite)

12 oz. shortcrust pastry (12 oz. flour, etc.)
1 lb. smoked haddock fillets
1 small onion
grated rind of 1 lemon
juice of ½ a lemon
6 oz. butter
8 oz. full-fat cream cheese
2 oz. white breadcrumbs
2 level tbsps. chopped parsley

TO MAKE: Roll out the pastry to a rectangle approx. 14 in. by 9 in. Poach the haddock by placing in a frying pan, covering with water and bringing slowly to the boil; switch off the heat, cover with a lid and leave to stand for 5–10 min. Drain and cool, discard the skin and flake the fish. Peel and finely chop the onion and add to the fish, with the lemon rind and juice. Blend thoroughly together. Work the butter and cream cheese together until a soft paste is obtained, add the breadcrumbs and combine with the fish. Stir in the parsley. Place the filling lengthwise down the centre of the pastry. Damp the edges with water, fold the pastry over and seal edges. From the

trimmings cut out pastry leaves or other shapes, and use to decorate the roll.

TO PACK: Line a baking sheet with foil large enough to wrap entirely around roll.

TO FREEZE: Place roll on foil but do not package. Freeze rapidly, lightly covered. When solid, wrap roll securely around. Place in a polythene bag, seal and label.

TO USE: Thaw overnight in the refrigerator covered. Glaze the pastry with egg, sit the roll on the foil and support the sides with foil; bake near the top of the oven at 400°F (mark 6) for 10 min. to brown the pastry, then reduce to 375°F (mark 5) for a further 25 min. Serve with wedges of lemon and watercress or parsley.

Apple snow

1 pt. frozen unsweetened apple purée
2 oz. caster sugar (optional)
green colouring (optional)
2 egg whites
½ oz. Demerara sugar
2 red apples, sliced
lemon juice

TO MAKE: Thaw the apple purée overnight in the refrigerator. Put into a bowl and combine with the sugar, if used. Tint with colouring if wished. Whisk the egg whites stiffly and fold into the apple. Spoon into 6 tall stemmed glasses. Sprinkle Demerara sugar over and top with unpeeled slices of apple, previously dipped in lemon juice. Chill. Serve with sponge fingers.

Menu for four

Cream of celery soup   Croûtons
Sweet-sour gammon   Casseroled rice   Green salad   French dressing
Strawberries and cream

THE PLAN

Put the frozen whole strawberries (see page 216) into a bowl and leave to thaw at room temperature for about 1½ hr. before they are required. Re-heat the gammon from frozen

at 375°F (mark 5) for about 1¼ hr. Alongside it put 8 oz. long-grain rice with 1 level tsp. salt and 1 pt. *boiling* water in a covered casserole for about 30 min., or until the water

Cheesy haddock roll with potato nests and peas

is absorbed. Stir in a lump of butter. Re-heat the soup (see page 138) in a double boiler or in an easy-clean pan over a low heat, stirring frequently. When it is hot, whisk in $\frac{1}{4}$-pt. single cream; re-heat, but don't boil. Garnish with tiny celery leaves. Serve $\frac{1}{4}$–$\frac{1}{2}$ pt. single cream and some grated chocolate to spoon over the fruit.

Menu for four

Cream of avocado soup   *Croûtons*
Beef with horseradish   *Rice with paprika*   *Baked tomato halves*
Buttered Spinach
Lattice almond sponge   *Custard sauce*

THE PLAN

Beef with horseradish needs overnight defrosting in the refrigerator. Start the meal preparation about $1\frac{1}{2}$ hr. before it is required. Set the oven at 375°F (mark 5), put the beef towards the top and the almond sponge in the centre for about $1\frac{1}{4}$ hr. The tomatoes can go towards the lower part of the oven for 15–20 min. Re-heat 1–$1\frac{1}{2}$ pt. soup (*see page* 137).

Sweet-sour gammon

(*see picture below*)

4 even-sized gammon steaks
$\frac{1}{2}$ oz. butter
a 15-oz. can of peach halves
$1\frac{1}{2}$ level tbsps. cornflour
3 oz. sugar
3 tbsps. distilled malt vinegar
1 tbsp. soy sauce

TO MAKE: Trim the gammon steaks free of excess fat. Put them in an ovenproof dish, dot with butter, cover and cook in the oven at 375°F (mark 5) for about 25 min., until the gammon is fork-tender. Drain the peaches and cut each cap in half again. Make the peach syrup up to $\frac{1}{2}$ pt. with water and blend with the cornflour. Put into a pan with the sugar, vinegar and soy sauce. Bring to the boil, stirring, then simmer for 5 min. Add the peach quarters. Remove from heat and cool.

TO PACK: Arrange the cooked gammon in a shallow rectangular foil container of $3\frac{1}{2}$ pt. capacity. Pour the sauce over; cool quickly.

TO FREEZE: Cover with lid, seal and label. Freeze; store for up to 1 month.

TO USE: Re-heat from frozen. Loosen the lid and re-heat in the oven at 375°F (mark 5) for about $1\frac{1}{4}$ hr., until bubbling; baste occasionally. To garnish, sprinkle $1\frac{1}{2}$ oz. browned toasted almonds over the gammon.

Sweet-sour gammon

When hot, add $\frac{1}{4}$ pt. single cream, bring back to serving temperature but don't boil. Garnish with chopped parsley. Refresh frozen croûtons (see page 163).

Beef with horseradish

1 large onion
1 green pepper
4 oz. button mushrooms
1 pt. ready-made Béchamel sauce (see page 43)
2 level tbsps. corn oil
1½ lb. topside or forerib
3 level tbsps. horseradish relish

Serves 4–6

TO MAKE: Peel and slice the onion. Discard the stem end of the pepper and the seeds, then cut the flesh into strips. Wipe and quarter the mushrooms. Remove the frozen sauce from its container and put in a saucepan, over a low heat; stir until thawed; gradually bring to the boil and beat well until smooth. Heat the oil in a flameproof casserole and fry the onion until it begins to brown. Cut the meat into thin strips $\frac{1}{2}$ in. by $1\frac{1}{2}$ in. Add to the onion and continue to fry until sealed. Stir in the green pepper and mushrooms, add the Béchamel sauce and horseradish. Cover tightly and cook in the oven at 325°F (mark 3) for 2–2½ hr. when using forerib, or 375°F (mark 5) for 1 hr. when using topside. Cool rapidly.

TO PACK: Pack in a large 9 in. square foil container with lid.

TO FREEZE: Seal container and label.

TO USE: Thaw overnight in the refrigerator, remove lid and cover with foil. Re-heat in the oven at 375°F (mark 5) for about 1¼ hr.; stir well. Transfer to a suitable-sized serving dish, and garnish with parsley.

Lattice almond sponge

4 oz. shortcrust pastry
4 level tbsps. seedless raspberry jam
2 oz. margarine
2 oz. caster sugar
$\frac{1}{4}$ level tsp. almond essence (optional)
1 egg
2 oz. plain flour

Serves 4–6

TO MAKE: Roll out the pastry and thinly line a $7\frac{1}{2}$-in. pie plate, reserving the trimmings for a lattice design. Spread the bottom of the pastry with jam. Cream the fat and sugar until pale and fluffy, add the essence and beat well. Add the egg a little at a time and beat after each addition. Fold in the flour; the mixture should be of a soft dropping consistency. Spread over the jam and smooth the surface with a knife. Add pastry strips to make a lattice design.

TO PACK: Pack uncovered until frozen. When firm, double-wrap in foil, label and seal.

TO FREEZE: Freeze rapidly until solid.

TO USE: Remove the wrappings, place on a baking tray and bake in the centre of the oven at 375°F (mark 5) for about 1¼ hr.

HUSBAND ON HIS OWN

Simple menus for when that helpless male has to fend for himself (perhaps you've gone to visit a sick relative or fallen ill yourself). So simple in fact, that he ought to be able to feed the rest of the family if necessary—that's why the menus are for four.

Incidentally, if he's really on his own and really helpless, better see the plate meals in 'Straight from the Freezer'.

Menu for four

Kidneys in red wine   Creamed potatoes   Tossed green salad
Whole peaches in syrup

Start re-heating the kidneys from frozen 1½ hr. before they are required. The peaches can be home-frozen (see page 217) or canned; to sharpen the syrup, add a little lemon juice; a dash of brandy or orange liqueur is a very special extra.

Kidneys in red wine

2 oz. butter
1 onion, peeled and chopped
10 sheeps' kidneys
3 level tbsps. flour
¼ pt. red wine
¼ pt. stock
a bouquet garni
1 level tbsp. tomato paste
½ level tsp. salt
freshly ground black pepper
4 oz. button mushrooms, quartered
4 oz. raisins
1 level tbsp. chopped chives

Serves 4–6

TO MAKE: Melt the butter and fry the onion until golden-brown. Wash, skin and core the kidneys; cut into manageable pieces. Add to pan and cook for 5 min., stirring occasionally. Stir in the flour. Pour in the wine and stock, bring slowly to the boil, then add bouquet garni, tomato paste and seasoning. Simmer for a further 5 min. Add the mushrooms and raisins and continue to cook for a few min. Remove from heat and allow to cool. Discard the bouquet garni.

TO PACK: Pour into a 5½ in. by 8 in. foil container; sprinkle the chives over.

TO FREEZE: When cold, freeze until firm. Cover with the lid, overwrap, seal and label. Return to freezer.

TO USE: Remove wrapping and re-heat from frozen in a covered foil container. Place in the oven at 400°F (mark 6) for about 1½ hr. until bubbling hot. Garnish with chopped parsley.

Upside-down beef and potato pie

Menu for four

Grapefruit juice

Upside-down beef and potato pie
Buttered savoy cabbage

Individual caramel custards
Pouring cream

Concentrated frozen grapefruit juice is a good-for-you starter to have always on hand; make it up early in the day and keep chilled in the refrigerator. Upside-down pie and the caramel custards cook in the oven at the same temperature. Take 8 individual custards from those made up in the bulk cooking section (see page 51), allowing two per person. Cook the custards from frozen, using a waterbath in the oven at 375°F (mark 5) for 30–45 min. Remove from water, ease around the custard edge and turn out; serve warm. Shredded cabbage cooked in the minimum of water will need last-minute attention.

Upside-down beef and potato pie

(*see picture overleaf*)

3 oz. butter
4 oz. fresh white breadcrumbs
2 lb. old potatoes
1 large onion
1 clove of garlic
6 gherkins
$\frac{1}{2}$ lb. button mushrooms
salt and pepper
1 lb. lean minced beef
1 level tbsp. mild curry powder
1 level tbsp. flour

TO MAKE: Line a $2\frac{1}{2}$-pt. ovenproof dish with foil, leaving enough to enclose the contents later; butter lightly. Heat 2 oz. butter in a frying-pan, add the breadcrumbs and fry, stirring, until golden. Place in the lined dish. Peel and evenly slice the potatoes. Peel and chop the onion, peel the garlic clove. Chop the gherkins and slice the mushrooms. Boil the potatoes carefully until just tender when pierced with a skewer; drain, and season with salt and pepper. Heat remaining butter and fry onion until golden. Add the crushed garlic, minced beef, curry powder, gherkins and mushrooms and fry for 10 min., stirring frequently. Add the flour and mix well. Arrange half the potatoes over the crumbs. Cover with meat mixture and remaining potatoes, press well down. Cool quickly.

TO PACK: Seal foil over the top potato layer to enclose completely.

TO FREEZE: Freeze rapidly until firm. Ease the foil pack from the dish and overwrap.

TO USE: Remove the overwrap, and carefully return the food to the original dish. Open up the foil and cook the pie from frozen in the oven at 375°F (mark 5) for about $1\frac{1}{2}$ hr. To serve, invert onto a serving dish and garnish with tomato and parsley.

Menu for four

Grapefruit juice
Barbecued spare ribs   Casseroled rice   Dressed chicory
Iced strawberry mousse

THE PLAN

The spare ribs are cooked from frozen at 375°F (mark 5); start $1\frac{1}{2}$ hr. before they are required. Put 8 oz. long-grain rice in a casserole, pour on 1 pt. boiling water, add 1 level tsp. salt and stir. Cover with the lid and cook alongside the ribs for about 30 min. Test the rice, and if it is not quite tender, or if the water is not completely absorbed, cover and cook for another few minutes. Fluff the grains lightly with a fork. Take the sweet from the freezer and put in the refrigerator $\frac{1}{2}$ hr. before the meal.

Barbecued spare ribs

(*see picture opposite*)

2 tbsps. oil
6 oz. onion, peeled and chopped
1 clove of garlic, peeled
2 level tbsps. tomato paste
4 tbsps. malt vinegar
$\frac{1}{4}$ level tsp. dried thyme
$\frac{1}{8}$–$\frac{1}{4}$ level tsp. chilli powder
3 level tbsps. clear honey
1 beef cube and $\frac{1}{4}$ pt. hot water
2 lb. spare ribs (American cut)

TO MAKE: Heat the oil in a saucepan, add the onion and sauté until tender; add the crushed garlic, tomato paste, vinegar, thyme, chilli powder, honey and beef cube, dissolved in hot water. Bubble gently for 10 min. Place the spare ribs in a roasting pan just big enough to take them in a single layer. Brush with a little sauce. Roast at 375°F (mark 5) for 30–40 min. Pour off the fat and re-coat the ribs with the sauce remaining in the base of the container. Brush the rest of the sauce from the pan over the meat. Allow to cool.

TO PACK: Pack a 9½-in. by 6½-in. rectangular foil container (3½-pt. capacity). Cover with the lid and overwrap in a polythene bag. Seal, label and freeze.

TO USE: Cook from frozen. Remove the wrappings and cook at 375°F (mark 5) for about 1½ hr. Cover if necessary.

Note: ⅛–¼ level tsp. chilli powder is mentioned; for a strong flavour use ¼ level tsp., but remember that during the freezing the flavour is accentuated. For a mild flavour, use ⅛ level tsp.

Barbecued spare ribs

Iced strawberry mousse

½ lb. strawberries (or ¼ pt. purée)
1 oz. caster sugar
4 egg yolks
¼-pt. double cream
lemon juice (optional)
2 egg whites

Hull the strawberries and put through a nylon sieve (or a liquidiser). In a deep bowl over hot water whisk together the strawberry purée, 1 oz. sugar and the egg yolks, until thick. Remove from the heat and whisk from time to time while the mixture is cooling.

Half-whisk the cream until it just holds its shape; lightly fold it into the strawberry mixture. Add more sugar to taste, or sharpen with lemon juice. Fold in the stiffly whisked egg whites—these should look glossy, and not be whisked as far as the 'dry' stage.

TO PACK: Spoon the mixture into individual soufflé dishes or into one large one. Cover tightly with foil.

TO FREEZE: Freeze until firm. Overwrap in a polythene bag, seal, label and return to the freezer.

TO USE: Unwrap and put in the refrigerator ½ hr. before required.

OUT ALL DAY

Everyone deserves to come home to a good meal after a hard day's work at the office. Cook one or two good meals on a Saturday to slot in during the week—and you'll be able to sip a civilised glass of sherry while they're heating up.

Menu for four

Chilled minted tomato juice
Cornish pasties   Chunky green beans with butter
Cornish ice cream   Hot chocolate sauce

THE PLAN

The pasties are cooked from frozen and take about 1 hr. Stock or gravy to serve with them can be frozen in cubes. Take 4 portions of beans from a bulk buy; don't overcook, and when serving add a good knob of butter and freshly ground pepper from the mill. For the starter use canned or home-frozen tomato juice, with a dash of lemon and fresh-chopped mint or a mint ice cube. The recipe for rich chocolate sauce to go with the ice cream is on page 154.

Cornish pasties

1 lb. lean chuck steak
4 oz. raw peeled potato
1 small onion, peeled and chopped
salt
freshly ground black pepper
10 oz. shortcrust pastry (10 oz. plain flour, etc.)

TO MAKE: Cut the steak into small pieces, about $\frac{1}{2}$-in. cubes. Add the finely diced potato and onion and season well. Divide the pastry into 4 and roll each piece into a round about 6 in. in diameter. Divide the meat mixture between the pastry rounds, damp the edges, draw the edges of the pastry together to form a seam across the top, and flute the edges with the fingers.

TO PACK AND FREEZE: Place each pasty on a large square of foil. Freeze uncovered until firm, before packaging in foil. Overwrap in a polythene bag, seal and label. Return to the freezer.

TO USE: Remove the wrappings. Place the frozen pasties on a baking sheet, glaze with egg and bake lightly covered at 400°F (mark 6) for 20 min., to set the pastry. Reduce the heat to 325°F (mark 3) and cook for about a further 1 hr.

Menu for four

Veal and leek pie   Glazed vegetables
Fruit and nut ice cream sundae

THE PLAN

Take the veal and leek pie out of the freezer overnight and thaw in the refrigerator. Put 4 oz. dried apricots to soak for the sundae.

The pie will take about $1\frac{1}{2}$ hr. to cook, first at 375°F (mark 5) for 1 hr., then at 400°F (mark 6) for about a further 30 min. Make a slit in the pastry lid after about 30 min. For the sundae use vanilla ice cream from a bulk supply in the freezer (see page 150). Cover the drained apricots with water and cook gently for 15–20 min., until soft. Drain and sieve, or purée in a blender. Add 2 level tbsps. sugar and leave until cold. Sharpen with lemon juice and fold in 1 oz. seedless raisins and 1 oz. flaked almonds. Use to top the ice cream, in tall glasses.

Veal and leek pie

Veal and leek pie

(*see picture on right*)

1 oz. butter
4 oz. celery, finely chopped
1 lb. pie veal, minced
2 oz. fresh white breadcrumbs
salt and pepper
1 egg, beaten
1 oz. flour
2 tbsps. oil
1 lb. leeks, washed and finely sliced
$\frac{3}{4}$ pt. white sauce ($\frac{3}{4}$ pt. milk, 1 oz. butter, 1 oz. flour)
3 oz. Cheddar cheese
6 oz. shortcrust pastry (6 oz. flour etc.)

TO MAKE: Heat the butter and fry the celery for 5 mins. Mix together the celery, veal, breadcrumbs, seasoning and egg. Form into 30 little balls and toss in flour. Heat the oil, add the balls and fry gently for 10 min. Drain. Slice the leeks finely and add to $\frac{3}{4}$ pt. white sauce; season well. Blend thoroughly, add the cheese and stir over the heat until the cheese has melted. Put in a 2-pt.oval pie dish or foil container. Place the meat balls on top. Cool. Make up the pastry in the usual way and use to cover pie. Make leaves with the trimmings.

TO PACK: Loosely, and cover with foil.

TO FREEZE: Freeze rapidly until firm. When solid, secure the foil firmly around the dish. Double wrap, label and seal.

TO USE: Thaw overnight in the refrigerator. Remove wrappings. Lightly cover pie with foil and bake at 375°F (mark 5) for 1 hr. Increase the heat to 400°F (mark 6) and cook for about a further 30 min., to crisp the pastry to a golden-brown.

Menu for four

Cream of broccoli soup
Lamb parcels with fruit sauce   Duchesse potatoes
Green beans or young whole carrots
Chocolate éclairs

Take 4 éclairs from the freezer (see page 50), place on a baking sheet and 'refresh' at 350°F (mark 4) for 4–5 min. Cool on a wire rack. Cut in half horizontally. Whip 6 tbsps. double cream and sandwich the halves together with this. Melt about 1½ oz. plain chocolate and use to coat the cream-filled éclairs. (If you prefer, use ready-made éclairs.)

Raise oven temperature to 375°F (mark 5) and put in lamb parcels; after about 30 min. add duchesse potatoes (see page 49). Re-heat 1 pt. of frozen broccoli soup (see page 140);

if you like, add a spoonful of single cream, but don't re-boil. Cook the second vegetable according to type; add a knob of butter before serving.

Lamb parcels with fruit sauce

(see picture opposite)

6 lamb cutlets, trimmed
salt
freshly ground black pepper
1 egg, beaten
2 oz. fresh white breadcrumbs
3 oz. butter
1 lb. eating apples, peeled and cored
$\frac{1}{2}$ lb. fresh or frozen gooseberries
1 level tbsp. sugar
2 level tbsps. chopped mint, or a whole mint sprig

TO MAKE: Season the cutlets, dip in beaten egg and coat with the breadcrumbs. Place under a hot grill to brown the crumbs for a few sec., then either reduce the heat and grill for 20 min., turning them halfway through, or place in the oven at 375°F (mark 5) for 20 min. Cool quickly. For the sauce, melt 2 oz. butter, add the fruit and stew until soft and mushy; put through a sieve or purée in a blender and add the sugar. Divide the thick sauce between squares of kitchen foil large enough to take one cutlet each. Place cutlets diagonally on top of sauce; sprinkle with mint or add a sprig. Divide the remaining butter between the cutlets. Parcel up loosely.

TO PACK: Overwrap parcels with polythene bags, singly or in pairs. Seal, label and freeze.

TO USE: Remove from polythene bags, loosen foil, place frozen cutlets on a baking sheet in the oven at 375°F (mark 5) for about 1 hr. Add a cutlet frill to each before serving.

Menu for four

Cream of carrot soup   Breadsticks
Liver balls en casserole   Duchesse potatoes   Green beans
Cinnamon-apple pie

THE PLAN

No thawing time is required for this menu; start cooking $1\frac{1}{2}$ hr. before the meal is to be served. Recipes and directions for freezing cream of carrot soup and duchesse potatoes are on pages 137 and 49 respectively.

Liver balls en casserole

1 lb. lambs' liver
6 oz. back bacon rashers, rinded
$\frac{1}{2}$ lb. onions
4 oz. fresh white breadcrumbs
1 egg, beaten
$\frac{1}{4}$ level tsp. salt
freshly milled pepper
2 oz. flour
2 oz. butter
a 14-oz. can of tomatoes
$\frac{1}{3}$ pt. stock
A sprig of fresh rosemary

TO MAKE: Mince the liver with the bacon. Peel and finely chop or mince the onions. In a bowl combine the liver, bacon, onion, breadcrumbs, egg and seasoning. Shape into 12 balls, pressing the mixture lightly together, and coat with flour. Melt the butter in a frying-pan and fry the balls until evenly browned. Remove from pan and allow the balls to cool. Meanwhile sprinkle any remaining flour into the pan and stir to loosen the residue. Add the tomatoes with their juice, the stock and rosemary. Stir to blend, then pour into a suitably-sized rigid foil container. Add the liver balls and cool rapidly.

TO FREEZE: Freeze rapidly, uncovered, until firm. Cover with lid or foil, seal and label.

TO USE: Re-heat from frozen. Cover suitably and place in the oven at 400°F (mark 6) for about $1\frac{1}{4}$ hr., turning the liver balls halfway through cooking. Adjust seasoning before serving.

Cinnamon-apple pie

8 oz. plain flour
½ level tsp. powdered cinnamon
2 oz. butter or margarine
2 oz. lard
water to mix
1½ lb. cooking apples
½ a lemon
2 oz. caster sugar
a 5-fl.-oz. carton of soured cream

Serves 4–6

TO MAKE: Sift together the flour and cinnamon. Rub in the fat till the mixture resembles fine breadcrumbs. Add water to give a firm but pliable dough. Divide the mixture in half. Roll out half and line a shallow 7½ in. round pie plate. Peel, core and evenly slice the apples. Place half the apples in the base of the plate, with the rind and juice of the lemon. Sprinkle with sugar and spread the soured cream over; top with the remaining apples. Roll out the remaining pastry for a lid. Flute the edges, and use any trimmings for leaves to decorate the pie.

TO PACK: Place in a polythene bag, excluding as much air as possible. Seal and label.

TO FREEZE: Freeze away from other packages until firm.

TO USE: Thaw overnight in a refrigerator. Brush with milk and bake in the oven on a baking sheet, uncovered, at 400°F (mark 6) for about 25–30 min., until the pastry is golden-brown. Allow to cool slightly, then dust heavily with icing sugar.

Menu for four

Lamb and aubergine casserole   Jacket potatoes   Cauliflower florets
Apple crumble   Pouring custard

THE PLAN

Here both main courses are cooked from frozen. Allow about 1½ hr. before serving time to start the cooking. Set the oven to 400°F (mark 6) and put the casserole on the centre shelf; after ½ hr. place the potatoes above the casserole. Halfway through the cooking time add the crumble, alongside the potatoes. Cauliflower florets take only about 10 min. to cook in boiling salted water.

Lamb and aubergine casserole

1½ lb. lamb fillet
1 oz. butter
2 onions, peeled and chopped
½ lb. carrots, pared and thickly sliced
1 large aubergine, prepared and sliced
1 meat cube
½ pt. hot water
¼ pt. dry Chablis
1 level tbsp. flour
salt
freshly milled pepper

Lamb parcels with fruit sauce, duchesse potatoes and young whole carrots

TO MAKE: Slice the meat into strips about $\frac{1}{2}$ in. wide. Melt the butter in a pan and add the onion; cook until tender. Add the meat and fry lightly, drain well and remove to a casserole. Add the carrots and aubergine and fry lightly; transfer to the casserole. Dissolve the meat cube in hot water and add the wine. Stir the flour into the remaining fat in the pan. Remove from heat and gradually add the prepared stock and wine, stirring all the time; bring to the boil. Pour over the ingredients in the casserole and adjust the seasoning. Cook in the oven at 300°F (mark 2) for 1 hr. Allow to cool.

TO PACK: Turn into a shallow family-size foil container ($3\frac{1}{2}$-pt. capacity), or use a foil-lined casserole dish.

TO FREEZE: Cover and freeze rapidly until firm. Remove foil pre-former from casserole, overwrap, label and seal. Return the package to the freezer.

TO USE: Discard the wrappings, leave lightly covered and re-heat from frozen at 400°F (mark 6) for about $1\frac{1}{2}$ hr.

Apple crumble

$1\frac{1}{2}$ lb. cooking apples, peeled and cored
$\frac{1}{2}$–1 oz. caster sugar
grated rind of $\frac{1}{2}$ a lemon

For the Crumble
3 oz. margarine
6 oz. plain flour
2 oz. caster sugar
$\frac{1}{2}$ oz. Demerara sugar

TO MAKE: Slice the apples thickly. Blanch in usual way for 1 min., drain and cool. Place apples in a 9-in. square foil container ($3\frac{1}{4}$ pt. capacity). Sprinkle the sugar and lemon rind over. Rub the fat into the flour until of a fine breadcrumb consistency and mix in the caster sugar. Sprinkle this crumble over the apples and press down lightly. Top with the Demerara sugar.

TO FREEZE AND PACK: Freeze uncovered until firm. Top with foil lid, overwrap in a polythene bag, seal, label and return to freezer.

TO USE: Remove wrappings and bake at 400°F (mark 6) for $\frac{3}{4}$–1 hr., until crumble is crisp and golden-brown.

2. Bulk Cooking

Bulk cooking doesn't mean churning out steak and kidney puddings till you feel as if you're on a factory production-line. It does mean getting into an 'eat one, freeze one' routine—and ringing the changes on what you've frozen. That way you save time and effort and achieve greater variety in your menus over the weeks ahead, at the price of an initial biggish cooking session.

Sauces—savoury and sweet—stuffings, savoury mince, chicken portions and good old apple purée are among the most valuable bulk stocks to have in your freezer, and we give here all the freezing know-how, followed by some typical recipes using them to advantage.

Béchamel sauce

4 pts. milk
1 large carrot, peeled and roughly cut
1 medium-size onion, studded with 8 cloves
1 large sprig of parsley, including the stem
a bouquet garni
1 level tsp. salt
$\frac{1}{2}$ level tsp. freshly ground black pepper
8 oz. butter
8 oz. plain flour

Makes 8 $\frac{1}{2}$ pt. portions

TO MAKE: Heat the milk with the carrot, clove-studded onion, parsley, bouquet garni, salt and pepper. Bring almost to the boil, remove from the heat and leave to infuse for $\frac{1}{4}$ hr. In a large pan melt the butter, but don't over-heat it. Remove from the heat, add the flour and blend well together. Cook the roux for 3 min., remove from the heat and gradually add the warm strained milk. Cool quickly. Divide into $\frac{1}{2}$-pt. portions and pack in pre-formed polythene bags; seal, label and freeze.

TO USE: as a sauce, immerse the polythene bag(s) in hot water just long enough to loosen the contents. Slip them into an easy-clean pan and, over a low heat, stir until the sauce has softened. Bring to the boil and boil for about 3 min., beating well to give a good gloss. Adjust the general seasoning and add additional flavourings as desired—for instance, capers, sherry, cheese, tomato paste, anchovy.

Other sauces given here are thawed in the same way.
Note: If you have the sauce in one of the special "boil-in-the-bag" freezer packs now available, the unopened bag can be slipped into a pan of boiling water to thaw and re-heat—allow extra heating time.

Espagnole sauce

This classic brown sauce is often used in French dishes, and also makes the base for a number of other exciting sauces such as Madeira, Marengo, Bordelaise, Lyonnaise, but when made in small quantities for each dish it is time-consuming and—surprisingly enough—never tastes quite as good as when made in bulk. Pack the sauce in $\frac{1}{2}$-pt. portions for the freezer. The following recipe makes about 2 pts.

4 oz. butter or good dripping
4 oz. green bacon, chopped
1 large onion, peeled and chopped
$\frac{1}{2}$ lb. carrots, peeled and finely sliced
2 stalks of celery, finely sliced
6 mushrooms or $\frac{1}{4}$ lb. stalks, sliced
  (optional)
3 oz. plain flour
3 pts. good meat stock
a bouquet garni
4 level tbsps. tomato paste

Makes 4 $\frac{1}{2}$-pt. portions

TO MAKE: Melt the fat in a large pan and fry the bacon, onion, carrot and celery slowly until a deep golden-brown, stirring occasionally. Add the mushrooms and cook for 5 min. more. Sprinkle with the flour and cook slowly, stirring often, until well-browned but not burnt. Add 1 pt. boiling stock, stirring, then the bouquet garni. Bring to the boil and add a further 1 pt. of hot stock, stirring. Continue to simmer—with just the occasional bubble rising—without the lid for about $1\frac{1}{2}$ hr., stirring occasionally. Skim off any fat as it rises. Add the tomato paste and cook for 15 min. more. Strain the mixture into a clean pan, add the remaining 1 pt. stock and continue to cook to reduce the sauce to about 2 pts. Adjust the seasoning at this point. Cool quickly by standing the pan in a bowl of ice-cold water.

Divide into $\frac{1}{2}$-pt. portions; pack in pre-formed polythene bags, seal, label and freeze.

TO USE: When using—say, for a Madeira sauce—you need to add a fair quantity of liquid, then to reduce the sauce by boiling to give the required consistency.

Tomato sauce

8 oz. green streaky bacon, rinded and chopped
1 small onion, peeled and chopped
1 clove of garlic, peeled and crushed
2 oz. plain flour
a $2\frac{1}{4}$-oz. can of tomato paste
3 lb. fresh tomatoes, peeled and seeded
3 pts. chicken stock (fresh or cube)
a bouquet garni
2 level tsps. salt
freshly milled black pepper

Makes 6 $\frac{1}{2}$-pt. portions

TO MAKE: Fry the bacon in a large saucepan until the fat begins to run. Add the onion, garlic and flour, cook 5 min. longer, blend in the tomato paste, tomatoes and stock and add the bouquet garni and seasonings. Stir well together, bring to the boil, then simmer for about 15 min. Cool quickly.

Pack in $\frac{1}{2}$ pt. portions in pre-formed polythene bags, seal, label and freeze.

LARGE UTENSILS *are almost a must for bulk cookery—everyday sizes are really not satisfactory unless you usually cook for large numbers. We suggest the following as good buys: a pressure cooker (handy as a sturdy large pan, too); double roaster with easy-clean surface (good also for casseroling); a sauté-type paella pan (about 12$\frac{1}{2}$-in. base and with easy-clean finish); a fish kettle; a really large (6–8-pt.) well-lidded casserole; a 14-pt. maslin pan; a good-sized colander*

Barbecue sauce

1 pt. frozen bulk tomato sauce (see previous recipe)
2 level tbsps. cornflour
2 tbsps. water
1 tbsp. vinegar
1 oz. soft brown sugar
a dash of Worcestershire sauce

Makes 1 pack of $\frac{3}{4}$-pt. and 1 of $\frac{1}{2}$-pt.

TO MAKE: Thaw the tomato sauce in a saucepan over a low heat. Blend the cornflour with the water to a smooth paste, add the vinegar, then stir into the warm tomato sauce. Add the sugar and Worcestershire sauce to taste. Bring to the boil and boil for a few minutes, stirring. Cool quickly.

Pack in pre-formed polythene bags in 1 $\frac{3}{4}$-pt. and 1 $\frac{1}{2}$-pt. portion, seal, label and freeze.

Dried roux mix

8 oz. unsalted butter
8 oz. plain flour
$\frac{1}{2}$ level tsp. salt
1 level tsp. freshly ground black pepper
8 oz. dried skimmed milk powder

Sufficient for 8 $\frac{1}{2}$-pt. portions of sauce

TO MAKE: Melt the butter, add the flour, remove from the heat and combine to form a roux; season. Allow to cool on a flat plate, then roughly chop the roux into tiny cubes or rough pieces. Add the milk powder and blend together to make granules. Divide into 8 even-sized portions, about 3 oz. each. Pack in polythene bags, seal, label and freeze.

TO USE: To the contents of 1 bag simply add $\frac{1}{2}$ pt. water in a saucepan. Gently heat, stirring all the time. Bring to the boil and cook for 2–3 min., still stirring. Serve as a basic savoury white sauce, or add other flavours such as sautéed mushrooms, grated cheese, herbs, anchovy paste or sauce, shrimps, etc.

USING SAUCES FROM THE FREEZER

Chicken fricassee

using Béchamel sauce

A $2\frac{1}{2}$-lb. oven-ready chicken
2 medium-size onions, peeled and sliced
a bouquet garni
$\frac{1}{2}$ pt. frozen Béchamel sauce
4 oz. button mushrooms
1 egg yolk
single cream (optional)

Serves 4

TO MAKE: Reserve the chicken giblets to make some stock to store in the freezer for use later. Place the chicken, onion and bouquet garni in a pan just large enough to take them; add enough water to come halfway up; cover, bring to the boil, reduce the heat and simmer for about 1 hr. until the chicken is nearly tender. Remove the chicken, discard the skin and cut the meat from the carcase in serving-size pieces. Discard the bouquet garni. Reduce the chicken stock to $\frac{1}{2}$-pt. by rapid boiling. Skim off any fat. At this stage, if you wish to freeze the fricassee, combine the chicken meat with the reduced stock, pack in a rigid container or foil-lined casserole dish, seal, label and freeze.

If you wish to serve the fricassee at once, heat the Béchamel sauce, stirring, bring to the boil and add the chicken stock, chicken meat and mushrooms, pre-sautéed in a little butter. Cook gently for about 15 min. Adjust

the seasoning. Blend the egg yolk with about 2–3 tbsps. cream (or top of the milk) and add to the fricassee; re-heat but don't boil. Serve in a ring of rice, with a garnish of chopped parsley.

Vegetable pie

using Béchamel sauce

6 oz. shortcrust pastry (6 oz. flour, etc.)
1 oz. butter
4 oz. leek, cleaned and sliced
4 oz. onion, peeled and sliced
8 oz. carrots, peeled and thinly sliced
4 oz. frozen shelled peas
$\frac{1}{2}$ lb. tomatoes, peeled, quartered and seeded
$\frac{1}{2}$ pt. frozen Béchamel sauce, thawed
salt and freshly ground black pepper

Serves 4

TO MAKE: Make up the pastry (or use a ready-shaped frozen pie lid—see page 50) to fit a $1\frac{1}{4}$ pt. pie dish. Melt the butter and sauté the leeks, onion and carrots until beginning to soften without colouring. Add the peas and continue to cook for 5 min. Remove from the heat and add the tomatoes and Béchamel sauce. Adjust the seasoning and turn the mixture into the pie dish—using a pie funnel if needed. Top with a pastry lid. Bake in the centre of the oven at 375°F (mark 5) for about $1\frac{1}{2}$ hr., until the filling is bubbling and the pastry crisp and golden. Cover pastry with foil if it is becoming too brown.

Stuffed cannelloni au gratin

using tomato and Béchamel sauce

6 cannelloni
$\frac{3}{4}$ lb. lean minced beef
4 oz. back bacon, rinded and chopped
1 medium-size onion, peeled and chopped
salt and freshly ground black pepper
1 egg, beaten
1 pt. frozen tomato sauce
$\frac{1}{2}$ pt. frozen Béchamel sauce
2 oz. Cheddar cheese, grated
$\frac{1}{4}$ level tsp. grated nutmeg

Serves 3–4

TO MAKE: Cook the cannelloni in boiling salted water until just soft; drain and refresh them in cold water. In a frying pan fry together the beef, bacon and onion until beginning to take on colour—about 10 min. Adjust the seasoning, cool a little, then add the beaten egg. Stand the cannelloni upright on a flat surface and stuff them well with the beef mixture, using a teaspoon. Place in a single line in a shallow heatproof dish. Heat the tomato sauce and use to mask the cannelloni. Heat the Béchamel sauce, flavour well with cheese and spoon down the centre of the dish; sprinkle with nutmeg. Cook in the oven at 400°F (mark 6) for 30–40 min.

Swiss steak

using tomato sauce

3 level tbsps. flour
1–2 level tsps. salt
$\frac{1}{4}$ level tsp. pepper
$1\frac{1}{2}$ lb. chuck or blade-bone steak
2 oz. lard or dripping
2 medium-size onions, peeled and sliced
1–2 stalks of celery, chopped
1 small clove of garlic, peeled and crushed
$\frac{1}{2}$ pt. tomato sauce (see page 44)
3 level tsps. tomato paste
6 tbsps. water

TO MAKE: Season the flour with the salt and pepper. Trim the meat and rub in all the flour. Cut it into $\frac{1}{2}$-in. cubes. Melt half the fat add the onions and brown lightly; remove them from the pan. Melt the rest of the fat in the pan and brown the steak on all sides. Reduce the heat, and add the celery, garlic, tomato sauce and paste. Stir, cover and simmer very gently for $1\frac{1}{2}$ hr. Add the onion to the meat. Re-heat before serving.

Stuffing mix

1 lb. fresh white breadcrumbs
2 oz. parsley, stalked and finely chopped
1 level tsp. salt
1 level tsp. freshly ground black pepper
grated rind of 1 lemon
4 oz. butter, diced

Makes 4 4-oz. portions

TO MAKE: Mix all the ingredients together, rubbing in the butter lightly as when making pastry. Divide into 4 even-sized portions and pack in polythene bags, removing as much air as possible; seal, label and freeze.

TO USE as a basic stuffing, add 1 beaten egg to each portion of thawed stuffing.

Note: The bulk mix can be made up with shredded suet instead of butter, but don't use this version for the fish stuffing variation.

Sage and onion stuffing

At time of using, take one portion of dry bulk mix and add 2 large onions (peeled, chopped, cooked in boiling water until tender and well-drained) and 2 level tsps. chopped sage; bind with 1 beaten egg.

Note: If you wish, this stuffing, (without the egg) can be frozen in its entirety, but it requires 3–4 hr. thawing at room temperature before use.

Cheese and tomato stuffing for fish

At time of using, take one portion of dry bulk mix and add 3 large tomatoes, skinned and chopped, 3 oz. grated cheese and 1 level tsp. dried mixed herbs; bind with 1 beaten egg.

Note: If you wish, this stuffing (without the egg) can be frozen in its entirety, but it requires thawing slightly (for about 1 hr. at room temperature) before use.

Peanut stuffing balls

6 oz. fresh white breadcrumbs
$\frac{1}{2}$ oz. chopped parsley
$\frac{1}{2}$ level tsp. freshly ground black pepper
4 oz. salted peanuts, ground
2 oz. butter
1 egg, beaten

Serves 6–8 (about 16 balls)

TO MAKE: Combine the first four ingredients. Rub in the butter as when making pastry. Bind with the beaten egg. Roll into balls about the size of a walnut. Pack in rigid foil containers or polythene bags. Label, seal and freeze.

TO USE: Add, still frozen, to casseroles for the last 15–20 min. of the cooking time, or gently fry in a little shallow fat to crisp and thaw.

Savoury mince

2 oz. butter
1 lb. onions, peeled and chopped
2 cloves of garlic, peeled and crushed
a 2¼-oz. can of tomato paste
2 level tsps. salt
2 level tsps. pepper
7 lb. lean minced beef

Makes 8–9 lb.

TO MAKE: Heat the butter in a large preserving or paella-type pan. Add the onions, stir and fry over a low heat until soft and lightly coloured. Stir in the garlic and tomato paste. Add the seasoning and the beef and cook, stirring frequently, until the mince has separated and has taken on colour—about 15 min. Remove from the heat and cool rapidly.

Either make up into individual dishes for the freezer (see recipes which follow), or pack into 1-lb. and/or 2-lb. portions (to use later as the basis of various dishes. Seal, label and freeze rapidly until solid.

Cabbage parcels

using savoury mince

5 large Savoy cabbage leaves
1 lb. bulk savoury mince
3 oz. cheese, grated
1 oz. rice, cooked (raw weight)
½ level tsp. salt
½ level tsp. pepper

Serves 5

TO MAKE: Blanch the cabbage leaves for 5 min., 'refresh' in cold water and drain well. If necessary, cut away the coarse stem with scissors. Combine the remainder of the ingredients. Put 1 heaped tbsp. of the filling on each cabbage leaf and fold the sides, top and bottom over to form a square parcel. Pack close together in a shallow rigid foil container. Cover, overwrap, seal and label. Freeze.

TO USE: Remove overwrap and thaw overnight in the refrigerator. Place the parcels in an ovenproof dish, brush with melted butter, cover with foil and cook in the oven at 350°F (mark 4) for about 45 min. Uncover for the last 10 min. of the cooking time. Serve with a rich gravy or tomato sauce.

Beef loaf

using savoury mince

1 lb. bulk savoury mince
½ lb. sausage-meat
1 level tsp. mixed herbs
1 tbsp. tomato paste
1 tbsp. Worcestershire sauce
¼ level tsp. garlic salt
1 oz. fresh or frozen white breadcrumbs
1 egg, beaten

Serves 4–6

TO MAKE: Foil-line a loaf tin, top measurements 8½ in. by 4¼ in. Combine the mince with all the other ingredients; blend thoroughly with a fork. Turn the mixture into the prepared tin, wrapping the excess foil over. Freeze until firm, then remove the foil-covered loaf from the tin and overwrap. Seal, label and return it to the freezer.

TO USE: Thaw overnight in the refrigerator. Remove the wrapping and replace in tin, still in its foil wrap. Bake in the oven at 350°F (mark 4) for 1–1½ hr., until the loaf shrinks from the tin. Turn out and serve hot, cut in thick slices, or leave it in the tin and unmould to serve cold.

Chilli beef

using savoury mince

2 lb. bulk savoury mince
a 15-oz. can of baked beans
a 15-oz. can of broad beans
1 level tbsp. Worcestershire sauce
1 level tsp. chilli powder
an 11-oz. can of plum tomatoes

Serves 4–6

TO MAKE: Combine all the ingredients in a saucepan, cover with a lid and simmer for

10–15 min. Cool rapidly. Turn the mixture into a party-size rigid foil container 9 in. by 9 in. (4¼-pt. size). Cover and seal lid; overwrap in a polythene bag. Seal, label and freeze.

TO USE: Cook from frozen. Discard the wrapping and place in the oven, uncovered, at 400°F (mark 6) for 1½–2 hr. (stir occasionally). Half an hour before the end of the re-heating time, stir in the drained contents of a 15-oz. can of red kidney beans.

Bolognese sauce for pasta
using savoury mince

1 lb. bulk savoury mince
a 14-oz. can of whole tomatoes
2 level tsps. dried oregano
½ pt. beef or meat stock
¼ pt. dry red wine

Makes 2 4-serving packs

TO MAKE: Combine all the ingredients in a large saucepan, bring to the boil and simmer, covered, for about 20 min. Cool quickly. Divide into 2 and pack individually in pre-formed polythene bags. Seal, label and freeze. Remove from pre-former and overwrap.

TO USE: Immerse a polythene bag in hot water, then turn the contents into a saucepan and heat slowly until softening—break the sauce down from time to time with a wooden spoon. When thawed, bring to the boil and simmer for 10 min.

Cottage pie
using savoury mince

2 lb. bulk savoury mince
1 lb. carrots, peeled and grated
1 level tbsp. chopped parsley
½ level tsp. salt
½ level tsp. freshly ground pepper
1½ lb. old potatoes, boiled
1 oz. butter
2 level tbsps. milk

Serves 4–6

TO MAKE: Combine the mince, carrots, parsley and seasoning. Turn the mixture into a party-size rigid foil container 9 in. by 9 in. (4¼-pt. size). Sieve the drained potatoes and cream to a fluffy consistency with the butter and milk. Use to top the meat; level and mark with a fork. Freeze uncovered until firm. To pack, wrap in foil, cover with lid and overwrap, seal and label. Return to freezer.

TO USE: Remove wrapping and cook from frozen, uncovered, at 400°F (mark 6) for about 1¾ hr. If necessary, raise the oven temperature to brown the potato.

Chicken portions

Buy 4 3-lb. fresh chickens and divide as follows (reserving giblets for stock):

1. Drumsticks

Makes 4 servings

TO FREEZE: Remove the legs and upper thigh joints from the 4 birds. Remove the skin. Joint again, separating the lower leg from the upper thighs (which can be used as described in No. 4). Coat the drumsticks in beaten egg and toss in 2 oz. golden crumbs. (This egg-and-crumbing is not essential.) Place in a large party-size foil container 9-in. square (4¼-pt. capacity). Cover, label and seal. Freeze until solid.

TO USE: Remove wrappings, thaw overnight in the refrigerator, brush lightly with oil and bake in centre of oven at 375° (mark 5) for about 45 min. Add a cutlet frill before serving, with salad.

2. Chicken breasts

Makes 8 portions

TO FREEZE: Remove the breasts from the 4 birds. Peel away the outer skin. Place in 2 3-portion size foil containers (3½ in. by 7¼ in., 1⅛ pt. capacity). Layer with greaseproof or non-stick paper between the portions.

TO USE: See Chicken Kiev, page 101.

Note: Don't re-freeze thawed chicken breasts.

3. Chicken wings

Remove the wings from the 4 birds and make up a quick *chicken chasseur*:

8 chicken wings
¾ oz. seasoned flour
2 level tbsps. oil
3 oz. butter
1 medium-size onion, peeled and chopped
12 oz. button mushrooms
a 15-oz. can of cream of mushroom soup
¼ level tsp. salt
freshly ground black pepper

Serves 4

TO MAKE: Coat the chicken wings in seasoned flour and fry in the oil and 1 oz. butter for about 5 min. until golden-brown. Remove from the pan and put into a casserole dish. Fry the onion and mushrooms in the remaining 2 oz. butter and the pan juices for 5 min., until golden-brown. Place the vegetables in the casserole dish and pour the soup over. Season well, and cook in the centre of the oven at 350°F (mark 4) for 45 min.–1 hr., until tender. Remove from heat and allow to cool.

TO PACK: Pack in a shallow, foil-lined casserole dish or a 9 in. by 9 in. foil container (4¼ pt. capacity).

TO FREEZE: Freeze uncovered until firm. When solid, add the lid. Place in a polythene bag, label and seal.

TO USE: Re-heat from frozen. Remove wrappings and lid. Cover lightly with foil and re-heat at 375°F (mark 5) for about 1½ hr.

4. Chicken thighs

Makes 4 servings

This joint can be used for curry—see chicken curry, page 126, also chicken paprika, page 28 or Chicken Marengo, page 132.

5. Stock from bones and carcase

Makes about 3 ½-pt. portions of stock, or 2 full ice-cube trays.

TO MAKE: After jointing the birds, put bones, carcase and giblets in a large saucepan or preserving pan. Add 4 pts. water, 1 onion, peeled and stuck with 2–3 cloves, 2–3 carrots, peeled and roughly chopped, 2 bay leaves and a bouquet garni. Bring to the boil and cook gently for 2 hr. Strain the liquor from the bones, etc., and if necessary, boil to reduce. Allow it to cool, then place in a refrigerator to allow the fat to rise to the surface; skim it off. If the stock jellies whilst in the fridge, melt it in a saucepan to ease packing.

TO PACK: Put in ½-pt. quantities into polythene bags, or pour it into empty ice-cube trays and freeze until solid. When firm, remove the cubes and place in polythene bags.

Note: A pressure cooker, if available, may be used to cook the stock.

Duchesse potatoes

6 lb. old potatoes, peeled and boiled
2 oz. butter
1 egg
1 level tsp. salt
freshly ground black pepper
¼ level tsp. grated nutmeg

Serves 10

TO MAKE: Mash the potatoes, add the remaining ingredients (no milk) and beat well. Line a baking tray with non-stick paper. Using a forcing bag fitted with a large star nozzle, pipe onto the tray about 20 raised pyramids of potato, with a base of about 2 in.

TO FREEZE: Freeze uncovered until firm. Remove from freezer.

TO PACK: Slide the potato pyramids off the tray onto a foil plate or container. Cover with polythene film, seal and label.

TO USE: Grease some baking sheets or line with kitchen foil, transfer the frozen duchesse potato portions to the trays, brush lightly with egg glaze and put into a cold oven. Cook at 400°F (mark 6) for 20–30 min., or until heated and lightly browned.

Note: Milk has been omitted from the recipe because it is found that when defrosted, the potato mixture 'weeps' slightly, owing to the large amount of water present.

Pastry

It's not particularly practical to freeze short-crust in bulk, since it can take up to 3 hr. to thaw before you can roll it out, so it's quicker to make it from scratch. However, it's handy to have a store of pies, flan cases and pastry lids (see picture below), frozen either unbaked or baked—see page 207 for directions. It's also useful to freeze in bulk the flaky and puff types of pastry, which take a fair amount of time to prepare, and to make various kinds of cases.

FLAKY AND PUFF PASTRY
Prepare the dough up to the last rolling. Divide it into convenient amounts, such as $\frac{1}{2}$ lb. or 1 lb., and pack in polythene bags or heavy-duty foil. To thaw, leave it for 3–4 hr. at room temperature, or overnight in the refrigerator.

Pies and pie lids should be treated as for shortcrust pastry (see page 207). Vol-au-vent cases prepared in quantity store well. Simply freeze the shaped but uncooked cases on a flat baking sheet; when frozen, pack in

READY-MADE PIE LIDS: *Make a number of pastry lids for your favourite pie dishes, include a double rim of pastry and 'knock-up' the edges; interleave them with non-stick paper or waxed paper, freeze until firm on a flat baking tray and then wrap. To use, fill the pie dish with the required ingredients, damp the rim and top with a frozen pie crust; either cook from frozen, or thaw first in the refrigerator or at room temperature*

stacks in a sealed plastic container, in polythene bags or in heavy-duty foil. Store for up to 4 months. To use, place the frozen cases on a baking sheet and cook in the oven at 450°F. (mark 8) for about 15 min.

Baked vol-au-vent cases are very fragile and are also bulky, but if you wish to freeze them, pack carefully in rigid containers; store for up to 6 months. Thaw for about 1 hr. at room remperature, or 'refresh' quickly at 450°F (mark 8) for about 5 min.

HOT-WATER CRUST PASTRY is frozen only after being made up as raised pies.

CHOUX PASTRY can be frozen either unbaked or baked.

Choux paste

6 oz. butter
1 pt. water
10 oz. plain flour
8 standard eggs

Makes 24 profiteroles, or 14 éclairs, or 2 choux rings

TO MAKE: Melt the butter in the water and bring to the boil. Remove from the heat and quickly add the flour all at once. Beat until the paste is smooth and forms a ball in the centre of the pan. (Don't over-beat, otherwise the mixture becomes fatty.) Allow to cool slightly, then beat in the eggs gradually, adding just enough to give a smooth mixture of piping consistency.

If freezing before baking, line baking sheets with non-stick or greaseproof paper; otherwise, grease the baking sheets.

Using a large plain nozzle, pipe on to prepared baking sheets small dots of paste for profiteroles, or 2-in. lengths for éclairs, or a circle of approx. 7 in. diameter for a choux ring, consisting of piped balls joined together.

TO FREEZE AND PACK—*Unbaked:* Leave uncovered. When frozen, remove from baking sheet and pack in polythene or heavy-duty foil.

TO USE: Place the frozen shapes onto a greased baking sheet and bake at 400°F (mark 6), allowing 5 min. longer than for freshly-made pastry.

TO COOK AND PACK—*Baked:* Cook in the

oven at 425°F (mark 7) for about 20–25 min. Allow to cool; make a small hole to let the steam escape.

TO PACK: Pack on foil-lined baking trays.

TO FREEZE: Freeze rapidly, uncovered, until solid. Remove carefully and pack in polythene bags or heavy-duty foil. Seal, label and overwrap, then return them to the freezer. Store for up to 3 months.

TO THAW AND REFRESH: Leave in the packaging at room temperature for about 1 hr., then remove the wrappings and 'refresh' in the oven at 400°F (mark 6) for 5 min. Alternatively, unwrap and 'refresh' from frozen at 350°F (mark 4) for about 10 min.

TO FINISH: Allow to cool. Directions for finishing profiteroles are given on page 89 and for a choux ring on page 22. For éclairs, fill with whipped double cream (if you are using all 14 éclairs, allow ½ pt. cream—less if you are using only part of the batch). Dip the tops of the éclairs in melted chocolate.

Egg custard

3 pts. milk
12 eggs
4 oz. caster sugar

TO MAKE: Warm the milk in a saucepan but don't boil it. Whisk the egg, and sugar lightly in a basin and pour on the hot milk, stirring all the time. Strain the mixture and blend thoroughly together. Use as in the following sweets which can be frozen unbaked.

Large caramel custard

(*see picture on right*)

4½ oz. caster sugar
¼ pt. water
1 pt. fresh bulk egg custard

Serves 4

TO MAKE: Put the sugar and water in a pan. Allow the sugar to dissolve slowly and bring to the boil without stirring; boil until of a caramel colour. Pour into a 1½-pt. soufflé dish until the bottom is completely covered. Lightly coat the sides, too, turning the dish backwards and forwards. Pour in the custard.

Using custard mixture: Caramel custard and Individual egg custard tartlets; for Quiche Lorraine, see page 118.

TO FREEZE: Freeze uncovered until firm before packing.

TO PACK: Use double foil, label and seal.

TO USE: Remove wrappings and place in a warm water bath. Bake at 375°F (mark 5) for about 1½ hr. until the custard is firm to the touch.

Individual caramel custards

4½ oz. caster sugar
¼ pt. water
1 pt. fresh bulk egg custard

Makes 10

Have ready 10 foil tartlet cases, 3 in. wide.

TO MAKE: Prepare the caramel as for the larger custard. Pour a little into each tartlet case and run it round the edges to coat evenly. Divide the custard mixture between the cases, and place them on baking sheets.

TO FREEZE: Freeze uncovered until firm.

TO PACK: Invert one custard on top of another, wrap in foil, place in a labelled polythene bag and seal. Replace in the freezer.

TO USE: Unwrap and lay the custards in a single layer in a water-bath in the oven. Bake at 375°F (mark 5) for about 35–40 min. Remove from the water, and ease around the edges of the custard before turning out.

Egg custard tartlets

(*see picture on page 51*)

4 oz. shortcrust pastry (4 oz. flour, etc.)
½ pt. fresh bulk egg custard
nutmeg

Makes 6

TO MAKE: Roll out the pastry and cut into 6 rounds, using a 3½-in. plain cutter; line 6 foil tartlet cases (3-in. diameter). Divide the custard between the cases, and sprinkle with grated nutmeg.

TO FREEZE: Freeze uncovered until solid.

TO PACK: Invert one case on top of another, double-wrap in foil and place in a polythene bag to keep them together in the freezer. Label and seal.

TO USE: Re-heat from frozen. Unwrap and place on a baking sheet. The custards can be cooked at varying temperatures, depending on the cooking time of the meal you are preparing. Bake at either 325°F (mark 3) for 1–1¼ hr., which would suit a casserole, or bake at 375°F (mark 5) for 30–45 min. for a quicker meal. Both give a perfect custard set.

Large egg custard tarts

10 oz. shortcrust pastry (10 oz. flour, etc.)
1 pt. fresh bulk egg custard
nutmeg

Each tart serves 4–6

Have ready 2 8½-in. loose-bottomed French fluted flan cases

TO MAKE: Divide and roll out the pastry and line the flan cases. Divide the custard into ½-pt. portions and pour into the cases. Sprinkle nutmeg over. Place on a baking sheet for freezing.

TO PACK AND FREEZE: Leave uncovered until frozen. When solid, take the custards from the baking sheet and remove the flan cases; overwrap in foil, label and seal. Replace in the freezer.

TO USE: Simply remove wrappings and replace the flan case around the frozen custard. Bake from frozen on a baking sheet at 375°F (mark 5) for about 1 hr.

Vanilla custard

½ pt. fresh bulk egg custard
½ level tsp. cornflour
vanilla essence

Makes ½ pt. coating custard

TO MAKE: Combine the cornflour with the egg custard. Add 1–2 drops of vanilla essence.

TO PACK: Pour into a rigid plastic container.

TO FREEZE: Freeze until solid, label and seal.

TO USE: With lid in place, simply dip the container in hot water for 1–2 mins., remove and uncover. Place the frozen custard in a double boiler and gently re-heat until defrosted, stirring all the time. Bring almost to the boil, to thicken and cook the cornflour. Remove from the heat.

Use to cover trifles, or to serve alongside sponge puddings or fruit desserts.

Sweet apple purée

5 lb. cooking apples
¼ pt. water
2 oz. butter
juice and grated rind of 1 lemon
4 oz. sugar

Apple purée can be used for Apple fool, Apple snow and Apple cheesecake; apple slices combine well with other fruit, fresh or frozen, to make a winter sweet, as in this Blackberry and apple pie

TO MAKE: Wash, peel and core the apples. Roughly slice and put in a large pan—a preserving pan is very suitable. Add the water, butter, lemon juice and rind. Cook gently, stirring frequently. When the apples are pulped, add the sugar and beat with a wooden spoon. Either sieve, or purée in an electric blender. Cool quickly and pack in ½-pt. and 1-pt. portions, then freeze—the smaller packs can be thawed or re-heated more quickly.

Note: It is also most worthwhile to purée some apples without the addition of butter, lemon and sugar, for use as apple sauce to accompany roast pork, pork chops, sausages, etc.

Apple slices

TO PREPARE: Peel and core 5 lb. cooking apples; keep them under water whilst the preparation is in progress. Cut into ½-in. slices and blanch in boiling water for 1–2 min. Drain, and cool immediately in iced water, drain very thoroughly, and pack in 1-lb. portions in heavy-gauge polythene bags; freeze.

Apple cheesecake

3 large eggs, separated
3 oz. caster sugar
grated rind of 1 lemon
juice of ½ a lemon
2 level tsps. powdered gelatine
2 tbsps. water
8 oz. cream cheese
1 pt. frozen sweetened apple purée, thawed
green colouring (optional)
7½ oz. gingernut biscuits, crushed
4 oz. unsalted butter, melted

Serves 6

TO MAKE: Use kitchen foil to line an 8-in. round cake tin, preferably one with a loose bottom. Whisk the egg yolks in a bowl over hot water with the sugar, lemon rind and juice until thick. Dissolve the gelatine in the water—see page 167. Add a little whisked egg mixture to the gelatine until blended, then return this to the remaining egg mixture; fold through until blended. Cool the egg mixture until lukewarm, then add the cream cheese, blended with the apple purée. When evenly combined, add a little colouring if

Eve's pudding, made with apple slices

wished. Whisk the egg whites until stiff; fold evenly and lightly into the apple mixture to hold as much air as possible. Turn the mixture into the prepared tin and chill until firm. Combine the biscuits and butter and spread over the apple cake, pressing down gently with the back of a spoon.

TO FREEZE, etc.: Place in the freezer, uncovered, until firm. Remove from the tin, with the foil lining. Wrap in foil and overwrap in a polythene bag. Seal and label.

TO USE: Loosen wrappings but do not remove; thaw overnight in the refrigerator. To serve, decorate with whirls of whipped cream and fresh apple slices dipped in lemon juice.

Note: Cheesecake can be made while you are preparing bulk apple purée, or it can be made from thawed purée for immediate eating.

Eve's pudding
using apple slices

(*see picture above*)

1 lb. apple slices, thawed
3 oz. Demerara sugar
grated rind of 1 lemon
1 tbsp. water
3 oz. butter or margarine
3 oz. caster sugar
1 egg, beaten
4 oz. self-raising flour

Serves 4

TO MAKE: Place the apple slices in a greased 1½-pt. pudding basin and sprinkle the Demerara sugar and grated lemon rind over them. Add the water. Cream the fat and caster sugar together until pale and fluffy; add the beaten egg a little at a time, beating well after each addition. Fold in the flour with a metal spoon and spread the mixture over the apples.

TO PACK: Make a large centre pleat in some greaseproof paper and in a sheet of foil. Place first the paper, then the foil over the top of the basin and secure, either by folding the layers under with the hands, or by tying with string. (Remember to allow for expansion during cooking.)

TO FREEZE: Freeze uncooked until solid.

TO USE: Cook from frozen. Make a stand or rack in a saucepan by means of an inverted heatproof plate or some metal skewers placed crosswise. Put in the basin, half-fill the pan with boiling water and gently cook for about 1¾ hr. Serve with clotted cream.

3. *Straight from the Freezer*

Be prepared for the inevitable emergency with a few ready-and-waiting dishes that can whizz straight from the freezer to the oven; add some frozen vegetables and you have a complete meal.

To give you the general idea of what is possible, we've collected here some popular recipes for the no-time-to-think days. Label these packs clearly for instant identification—you might like to use special-coloured wrappings—and just in case you're not the one who will do the actual cooking, it's a good idea to add brief re-heating or serving directions.

Also included are some handy recipes which make use of commercially-frozen products you're sure to have in the freezer—even if your home-frozen supplies have run low.

Thick oxtail soup

4 tbsps. oil
1 lb. oxtail, cut into pieces
1 large onion, peeled and halved
1 carrot, peeled and halved
1 small turnip, peeled and halved
1 small leek, washed and chopped
1 level tbsp. flour
1 level tbsp. tomato paste
a bouquet garni
$\frac{1}{2}$ level tsp. salt
freshly ground black pepper
$3\frac{1}{2}$ pts. boiling water
1 level tbsp. cornflour
$\frac{1}{2}$ level tsp. curry powder
1 glass of sherry or red wine

Serves 8

TO MAKE: Heat the oil in a very large flame-proof casserole or saucepan and lightly brown the oxtail in it. Remove the meat, put in the vegetables and brown them lightly. Replace the meat and add the flour, tomato paste, bouquet garni, salt and pepper; mix well. Pour in the boiling water, cover and simmer for 4–5 hr. Leave to get cold, and skim off the fat. Remove and discard the bones, and chop the meat finely: return it to the soup and bring back to the boil. Mix in the cornflour, blended with a little water, add the curry powder and cook for 5 min. Add the sherry or wine.

TO PACK: Leave until cold, then pack in rigid plastic containers, allowing a 1-in. head-space.

TO FREEZE: Freeze rapidly until solid. Seal and label.

TO USE: Plunge the sealed container into hot water to loosen the frozen block of soup. Re-heat slowly in a saucepan until boiling. (Add small suet dumplings, and serve extra vegetables separately, to make a really substantial meal.)

Beef and mushroom rissoles

1 large onion, peeled and chopped
1 lb. lean minced beef
a 10$\frac{1}{2}$-oz. can of condensed cream of mushroom soup
2 tbsps. chopped parsley
salt and pepper
6 oz. fresh white breadcrumbs
2 oz. plain flour
oil for frying

Makes 10

TO MAKE: Put the onion, beef, soup, parsley, salt, pepper and breadcrumbs in a large bowl and combine, using a fork, until evenly mixed. Divide the mixture into 10 even-sized portions, form them into 'cork' shapes and roll them in flour. Pour sufficient oil into a frying pan to give a depth of $\frac{1}{2}$ in. When it is hot, add the rissoles and fry, turning them occasionally, for 15 min., until golden-brown. Drain on absorbent paper and allow to cool.

TO PACK: Pack alongside each other in a rigid container. Cover with a lid or double foil, seal and label.

TO FREEZE: Freeze rapidly until solid.

TO USE: Remove the wrapping, place the rissoles on a baking sheet, lightly cover with foil and re-heat from frozen at 400°F (mark 6) for about $1-1\frac{1}{4}$ hr., or until really hot.

Thatched burgers

$\frac{1}{2}$ lb. fresh minced beef, cooked
6 oz. onion, peeled
1 beef stock cube
a 3-oz. pkt. of potato powder
$\frac{1}{2}$ level tsp. dried thyme
$\frac{1}{2}$ level tbsp. tomato paste
$\frac{1}{2}$ tbsp. chopped parsley
a little beaten egg
salt and freshly ground black pepper
$\frac{1}{2}$ oz. flour
oil for frying
1 oz. butter
$\frac{1}{2}$ lb. tomatoes, peeled and roughly chopped
4 oz. button mushrooms, sliced
1 oz. cheese, coarsely grated

Makes 6

TO MAKE: Combine the cooked minced beef and 2 oz. of the onion. Pour $\frac{1}{2}$ pt. boiling

Plate meals—Mixed grill with creamed potatoes and peas (foreground) and Pork chop with duchesse potatoes and mixed vegetables (background)

water into a bowl and crumble in the stock cube; when it is dissolved, sprinkle over the potato powder and leave to cool. Stir the beef, onion, thyme, tomato paste, parsley and egg into the potato; season with salt and pepper. Divide into 6 and shape into flat cakes on a floured board. Pour into a frying-pan enough oil to coat the base, and fry the meat cakes until crisp and brown — about 3–5 min. Allow to cool. Meanwhile melt the 1 oz. butter in a frying-pan and add the tomatoes, mushrooms and rest of onion. Fry for 2 min; cool. Cut 6 squares of foil large enough to take the burgers and wrap round. Place 1 heaped tbsp. of the sautéed vegetables on top of each cooled burger, top with grated cheese and wrap the foil over.

TO PACK: Overwrap in a polythene bag, seal and label.

TO FREEZE: Freeze rapidly until solid.

TO USE: Remove the polythene bag, loosen foil slightly and place frozen parcels in a large frying-pan. Cook dry over a low heat for about 10–15 min. Unwrap the foil around the topping and grill under a pre-heated grill for about 5 min., to melt the cheese and crisp the burgers. Serve at once.

Pork parcels

4 pork chops
4 oz. turnip, peeled
4 oz. carrot, peeled
2 oz. butter

Serves 4

TO MAKE: Remove the rind from the chops and gently wipe the flesh, if necessary. Par-cook the chops by placing under a hot grill for 4–5 min. on each side. Meanwhile dice the turnips into $\frac{1}{4}-\frac{1}{2}$ in. cubes and cut the carrots into fine strips. Blanch the vegetables in a pan of fast-boiling water for 2–3 min., remove and drain well. Cut 4 squares of foil large enough to take a chop and wrap up like a small parcel. Place each chop on a square of foil and cup this round with the hands. Divide the blanched vegetables between the chops. To the drippings from the chops, add 1 oz. butter and gently heat until melted. Spoon the fat over the chops, and top with the remaining 1 oz. butter, cut into 4 knobs.

TO PACK AND FREEZE: Wrap the foil over, cool quickly and freeze until firm.

TO USE: Lightly loosen the foil, but leave the chops covered. Put on a baking sheet and bake from frozen at 375°F (mark 5) for about 1¼ hr. With the chops you can bake some jacket potatoes; choose evenly-matched, average-size ones, rub with butter and prick the skins with a fork before wrapping in foil.

Minced beef pielets

(*see colour picture facing page 129*)

½ oz. margarine
1 medium-size onion, peeled and sliced
12 oz. minced beef
1 tsp. Worcestershire sauce
salt and freshly ground black pepper
1 level tbsp. tomato paste
a 7½-oz. pkt. of frozen puff pastry, thawed
beaten egg to glaze

Makes 6

TO MAKE: Melt the margarine and fry the onion until lightly browned; add the minced meat and cook for a further 10 min. Season well with Worcestershire sauce, salt and pepper, stir in the tomato paste and cook for a further 5 min. Allow this filling to cool.

Roll out the pastry and line 6 pielet tins. Fill with the savoury mixture, place pastry lids on top and seal well. Glaze with egg and decorate with pastry leaves. Leave in the refrigerator for 10 min., then bake at 450°F (mark 8) for 10 min. Reduce the temperature to 350°F (mark 4) and bake for a further 15 min. Allow to cool.

TO PACK: Either pack in a rigid container and overwrap in foil, or double-wrap them in in foil; seal and label.

TO FREEZE: Freeze rapidly until solid.

TO USE: Remove wrappings, place frozen pies on a baking sheet, cover lightly with foil and re-heat at 350°F (mark 4) for about 30 min. These pies are ideal for picnics or snacks.

Plate meals

The trick in preparing plate meals is to carry on cooking your meals for the family in the normal way but, when opportunity offers, to get, say, 1 or 2 extra chops or sausages, which can be cooked along with the ones you are going to eat at once. Then, in the last stages of preparation, place the extra food on a suitable ovenproof plate or foil dish (re-used perhaps from a bought fruit pie); cover, seal, label and freeze. Similarly, you can reserve a one-plate portion of stew or casserole, or a single hamburger, to freeze for future use. Then, when the need arises, simply take one, two or more plate meals out, remove the wrappings, but leave the foil in place, and re-heat at 400°F (mark 6) for about 40 mins.

We list below some suitable foods, with notes as required.

ROAST MEAT: It's better to freeze this in slices than in cuts on the bone. Cut or slice the meat into pieces of even thickness. (It is preferable if beef is underdone—after being plated up, frozen and re-heated, it will be cooked through when it is eaten.) Any cut of meat or poultry, with its trimmings, in gravy or a suitable sauce, freezes well. For example, lamb with mint or onion sauce; pork with apple sauce, chicken with bread sauce. (In the last instance, make the bread sauce more liquid than usual—it thickens when frozen.)

BRAISING STEAK: Prepare in the usual way, but undercook slightly, to allow for the re-heating time.

SAUSAGES: It is better to grill these first, then place them in the oven for a short time, to dry out; you can if you like plate them up with a barbecue sauce.

MIXED GRILL: Chops, bacon rolls, sausages, mushrooms, frozen peas, creamed potato and firm tomatoes can all be included, but unfortunately it is not a good idea to plate chips, as they don't crisp up again when re-heated.

OFFAL: Choose really fresh, tender meat—if it is the slightest bit tough, the freezing and re-heating will accentuate this.

STUFFED TOMATOES: Very good for a snack plate meal. Choose really firm fruit, and fill with a mixture of breadcrumbs, grated cheese, chopped parsley and seasoning.

POTATOES: Most potatoes (except for chips or other fried kinds) freeze well. Creamed potatoes are very good. New potatoes must be fully cooked before being plated up.

PEAS: Plate up while still in the frozen state; add a knob of butter, and double-wrap in foil.

FRESH GREEN VEGETABLES: These are not suitable—they tend to dry out and burn on the plate.

ROOT VEGETABLES: Good, especially if not diced too small.

ONIONS: Button onions are very good.

Packaging material

Use any ovenproof plates, about 8–10 in. across, or an 8-in. foil plate. (These specially made foil plates are good because of the rim, which helps when wrapping up food.)

Seal by double-wrapping in foil; it is important to keep an even thickness and density of wrapping over the entire plate. Seal and label, giving the full menu and date. Meals packed in this way will keep quite satisfactorily for up to 3 months.

Cooking temperatures

As a general guide, for most meals you can start with a cold oven set at 400°F (mark 6); heat for about 40 min. Obviously, less time is needed if the oven is pre-heated, but since plate meals are essentially emergency meals—for unexpected guests, husbands fending for themselves, and so on—the oven will mostly be cold when the food is put in.

Plate meal 1—single mixed grill

(see picture on page 56)

1 lamb chump chop
2 chipolata sausages
2 bacon rashers, made into rolls
1 large firm tomato
salt and pepper
butter
creamed potato or instant potato
2–3 mushrooms
frozen peas

TO MAKE: Place the chop, sausage and bacon rolls on a grill tray and grill until the sausages are swollen and two-thirds cooked, the chop cooked, and the bacon rolls crisp and lightly browned. Remove the meats and place on a suitable plate. Cut the tomato in half, season with salt and pepper, put a small knob of butter on top and add to the plate. You can either use freshly creamed potato or make up the required amount of instant potato, according to the pkt. directions, and adding a knob of butter. In either case, place the potato in an even thickness on the plate. Sauté the mushrooms in a little fat for 1–2 min., remove from the heat whilst still crisp and add to the rest of the grill. Use a small (4-oz.) pkt. of frozen peas, or take a scoop from a bulk pack; place on the plate while still frozen. Add a generous knob of butter on top, or pour some gravy round, if available.

TO PACK: Cover the complete meal with double foil, seal and label.

TO FREEZE: Freeze rapidly until firm.

TO USE: Loosen the foil, but leave it lightly covering the meal. Bake from frozen at 400°F (mark 6) for about 40 min.

Plate meal 2—single pork chop

(*see picture on page 56*)

1 pork chop
creamed potato
macedoine of vegetables (frozen)
butter

TO MAKE: Place the chop on the grill rack and grill on both sides until the meat is coloured and two-thirds cooked. Arrange on an ovenproof or foil plate. Use either freshly creamed potato or instant potato, and pipe it into small whirls on the plate. Take sufficient frozen mixed vegetables for one serving and arrange in a flat, even layer on the plate. Add a generous knob of butter on top.

TO PACK: Double-wrap in foil, seal and label.

TO FREEZE: Freeze rapidly until solid.

TO USE: Loosen the wrapping but leave the foil in place; re-heat from frozen at 400°F (mark 6) for about 40 min., until really hot.

Lamb and carrot casserole

(*see colour picture facing page 129*)

2 tbsps. oil
1 oz. margarine
8 frozen lamb cutlets
salt and freshly ground black pepper
2 medium-size onions, peeled and sliced
4–6 medium-size carrots, scrubbed and
    sliced into julienne strips
2–3 level tbsps. flour
1 pt. chicken stock
$\frac{1}{2}$ level tsp. dried rosemary
juice of $\frac{1}{2}$ a lemon
2 level tbsps. tomato paste
an 8-oz. can of tomatoes

Serves 4

TO MAKE: Heat the oil in a large pan, add the margarine and heat gently. Season the cutlets well with salt and pepper and fry quickly to brown. Cover if necessary to prevent the fat spitting. Remove the cutlets, drain and place in a large casserole. Fry the onions and carrots for a few minutes, remove from the pan and drain well; place in the casserole. Add the flour to the fat remaining in the pan and cook for a few minutes; slowly add the stock and stir well until boiling. Add the rosemary, lemon juice and tomato paste, and adjust seasoning. Stir well and cook for a further few minutes. Pour this mixture on to the cutlets in the casserole; place this, covered, in the oven at 325°F (mark 3) and cook for about $1\frac{1}{4}$ hr. Meanwhile, drain the canned tomatoes well. When the casserole is almost cooked, quickly remove from the oven, arrange the tomatoes at intervals over the top and replace in the oven to heat through. Before serving, sprinkle with chopped parsley.

Chicken with sweet-sour sauce

(*see colour picture facing page 129*)

8 frozen chicken joints
salt
2 oz. butter

For the Sweet-sour Sauce
$\frac{1}{2}$ pt. stock, frozen, or made with a stock cube
Half the contents of a 15-oz. can of pineapple
    chunks
4 tbsps. vinegar
$\frac{1}{2}$–1 tbsp. soy sauce
1 oz. cornflour mixed with a little water
$\frac{1}{2}$–1 level tsp. caster sugar
a 7-oz. can of red peppers, drained
1 oz. flaked almonds

Serves 8

TO MAKE: Season the chicken joints well with salt. Melt the butter in a large pan and fry the chicken slowly until brown—about 20 min. Place in an ovenproof casserole dish. Meanwhile make up the sauce as follows: Combine the stock, the juice drained from the pineapple chunks, and the vinegar, add the soy sauce and the blended cornflour and boil, stirring well, for 2 min. Add sugar to taste. Cut the peppers into strips and add to the sauce; pour over the chicken joints and bake, covered, at 375°F (mark 5) for about 35 min., until bubbling hot. Remove from the oven, add the drained pineapple pieces and continue to cook for a further 10 min. Garnish with flaked almonds. (Reserve the remainder of the pineapple and juice for later use.)

Thatched haddock

(*see colour picture facing page 129*)

2 large frozen haddock fillets
oil
1 pack of dry bulk stuffing mix (see page 46)
3 large tomatoes, peeled and chopped
1 level tsp. dried mixed herbs
3 oz. cheese, grated
1 egg, beaten
lemon slices and parsley to garnish

Serves 2

TO MAKE: Brush the frozen haddock fillets with a little oil and place under a medium grill; cook for 7–10 min. To the portion of stuffing mix, add the tomatoes, herbs and cheese; mix thoroughly and add the beaten egg. Spread this topping over the fish and grill for a further 5 min. to crisp the 'thatching'. Serve with the lemon slices and parsley garnish.

Fish nuggets with tartare sauce

(*see colour picture facing page 129*)

10 frozen fish fingers
$\frac{1}{4}$ lb. streaky bacon rashers, rinded
4 oz. (approx.) bought Tartare sauce

Serves 4–6

TO MAKE: Cut each fish finger in half crosswise. Stretch the bacon, using the back of a knife, and remove any small bones. Wrap a piece of the bacon once round a fish finger half, cutting off the surplus to use on another fish finger. Secure each with a cocktail stick. When all have been prepared, place under a hot grill and cook gently for about 7 min., until the fish fingers are cooked and the bacon is crisp. Pour the tartare sauce into a small bowl and dip the fish nuggets in before eating.

Note: This dish is good for a quick supper savoury or a party dip.

Stuffed devilled pancakes

4 oz. flour (plain or self-raising)
$\frac{1}{4}$ level tsp. salt
1 egg
$\frac{1}{2}$ pt. milk
oil or butter for frying

For the Devilled Kidney Filling
1 medium-size onion, peeled and chopped
1 oz. butter
$\frac{1}{4}$ lb. bacon, rinded and chopped
8 oz. lambs' kidneys
1 oz. flour
$\frac{1}{2}$ pt. stock or water
4 level tsps. French mustard
2 tsps. Worcestershire sauce
salt and pepper

Makes 8 7-in. pancakes

TO MAKE: Sift together the flour and salt. Add the egg, then gradually beat in half the milk to make a smooth batter. Beat in the remaining milk and pour the batter into a jug. Lightly grease a frying-pan and heat it. Quickly pour in enough batter to coat the bottom of the pan thinly and tilt the pan so that the base is evenly covered. Cook until the underside of the pancake is golden-brown, then toss or turn it and cook on the other side. Repeat until the batter is all used. Layer the pancakes with kitchen paper between while you make the filling.

Cook the onion gently in the butter until soft, without browning. Add the chopped bacon and fry until cooked. Skin, core and dice the kidneys and toss them in the flour. Add the kidneys and flour to the onions and stir over a medium heat for 1 min. Stir in the stock or water gradually, then add the mustard and Worcestershire sauce, and season to taste. Simmer for 10 min. Divide between the 8 pancakes, roll up and arrange in a suitably-sized rigid container or heatproof dish. Any surplus sauce may be poured down the centre of the pancakes, or packed in a separate rigid container. Garnish if desired with small bacon rolls, grilled in the usual way.

TO PACK: Cover with a lid or double-wrap in foil; seal and label.

TO FREEZE: Freeze rapidly until solid.

TO USE: Remove the wrapping, but leave the lid in place, or cover lightly with foil. Re-heat at 400°F (mark 6) for about 1¼ hr. If the sauce was frozen separately, re-heat it to serve with the pancakes.

More straight-from-the-freezer recipes

which you will find elsewhere in this book— see the Index

Frikadeller with barbecue sauce
Moussaka
Cottage pie
Upside-down beef and potato pie
Steak, kidney and oyster pie
Individual steak and kidney puddings
Lamb parcels with fruit sauce
Barbecued spare ribs

Cheese-crusted beef roll
Beef with horseradish cream
Veal escalopes and sauce aurore
Sweet-sour gammon
Hot sausage flan
Marinaded venison
Coquilles St. Jacques
Salmon mousses
Cheesy haddock roll
Chicken Tettrazini
Chicken paprika
Chicken hash
Chicken Chablis
Lasagne
Quiches (various)
Cheese pudding
Curry sauce (use with freshly boiled eggs or prawns, etc.)

Sweets or desserts

Choose something that's really simple to prepare and serve for the inexperienced cook (that husband on his own, for example). Ice cream with a good sauce is always popular, as are mousses and fruit whips packed in small individual containers.

For those who can cope with some last-minute cooking or re-heating, here are three good recipes that would impress the unpremeditated guest.

Baked alaska
(using ice cream from freezer)

(see colour picture facing page 128)

2 eggs
2 oz. caster sugar
2 oz. plain flour
a 17-fl.-oz. pkt. of raspberry ripple ice cream
glacé cherries and shelled nuts to decorate

For the Meringue Mixture
2 egg whites
4 oz. caster sugar

Serves 4–6

TO MAKE: Lightly grease an oblong tin measuring 8 in. by 5½ in., and dust with a mixture of caster sugar and flour. Whisk the eggs and sugar together in a bowl over hot water until the mixture is thick and the whisk will leave a trail of the mixture on the surface. Gradually fold in the sifted flour with a metal spoon, until fully blended. Pour the sponge mixture into the prepared tin and bake at 375°F (mark 5) for 15–20 min. Remove from the tin and allow to cool. Turn the oven setting to 450°F (mark 8).

Whisk the egg whites until stiff, add half the sugar and continue whisking until the mixture regains its former stiffness. Fold in the remaining sugar. Place the frozen ice cream on the sponge base and quickly swirl the meringue mixture over, to enclose the ice cream completely. Decorate with cherries and nuts. Bake in the pre-heated oven for about 5 min., to colour the meringue lightly. Serve at once, or freeze unwrapped till solid, cover with non-stick paper, overwrap and return to freezer. Remove wrappings and re-heat at 450°F (mark 8) for 5 mins. before serving.

Double-crust fruit pie

(*see colour picture facing page 97*)

10 oz. plain flour
5 oz. fat (half lard, half margarine)
cold water
a 29-oz. can of apricot halves
1 level tbsp. cornflour

Serves 4–6

TO MAKE: Sift the flour into a large bowl. Add the fats and rub in with the fingertips until the mixture resembles fine breadcrumbs. Add sufficient water to bind together and give a smooth dough. Roll out half the pastry and line a foil-lined 8½-in. round ovenproof dish 1½ in. deep; trim the edges. Drain the apricots. Measure out ½ pt. of the syrup and combine a little of it with the cornflour to give a smooth paste. Add the remaining measured syrup and heat in a pan until boiling; boil gently for 1–2 min. to cook the cornflour. Remove from the heat and cool before mixing with the fruit. Fill the base of the pie with the fruit filling. Damp the pastry edge and top with the rest of the pastry, rolled out to make a lid. Knock up the edges and make a scalloped edging, using your thumb and a knife. Roll out the trimmings to make pastry 'leaves'.

TO PACK AND FREEZE: Place in the freezer on a baking tray until firm. When solid, remove the pie from the dish, overwrap in foil, seal and label. Return it to the freezer.

TO USE: Replace the pie in the original dish, and if possible allow it to 'rest' for 1–1½ hr. before baking. Glaze with a little milk and bake at 400°F (mark 6) for 1 hr. 5 min. If cooking from frozen, allow about 10 min. extra for cooking. Just before serving, dust lightly with a little caster sugar or icing sugar.

Cherry almond crumble

2 14-oz. cans of cherry pie filling
6 oz. plain flour
3 oz. butter or margarine
2 oz. caster sugar
2 oz. nuts, chopped
1 oz. flaked almonds

Serves 4–6

TO MAKE: Pour the cherry pie filling into a shallow ovenproof dish, which should be large enough to allow for the crumble topping. Put the flour into a large bowl and rub in the fat with the fingertips until the mixture resembles fine breadcrumbs. Fold in the sugar and chopped nuts. Sprinkle this topping over the fruit, and top with the flaked almonds.

TO PACK: Double-wrap in foil, seal and label.

TO FREEZE: Freeze rapidly until solid.

TO USE: Cook from frozen. Simply remove the wrappings and bake at 400°F (mark 6) for about 1 hr., until the top is crisp and golden, then cover top and bake for a further 15 min. (about 1¼ hr. in all). Serve the crumble with whipped cream.

4. Bake Now-Eat Later

If there's something about a sunny morning that makes you want to bake a cake (or a loaf or a pie), don't curb that creative urge. Carry on baking—cup cakes along with a big cake; rolls as well as a loaf; tarts as well as a pie. They're all a dream to freeze, and if your creative urges come rarely, you can always turn the weekly bake-day into a once-a-month bonanza.

Almost all baked goods freeze well. Some are better if frozen before they are baked, others are better if frozen after they are cooked. Freezing retains the fresh quality of baked products to a remarkable degree if they are properly handled. However, it cannot actually improve the flavour and texture—what goes in comes out, therefore for real freshness always freeze the goods on the day they are baked.

Cakes and gâteaux

Although both iced and un-iced cakes can be frozen, iced ones need careful attention. Swiss rolls, sponge cakes and fatless flan cases, which don't keep fresh for long after baking, freeze very well. Butter cream and fudge-type fillings and icings are very suitable; avoid cakes with boiled or seven-minute frostings. Avoid custard fillings, too, as they tend to break down. Un-iced cakes will remain in top condition for up to 6 months, and iced ones for up to 2 months, after which time they lose peak quality.

TO PACK AND FREEZE: Cool all cakes thoroughly before packaging. Wrap plain cakes or sandwich layer cakes separately in foil, and overwrap in plastic film or bags. If layers are to be packaged together, separate them with a double thickness of plastic film or waxed paper. Place fragile cakes in a rigid plastic or foil lidded container or a cardboard box for extra protection—this especially applies to iced cakes and gâteaux. Such cakes, whether whole or cut, should be frozen unwrapped until the icing and any piped decoration has set, and should then be wrapped and sealed. It's often a practical idea to cut a gâteau into portions before freezing—that

way, the cake can be thawed more quickly, or just a few pieces may be thawed and eaten while the rest stays frozen and fresh. Protect the cut edges of the cake with plastic film or waxed paper, then re-assemble them for packaging. Seal, label and freeze until solid.

TO THAW: Iced cakes are best unwrapped before thawing, to avoid the icing sticking to the wrappings. If they are in a container or cardboard box, take off the lid. Unfrosted cakes should be thawed wrapped, or moisture will collect on the surface of the cake and make the crust soggy.

Small cakes thaw in about 1 hr. at room temperature, sponge layers and flans take about $1\frac{1}{2}$–2 hr., and Swiss rolls $2\frac{1}{2}$ hr., while large plain cakes and gâteaux take up to 4 hr. (a little longer if extra large, and only about $2\frac{1}{2}$ hr. if cut in portions).

A cake that is decorated with cream is best thawed in the refrigerator; it takes 6–7 hr. (or overnight, if more convenient).

Biscuits and cookies

Any mixture with more than $\frac{1}{4}$ lb fat to 1 lb. flour can be frozen, either baked or unbaked. However, freezing biscuits or cookies in baked form is rather a waste of precious freezer space. Why not make up a large batch of the mixture, bake a third or half of it for immediate use, then freeze the rest of the dough unbaked? Either way, if correctly packaged, biscuits and cookies will keep perfectly for around 6 months.

TO PACK AND FREEZE: Pack baked un-iced biscuits or cookies in a rigid container. Unbaked dough can be stored either before or after shaping; in the latter case, pipe or shape it onto a baking sheet. Freeze until frozen solid—1–2 hr. Remove from the tray, then package, seal, label and return the package to the freezer. Bar-shaped cookies can be frozen in the baking tin. Refrigerator cookie dough can be shaped into rolls, packaged, sealed and frozen.

TO THAW OR BAKE: Thaw baked mixtures, still wrapped, for about 15 min. at room temperature. Cookies or biscuits (undecorated) which need to be crisp may be put on a baking sheet and 'refreshed' in the oven at 375°F (mark 5) for about 5 min. Unbaked cookies, piped, shaped or bar-type, can be baked without thawing; simply follow the ordinary recipe, adding a few min. extra to the baking time.

Refrigerator cookie dough
Slice off as many cookies as you need—thaw the dough slightly before cutting, if necessary. Return the surplus dough to the freezer.

Biscuit dough
Thaw at room temperature, or at the temperature required for easiest handling, and proceed to shape and bake as directed in the recipe.

FRUIT CAKES

Rich, heavily fruited cakes keep very satisfactorily in airtight wrappings without freezing, so there is little point in using up precious space in the freezer for them. It is, however, worthwhile freezing one or two of the family-style cut-and-come-again cakes which are more lightly fruited, so we give a few such recipes.

Caraway and cherry ring

6 oz. butter
6 oz. caster sugar
3 large eggs
4 oz. glacé cherries, halved
2 oz. chopped mixed peel
2–3 level tsps. caraway seeds
8 oz. self-raising flour
2–3 tbsps. top of the milk
caster sugar

TO MAKE: Well grease an 8¼-in. spring-release cake tin fitted with a fluted tubular base. Line the sides with a strip of greased greaseproof paper. Cream the butter, add the sugar and continue to cream until light and fluffy. Beat in the eggs one at a time; stir in the cherries, peel and caraway seeds. Fold in the flour with the milk. Turn into the prepared tin. Spread evenly. Bake just below the centre of the oven at 350°F (mark 4) for ½ hr., reduce temperature to 325°F (mark 3) and bake for about a further ½ hr. till well risen and firm to the touch. Remove sides of tin, invert cake onto a rack and leave to cool for a few minutes before removing the tin base.

TO PACK, etc.: Package, seal, label and freeze as directed on page 63.

Iced gingerbread

8 oz. plain flour
½ level tsp. salt
1½ level tsps. ground ginger
1½ level tsps. baking powder
½ level tsp. bicarbonate of soda
4 oz. Demerara sugar
3 oz. butter
3 oz. black treacle
3 oz. golden syrup
¼ pint milk
1 small egg
2 oz. stem ginger, chopped
2 oz. sultanas

TO MAKE: Grease and line a 7-in. square cake tin. Sift together the flour, salt, ginger, baking powder and bicarbonate of soda. Warm the sugar, butter, treacle and syrup to melt the butter, but do not over-heat. Stir into the dry ingredients, with the milk and beaten egg. Add the ginger and sultanas and beat well. Pour into the tin and bake at oven centre at 350°F (mark 4) for about 1 hr., until well risen and firm to the touch. Cool on a wire rack. Don't remove lining paper.

TO PACK, etc.: Package, seal, label and freeze as directed on page 63.

TO FINISH: Allow to thaw for 1 hr., then make up 6 oz. icing sugar, as for stiff glacé icing, and spoon over the cake top. Decorate with slices of stem ginger and leave to set.

Family fruit cake

4 oz. plain flour
4 oz. self-raising flour
$\frac{1}{2}$ level tsp. ground nutmeg
$\frac{1}{2}$ level tsp. ground ginger
6 oz. butter or margarine
6 oz. caster sugar
4 large eggs, beaten
grated rind of $\frac{1}{2}$ a lemon
2 oz. ground almonds
12 oz. mixed dried fruit
4 oz. glacé cherries, quartered
1 tbsp. milk
12 cubes of sugar, roughly crushed
1 oz. almonds, blanched and slivered

TO MAKE: Grease and line an 8-in. round cake tin. Sift together the flours, nutmeg and ginger. Cream the fat and sugar until light and fluffy. Gradually beat in the eggs. Fold in the flour mixture, with the lemon rind and almonds. Lastly, add the fruit and milk. Turn the mixture into the tin and slightly hollow the centre. Scatter the sugar and nuts on top. Bake at oven centre at 350°F (mark 4) for 1 hr., lower the temperature to 325°F (mark 3) and bake for a further $\frac{1}{2}$ hr. Leave for 15 min. in the tin, then remove onto a wire rack.

TO PACK, etc.: Package, seal, label and freeze as directed on page 63.

Genoa cake

3 oz. shelled Brazil nuts
4 oz. glacé cherries, quartered
4 oz. chopped mixed peel
8 oz. sultanas
12 oz. plain flour
2 level tsps. baking powder
juice and grated rind of 1 lemon
4 oz. margarine
4 oz. butter
8 oz. caster sugar
3 large eggs, beaten

TO MAKE: Grease and line an 8-in. square cake tin. Roughly chop 2 oz. of the nuts and pare the remainder in thin slices for decoration. Mix together the chopped nuts, cherries, peel and sultanas. Sift together the flour and baking powder and add the lemon rind.

Cream together the margarine, butter and sugar until light and fluffy. Gradually beat in the eggs. Fold in the flour and lemon juice; lastly, add the fruit. Turn the mixture into the tin and sprinkle with the sliced nuts. Bake at oven centre at 375°F (mark 5) for 1–1$\frac{1}{4}$ hr. Cool on a wire rack.

TO PACK, etc.: Package, seal, label and freeze as directed on page 63.

Wholemeal lunch cake

1 lb. wholemeal flour
a pinch of salt
1$\frac{1}{2}$ level tbsps. baking powder
2 level tsps. mixed spice
1 level tsp. powdered cinnamon
8 oz. butter or margarine
8 oz. granulated sugar
3 oz. currants
3 oz. sultanas
2 eggs, beaten
10 tbsps. milk, approx.

TO MAKE: Line an 8-in. round cake tin. Combine the flour, salt, baking powder and the spices in a basin. Rub in the fat, then stir in the sugar, currants and sultanas. Make a well in the centre, stir in the eggs and mix to a dropping consistency with the milk. Turn the mixture into the tin. Bake at oven centre at 350°F (mark 4) for about 1$\frac{3}{4}$ hr. Cool on a wire rack.

TO PACK, etc.: Package, seal, label and freeze as directed on page 63.

Tutti frutti cake

6 oz. self-raising flour
$\frac{1}{4}$ level tsp. salt
4 oz. caster sugar
2 oz. nibbed almonds
2 oz. glacé cherries, chopped
3 level tbsps. honey
4$\frac{1}{2}$ tbsps. vegetable oil
2 eggs, beaten
4 tbsps. milk

For the Topping
4 oz. icing sugar, sifted
water
1 oz. walnuts, chopped
1 oz. glacé cherries, chopped

TO MAKE: Grease and line a 7-in. round cake tin. Sift together the flour and salt. Add the sugar, almonds and cherries. Stir in the honey, oil, eggs and milk. Beat until creamy, then turn into the tin. Bake in the centre of the oven at 350°F (mark 4) for about 1 hr. Turn out and cool on a wire rack. Mix the icing sugar with very little water to make a fairly stiff icing. Add the nuts and cherries, and spread over the top of the cake.

TO PACK, etc.: See page 63.

GÂTEAUX

Delicious, but rather time-consuming in the making—so a home-made gâteau stashed away in the freezer can be the answer to an almost-spur-of-the-moment dinner party; it's just super for an extra special tea occasion, and fine for a buffet table too. Included here is one recipe for tartlets which are delicious and keep well.

Glazed pineapple gâteau

4 oz. butter, melted
3 oz. plain flour
1 oz. cornflour
4 large eggs
4 oz. caster sugar

For the Filling
6 oz. apricot glaze
½ pt. double cream

For the Decoration
an 8-oz. can of pineapple slices
2 level tbsps. caster sugar
6 glacé cherries
flaked almonds
2 oz. icing sugar
lemon juice

TO MAKE: Grease and base-line 2 shallow oblong tins measuring 12 in. by 4½ in. Heat the butter, without boiling, until it is melted; leave to cool but not set. Sift together the flour and cornflour. Place the eggs in a large, deep basin placed over a pan of hot—not boiling—water, whisk for a few seconds, add the sugar, and continue whisking over the heat until the mixture is very pale in colour and a trail will form a figure of eight. Remove

from the heat and whisk for a few seconds longer. Using a metal spoon, carefully fold in half the sifted flour, then fold in the butter, poured in round the side, alternately with the flour. Turn the mixture into the prepared tin and bake at 375°F (mark 5) just above the oven centre for about 20 min. Turn out and cool on a wire rack. To finish, sandwich the cakes together with a little apricot glaze and the whipped double cream. Brush the sides and top with more apricot glaze. Drain the pineapple, putting the juice in a saucepan; dissolve the 2 tbsps. caster sugar in it without boiling, then bring to the boil, add the pineapple slices and simmer gently for 20–25 min., until the fruit is clear and the juice almost completely reduced. Leave until cold. Arrange the pineapple slices on top of the cake, with a glacé cherry in the centre of each. Scatter the flaked almonds over, and coat with a thin lemon icing made by blending the icing sugar with a little lemon juice.

TO PACK, etc.: See page 63.

Hazelnut gâteau

6 oz. butter
6 oz. caster sugar
3 large eggs
5 oz. self-raising flour
1 oz. hazelnuts, ground

For the Icing
12 oz. icing sugar, sifted
3–4 tbsps. water

For the Decoration
1 oz. butter
4 oz. icing sugar, sifted
a little top of the milk
24 whole hazelnuts

TO MAKE: Lightly grease and base-line a 'moule-à-manqué' cake tin measuring 9½ in. across the top. Cream the butter and sugar until light and fluffy. Beat in the eggs one at a time. Sift the flour over the surface and stir into the creamed ingredients, together with the ground hazelnuts. Turn the mixture into the prepared tin and level off. Bake at the centre of the oven or just above at 350°F (mark 4) for about 40 min. Turn out and cool on a wire rack, narrow side uppermost.

Blend the icing sugar with enough water

to give a coating consistency. Pour over the cake and, using a round-bladed knife, ease it over the surface to coat evenly. Leave to set. Beat the 1 oz. butter to a cream and gradually beat in the remaining sugar, with just enough top of the milk to give a piping consistency. Using a large star nozzle, pipe 8 rosettes, one for each portion of cake. Top each rosette with 3 nuts.

TO PACK, etc.: See page 63.

Orange layer cake

6 oz. butter
6 oz. caster sugar
3 large eggs
grated rind of 1 orange
6 oz. self-raising flour
6 oz. ready-made almond paste
toasted flaked almonds

For the Orange Cream
6 oz. butter
9 oz. icing sugar, sifted
1 egg yolk
3 tbsps. orange juice
3 tbsps. double cream (optional)

TO MAKE: Line the base of an $8\frac{1}{4}$-in. spring-release cake tin and place it on a baking sheet. Cream the butter, add the sugar and beat together until light and fluffy. Beat in the eggs one at a time. Lightly beat in the orange rind and flour. Turn the mixture into the tin and level it. Bake just below the centre of the oven at 350°F (mark 4) for about 45 min. Turn it out and cool on a wire rack.

Cream the butter for the filling and add the icing sugar, alternately with the egg yolk, orange juice and cream (if used), beating well after each addition. Split the cake into 4 layers, using a sharp knife, and sandwich together with some of the filling; spread a thin layer of filling over the top and position the thinly-rolled almond paste to cover the top. Press down to fix and mark the top of the paste into 8 sections, cutting through the paste. Pipe a small whirl of filling in each section. Use the remainder of the filling to coat the sides of the cake, cover with flaked almonds and leave to set.

TO PACK, etc.: See page 63.

Caribbean cake

4 eggs, separated
6 oz. caster sugar
4 oz. self-raising flour

For the Filling
3 oz. butter
6 oz. icing sugar, sifted
1 oz. preserved ginger, chopped
1 oz. plain chocolate, grated
3–4 tsps. rum

For the Icing
8 oz. chocolate dots
8 oz. unsalted butter
1–2 tbsps. rum
walnut halves and preserved ginger to
  decorate

TO MAKE: Grease and line an 8-in. cake tin. Whisk the egg whites until stiff; very lightly fold in the caster sugar and beaten egg yolks. Sift in the flour and fold through gently. Turn the mixture into the tin. Bake in the oven at 350°F (mark 4) for about 45 min. until golden and shrinking from the tin. Turn out and cool on a wire rack.

Cream the butter, beat in the icing sugar a little at a time and cream until fluffy. Stir in the ginger and chocolate, with rum to taste. Slice cake into 3 even layers and sandwich together with filling. Melt the chocolate dots and butter in a basin over a pan of warm water; add rum to taste. Leave to cool until the mixture thickens (this takes a little time), then spread over top and sides of cake. Decorate and chill.

TO PACK, etc., See page 63.

Raspberry cream ring

3 large eggs
3 oz. caster sugar
3 oz. plain flour, sifted
2 tsps. glycerine

Filling and decoration—see end of recipe

TO MAKE: Grease and flour a $3\frac{1}{2}$-pt. fluted ring mould. Whisk together the eggs and sugar over a bowl of hot (not boiling) water, until the mixture is thick and pale in colour. Remove from the heat and continue whisking until cool. Re-sift half the flour over the egg mixture and fold in quickly and lightly. Repeat with the remaining flour and the glycerine. Turn the mixture into the mould and bake above the oven centre at 375°F (mark 5) for about 30 min. Turn out and cool on a wire rack.

TO PACK, etc. : See page 63.

TO FINISH : Prepare a thin syrup by heating 2 level tbsps. sugar with 2 tbsps. water; add 2 tbsps. sherry. Split the cake in half and moisten the cut surface with the sherry syrup. Whisk $\frac{1}{2}$ pt. double or whipping cream until it holds its shape. Spoon over the sponge halves and embed $\frac{1}{2}$ lb. fresh or half-thawed raspberries in the cream on the base. Top with second part. Dust with icing sugar.

Caramel pistachio gâteau

4 oz. butter
5 oz. caster sugar
4 eggs, beaten
3 oz. plain flour
3 oz. cornflour
2 level tsps. baking powder
grated rind of 1 lemon
6 oz. sugar for caramel

For the Rich Butter Filling
4 oz. caster sugar
3 egg yolks
$\frac{1}{4}$ pt. milk, warmed
$\frac{1}{2}$ lb. butter

TO MAKE : Grease and flour a 3-pt. ring mould. Cream together the butter and sugar until pale and fluffy. Add the eggs a little at a time, beating well. Sift the flour with the cornflour and baking powder, and fold into the creamed mixture, with the lemon rind. Turn the mixture into the ring mould and bake in the centre of the oven at 350°F (mark 4) for about 50 min. Turn out and cool on a wire rack. While the cake is baking, make the filling and caramel—see below.

Slice the cake into 3 layers. Sandwich with some of the filling and mask with the remainder. Decorate the top of the ring with rosettes of piped filling.

TO MAKE FILLING : Cream the sugar and egg yolks until thick and pale. Add the warm milk, return the mixture to the saucepan or double boiler and cook over a low heat, stirring, until thick enough to well coat a wooden spoon, but don't boil; cool. Well cream the butter and gradually beat in the cool (not cold) egg mixture. Beat until fluffy.

TO MAKE CARAMEL : Put the 6 oz. sugar in a pan and set on a low heat until it melts. When it is turning brown, stir and continue to heat until dark golden. Cool on an oiled slab or greased tin and when set, crush.

TO PACK AND FREEZE : See page 63. Alongside the cake pack the crushed caramel in a small sealed plastic bag.

TO THAW : See page 63. Coat the cake sides with caramel and decorate the cream rosettes with blanched pistachio nuts.

Brandy ginger ring

5 oz. butter
4 oz. soft brown sugar
6 oz. plain flour
1 level tsp. bicarbonate of soda
2 level tsps. ground ginger
2 large eggs, beaten
1 level tbsp. ginger marmalade
1 level tbsp. golden syrup
1 tbsp. milk

For the Brandy Butter and Decoration
6 oz. butter
9 oz. icing sugar, sifted
3 tbsps. brandy
brandy cornets (see below) and stem ginger

TO MAKE : Grease a flat-based, sloping-sided angel cake ring tin, measuring $7\frac{1}{2}$ in. in diameter (top measurement), or of $2\frac{1}{2}$ pt. capacity ; line the base.

Cream the butter, add the sugar, and cream until light and fluffy. Sift together the flour, soda and ginger. Beat the eggs one at a time into the creamed ingredients. Fold in the marmalade and syrup, then the sifted ingredients, together with the milk. Turn the mixture into the tin. Bake just below the centre of the oven at 325°F (mark 3) for about 1 hr., turn it out and cool on a wire rack. Split the cake into 4 layers and sandwich together with brandy butter (reserve a little brandy butter in a sealed container for filling the cornets at the time of serving).

TO PACK, FREEZE AND THAW : See page

63. When thawed, decorate the top with brandy cornets (see below) filled with piped rosettes of thawed filling and some pieces of stem ginger.

Brandy butter
Cream the butter and gradually beat in the icing sugar and the brandy, until light and fluffy.

Brandy cornets (make these the day before the cake comes out of the freezer)
Melt 1 oz. butter with 1 oz. caster sugar and 1 tbsp. golden syrup in a small pan. Remove from the heat, add 1 oz. plain flour, a pinch of ground ginger, a few drops of brandy and a little grated lemon rind; mix well. Drop in teaspoonfuls (not more than 4, placed well apart) on a baking sheet lined with non-stick paper. Bake towards the top of a moderate oven (350°F, mark 4) for 7–10 min., until bubbly and golden. When beginning to firm, carefully lift each snap with a palette knife and shape round a greased cream horn tin. When set, slip off the tins. Store in an airtight tin till required, and fill as desired.

Mocha gâteau (foreground) and meringue layers and shell shapes for use in a vacherin (see Raspberry vacherin, page 93)

Mocha gâteau

(*see picture on the right*)

3 oz. butter
3 eggs
4 oz. caster sugar
2 oz. plain flour
$\frac{1}{2}$ oz. cornflour
1 oz. walnuts, chopped
8–9 walnut halves

For Coffee Crème au Beurre
3 oz. caster sugar
4 tbsps. water
2 egg yolks, beaten
4–6 oz. unsalted butter
1–2 tbsps. coffee essence

For Coffee Glacé Icing
12 oz. icing sugar
3–6 tbsps. warm water
3 tsps. coffee essence

TO MAKE: Grease and base-line a $9\frac{1}{2}$-in. 'moule-à-manqué' cake tin (top measurement). Heat the butter gently until just melted, remove from heat and let it stand for a few min. Whisk the eggs and sugar until thick over a pan of hot water off the heat. Continue to whisk until the mixture is lukewarm.

Carefully fold in the sifted flour and cornflour, alternately with the melted butter and chopped walnuts. Turn the mixture into the prepared tin and bake just above the centre of the oven at 375°F (mark 5) for about 25 min. Turn out and cool on a wire rack.

For the crème au beurre, place the sugar in a heavy-based pan. Add the water and leave over a low heat to dissolve the sugar without boiling. When completely dissolved, bring to boiling point and boil steadily for 2–3 min., to 225°F. Pour the syrup in a thin stream on the egg yolks, whisking all the time. Continue to mix until the mixture is thick and cold. Gradually add to the creamed butter. Beat in the coffee essence. When the cake is cold, split and sandwich with a little of the crème au beurre, reserving some to use later for decoration. Make the coffee glacé icing in the usual way. Coat the cake completely with it, then leave to set. When the glacé icing is firm, put the reserved crème au beurre into a forcing bag fitted with a large rose nozzle to pipe rosettes round the edge. Finish with the walnut halves.

TO PACK, etc.: See page 63.

Chestnut gâteau

3 eggs
3 oz. caster sugar
3 oz. plain flour, sifted
1 tbsp. warm water
apricot jam
4 oz. nibbed almonds, toasted
¼ pt. double cream, whipped
sweetened chestnut spread from a tube

TO MAKE: Grease and line a straight-sided Swiss roll tin 12 in. by 8 in. Whisk the eggs and sugar until thick enough to leave a trail. Sift the flour over the egg mixture and fold it in, along with the water. Turn the mixture into the prepared tin and bake above the oven centre at 450°F (mark 8) for 10–15 min., until well-risen and golden. Turn onto a wire rack and remove the paper. When cold, cut horizontally into three. Sandwich together in layers with apricot jam. Coat the sides with jam and press in the toasted nuts. Decorate the top with alternate lines of piped cream and chestnut spread straight from the tube.

TO PACK, etc.: See page 63.

Malakoff cake

1½ pkts. of boudoir biscuits (approx.)
5 oz. whole almonds, blanched and chopped
4 oz. caster sugar
6 oz. butter
2 egg yolks
6 tbsps. brandy
5 tbsps. milk

TO MAKE: Line a loaf tin 8½ in. by 4½ in. (top measurement) with non-stick or waxed paper. Cover the base with boudoir biscuits. Place the almonds and 2 oz. of the sugar in a thick-based frying-pan and heat gently; stir occasionally until the sugar caramelises and the almonds are golden; allow to cool, then chop finely. Cream the butter and the remaining sugar until light and fluffy; beat in the egg yolks and 3 tbsps. brandy, alternately. Stir in the nuts. Blend the remaining brandy with the milk and sprinkle 2 tbsps. over the first layer of biscuits. Cover with half the nut filling. Continue with another layer of biscuits, 2 tbsps. brandy/milk mixture, the re-maining nut filling and final layer of biscuits and the rest of the brandy/milk mixture.

TO PACK, etc.: Place in the freezer in the tin until frozen hard. Lift from the tin and package in foil, then in a polythene bag, seal and label.

TO THAW: See page 63 as for gâteaux. To serve, mask with ½ pt. whipping cream and decorate with chopped toasted almonds.

Almond tartlets

4 oz. shortcrust pastry (4 oz. flour, etc.)
1½ oz. butter
2 oz. caster sugar
1 egg
2 oz. ground almonds
apricot or raspberry jam
glacé icing and glacé cherries to decorate

Makes 12

TO MAKE: Line a dozen 2½-in. patty tins with thinly rolled pastry. Cream the butter and sugar until light and fluffy. Beat in the egg and then stir in the almonds. Place a little jam in the base of each pastry case, and divide the almond mixture between the cases. Bake just above the centre of the oven at 400°F (mark 6) for about 15 min., until golden and firm to the touch. Cool on a wire rack. Decorate with a little glacé icing in the centre of each and top with half a small glacé cherry.

Coconut tartlets
Use 2 oz. desiccated coconut in place of the almonds.

TO PACK, etc.: When the icing is set, pack in a single layer in a shallow tin, overwrap in foil and place in a polythene bag, excluding as much air as possible. Label and freeze.

TO THAW: Remove polythene bag and leave the tartlets at room temperature for about 2 hr.

TEABREADS

Teabreads are particularly good 'keepers' for the freezer, so always have a couple to hand. To package, use kitchen foil and overwrap in a polythene bag. To thaw, remove the polythene bag and leave in the foil for about 2 hr. at room temperature. Slice thickly and spread with plenty of butter.

Date and raisin teabread

4 oz. butter or margarine
8 oz. plain flour
4 oz. stoned dates, chopped
2 oz. walnut halves, chopped
4 oz. seedless raisins
4 oz. Demerara sugar
1 level tsp. baking powder
1 level tsp. bicarbonate of soda
$\frac{1}{4}$ pt. milk, approx.

TO MAKE: Grease and line a loaf tin, top measurement $9\frac{3}{4}$ in. by $5\frac{3}{4}$ in. Rub the fat into the flour to resemble fine breadcrumbs. Stir in the dates, walnuts, raisins and sugar. Mix the baking powder, bicarbonate of soda and milk in a measure and pour into the centre of the dry ingredients; mix well together. Turn the mixture into the prepared tin and bake in the centre of the oven at 350°F (mark 4) for about 1 hr., until well risen and just firm to the touch. Cool on a wire rack.

TO PACK, etc.: Package, seal, label and freeze as directed above.

Bran teabread

3 oz. All-Bran
8 oz. sultanas
8 oz. soft brown sugar
$\frac{1}{2}$ pt. milk
6 oz. self-raising flour
1 level tsp. baking powder

TO MAKE: Mix the bran, sultanas, sugar and milk well together and leave to soak for about 4 hr. Grease and line a loaf tin $9\frac{3}{4}$ in. by $5\frac{3}{4}$ in. (top measurement). Add the flour and baking powder sifted together. Stir well and turn the mixture into the prepared tin.

Bake in the centre of the oven at 375°F (mark 5) for $1–1\frac{1}{4}$ hr. Turn out, remove the paper and cool on a wire rack.

TO PACK, etc.: Package, seal, label and freeze as directed on left.

Apricot tea loaf

8 oz. dried apricots
$\frac{1}{2}$ pt. water, less 2 tbsps.
6 oz. caster sugar
3 oz. lard
$\frac{3}{4}$ level tsp. mixed spice
$\frac{1}{2}$ level tsp. salt
8 oz. plain flour
1 level tsp. bicarbonate of soda
2 eggs, beaten

TO MAKE: Grease a loaf tin $9\frac{3}{4}$ in. by $5\frac{3}{4}$ in. (top measurement). Cut the apricots into small pieces and place in a pan with the water, sugar, lard, spices and salt. Simmer for 5 min., then leave till cold. Sift together the flour and bicarbonate of soda. Make a well in the centre and stir in the apricot mixture and beaten eggs. Mix well, then pour into the prepared tin. Bake in the centre of the oven at 350°F (mark 4) for about $1–1\frac{1}{4}$ hr. Cool on a wire rack.

TO PACK, etc.: Package, seal, label and freeze as directed above.

Banana teabread

7 oz. self-raising flour
$\frac{1}{4}$ level tsp. bicarbonate of soda
$\frac{1}{2}$ level tsp. salt
3 oz. butter
6 oz. sugar
2 eggs, beaten
1 lb. bananas, mashed
4 oz. nuts, coarsely chopped

TO MAKE: Grease and line a loaf tin 8 in. by $4\frac{1}{2}$ in. (top measurement). Sift together the flour, soda and salt. Cream the butter and sugar, add the eggs and beat well. Add the bananas and beat. Stir in the flour and nuts. Turn the mixture into the prepared tin and bake in the centre of the oven at 350°F (mark 4) for about $1\frac{1}{4}$ hr., until well risen and just firm. Turn out and cool on a wire rack.

TO PACK, etc.: Package, seal, label and freeze as directed on page 71.

Cranberry nut loaf

8 oz. plain flour
$1\frac{1}{2}$ level tsps. baking powder
$\frac{1}{2}$ level tsp. bicarbonate of soda
1 level tsp. salt
2 oz. margarine
6 oz. sugar
$\frac{1}{4}$ pt. orange juice
1 tbsp. grated orange rind
1 egg, beaten
3 oz. walnuts, chopped
4 oz. cranberries, chopped

TO MAKE: Grease and line an oblong cake tin 8 in. by $4\frac{1}{4}$ in. (top measurement). Sift together the flour, baking powder, bicarbonate of soda and salt. Rub in the margarine and add the sugar. Mix the orange juice, grated rind and egg. Pour into the dry ingredients and mix lightly. Fold in the walnuts and cranberries. Turn into the tin and bake in the centre of the oven at 350°F (mark 4) for $1-1\frac{1}{4}$ hr. until risen, golden-brown and firm to the touch. Turn out and cool on a wire rack.

TO PACK, etc.: Package, seal, label and freeze as directed on page 71.

Orange teabread

2 oz. butter
6 oz. caster sugar
1 egg, beaten
grated rind and juice of $\frac{1}{2}$ an orange
2 tbsps. milk
8 oz. plain flour
$2\frac{1}{2}$ level tsps. baking powder
pinch of salt

TO MAKE: Grease and bottom-line a loaf tin 8 in. by $4\frac{1}{4}$ in. (top measurement). Cream the butter, add sugar and beat until well mixed; gradually beat in the egg until smooth and creamy. Slowly add the orange rind and juice; do not worry if the mixture curdles. Lightly beat in the milk alternately with the sifted flour, baking powder and salt. Turn into the prepared tin. Bake in the centre of the oven at 375°F (mark 5) for 40–50 min. Turn out and cool on a wire rack.

TO PACK, etc.: Package, label, seal and freeze as directed on page 71.

SCONES

So useful for emergencies when the cake tin is empty! Bake them as usual, but avoid over-browning; cool on a wire rack, and package in foil or plastic trays. To use, either leave the frozen scones at room temperature for $1-1\frac{1}{2}$ hr., or put them in the oven at 400°F (mark 6) while still frozen and wrapped in foil, and 'refresh' them for about 10 min.; leave to cool on a rack, or serve warm.

Sultana round

8 oz. plain flour
2 level tsps. baking powder
2 oz. margarine
1 oz. sultanas
$\frac{1}{4}$ pt. milk, approx.

TO MAKE: Sift together the dry ingredients. Lightly rub in the margarine and add the sultanas. Bind the mixture together with the milk. Knead lightly on a floured board, shape into a flat 6-in. round and mark with the back of a floured knife into 6 triangles. Place on a baking sheet and bake at once near the top of the oven at 450°F (mark 8) for about 15 min. Cool on a wire rack.

TO PACK, etc.: Package, seal, label and freeze as directed above.

Treacle scones

8 oz. plain flour
1 level tsp. bicarbonate of soda
1 level tsp. cream of tartar
$\frac{1}{2}$ level tsp. mixed spice
a pinch of salt
1 oz. margarine
1 level tsp. sugar
2 tbsps. black treacle
$\frac{1}{4}$ pt. milk, approx.
milk to glaze

TO MAKE: Sift together the dry ingredients. Rub the margarine until the mixture resembles fine breadcrumbs. Add the sugar and treacle. Bind the mixture together with the milk. Knead lightly on a floured board and roll to $\frac{1}{2}$ in. thickness. Using a 2-in. fluted cutter, cut 8 rounds. Place on a greased baking sheet, brush tops with milk and bake at 450°F (mark 8) for about 15 min. Cool on a wire rack.

TO PACK, etc.: Package, seal, label and freeze as directed opposite.

Plain scones

2 oz. margarine
8 oz. self-raising flour
1 level tsp. baking powder
$\frac{1}{2}$ level tsp. salt
$\frac{1}{4}$ pt. milk (approx.)
beaten egg

TO MAKE: Grease a baking tray. Rub the fat into the sifted flour, baking powder and salt until the mixture resembles fine bread-crumbs. Make a well in the centre and stir in enough milk to give a fairly soft dough. Turn onto a floured board, knead lightly, then roll to about $\frac{3}{4}$ in. in thickness. Cut into 8 rounds with a 2-in. cutter. Place on a pre-heated baking sheet, brush with beaten egg and bake near the top of the oven at 450°F (mark 8) for 8–10 min., until lightly brown. Cool on a wire rack.

TO PACK, etc.: Package, seal, label and freeze as directed opposite.

Drop scones
(SCOTCH PANCAKES)

4 oz. self-raising flour
$\frac{1}{2}$–1 oz. caster sugar
1 egg
$\frac{1}{4}$ pt. milk

Makes 15–18

TO MAKE: Prepare a special girdle or griddle, a heavy frying-pan, or the solid hot-plate of an electric cooker, by rubbing the surface with salt on a pad of kitchen paper, wiping clean and then greasing lightly. Just before cooking the scones, heat the girdle (or frying-pan etc.) until the lard is 'hazing'. Wipe the surface with a piece of kitchen paper.

Put the flour and sugar in a bowl, add the egg and half the milk and beat until smooth. Add the remaining milk and beat until bubbles rise to the surface. Spoon the mixture onto the heated girdle from the top of the spoon into rounds, spacing them well. When bubbles rise on the surface, turn the scones with a palette knife and cook for a further $\frac{1}{2}$–1 min., or till golden-brown. Place on a cooling rack while the rest are cooked.

TO FREEZE, etc.: When cold, place on a flat surface, freeze until firm, then stack together and package neatly, seal, label and return to the freezer.

TO THAW: Spread out on a tray and put in a cold oven set at 400°F (mark 6) for 10–15 min., until warmed through. Serve buttered, while still warm.

Date scone bar

8 oz. plain flour
$\frac{1}{2}$ level tsp. of bicarbonate of soda
1 level tsp. cream of tartar
a pinch of salt
2 oz. butter or margarine
1 oz. sugar
3 oz. dates, stoned
$\frac{1}{4}$ pt. milk (approx.)

TO MAKE: Sift together the dry ingredients. Rub in the fat to resemble fine breadcrumbs and add the sugar. Using kitchen scissors, snip the dates into small pieces and add to the mixture. Mix to a light dough with the milk. Roll out into an oblong 12 in. by 4 in. Brush with milk and place on a greased baking sheet. Mark through into 8 bars, using the back of a knife. Bake towards the top of the oven at 450°F (mark 8) for about 15 min. Break apart, and cool on a wire rack.

TO PACK, etc.: Package, seal, label and freeze as directed opposite.

Cheese scones

8 oz. self-raising flour
a pinch of salt
1½ oz. margarine
3 oz. cheese, grated
1 level tsp. dry mustard
¼ pt. milk (approx.)

TO MAKE: Grease a baking tray. Sift the flour and salt and rub in the margarine until the mixture resembles fine breadcrumbs. Stir in 2 oz. cheese, the mustard and enough milk to give a fairly soft, light dough. Roll out to ½–¾ in. in thickness and cut into 2-in. rounds. Sprinkle with the rest of the cheese. Put on the greased baking tray and bake towards the top of the oven at 450°F (mark 8) for about 10 min. Cool on a wire rack.

TO PACK, etc.: Package, seal, label and freeze as directed on page 72.

BREADS, ROLLS, YEAST CAKES

Both baked and unbaked dough may be frozen, and so may most of the favourite fancy yeast goods, like babas and Danish pastries.

Bread

All bread, bought or home-baked, freezes well provided it is freshly baked when frozen. Storage times vary with the type of bread.

TO FREEZE: Wrap the bread in foil or polythene bags. If it is likely to be required quickly, wrap it in foil so that it can be placed while still frozen into a hot oven to thaw and 'refresh'. Sliced bread may be toasted from frozen.

Storage times
White and brown bread—up to 4 weeks. Enriched bread and rolls (milk, fruit, malt and soft rolls) up to 6 weeks. Crisp-crusted loaves and rolls: the crusts begin to 'shell off' after 1 week, white Vienna-type loaves and rolls keep for 3 days only.

TO THAW: Loaves: leave in wrapping at room temperature for 3–5 hr., depending on size, or leave overnight in the refrigerator, or place the frozen loaf, wrapped in foil only, in the oven at 400°F (mark 6) for 45 min.
Rolls: leave in wrapping at room temperature for 1½ hr. or place frozen rolls, wrapped in foil only, in the oven at 450°F (mark 8) for 15 min.
Crusty loaves and rolls: thaw at room temperature and 'refresh' in the oven, without wrapping, at 400°F (mark 6) for 5–10 min. until crust is crisp.

Unbaked bread doughs

All standard bread mixtures can be frozen, either after or before rising, but the best results are obtained from doughs made with 50% more yeast than given in the basic recipe, e.g. increase ½ oz. yeast to ¾ oz. Freeze the dough in the amounts you are most likely to use—e.g. 1 lb. 2 oz. dough for a 1-lb. loaf. Heavy-gauge polythene bags, lightly greased, are the best packing. Exclude as much air as possible from the bag before sealing, but if there is any chance of the dough rising a little before freezing, leave 1 in. headspace. Choose bags that are large enough to allow the dough to rise later, but keep the seal close to the filled portion of the bag, leaving any unfilled part beyond the seal.

Unrisen dough

TO FREEZE: After kneading, form the dough into a ball. Place in a greased polythene bag, seal and freeze at once. Store plain white and brown doughs for up to 8 weeks. Enriched dough keeps for 5 weeks.

TO THAW: Unseal bag and re-tie loosely at the top, to allow space for rising. Leave for 5–6 hr. at room temperature, or overnight in the refrigerator. Knock back the risen dough, shape, rise and bake.

Risen dough

Place the dough in a large lightly-greased polythene bag, tie loosely at the top and put to rise in the usual way. Turn the risen dough onto a lightly floured surface, knock out any air bubbles and knead until firm. Return it to the polythene bag and tightly seal.

FREEZE at once. Plain and enriched white and brown doughs store frozen for up to 3 weeks.

TO THAW: Follow unrisen dough directions for thawing and baking.

Par-baked breakfast rolls

A handy and successful way of freezing; the rolls are ready to put straight from the freezer into the oven to complete baking.

TO MAKE: Place the shaped and risen rolls in the oven at 300°F (mark 2) for about 20 min. They should be set but still pale. Cool on a wire rack.

TO FREEZE: Pack in usable quantities, seal, label and freeze—don't pack rolls too tightly together, to avoid squashing. Storage time in the freezer up to 4 months.

TO THAW: Unwrap and place on a baking sheet in the oven for about 20 min.—white rolls at 400°F (mark 6), brown rolls at 450°F (mark 8).

Note: Commercial par-baked loaves and rolls now available from some shops freeze well, if frozen immediately after purchase. Leave loaves in their wrapping, and pack rolls as above. Store for up to 4 months. To thaw: remove wrapping from loaves and complete cooking in the oven at 425°F (mark 7) for 40 min. Cool before slicing. Place unwrapped frozen rolls in the oven at 400°F (mark 6) for 15 min.

Brioches

8 oz. plain flour
$\frac{1}{2}$ level tsp. salt
$\frac{1}{2}$ oz. caster sugar
2 level tsps. dried yeast
$\frac{1}{4}$ level tsp. caster sugar for yeast
3 tbsps. warm water
2 eggs, beaten
2 oz. butter, melted and then cooled but not firm
beaten egg to glaze

TO MAKE: Grease 12 3-in. brioche or deep bun tins. Sift the flour, salt and sugar together into a bowl. Sprinkle the yeast and $\frac{1}{2}$ level tsp. sugar onto the warm water in a small cup and leave in a warm place for about 10 min., until frothy. Add the yeast liquid, eggs and butter to the dry ingredients and work to a soft dough. Turn out onto a floured surface and knead for 5 min. Place the dough in a lightly greased polythene bag, close and allow to rise in a cool place for 2–3 hr. (or in a refrigerator for up to 12 hr.—a cool rising makes the dough easier to shape).

Divide the risen dough into 4 pieces and each quarter portion into 3 pieces. From each piece take three-quarters to form a ball; place the larger part in one of the prepared tins and firmly press a hole in the centre. Form the remaining quarter into a knob and place it in the centre. Place the tins on a baking sheet and put the baking sheet inside a large greased polythene bag. Close, and put to rise in a warm place for about 1 hr., until light and puffy. Brush the risen brioches lightly with egg glaze. Bake in the centre of the oven at 450°F (mark 8) for about 10 min. Cool on a wire rack.

TO PACK AND FREEZE: Place in a polythene bag, seal and label. Freeze and store for up to 4 weeks.

TO THAW: Place the frozen brioches, wrapped in foil, on a baking sheet and 'refresh' in the oven at 450°F (mark 8) for 10 min. Serve at once.

Croissants

1 oz. fresh baker's yeast
$\frac{1}{2}$ pt. water, less 4 tbsps.
1 lb. strong plain flour
2 level tsps. salt
1 oz. lard
1 egg, beaten
4–6 oz. butter or hard margarine
egg to glaze

TO MAKE: Blend the yeast with the water. Sift together the flour and salt and rub in the lard. Add the yeast liquid and egg and mix well together. Knead on a lightly floured surface until the dough is smooth—10–15 min. Roll the dough into a strip about 20 in. by 8 in. and $\frac{1}{4}$ in. thick. Keep the edges straight and the corners square. Soften the butter or margarine with a knife to the consistency of the dough, and then divide into three. Use one part to dot over the top two-thirds of the dough, leaving a small border clear. Fold in three by bringing up the plain (bottom) third first, then folding the top third over. Turn the dough so that the fold is on the right-hand side. Seal the edges with a rolling pin. Reshape to a long strip by gently pressing the dough at intervals with a rolling pin. Repeat with the other two portions of fat. Place the dough in a greased polythene bag to prevent it forming a skin or cracking. Allow to rest in the refrigerator for 30 min. Roll out as before, and repeat the folding and rolling three more times. Place in the refrigerator for at least 1 hr. Roll the dough out to an oblong about 23 in. by 14 in. Cover with lightly greased polythene and leave for 10 min. Trim with a sharp knife to 21 in. by 12 in. and divide in halves lengthwise. Cut each strip into 6 triangles 6 in. high and with a 6-in. base. Brush each triangle with egg glaze, then roll up loosely from the base, finishing with the tip underneath. Place the shaped croissants onto ungreased baking sheets. Brush the tops with egg glaze. Put each baking sheet inside a large lightly greased polythene bag, close and leave at room temperature for about 30 min., until the croissants are light and puffy. Brush again with egg glaze before baking in the centre of a hot oven (425°F, mark 7) for about 20 min.

TO PACK, etc.: Cool on a wire rack. Wrap in a single layer in a polythene bag or kitchen foil or place in a rigid foil container. Seal, label and freeze, and store for up to 2 months.

TO THAW: Leave in packaging at room temperature for 1½–2 hr., then 'refresh', wrapped in foil, in the oven at 425°F (mark 7) for 5 min., or place still frozen and wrapped only in foil, in the oven at 350°F (mark 4) for 15 min.

Savarin

TO MAKE: Make up the basic yeast mixture as for babas, omitting the currants. Grease an 8-in. ring mould or 2 6-in. ones and fill the rings half-full with the mixture. Place inside an oiled polythene bag, close, and leave in a warm place to rise until the moulds are two-thirds full. Bake in the centre of the oven at 400°F (mark 6) for about 20 min. Cool on a wire rack.

TO PACK, etc.: Pack, seal, label and freeze as directed on page 74 under 'Bread'.

TO THAW AND FINISH: Leave wrapped at room temperature for 2–3 hr. Place on a serving dish, prick with a fine skewer or clean hat-pin and soak either with a honey and rum (or honey and kirsch) syrup, or with lemon syrup, or with white wine and thick fruit syrup. Serve with lightly whipped cream.

Alternative finishes:
1. Fill the centre of the savarin with fruit, fresh or canned, and pile whipped cream on top.
2. Sprinkle heavily with caster or icing sugar and fill the centre with whipped cream.
3. Brush with apricot glaze and decorate with glacé cherries, chopped nuts and angelica, then re-brush with glaze and serve with thick pouring cream.

Rum babas

1 oz. fresh baker's yeast (or 1 level tbsp. dried yeast)
6 tbsps. warm milk
8 oz. plain strong flour
½ level tsp. salt
1 oz. caster sugar
4 eggs, beaten
4 oz. butter, soft but not melted
4 oz. currants

TO MAKE: Grease about 16 small ring tins with lard. In a bowl blend together the yeast, milk and 2 oz. of the flour, until smooth. Allow to stand in a warm place until frothy —about 20 min. for fresh yeast, 30 min for dried. Add the remaining flour, the salt, sugar, eggs, butter and currants, and beat thoroughly for 3–4 min. Half-fill the tins with the baba dough, cover with oiled polythene sheeting or a bag and allow to rise till the moulds are two-thirds full. Bake near the top of a fairly hot oven (400°F, mark 6) for 15–20 min. Cool for a few min. and turn out onto a wire tray and leave until cold.

TO PACK, etc.: Wrap carefully in foil, polythene bags or rigid containers. Store in the freezer for up to 3 months.

TO THAW AND FINISH: Place, frozen and wrapped in foil, in the oven at 400°F (mark 6) for 10–15 min. Whilst still hot, spoon over each baba sufficient warm honey and rum syrup to soak it well. Brush with apricot glaze and leave to cool. Transfer to a serving plate, and top with a whirl of whipped cream and a glacé cherry.

Rum syrup
Warm 4 tbsps. clear honey, 4 tbsps. water and rum to taste. Adjust the quantities to suit individual requirements.

Swedish tea ring

8 oz. strong plain flour
½ level tsp. caster sugar
1 level tsp. dried yeast
4 fl. oz. warm milk
½ level tsp. salt
1 oz. margarine
½ an egg, beaten
½ oz. butter, melted
2 oz. brown sugar
2 level tsps. powdered cinnamon

TO MAKE: In a large bowl blend together 2½ oz. of the flour, the sugar, dried yeast and milk. Set aside in a warm place until frothy—about 20 min. Mix the remaining flour with the salt and rub in the margarine. Add the egg and the flour mixture to the yeast batter and beat well to give a fairly soft dough that will leave the sides of the bowl clean. Turn the dough onto a lightly floured surface and knead until it is smooth and no longer sticky —about 10 min. (no extra flour should be necessary). Place the dough in a lightly-greased polythene bag, tie loosely and put to rise until twice its size. Turn the dough onto a floured surface and knead lightly. Roll the dough to an oblong 12 in. by 9 in. Brush with melted butter, then sprinkle the mixed brown sugar and cinnamon over the dough. Roll up tightly from the long edge and seal the ends together to form a ring. Place on a greased baking sheet. Using scissors, cut slashes at an angle 1 in. apart and to within ½ in of the

centre. Turn the cut sections to one side. Cover with a lightly greased polythene bag and put to rise in a warm place for about 30 min. Bake just above the centre of a fairly hot oven at 375°F (mark 5) for 30–35 min. Cool on a wire rack.

TO PACK, etc.: Pack, seal, label and freeze —see page 74.

TO THAW: See page 74.

TO FINISH: Blend 4 oz. icing sugar with lemon juice and a little water to give a coating consistency. Drizzle icing over the yeast ring and decorate with glacé cherries, angelica leaves and flaked almonds. Leave to set.

Danish pastries

1 level tsp. caster sugar for yeast
5 tbsps. warm water
1½ level tsps. dried yeast
1 oz. lard
8 oz. soft plain flour
a pinch of salt
1 egg, beaten
½ oz. caster sugar
5 oz. Danish butter

TO MAKE: Add the 1 tsp. sugar to the water, sprinkle the yeast on top and leave in a warm place until frothing—about 10 min. Meanwhile rub the lard into the sifted flour and salt and make a well in the centre. Stir in the yeast mixture, the egg and ½ oz. sugar. Mix to a soft dough and knead on a floured surface until smooth. Place in a greased polythene bag, close and leave to rest in a cool place—preferably the refrigerator—for 10 min. Work the butter to a thin oblong block measuring 9 in. by 3 in. Roll out the dough to a 10-in. square, place the butter in the centre and fold the sides of the dough over to just overlap. Seal the top and bottom. Roll out to an oblong 15 in. by 5 in. Fold the top one-third down and the bottom one-third up, place in the polythene bag and leave for 10 min. Repeat the rolling, folding and resting twice more. Lastly, leave the dough in a cool place for ½ hr. before use.

Finishes for Danish pastries:
Crescents
Roll out half the dough to a 10-in. square. Cut

into 4 squares. Cut each square in two diagonally. Place a small piece of almond paste at the base of each triangle, roll up from the base, shape into a crescent and put on a baking sheet. Leave, lightly covered, in a warm place for about 20 min., until puffy. Brush with beaten egg and bake towards the top of a hot oven (425°F, mark 7) for about 10 min. Cool on a wire rack (*Makes 8*).

Windmills
Roll out half the dough to an oblong measuring 12 in. by 8 in. Cut into 4-in. squares. Make diagonal cuts from each corner to within $\frac{1}{2}$ in. of the centre. Put a piece of almond paste in the middle and fold alternate corners to the centre, overlapping each other. Continue as for crescents but bake for about 20 min. (*Makes 6*).

Fruit pinwheels
Roll out as for windmills. Spread with spiced butter (1 oz. butter, 1 oz. caster sugar and 1 level tsp. powdered cinnamon, creamed together) and scatter with a few currants and finely chopped peel. Cut in halves lengthwise. Roll each piece from a short end to form a thick roll. Cut into 1-in. slices and place, cut slightly and continue as for crescents. (*Makes 8*).

TO PACK, etc.: As for croissants (see page 76), but use within 4 weeks.

TO THAW: Loosen packaging and leave at room temperature for $1\frac{1}{2}$ hr., then 'refresh' in the oven at 350°F (mark 4) for 5 min. or place frozen, without wrapping, at the same temperature for 10 min. While still hot, brush with glacé icing. Cool, and eat while fresh.

5. Parties and Entertaining

Take the terror out of entertaining by preparing the food in advance. This way, you'll *know* it's going to be all-right-on-the-night—have time to set the house to rights—and possibly even go and get your hair done.

All made-up dishes, meat, fish and poultry, etc., are best thawed in the refrigerator. However, when you thaw at room temperature, ensure an even temperature and cover the food lightly.

Dip and spread parties

Taramasalata*   Frikadeller*
Guacamole*   Smoked Salmon*
Ceviche*   Cheese Straws*

Dinner Parties

MENU FOR FOUR
Jellied Consommé
Chopped Hard-boiled Egg
and Onion   French Bread
Steak au Poivre*
Green Salad
Cheeseboard*

MENU FOR SIX
Home-made Cream of Vegetable Soup
with Chives*   French Bread
Shoulder of Lamb with
Apricot and Ginger Stuffing*
Roast Potatoes
Cauliflower Sprigs à la Polonaise
Crêpes Suzette*

MENU FOR FOUR
Gazpacho*
Trout Meunière*
Tiny New Potatoes
Courgettes with Parsley
Profiteroles*
Chocolate and Rum Sauce*

MENU FOR SIX
Salmon Mousse*   Fresh Toast
Boeuf en Croûte   Potatoes with Chives
Tomato, Chicory and Lettuce Salad
Lemon and Blackcurrant Sorbets*

MENU FOR SIX
Smoked Trout or Mackerel*
Chicken and Lemon Pie*
Leaf Spinach   Lyonnaise Potatoes
Raspberry Vacherin*

MENU FOR FOUR
Individual Ratatouilles*   Grissini
Beef Goulash with Soured Cream*
Buttered Rice
Baby Brussels Sprouts*
Chilled Poached Pears
with Melba Sauce*
Crème Chantilly*

MENU FOR SIX
Ratatouille with Garlic*
Steak, Kidney and Oyster Pie*
Buttered Spring Greens
Creamy Buttered Potatoes
Caramel Custard*
Sponge Fingers

MENU FOR EIGHT
Chicken Liver Pâté*
Grilled or Fried Mackerel
Gooseberry Sauce*
and Horseradish Cream*
New Potatoes   Salad Greens
Danish Peasant Girl with Veil*

MENU FOR FOUR
Courgettes à la Grecque*
Chicken Kiev*
Minted New Potatoes
Dressed Green Salad or Broccoli
Apricot Soufflé*

MENU FOR SIX
Bortsch with Soured Cream*
Moussaka*   Boiled Potatoes with Parsley
Salad Greens with Lemon Dressing
Summer Fruit Salad*   Thick Pouring Cream

Dinner Parties (contd)

MENU FOR SIX
Prawn and Cod Bisqui*
Veal Escalopes*   Sauce Aurore*
Fluffy Whipped Potatoes
Petits Pois
Pineapple Creams*   Brandy Snaps

MENU FOR SIX
Kipper Pâté*   Melba Toast
Coq au Vin*   Creamed Potatoes
Broccoli Spears*   or Baby Carrots*
Orange Sorbet*

MENU FOR EIGHT
Individual Mixed Fish Pâtés*
Hot Toast Fingers
Jugged Hare
with Forcemeat Balls*
Boiled Potatoes
Buttered Green or Red Cabbage
Oranges with Caramel*

MENU FOR SIX
Coquilles St. Jacques*
Noisettes of Lamb*
Buttered New Potatoes
Tossed Green Salad
Pavlova*

MENU FOR FOUR
Fresh Tomato Salad
with French Dressing*
Chicken with Curry and Lemon*
Fluffy Boiled Rice*
Cucumber Slices
with Yoghurt Dressing
Meringues Chantilly*

MENU FOR SIX
Country-style Pâté*
Melba Toast or French Bread
Boeuf Bourguignonne* Plain Boiled Potatoes
Leeks and Carrot Sticks
Melon, Strawberry and Almond Salad*

MENU FOR EIGHT
Chilled Watercress Soup*
French Bread or Croûtons*
Boeuf Stroganoff*
Freshly Boiled Rice
Sliced Courgettes or Tossed Green Salad
Cheesecake Topped with Fruit*

Quiche Party for 25

Quiche Lorraine*
Quiches with alternative fillings*
Rice Salad with Lemon Dressing
Green Salad with French Dressing

Tomato and Onion Salad with Garlic Dressing
French Bread and Butter
Orange Salad and Caramel*
Vacherin with Raspberries and Cream*
or Strawberries and Cream*

Buffet-style meals for a dozen or over

BUFFET-STYLE MENU FOR 15
Sweet-sour Pork*
Freshly Boiled Rice   Green Salad
Oranges with Caramel*
and Pouring Cream
Profiteroles*   Chocolate Rum Sauce*

INFORMAL BUFFET MENU FOR 12
Stuffed Pancakes*
Dressed Salad of Red and Green
Peppers, Chicory and Watercress
Pavlova with Peaches*

WEDDING BUFFET FOR 35–40
Baked Salmon Trout*
Boeuf en Croûte*   Horseradish Cream*
Boned Turkey* with Apricot and
Ginger Stuffing*
Smoked Trout and/or Mackerel*
Mustard Cream
Cole Slaw, Celery and Potato Mayonnaise

Chicory and Orange Salad with
French Dressing
Garlic-dressed Tomato and Onion Salad
French Bread and Butter
Pavlova*
Charlotte Russe*
Summer Fruit Salad* with Pouring Cream

Teenage Parties

SOUTH AMERICAN PARTY FOR 12
Chilli con Carne*
Freshly Boiled Rice
Cucumber Salad
Summer Fruit Salad with Cream*
Home-made Ice Cream* and Melba Sauce*

GREEK PARTY FOR 12
Taramasalata*   Freshly made Toast
Moussaka*
Iced Cucumber and Mint Salad
Ice Cream* with Honey and Chopped Nuts
Fresh Fruit

ITALIAN PARTY FOR 12
Iced Cream of Tomato Soup*
Quick Pizza*
Watercress and Chicory Salad
French Dressing
Iced Zabaione* or Lemon Sorbet*

Hot Fork Suppers

CURRY PARTY
Beef, Chicken and Prawn Curries*
Freshly Boiled Rice   Side Dishes
Fresh Fruit Salad or Orange Salad or
Strawberries and Cream or
Lemon Sorbet*

PASTA PARTY
Chicken Tettrazini*
Lasagne*
Macaroni Cheese*
Dressed Green Salad
Tomato & Onion Salad
French Bread and Butter
Fresh Pineapple Slices
Fresh Fruit
Cherries in Wine

PAELLA PARTY FOR 12
Gazpacho*
Paella*   Dressed Mixed Salad
French Bread
Pineapple Cream*
Vacherin
with Raspberries and Cream*

The well-ordered Christmas and other occasions

CHRISTMAS MENUS
Suggestions for newer and more
traditional fare; recipes for
Mince Pies   Brandy and Rum Butters

SIT-DOWN MEAL FOR 15 GUESTS
Chilled Watercress Soup*
Chicken Marengo*
Saffron-flavoured Rice   Cucumber Salad
Pineapple Creams*

Tea Parties

Asparagus Rolls   Smoked Salmon Pinwheels*
Stuffed Olive Pinwheels*
Chequerboard and Ribbon Sandwiches*
Devil's Food Cake*
Meringues*
Gateau Marguerite*

Toddler's Party

Sandwich Specials
Teddy Bears Cake*
Crisps
Milk Shakes and Fruit Squash

Dip and spread parties

For people who love to experiment with food, flavours and texture, but don't want to do too much cooking, for the hostess who enjoys the challenge of presenting food in an imaginative way—this is the ideal party.

Our recipes will see an evening party through for about twenty people. You can add or subtract or multiply to suit yourself, for, say, a drinks and nibblers cocktail occasion. One hot-flavoured dip—like the barbecue sauce on page 44—is a sure winner with meatballs or sausages. The cool, creamy dips ask for a good choice of dunkers—whole radishes, cauliflower florets, carrot sticks, celery, spring onions—as well as pretzels, crisps and crackers. The rough meaty texture of our country-style pâté is an excellent foil for the lighter dips. With this, as with the smooth liver pâté and the Taramasalata, the right accompaniments are coarse brown bread, pumpernickel, oatcakes, Dorset knobs and assorted plain crispbreads.

QUANTITY GUIDE		
	Item	Serves
Pâtés	chicken liver pâté	10
	simple chicken liver pâté	4–6
	country-style pâté	6
	kipper pâté	6
	taramasalata	8
	pâté de Bruxelles	6–8
	Peter's pâté	8
	farmhouse pâté	4–6
	meat pâté	8–10
	hunter's pâté	10
	fresh salmon pâté	6–8
Dips	guacamole	8
	ceviche	6
Nibblers	frikadeller with barbecue sauce	Makes 60
	smoked salmon fingers	Makes 16
	cheese straws	Makes 40
Note	See Index for pâtés in other chapters.	

Taramasalata

8 oz. smoked cod's roe, skinned
12 tbsps. olive oil
juice and a little grated rind of 1 lemon
1 level tsp. grated onion
1 level tbsp. chopped parsley
freshly ground black pepper

Serves 8

TO MAKE: Place the roe in a bowl with half the olive oil and leave for 10 min. Pass it through a fine sieve, or blend in an electric blender until smooth, gradually adding the lemon juice and the remaining oil. Turn the mixture into a bowl, then stir in the lemon rind, onion, parsley and freshly ground black pepper.

TO PACK: Turn into a $\frac{3}{4}$–1-pt. foil dish.

TO FREEZE: Cover with lid or foil, label and seal.

TO THAW: Allow to thaw in the refrigerator for 8 hr. or overnight, or for about $4\frac{1}{2}$ hr. at room temperature.

TO SERVE: Unwrap and turn into a serving dish. Sprinkle with more parsley, or add twists of lemon. Eat with hot toast or crackers.

Note: Canned cod's roe cannot be substituted for smoked in this recipe.

Guacamole

3 small ripe avocados
3 tbsps. fresh lemon juice
an 8-oz. pkt. of full-fat soft cheese
a dash of Tabasco sauce
a good pinch of Cayenne pepper

Serves 8

TO MAKE: Cut each avocado in half, twist the halves in opposite directions and remove the stones. Scoop out the flesh into an electric blender goblet, add the lemon juice and cheese and blend until smooth in texture. (Alternatively, pass the avocado through a sieve before beating in the lemon juice and cheese.) Add the tabasco sauce and cayenne pepper; beat again.

TO PACK: Turn the mixture into a 1-lb. pudding dish (to serve 6) and put the remainder into a $4\frac{1}{2}$-in. round foil dish (to serve 2). Overwrap, or cover with a lid, seal and label.

TO FREEZE: Freeze rapidly until solid.

TO THAW: Leave overnight in the refrigerator or for 4–6 hr. at room temperature.

TO SERVE: Stir in a little onion salt, if you like it; dust with paprika pepper and garnish with stuffed olives. Serve with crisp biscuits.

Ceviche

1¼ lb. filleted mackerel
juice of 2 lemons
1 large tomato
1 small onion
1 small green chilli (or ¼ level tsp. chilli
  powder)
4 tbsps. olive oil
1½ tbsps. wine vinegar

Serves 6

TO MAKE: Wipe and skin the fish and remove any remaining bones. Place in a shallow
dish. Pour the lemon juice over, cover and
leave for 24 hr. in the refrigerator, basting
occasionally. Place the fish and juices in an
electric blender with the peeled and quartered
tomato and the peeled and sliced onion. Cut
a slice from the stalk end of the chilli; slice
the chilli in half, discarding all seeds and pith,
and cut in small pieces. Place in the blender
(or add the chilli powder), with the other
ingredients. Add the oil and vinegar, and
blend until quite smooth.

TO PACK: Place in 2 small foil containers
(each sufficient for 3 persons, as a starter).
Overwrap in a polythene bag or cover with
a lid. Seal and label.

TO FREEZE: Freeze rapidly until solid.

TO THAW: Leave in the refrigerator overnight, or for about 8 hr.

TO SERVE: Return the mixture to the blender
and season to taste. Turn it into a serving
dish and garnish with black or green olives,
chopped parsley and a twist of lemon if liked.
Serve with crisp savoury biscuits for
spreading.

Frikadeller

2 lb. lean pork, finely minced
2 small onions, peeled and minced
1 level tsp. salt
freshly ground black pepper
4 level tbsps. flour
2 eggs, beaten
a little milk if necessary
fat for deep frying

Makes approx. 60

*Assorted dips, spreads and dunks: chicken liver
pâté, taramasalata, ceviche, guacamole, barbecue
sauce; frikadeller, cheese straws and smoked
salmon fingers*

TO MAKE: Place the minced pork in a bowl.
Add the onions, salt, pepper and flour. Bind
with beaten egg and sufficient milk to give a
soft but manageable mixture. Roll into small
balls the size of a walnut. Heat the fat until
it will brown a cube of bread in 1 min. Cook
the meatballs until brown—allow about 6
min. Drain on absorbent kitchen paper and
cool.

TO PACK AND FREEZE: Place the cold
frikadeller in a polythene bag. Freeze rapidly
until solid. Overwrap by placing inside another polythene bag. Seal and label.

TO RE-HEAT: Unwrap and place on a
greased baking sheet. Re-heat from frozen in
the oven at 400°F (mark 6) for 15–20 min.

TO SERVE: Use to dip into home-made barbecue sauce (see page 44) or mustard or
tomato sauce. Alternatively, serve on pasta
with sauce, as a supper dish or snack.

Smoked salmon

Buy 2 oz. per head for use as a starter.

TO PACK: Place the slices of smoked salmon between layers of freezing paper; make into a parcel, using foil.

TO FREEZE: Place the parcel inside a polythene bag. Seal and label. Freeze rapidly.

TO THAW: Allow 8 hr. in refrigerator or 4 hr. at room temperature.

TO SERVE: As a cocktail nibbler, serve on fingers of thinly cut brown bread and butter; 4 oz. smoked salmon will cover 4 small slices of bread, and each can then be cut into 4 fingers. Squeeze a little lemon juice on each, add freshly ground black pepper to taste and garnish with lemon butterflies. As a starter, serve with lemon wedges and brown bread and butter.

Cheese straws

4 oz. plain flour
salt and cayenne pepper
2 oz. butter
2 oz. mature Cheddar cheese, grated
1 egg yolk
cold water to mix

Makes 40

TO MAKE: Season the flour with salt and cayenne and rub in the butter to give the texture of fine breadcrumbs. Mix in the cheese and egg yolk, with enough cold water to give a stiff dough. Roll out the pastry thinly and trim into oblongs 8 in. long and $2\frac{1}{2}$ in. wide. Put onto a greased baking tray and cut each into straws $2\frac{1}{2}$ in. long and $\frac{1}{4}$ in. wide, separating them as you cut. Roll out the remaining pastry and cut rounds with a 2-in. plain cutter, then cut out the centre of the rounds with a $1\frac{1}{2}$-in. plain cutter. Put all onto the baking tray. Bake towards the top of the oven for 10–15 min. at 400°F (mark 6) until pale golden in colour—watch carefully. Remove from the oven and cool slightly on the tray before cooling completely on a wire rack.

TO PACK: Line a plastic box or foil container with freezer paper. Lift the straws into box and cover each layer with a piece of freezer paper. Cover with lid.

TO FREEZE: Label, seal and freeze.

TO RE-HEAT: Return frozen straws to baking sheet. Whisk 1 egg white until frothy, then use to brush the straws lightly. Sprinkle with Parmesan cheese and dust with paprika pepper, if liked. 'Refresh' in the oven at 450°F (mark 8) for 10 min., until crisp and brown. Cool, then put a few straws into each ring before serving.

Dinner Parties

Menus for four, for six and for eight people, all built around first-class food from the freezer.

Menu for four

Jellied consommé
Chopped hard-boiled egg and onion   *French bread*
Steak au poivre   *Green salad*
Cheeseboard

Skip the French bread, and you have the perfect slimmers' lunch or dinner. If calories don't worry you, the cheese could be replaced by a sorbet, by ice cream and chocolate sauce or by an iced zabaione, for a super in-haste meal.

COUNTDOWN

TWO DAYS BEFORE: Take cheese from freezer, unwrap and leave in refrigerator.

MORNING: Take cheese from refrigerator and leave at room temperature. (If you prefer a sweet, see separate recipes for thawing times.)

AT APPROPRIATE HOUR (according to whether you are serving lunch or dinner): Set table. Select wines. Set plates to warm for steak. Make up green salad. Spoon jellied consommé into bowls and leave in fridge until required. Hard-boil and chop egg and chop onion finely. Place in separate bowls, as accompaniments to the consommé. Arrange cheeseboard. Dress salad just before taking it to table. Start cooking steaks, if fully frozen, before serving the consommé.

Steak au poivre

4 fresh rump steaks (8–10 oz. each)
½ oz. whole black peppercorns

TO MAKE: Wipe the steaks. Crush peppercorns with a rolling pin between sheets of greaseproof, or use a pestle and mortar. Coat each side of steaks lightly with crushed peppercorns, pressing them on lightly with the palm of the hand.

TO PACK: Place on a large sheet of foil with freezer paper between them so that the steaks can be easily separated. Make into a neat parcel.

TO FREEZE: Overwrap, using a polythene bag or foil. Seal and label. Freeze rapidly.

TO THAW: Allow 8–9 hr. in the refrigerator or 4 hr. at room temperature, or cook straight from frozen state.

TO COOK: Heat 3 oz. butter and 1 tbsp. oil in a large frying pan. Add the steaks, turn

once and cook 5–8 min. in all if thawed, or 12–15 min. if frozen. Keep warm on a serving plate. At this stage, if you wish, add 2 tbsps. brandy to the juices in the pan, flambé, remove from heat and stir in ¼ pt. double cream. Heat gently, adjust seasoning, then pour over the steaks.

TO SERVE: Garnish with watercress.

Cheeseboard

(*see picture below*)

Make a selection for the freezer from a ripe Camembert, Boursin with garlic, and a cream cheese with herbs. Valmeuse or Brie, when ripe, can also be frozen successfully. It is not advisable to freeze hard or blue cheeses,

Cheeseboard

since they develop a crumbly texture which is not suitable for a cheeseboard, though as there is no flavour change they can be used for cooking or for using in sandwiches and salads.

TO PACK: Wrap closely in a double layer of foil.

TO FREEZE: Overwrap, using a polythene bag. Seal and label the packs. Freeze rapidly.

TO THAW: Allow 1–2 days in the refrigerator, then allow time to 'come to' at room temperature before serving.

TO SERVE: Arrange attractively on a board (or platter) and add a touch of garnish-cum-accompaniment, such as small radishes, celery or watercress.

Menu for six

Home-made cream of vegetable soup with chives   French bread
Shoulder of lamb with apricot and ginger stuffing
Roast potatoes   Cauliflower sprigs à la polonaise
Crêpes Suzette

A warm and welcoming cold-weather menu suitable for lunch or dinner. The home-made vegetable soup is made up in bulk when vegetables are plentiful/and cheap: for recipe see page 140. The boned and stuffed shoulder of lamb will keep for up to a month in the freezer. With the aid of the freezer, crêpes Suzette—sometimes thought to be a restaurant-only speciality—become quite possible, as the last-minute work is greatly simplified. Don't be frightened of the spectacular flambé act—it's not really difficult.

COUNTDOWN

EARLY EVENING: 3 hr. before guests arrive start cooking the joint of lamb. Set table, select wines. Ask the man of the house to sharpen the carving knife. Take soup from freezer and turn it into a pan. Prepare vegetables. Set plates to warm. Remove cover from meat $\frac{1}{2}$ hr. before end of cooking time. Baste meat and potatoes (which should be added at the usual time). Make gravy. Heat the soup slowly; stir occasionally. Transfer crêpes Suzette from the freezer container to a well-buttered ovenproof dish and dot with extra orange butter; cover with foil. Add cream to the warm soup and re-heat but don't boil; garnish with chives before taking to the table. Cook vegetables. Set crêpes in the oven as the meat is removed; flambé them before serving.

Stuffed shoulder of lamb

a $3\frac{1}{2}$-lb. shoulder of lamb, boned

For the stuffing
4 oz. fresh white breadcrumbs
2 oz. shredded suet
4 pieces of stem ginger, finely chopped
4 oz. drained canned apricot halves, chopped,
   or 8 oz. dried apricots, soaked overnight
   in water
1 large egg, beaten
seasoning

Note: As the lamb is being frozen uncooked,

do make sure that it has not been frozen and thawed before sale.

TO MAKE: Wipe the meat. Prepare the stuffing: mix the breadcrumbs and suet together, add the ginger and apricots, then bind with the egg; add a little seasoning. Stuff the lamb, using skewers to secure the joint into a good shape; tie with fine string, then withdraw the skewers.

TO PACK: Wrap in foil, making a neat parcel. Overwrap in a polythene bag, seal and label.

TO FREEZE: Freeze rapidly until solid.

TO SERVE: Cook uncovered from frozen at 350°F (mark 4) in the centre of the oven, allowing 40 min. per lb. and 40 min. over.

Crêpes Suzette

Crêpes Suzette

(*see picture on right*)

butter or oil for frying
¾ pt. rich pancake batter (see below)
6 oz. butter
6 oz. caster sugar
grated rind of 2 large lemons
juice and grated rind of 2 large oranges
8 tbsps. Cointreau

TO MAKE: Heat a little butter in a 7-in. thick-based frying-pan; pour off excess and cook each pancake in the usual way, making 12 altogether. Transfer each one onto a square of freezer paper. Cream together the butter and sugar until light and fluffy. Gradually beat in the grated rinds, orange juice and Cointreau.

Note: If at this stage the mixture separates,

put the bowl over hot water and whisk rapidly, then place over cold water and whisk again, until smooth and well blended. Spread half the filling across the pancakes; fold each in half and then in half again. Layer up the pancakes with freezer paper between them.

TO PACK AND FREEZE: Wrap the pancakes in foil and then overwrap, or place in a rigid container. Seal and label. Pack the remainder of the orange butter in a small plastic container. Freeze until solid.

TO COOK: Transfer the frozen crêpes to a shallow buttered ovenproof dish, dot with the reserved orange butter, then cover with foil. Heat through in the oven at 400°F (mark 6) for ½ hr.

TO SERVE: Warm 2–3 tbsps. brandy in a small pan and ignite; pour it flaming over the crêpes, and serve at once, decorated with a twist of orange.

RICH PANCAKE BATTER: Sift 6 oz. plain flour and a pinch of salt into a bowl. Make a well in the centre and break in 2 small eggs. Add ½ pt. milk and gradually incorporate the flour, beating. Add a further ¼ pt. milk and ¾ oz. melted butter, and beat until smooth and bubbly.

TO COMPLETE DISHES FROM THE FREEZER YOU WILL NEED

For Soup
¼ pt. single cream · chives

For Shoulder of Lamb
butter to baste · gravy

For Crêpes Suzette
brandy · orange twist to decorate

Menu for four

Gazpacho

Trout meunière
Tiny new potatoes
Courgettes with parsley

Profiteroles
Chocolate and rum sauce

Gazpacho

A good menu for the cook who doesn't like spending too much time in the kitchen at the last minute. Have a salad in lieu of the courgettes if you prefer.

COUNTDOWN

IN THE MORNING: Take trout from the freezer. Leave wrapped and set it on a large plate in the refrigerator for about 12 hr. to thaw. Take gazpacho from the freezer, unwrap and place in a bowl. Thaw at room temperature for about 6 hr.

TO COMPLETE DISHES FROM THE
FREEZER YOU WILL NEED
For Gazpacho
1 clove of garlic
a 15-oz. can of tomato juice
chopped parsley · fried bread croûtons
onion · red and green peppers
hard-boiled egg
For Trout
seasoned flour · butter and oil
2 lemons · watercress
For Profiteroles
½ pt. double cream, whipped
icing sugar

LATE AFTERNOON Put profiteroles on a baking sheet and refresh in the oven at 350°F. (mark 4) for about 10 min. to crisp up; cool on a wire rack. Fill with whipped cream just before guests arrive. Chocolate and rum sauce can be unwrapped and heated through straight from the freezer in a double boiler.

Prepare selected vegetables. Prepare accompaniments for gazpacho. Set table and chill wine. When guests arrive, set vegetables to cook. Cook fish on one side, turn it, then serve first course immediately while it is cooking gently on the other side.

Gazpacho

(*see picture above*)

1 lb. tomatoes, peeled, quartered and seeded
1 small onion, peeled and quartered
½ a cucumber, cut into chunks
4 tbsps. wine vinegar
2 tbsps. olive oil
2 tbsps. red wine

TO MAKE: Purée the tomatoes, onion and cucumber in an electric blender. Pour the mixture into a bowl and stir in the vinegar, oil and wine.

TO PACK AND FREEZE: Line a 2-pt. container with a polythene bag and pour in the gazpacho. When it is frozen, remove the polythene bag from the pre-former, place inside another polythene bag, seal and label.

TO THAW: Leave at room temperature for about 6 hr.

TO SERVE: Add 1 clove of garlic, peeled and crushed, stir in a 15-oz. can of tomato juice, adjust the seasoning and add 1 tbsp. chopped parsley. Serve with fried bread croûtons (fresh or frozen—see page 163), finely chopped onion, chopped red and green peppers and chopped hard-boiled egg.

Trout meunière

(*See picture below*)

4 rainbow trout about 8 oz. each (they must be absolutely fresh and not previously frozen; ask the fishmonger to clean them)

TO PREPARE AND PACK: Wipe each fish with a damp cloth. Either wrap in freezer paper, then in foil, *or* treat as follows: Place the fish in a shallow bowl of water with plenty of ice cubes. Turn each fish over and over in the water, then place on a wire tray in the freezer till frozen. Repeat, immersing the fish in more iced water, and then returning it to the freezer; do this 5 times altogether. Gradually a coat of ice builds up which prevents evaporation. Overwrap in double foil on mutton cloth and then place in a polythene bag. Seal and label.

TO THAW: Set the fish on a large plate. Allow 12 hr. in the refrigerator, still in the wrappings. Only if time is very short should you thaw the fish at room temperature, in a bowl of cold water, or cook them from frozen; in this case, allow $\frac{1}{2}$ hr. cooking time. and use a large pan, as the fish, being rigid, will not 'give' to the shape of a smaller pan.

TO COOK: Place the fish on absorbent kitchen paper and toss in 2 oz. seasoned flour. Fry in 2–3 oz. hot butter and 2 tbsps. oil, allowing 5 min. on each side. Turn the fish carefully. Lift them out onto a serving plate. Add the juice of 1 lemon to the pan juices, allow to boil, then pour over the fish immediately.

TO SERVE: Garnish with lemon wedges and sprigs of watercress.

Profiteroles

Make according to the recipe on page 50 (about 22). Fill with the whipped double cream, sprinkle with icing sugar and pile on to a serving dish. Serve with chocolate and rum sauce.

Chocolate and rum sauce

8 oz. plain chocolate
2 oz. unsalted butter
4 tbsps. milk
2 tbsps. rum

Makes $\frac{1}{2}$ pt.

TO MAKE: Break chocolate into small pieces and place in a bowl over a pan of hot water. Add the butter and milk. Stir occasionally until glossy and smooth. Stir in the rum.

TO PACK: Pour into a foil container or plastic tub. Overwrap, label and seal.

TO FREEZE: Freeze until solid.

TO USE: Unwrap then place in a double boiler and cook gently, stirring, till the sauce is smooth. Pour over the profiteroles, or serve separately.

Notes: The sauce separates out during freezing, but returns to a good consistency on being re-heated.

If you should have a quantity of sauce left over after the meal, cool it, then pack, seal and label, and return it to the freezer.

TO FREEZE WHOLE FISH—*prepare in the usual way, retaining or removing the tail, fins and eyes, as you prefer Chill the fish, then at frequent intervals dip in iced water and return it to the freezer, so building up about $\frac{1}{4}$ in. of ice to cover it entirely; see Trout Meuniere*

Menu for six

Salmon mousse   Fresh toast
Boeuf en croûte   Potatoes with chives   Tomato, chicory and lettuce salad
Lemon and blackcurrant sorbets

A really impressive dinner party—for very special friends or to win your husband a promotion ? The salmon mousse looks attractive presented individually in little soufflé dishes. The *pièce de résistance*, boeuf en croûte, does not mean hours of preparation and will certainly set the seal of success on any party. Lemon and blackcurrant make a perfect combination of flavours to round off a memorable evening.

COUNTDOWN

EARLY THE PREVIOUS DAY: Take the boeuf en croûte out of the freezer; leave wrappings in place but loosen the seal. Set on a plate in the refrigerator for about 35 hr. before cooking so that it will be totally thawed.

LATE AFTERNOON ON THE DAY: Take individual salmon mousses from freezer, unwrap and leave at room temperature to thaw. Set table, select wines. Prepare potatoes and ingredients for salad. Pour dressing ingredients into jar but don't shake up. Garnish the salmon mousses. Cut bread ready for toasting to serve with mousse. Arrange salad in bowl. Pop boeuf en croûte in oven as guests arrive, then the potatoes a few min. later. Dress salad before taking it to the table and take sorbets from freezer just before serving main course.

Salmon mousse

2 7½-oz. cans of red salmon
juice and grated rind of 1 lemon
3 level tsps. powdered gelatine
¼ pt. water
½ pt. double cream, whipped
salt and freshly milled pepper

TO MAKE: Remove any dark skin from the salmon and mash, with the juices, on a large plate (even better, purée, using an electric blender). Turn it into a bowl. Add the lemon juice and grated rind. Dissolve the gelatine in the water in a small bowl set in a pan of gently bubbling water. When cool but still liquid, stir into the fish mixture. Fold in the cream, which should just hold its shape. Adjust the seasoning.

TO PACK AND FREEZE: Put into 6 individual ramekin dishes; cover with foil caps. Overwrap with a double layer of foil, or use a polythene bag to group the dishes together; seal, label and freeze until solid.

TO THAW: Place in the fridge to thaw overnight or allow 4 hr. at room temperature.

TO SERVE: Garnish with cucumber slices or twists and some chopped parsley.

Boeuf en croûte

(*see colour picture facing page 128*)

2 lb. fillet of beef
2 rashers of bacon, rinded
salt and pepper
½ lb. button mushrooms, sliced
2 oz. butter
¾ lb. ready-made puff pastry

TO MAKE: Place the beef in a roasting tin with the bacon rashers laid across the surface. Cook in the oven at 400°F (mark 6) for 15 min. Take from the oven and remove the bacon; leave to cool rapidly. Sauté the seasoned mushrooms in butter for 3–4 min.; drain. Either sieve the mushrooms or chop very finely. Leave to become cold. Roll out the pastry into an oblong 14 in. long, and the width of the fillet plus 3 in. Cover centre area of pastry with mushrooms, then place the beef on top. Damp the edges of the pastry, then bring up the edges over the ends of the fillet to form a neat parcel—make sure that the edges are well sealed. Invert só that the sealed edges are underneath. Decorate with the pastry trimmings.

TO PACK: Set on a double thickness of kitchen foil placed over a baking sheet; chill until the pastry is firm, then wrap neatly in foil.

TO FREEZE: Overwrap in a polythene bag, label and freeze until solid.

TO THAW: Loosen seal, but leave wrapped in the refrigerator for about 36 hr.

TO COOK: Place on a wetted baking sheet in the oven, pre-heated to 450°F (mark 8) and bake for 15 min. Brush with beaten egg and continue to cook for a further 20–30 min.

TO SERVE: Garnish with sprigs of watercress. Slice at the table, using a sharp knife.

Blackcurrant sorbet

½ pt. water
4 oz. sugar
½ lb. fresh or frozen blackcurrants
1 tsp. lemon juice
2 egg whites

Serves 4–6

TO MAKE: Place the water in a saucepan with the sugar, bring to the boil and boil gently for 10 min. Cool. Meanwhile stew the blackcurrants in the minimum amount of water for about 10 min., then sieve and if necessary make the pulp up to 1 pt. with

---

TO COMPLETE DISHES FROM THE
FREEZER YOU WILL NEED
For Salmon Mousse
bread for toast · cucumber · parsley

For Boeuf en Croûte
egg to glaze · watercress

For Sorbets
a mint leaf to decorate

---

water. Cool. Mix together the sugar syrup, lemon juice and fruit pulp. Pour into an ice tray and freeze until nearly firm. Whisk the egg whites until stiff but not dry. Turn the frozen fruit mixture into a chilled bowl, break down with a fork and fold in the egg whites. Return the sorbet to the ice tray and freeze until firm.

TO PACK: Turn the sorbet into a rigid plastic container or foil tray, cover, seal and return it to the freezer.

TO SERVE: Soften the sorbet for a short time in the refrigerator—say, while serving the starter or main course of the meal. Scoop it out into glasses and serve alone, or combine it with a lemon sorbet.

Lemon sorbet

3 juicy lemons
8 oz. caster sugar
1 pt. water
1 egg white

Makes 3 3-portion packs

TO MAKE: Pare the rind from the lemons free from all trace of white pith, and squeeze out the juice. Put the sugar, water and lemon rind in a pan. Dissolve the sugar over a low heat, bring to the boil and boil gently, uncovered, for 10 min. Leave to cool. Remove lemon rind, then add the lemon juice and pour into one or more ice-cube trays. Place in the freezer until mushy. Turn the mixture into a bowl, whisk the egg white until stiff but not dry and fold into the half-frozen lemon ice.

TO PACK: Turn into 3 1⅛-pt. rigid foil freezer trays or plastic containers.

TO FREEZE: Cover with a lid and seal. Label and, if necessary, overwrap in a polythene bag. Freeze until solid.

TO SERVE: Place in the refrigerator just before serving the starter or main course, so that the ice softens slightly. Decorate with a mint leaf, and serve half and half with blackcurrant sorbet, as here. Two delicious alternatives are (1) Serve it with Melba sauce (see page 95) or (2) Pour a little champagne round the water ice just before it is served.

Menu for six

Smoked trout or mackerel
Chicken and lemon pie   Leaf spinach   Lyonnaise potatoes
Raspberry vacherin

This menu needs little last-minute attention, so it is just right for the busy mother-cum-hostess. Smoked trout are not as widely available as other fish, so if you spot them they're good buys for freezer storage; for economy, they may be filleted so that one fish gives two portions.

COUNTDOWN

FIRST THING IN THE MORNING: Take trout or mackerel and chicken pie from the freezer. Loosen wrappers from fish, but leave in polythene bag. Remove foil wrappings from pie, and set it on baking sheet in a large polythene bag. Set both low down in the refrigerator. Leave for about 10–12 hr. to thaw.

NOON: Take vacherin from the freezer, unwrap and set on a serving dish. Leave in a cool place for 7–8 hr., so that the cream and the fruit are quite thawed out in the centre.

TO COMPLETE DISHES FROM THE FREEZER YOU WILL NEED

For Trout
lettuce · lemon · brown bread
butter · ¼ pt. double cream
plus creamed horseradish, *or*
thick mayonnaise · mild made mustard
lemon juice

For Chicken and Lemon Pie
egg to glaze

For Vacherin
¼ pt. double cream, whipped
fresh or frozen raspberries (optional)

LATE AFTERNOON: Prepare vegetables of your choice. Set table. Put plates to warm. Select wines. Make simple sauces for fish. Select raspberries (if used) for top of vacherin and pipe whipped cream round its sides or top.

TWO HOURS BEFORE MEAL: Skin fish, leaving on heads and tails, if serving whole. Wash lettuce for garnish, to arrange at the last minute, plus lemon wedges. Cut bread, butter it and arrange on a plate. Put the chicken pie in the oven (first removing the polythene bag). Start cooking the potatoes ¾ hr. before the guests arrive. The smoked fish can be taken to the table before the guests are seated. Cook the other vegetables.

Smoked trout or mackerel

allow 1 fish or 1 large fillet per person

TO PACK: Wrap each fish in freezer paper so that they can be easily separated. Then overwrap in foil.

TO FREEZE: Overwrap all fish, using a polythene bag. Seal, label and freeze rapidly.

TO THAW: Allow 10–12 hr. in the refrigerator or 8 hr. at room temperature.

TO SERVE: When thawed, lift off skin from body of fish, leaving head and tail intact if serving whole. Serve on lettuce, with lemon wedges and either horseradish cream or mild mustard sauce.

Horseradish cream

To ¼ pt. double cream fold in 1 tsp creamed horseradish.

Mustard sauce

To 4 tbsps. thick mayonnaise add 1 level tsp. made mild mustard and a squeeze of lemon juice.

Chicken and lemon pie

1 pt. milk
juice and thinly pared rind of 1 lemon
2 oz. butter
2 oz. plain flour
½ pt. chicken stock
½ level tsp. sugar
seasoning
1 lb. cooked chicken meat
an 11-oz. can of sweet corn kernels
8 oz. shortcrust pastry (8 oz. flour, etc.)

TO MAKE: Infuse milk and lemon rind in a pan over a gentle heat for 10 min. Remove from the heat and cool; discard the lemon rind. Melt butter in a saucepan, stir in the flour and cook this roux over a low heat for 1 min. Gradually add the infused milk and stock, beating. Return to the heat and stir whilst bringing to the boil; cook for a few min. Add sugar, lemon juice and seasoning to taste; cover and cool, stirring occasionally. Cut chicken meat into small pieces. Add drained sweet corn and turn the mixture into a 2½-pt. pie dish. Spoon lemon sauce over the chicken and cover with a pastry lid. Decorate with pastry trimmings. (Don't make a hole in the centre of the pastry.)

TO FREEZE AND PACK: Freeze uncovered. When firm, overwrap in double foil or 2 polythene bags. Seal and label.

TO THAW: Remove all wrapping. Place pie on a baking sheet and cover loosely in a polythene bag. Leave in the refrigerator for 10–12 hr.

TO COOK: Remove polythene bag. Brush pastry with beaten egg and cook in the oven at 400°F (mark 6) for 15 min. Make a hole in the centre of the pastry, return pie to the oven and continue to cook for a further ½–¾ hr., until pastry is brown and the filling bubbling. Cover loosely with foil if showing signs of over-browning.

Raspberry vacherin

6 egg whites
12 oz. caster sugar
½ tsp. lemon juice
½–1 pt. double cream, whipped
½ lb. raspberries, fresh or frozen

TO MAKE: You will need 3 baking trays of equal size. Cut 3 pieces of non-stick paper to fit them, and on each mark a circle, using a 7-in. plate as guide.

The meringue may be made in a mixer, as follows: Whisk the egg whites until stiff. Gradually add all the sugar and re-whisk until the mixture regains its former stiffness; at the end, when the meringue is quite stiff, fold in the lemon juice.

Pipe the meringue, using a forcing bag and a large vegetable star pipe, or spoon it within the circles on the 3 lined baking sheets: make 1 layer decorative for the top, but keep the other layers as flat discs. Alternatively, keep all the layers plain, but pipe a few separate shell shapes to use as decoration—see picture below. Place in the oven at the lowest setting—with the door ajar if oven is on the hot side—for about 5 hr., until the meringue layers have dried out. Peel the paper away and leave to cool. Sandwich the layers together with fresh whipped cream and fresh or frozen (un-thawed) raspberries.

Raspberry vacherin

TO PACK: On a baking sheet, place two long strips of non-stick or freezer paper in a cross; carefully lift the vacherin onto the paper.

TO FREEZE: Freeze uncovered until firm. Using the paper strips, lift it into a rigid box. or slip the vacherin inside 2 polythene bags. Seal, label and return it to the freezer. Take care during storage that nothing heavy is placed on top of it.

TO SERVE: Unwrap, place on a serving plate and remove the paper. Allow to thaw for 8 hr. at room temperature. Decorate with fresh whipped cream, adding a few raspberries if you wish.

Menu for four

Individual ratatouilles   Grissini
Beef goulash with soured cream   Buttered rice   Baby Brussels sprouts
Chilled poached pears with Melba sauce   Crème Chantilly

An adaptable starter—ratatouille is equally delicious eaten hot or cold—precedes a worry-free meal that even the most in-experienced cook-hostess could tackle. The goulash will happily oblige even if guests are a little late, and only the sprouts need last-minute attention.

COUNTDOWN

THE DAY BEFORE: Take goulash from freezer and loosen lid. Put in the fridge.

AFTERNOON: Take ratatouilles from freezer, loosen wrappings and leave to thaw at room temperature for 4 hr. Set table, select wines. Prepare vegetables for main course. Take Melba sauce and crème Chantilly from freezer, uncover both and leave the Melba sauce to thaw at room temperature, but put the crème Chantilly in the fridge. If you have the pears in the freezer, take these out also and leave, covered, to thaw at room tempera-ture. Set the oven to 375°F (mark 5) $1\frac{1}{2}$ hr. before the guests arrive. Pop in the ratatou-illes, then the goulash $\frac{1}{4}$ hr. later. Blend the cornflour for thickening the goulash. Put the plates for the main course to warm. Cook and drain the rice, leaving it in the colander over steaming hot water and forking it through to keep the grains separate. Cook the sprouts for the main course and thicken the goulash just before serving.

Individual ratatouilles

$\frac{3}{4}$ lb. courgettes
1 lb. aubergines
salt
1 large red pepper
1 small green pepper
3 small onions
$\frac{1}{2}$ lb. tomatoes
4 tbsps. dry white wine
12 tbsps. olive or cooking oil
2 bay leaves

TO MAKE: Follow the same method as that given on page 96 for ratatouille with garlic, but omitting the garlic.

TO PACK AND FREEZE: Turn the mixture into 4 foil-lined dishes ($\frac{1}{2}$-pt. capacity). Freeze until firm, then remove from the dishes, wrap in foil, overwrap in a polythene bag, seal and label. Return them to the freezer.

TO THAW: Unwrap and return to the original ovenproof dishes to thaw at room temperature for 4 hr.

TO USE: Cover the dishes and put in the oven at 350°F (mark 4) for 1 hr., forking the mixture through occasionally. If cooking from frozen, put in the oven at the same temperature, but allow $1\frac{1}{2}$ hr.

TO SERVE: Serve hot or cold; top with some chopped parsley, and serve with grissini.

Beef goulash

$1\frac{1}{2}$ lb. best stewing steak
2 oz. lard
1 medium-size onion, peeled and chopped
1–2 level tbsps. paprika pepper
1 level tbsp. tomato paste
just under $\frac{1}{2}$ pt. beef stock made from a cube

TO MAKE: Wipe, trim and cube the beef. Fry it in hot lard until brown on all sides. Add the onion, and cook for 2–3 min. Stir in the paprika pepper, tomato paste and beef stock, bring to the boil, then transfer to an oven-proof casserole. Cover and cook towards the centre of the oven at 325°F (mark 3) for $1\frac{1}{2}$ hr. Cool quickly.

TO PACK: Transfer to a 4-portion-size rigid foil freezer tray, or freeze in a pre-former.

TO FREEZE: Cover, seal, label and freeze.

TO THAW: Allow 15 hr. in the refrigerator or place direct in a hot oven at 375°F (mark 5) for about $1\frac{1}{4}$ hr.; if already thawed, allow about $\frac{3}{4}$ hr.

TO SERVE: Blend $\frac{1}{2}$ oz. cornflour with 2 tbsps. water and stir into the hot goulash to thicken. Serve the soured cream separately, to spoon onto each helping.

Melba sauce

1 lb. fresh or frozen raspberries
1 level tbsp. cornflour
1 tbsp. water
2 oz. sugar
finely grated rind and juice of 1 lemon

Makes $\frac{1}{2}$ pt.
Serves 8–10 with ice cream

TO MAKE: Hull raspberries, if necessary. Cook with liquid in a covered pan (preferably easy-clean) over gentle heat for about 10–15 min. until reduced to a pulp. Pass through a nylon sieve into the rinsed pan. Blend cornflour and water to a cream and stir into fruit purée; cook over a gentle heat, stirring until the sauce thickens—1–2 min. Add sugar, lemon juice and rind. Allow to become cold.

TO PACK: Pour into a $\frac{3}{4}$-pt. foil dish or other rigid container.

> **TO COMPLETE DISHES FROM THE FREEZER YOU WILL NEED**
>
> *For Ratatouille*
> parsley
>
> *For Goulash*
> cornflour · a 5-fl.-oz. carton of soured cream
>
> *For Sweet*
> 8 half pears, poached

TO FREEZE: Cover with lid, seal, label and freeze till solid.

TO THAW: If to be served cold allow 7 hr. in refrigerator or $3\frac{1}{2}$ hr. at room temperature.

If to be served hot, turn into a bowl over a pan of hot water and allow to thaw, breaking up occasionally, until the sauce is smooth and hot. Alternatively turn the frozen 'block' into an easy-clean pan and heat directly over a low heat until it thaws; stir frequently.

TO SERVE: Pour the sauce over chilled poached pears, over ice cream or water ice, or with banana splits and so on; it is of course traditional with peach Melba.

Crème Chantilly

$\frac{1}{2}$ pt. fresh double cream
1 large egg white (optional)
1 oz. icing sugar
a few drops of vanilla essence

TO MAKE: Whip cream until thick but not stiff. Fold in stiffly whisked egg white and icing sugar with a metal spoon. Stir in vanilla essence lightly.

TO PACK: Spoon into a $1\frac{1}{8}$-pt. foil dish or plastic container.

TO FREEZE: Cover with lid. Label, seal and freeze until solid.

TO THAW: Allow 3 hr. in the refrigerator.

TO SERVE: Place in a glass dish to serve as an accompaniment to the pears. Crème Chantilly can also be used as a filling for a Pavlova or meringue case, and as a topping for trifles (freeze it in whirls—see page 165—if you like a piped decoration).

Menu for six

Ratatouille with garlic

Steak, kidney and oyster pie
Buttered spring greens
Creamy buttered potatoes

Caramel custard
Sponge fingers

Ratatouille with garlic

A good menu to choose if you are at home all day. Cook the caramel custard during the morning, chill it in the refrigerator and un-mould just before serving. Cook the ratatouille early in the evening and serve warm, or, if more convenient, cook it early on and re-heat alongside the pie for about ½ hr. before serving.

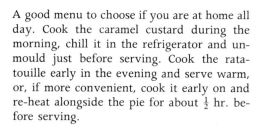

EARLY IN THE MORNING: Take the ratatouille and the steak, kidney and oyster pie from freezer. Remove seals and covers and set in refrigerator to thaw. Cook caramel custard; leave to cool, then set in refrigerator to chill.

LATE AFTERNOON: Set table, arrange

TO COMPLETE DISHES FROM THE
FREEZER YOU WILL NEED
For Ratatouille
1 lb. firm tomatoes · parsley
1 clove of garlic
grated Parmesan cheese
For Steak Pie
parsley
For Caramel Custard
⅓ pt. single cream

---

flowers, select wine. Prepare vegetables of your choice. Set ratatouille to cook. Peel and cut tomatoes into small pieces. Chop the parsley. Add tomatoes to ratatouille as directed. Cook potatoes when your guests arrive, then drain and mash. Put greens to cook whilst eating ratatouille. Drain thoroughly before serving and pour a little melted butter over before taking them to the table.

Ratatouille with garlic

(*see picture above*)

1¼ lb. aubergines
1 lb. courgettes
2 level tbsps. salt
1 red pepper
1 green pepper
1 large onion
¼ pt. oil plus 2 tbsps.
4 tbsps. dry white wine

TO MAKE: Wash, dry and thinly slice the aubergines and courgettes, using a stainless steel knife. Spread out on a large tray or plate, sprinkle with salt and leave for 1 hr. Drain away any excess liquid, then dry the aubergines and courgettes with absorbent paper. Meanwhile cut a slice from the stalk end of the peppers; scoop out and discard the seeds and pith. Cut the flesh into rings. Peel and slice the onion thinly. Heat half the oil in a pan. Add the peppers and onion, then cook for 2–3 min. Lift out with a draining

Dinner Party Menu: see pages 116–117

spoon into a rigid foil container. Add the remaining oil to the pan and cook aubergines and courgettes for 5–8 min., stirring occasionally. Lift from pan as for peppers, add to the container and spoon in the wine, allow to cool

TO PACK AND FREEZE: Cover with the lid or a double layer of foil and freeze until firm; Seal and label.

TO THAW: Leave in the refrigerator for 12 hr.

TO COOK: Cover and put in the oven at 400°F (mark 6) for $\frac{1}{2}$ hr. Remove the cover. Add 1 lb. fresh firm tomatoes, peeled and cut into 6 or 8 pieces, and 1 clove of garlic, peeled and crushed. Season to taste and stir lightly. Cook uncovered for a further 30–40 min.

TO SERVE: Sprinkle with chopped parsley and serve hot or cold. Hand grated Parmesan cheese separately.

Steak, kidney and oyster pie

2 lb. best stewing steak
8 oz. ox kidney
1 oz. seasoned flour
2 oz. lard
2 medium-size onions, peeled and chopped
2 level tbsps. tomato paste
$\frac{1}{2}$ pt. beef stock
1 bay leaf
seasoning
6 fresh oysters
$\frac{3}{4}$ lb. ready-made puff pastry

TO MAKE: Wipe, trim and cube the beef. Rinse and trim the kidney and cut into small pieces. Toss meat and kidney in seasoned flour in a large polythene bag until well coated. Fry quickly in melted lard until brown on all sides. Add onion and cook for 3 min. Stir in tomato paste blended with stock; add the bay leaf and a little seasoning. Pour into an ovenproof casserole, cover and cook in oven at 325°F (mark 3) for $1\frac{3}{4}$ hr., until tender. Cool quickly. Remove the bay leaf, then place pie filling in a $2\frac{1}{2}$-pt. pie dish; drop in the fresh oysters. Roll out pastry and use to cover the pie dish. Decorate with pastry leaves. Do not make an air vent in the pastry.

TO PACK AND FREEZE: Put in a polythene bag and freeze, taking care not to damage pastry. Remove from freezer and overwrap with heavy-duty foil, or place inside another polythene bag. Seal well and label.

TO THAW: Remove foil and loosen seal, then set pie in refrigerator on a baking sheet for 12–16 hr.

TO COOK: Remove polythene bag and bake pie in the oven at 450°F (mark 8) for 20 min., then make an air vent in the centre of the top, and return the pie to the oven. Reduce the temperature to 325°F (mark 3) and bake for a further 20 min. Cover the top of the pie with foil if there is a danger of over-browning.

TO SERVE: Garnish with a sprig of parsley.

Caramel custard

$4\frac{1}{2}$ oz. sugar
$\frac{1}{4}$ pt. water
1 pt. milk
4 large eggs

TO MAKE: Put 4 oz. of the sugar and the water in a small pan and dissolve the sugar slowly; bring to the boil and boil without stirring until it caramelises, i.e. becomes a rich golden-brown colour. Pour the caramel into a 6-in. (2-pt.) soufflé dish, turning the dish until the bottom is completely covered. Warm the milk, pour on to the lightly beaten eggs and remaining sugar and strain over the cooked caramel.

TO PACK: Allow to cool completely, and cover with a foil cap.

TO FREEZE: When quite frozen, overwrap in a polythene bag. Seal and label.

TO COOK: Remove coverings. Set frozen custard in a roasting tin of warm water, which should come half-way up the sides of the dish. Put in the oven at 375°F (mark 5) and cook for about $1\frac{1}{4}$ hr. until set.

TO SERVE: Serve cold— leave in dish in the refrigerator until cold before unmoulding. Serve with pouring cream.

Menu for eight

Chicken liver pâté
Grilled or fried mackerel
Gooseberry sauce and horseradish cream
New potatoes   Salad greens
Danish peasant girl with veil

Mackerel are rarely given the praise they deserve: when in season—October to July, but at their best in April, May and June—they are real value for money. For the sauce freeze a good stock of gooseberries when they are in season, and either just dry-pack for sauce-making, or make up as sauce from the beginning. The recipe for chicken liver pâté allows for two extra servings for a later occasion, or for using as a delicious piped topping for buttered savoury biscuits for a pre-dinner nibble with sherry.

COUNTDOWN

THE DAY BEFORE: Order fish, to collect on the day. Take sweet from freezer if thawing in refrigerator—see recipe. Next day, take pâté and gooseberry sauce from freezer, if to be thawed in the refrigerator; loosen all wrappings and leave at room temperature during the day.

EARLY EVENING: Set table, select wine, put plates to warm. Flood top of pâté with melted butter and set in refrigerator. Take horseradish cream from freezer, unwrap and leave

> **TO COMPLETE DISHES FROM THE FREEZER YOU WILL NEED**
> *For Pâté*
> butter for topping · parsley
> bread for Melba toast *or* crisp crackers
>
> *For Sweet*
> ½ pt. double cream, whipped
> grated chocolate
> raspberry jelly or strawberry jam
> (optional)

at room temperature to thaw. Top sweet with jam, whipped cream and chocolate; leave in refrigerator or cool place till required. Prepare potatoes. Wipe and dry fish. Wash salad ingredients, drain and pop in a polythene bag or a bowl in the refrigerator until required. Measure ingredients into jar for French dressing; when required, shake well together and pour over salad. Transfer sauces for fish to serving dishes. Set potatoes to cook after guests have arrived. Start cooking mackerel on one side, turn them and leave to cook on second side whilst eating pâté.

Chicken liver pâté

(see picture on page 83)

1½ lb. chicken livers
1 medium-size onion
2 small cloves of garlic
3 oz. butter
1 tbsp. double cream
2 tbsps. tomato paste
3 tbsps. sherry or brandy
a little salt and freshly ground black pepper

Makes an 8-portion and a 2-portion pack

TO MAKE: Rinse the chicken livers in a colander. Dry on absorbent paper. Peel and chop the onion finely. Peel and crush the cloves of garlic. Fry chicken livers in the hot butter until they change colour. Reduce heat, then add the onion and garlic, cover and cook for 5 min. Remove from the heat and cool slightly. Add the double cream, tomato paste, sherry or brandy, and season to taste. Purée in an electric blender, or pass the mixture through a sieve to make a smooth texture.

TO PACK: Turn two-thirds of the mixture into a ¾-pt. soufflé dish or similar-sized rigid

Grilled or fried mackerel, Gooseberry sauce and Horseradish cream

foil container, to give 8 portions. Package the remainder of the mixture for 2 portions.

TO FREEZE: Allow to become cold before overwrapping or covering with lid. Seal and label. Freeze until solid. Store for up to 1 month.

TO THAW: Unwrap. Leave in soufflé dish or transfer to serving dish. Thaw overnight (15 hr.) in the refrigerator and leave at room temperature for 1 hr. before serving. When thawed, flood the top with melted butter and put in the refrigerator to set.

TO SERVE: Garnish with a sprig of parsley. Serve with freshly made Melba toast or crisp crackers.

Gooseberry sauce

2 lb. gooseberries, topped and tailed
4 tbsps. water
4 oz. butter
sugar to taste

Makes 1½ pts.

TO MAKE: Place gooseberries in a colander and rinse well. Turn into a saucepan with the water and half the butter. Cover, and cook until the gooseberries are soft and pulpy. Pass them through a sieve or purée in an electric blender. Stir in the remaining 2 oz. butter, cut into small pieces. Add a little sugar to taste if wished (though this can be added when the mixture is being re-heated), but do keep the sauce on the sharp side. Allow to cool.

TO PACK: Divide into two ¾-pt. portions (¾ pt. is enough for 8 mackerel) and pack in rigid plastic containers or pre-formed polythene bags.

TO FREEZE: Seal and label; freeze until solid.

TO THAW: If serving hot, re-heat if wished from frozen—see page 43. Allow to thaw in the refrigerator for up to 12 hr., or at room temperature for 6 hr.

TO COOK: Serve cold, or re-heat in a heavy-based pan over a gentle heat, adding extra sugar if liked.

HORSERADISH CREAM: See page 163

Danish peasant girl with veil

12 oz. fresh breadcrumbs
6 oz. soft light brown sugar
4½ oz. butter
2 lb. cooking apples, peeled, cored and sliced
juice of ½ a lemon
sugar to taste

Note: The apples, lemon and sugar may be replaced by ½ pt. prepared apple purée.

TO MAKE: Mix the breadcrumbs and sugar together. Fry in hot butter for 1 min., then reduce the heat and cook, turning all the time, for about 10 min., till crisp and golden. Spoon onto absorbent kitchen paper. Meanwhile cook the apples in very little water with the lemon juice and sugar to taste, to give a *thick* pulp—about 10–15 min. Purée if wished. Cool thoroughly.

TO PACK: Use either of these methods: (a) put half the crumb mixture in a layer in a serving dish, then the purée, and top with the remaining crumb mixture. For quicker thawing, use a shallow rather than a deep dish. (b) Pack the crumbs and fruit purée in separate containers and make up in individual glasses when lightly thawed, then re-chill.

TO FREEZE: Freeze until solid. Overwrap (a) when frozen. Seal and label.

TO THAW: (a) Thaw out in refrigerator overnight, i.e., 10–12 hr. (b) Allow 8–10 hr. in refrigerator or 6 hr. at room temperature.

TO SERVE: Decorate with whipped double cream, and sprinkle with grated chocolate. A thin layer of raspberry jelly or strawberry jam may be spread over the crumbs before topping with cream.

Menu for four

Courgettes à la Grecque
Chicken Kiev New minted potatoes Dressed green salad or broccoli
Apricot soufflé

Ideal for a summer evening: the cold starter and dessert allow the hostess to spend the maximum time with her guests. The only last-minute attention required is for the Chicken Kiev, which can successfully be cooked straight from the freezer.

If you serve salads often, keep in your fridge (not freezer) a jar of basic French dressing, to which you can add any number of different flavourings to give variety.

COUNTDOWN

DURING THE MORNING: Remove courgettes from freezer, loosen seal, set polythene bag in bowl in refrigerator, or leave at room temperature to thaw.

LATE AFTERNOON: Take soufflé from freezer, unwrap and leave at room temperature. Set table and select wine. Prepare vegetables and salad ingredients, placing salad items in a polythene bag in the fridge to become crisp. Decorate soufflé. Peel and seed tomatoes. Chop parsley for courgettes.

BEFORE GUESTS ARRIVE: Pour oil into deep pan for the Chicken Kiev. Turn the courgettes into a serving dish. Arrange salad. Cook potatoes.

WHEN GUESTS ARRIVE: Cook Kiev and keep warm whilst the starter is being eaten. Dress and serve salad.

TO COMPLETE DISHES FROM THE FREEZER YOU WILL NEED
For Courgettes
½ lb. tomatoes, peeled and seeded
chervil or parsley

For Chicken Kiev
fat for deep frying · watercress

For Apricot Soufflé
¼ pt. double cream, whipped
a small can of apricot halves, drained

Courgettes à la Grecque

2 small onions, peeled and thinly sliced
3 tbsps. olive oil
1 clove of garlic, peeled and crushed
just over ¼ pt. dry white wine
seasoning
1½ lb. courgettes
½ lb. tomatoes
a pinch of dried chervil (optional)

TO MAKE: Sauté onions in the hot oil until soft but not coloured; add garlic, wine and a little seasoning. Wipe courgettes and discard end slices. Cut remainder into rings. Peel and quarter tomatoes, discarding seeds. Add courgettes and tomatoes to the pan and cook gently, without covering, for 10 min. Cool quickly. Add a little chervil if liked (or add fresh chervil, if available, when serving).

TO PACK: Spoon into a polythene bag, set in a pre-former to shape it up. Put in freezer.

TO FREEZE: When set in shape, remove from

pre-former and overwrap with foil, or place inside another polythene bag, seal and label. Return the pack to the freezer.

TO THAW: Allow 12–14 hr. in refrigerator or 6–8 hr. at room temperature.

TO SERVE: Add a further $\frac{1}{2}$ lb. peeled and seeded tomatoes. Adjust seasoning if necessary. Sprinkle with chopped fresh chervil (if available, and provided dried chervil was not included before freezing) or with chopped parsley.

Chicken Kiev

(see colour picture facing page 128)

4 fresh (unfrozen) chicken breasts
2 oz. garlic butter (see page 161)
1 oz. seasoned flour
2 eggs
6 oz. fresh white breadcrumbs

TO MAKE: Ask your butcher to beat out the flesh from the chicken breasts like an escalope. Make the garlic butter, form into a sausage shape and pop into freezer to set. Divide the butter between the 4 pieces of chicken, roll up and secure with cocktail sticks. Coat in seasoned flour, dip in egg, then toss in breadcrumbs. Repeat the egg and crumbing process a second time.

TO PACK: Place on a small baking tray inside a large polythene bag.

TO FREEZE: When the chicken is completely frozen, wrap up individually in heavy-duty foil, place together in a polythene bag, seal and label. Store for up to 1 month.

TO THAW: Allow 8 hr. in refrigerator, or cook from frozen as directed below (the crumb coating becomes darker in this case, due to the longer cooking time).

TO SERVE: When thawed, deep-fry at 350°F for about 10 min.; if still frozen, allow about 20 min., depending on size; fry at 350°F to start, then reduce to 300°F. Remove cocktail sticks. Prick with a fork or skewer before taking to the table, or the butter may splutter. Garnish with sprigs of watercress.

Apricot soufflé

a 15-oz. can of apricot halves, drained
5 egg yolks
6 level tbsps. caster sugar
1 level tbsp. gelatine
2 tbsps. water
5 tbsps. apricot brandy
2 tbsps. lemon juice
3 egg whites
whipped cream and poached or drained canned apricots for decoration

TO MAKE: Line a 6-in. ($1\frac{1}{2}$-pt.) soufflé dish with non-stick paper to extend 3 in. above the dish rim. Pass the apricots through a sieve or purée them in an electric blender; add the apricot juice. Place with the egg yolks and sugar in a basin over a pan of hot water and whisk until the mixture thickens and leaves a trail when the whisk is removed.

Dissolve the gelatine in the water; add the apricot brandy and lemon juice. Stir a little of the whisked mixture into the gelatine, return all to the bulk of the whisked mixture and fold in. Chill until on the point of setting. Stiffly whisk the egg whites and swiftly fold them into the apricot mixture. Turn it into the prepared soufflé dish and allow to set.

Note: The canned fruit may be replaced by either $\frac{1}{2}$ pt. fresh apricot purée, or by purée made by soaking $\frac{1}{2}$ lb. dried apricots for a short time in water to just cover, cooking gently in a covered pan till tender and purée-ing as for fresh fruit.

TO PACK: Cover the dish loosely in foil.

TO FREEZE: When quite frozen, remove foil and place the dish inside 2 polythene bags, one inside the other. Seal and label. Place carefully in freezer so that no heavy weights will at any time rest on it. If more practical, place soufflé inside a rigid container such as a plastic box or cake tin as protection.

TO THAW: Allow 12 hr. in refrigerator or 4–5 hr. at room temperature.

TO SERVE: Remove paper collar. Decorate with $\frac{1}{4}$ pt. whipped cream, and more drained apricot halves if liked.

Makes 4–6 servings.

Menu for six

Bortsch with soured cream
Moussaka Boiled potatoes with parsley
Salad greens with lemon dressing
Summer fruit salad with cream

An interesting menu with a Continental slant; for the delicious sweet, catch the summer berries at the height of their season and store them in the freezer, to bring out on a dreary day in winter. The moussaka is best placed on a large, shallow dish, as a deeper casserole takes so long to thaw and cook—sometimes spoiling the texture.

COUNTDOWN

THE DAY BEFORE: Take the bortsch, the moussaka and its cheese sauce and the summer fruit salad from the freezer and thaw in the refrigerator or at room temperature—see thawing times given in the recipes.

DURING THE AFTERNOON: Prepare the potatoes and leave covered in cold water. Prepare the salad ingredients; pop them in the refrigerator in a polythene bag or box to crisp up. For the lemon dressing, measure out the ingredients as for French dressing, but replace the vinegar by lemon juice; put into a screw-top jar, but don't shake up until required. Put the plates to warm, lay the table and arrange a bowl of flowers, if liked. Set the moussaka to cook in the oven, then top with cheese sauce as directed in the recipe.

Spoon the summer fruit salad into glass bowls and leave in the refrigerator. Pour the cream into a jug. Put the potatoes on to cook when the guests arrive; drain just before the serving of the soup, and keep warm. Serve the bortsch with the soured cream and chopped chives.

Bortsch

(*see picture opposite*)

6 small raw beetroot (2 lb.), peeled
2 medium-size onions, peeled and chopped
4 pts. seasoned beef stock

TO MAKE: Grate the beetroot coarsely (it's a good idea to wear rubber gloves for this job). Place the beetroot and the onion in a pan with the stock, bring to the boil and simmer without a lid for 45 min. Strain.

TO PACK: Allow to cool. Pour into a rigid plastic container, label and seal. Alternatively, pour into a polythene-lined pre-former and when frozen solid, remove the polythene bag from the pre-former, label and seal.

TO FREEZE: Freeze rapidly until solid.

TO USE: Defrost overnight in the refrigerator, or allow 8 hr. at room temperature. (A pre-formed package should be stood in a basin.) Bortsch is best served chilled. When it is fully defrosted, add 2 tbsps. lemon juice and 6 tbsps. dry sherry. Adjust seasoning, and serve in bowls, with a whirl of soured cream floating on top and a few scissor-snipped chives.

Moussaka

2 lb. aubergines, trimmed and thinly sliced
salt
8–10 tbsps. olive oil
2 oz. butter
5 medium-size onions, peeled and thinly
  sliced
2 lb. minced raw lean lamb
a $2\frac{1}{4}$-oz. can of tomato paste
seasoning
a 15-oz. can of plum tomatoes
1 bay leaf
1 pt. cheese sauce (see Béchamel sauce,
  page 43)

TO MAKE: Spread the aubergines out on a large plate or tray, sprinkle with salt and leave for at least 1 hr. Pour off the liquid which collects, and dry all the slices with absorbent kitchen paper. Fry the aubergines in several lots in the oil for about 10 min., turning them frequently. Meanwhile melt the butter in another pan and sauté the onion until soft. Place the minced lamb in a bowl and stir in the tomato paste and seasoning. Pass the plum tomatoes with their juice through a sieve, or purée in an electric blender. Line a large, shallow ovenproof casserole with foil. Arrange in it layers of aubergine, lamb and onion, adding the bay leaf and finishing with aubergine. Pour the puréed tomatoes over. (There should be enough room left for the cheese sauce to be poured on afterwards.) Cover, and cook in the oven at 350°F (mark 4) for 1 hr. Cool quickly.

TO PACK AND FREEZE: Freeze the moussaka in its casserole, then take out by easing the foil away from the dish; overwrap in a polythene bag. Seal and label.

TO THAW: Remove the packaging and return the moussaka to the original casserole. Cover with foil or a lid. Allow 24 hr. in the refrigerator, or if more convenient cook from frozen; in this case, set the dish on a baking sheet and cook in the oven at 375°F (mark 5) for $1\frac{1}{2}$ hr. (If thawed, for about 30 min.) Meanwhile prepare the cheese sauce. Pour the sauce over the oven-thawed or pre-thawed moussaka and sprinkle with a little Parmesan cheese. Return the moussaka to the oven and cook uncovered for a further $\frac{1}{2}$–1 hr., until the sauce is golden.

TO SERVE: Sprinkle with chopped parsley.

Summer fruit salad

1 lb. raspberries
1 lb. strawberries
4 oz. granulated sugar
1 pt. water
2 oranges

TO MAKE: Pick over the fruits, removing any stalks or hulls. Rinse only if it is felt necessary. Drain thoroughly, keeping the fruits separate. Dissolve sugar in water over gentle heat, stirring all the time. Finely pare rind from oranges, free of white pith, and add to the syrup; boil rapidly for 5 min. Allow to become completely cold. Remove orange rind and add squeezed orange juice.

Bortsch with soured cream

TO PACK: Pack strawberries in a rigid foil container; arrange raspberries in a family-size rigid foil container. Pour syrup over both and place container on a baking sheet.

TO FREEZE: Freeze uncovered until firm, then cover with a lid, seal and label.

TO THAW: Allow 18 hr. in the refrigerator or 8 hr. at room temperature. Try to catch the fruit with just the last traces of ice left. Allow $2\frac{1}{2}$ hr. for strawberries to thaw in refrigerator or $1-1\frac{1}{4}$ hr. at room temperature, add to the raspberries in syrup $\frac{1}{2}$ hr. before serving.

TO SERVE: Spoon into glass dishes and serve with thick cream.

TO COMPLETE DISHES FROM THE
FREEZER YOU WILL NEED
For Bortsch
lemon juice · dry sherry
5 fl. oz. soured cream · chives

For Moussaka
parsley · 1 oz. Parmesan cheese, grated

For Summer Fruit Salad
$\frac{1}{4}$ pt. double cream *or* $\frac{1}{3}$ pt. single
(pouring) cream

Menu for six

Prawn and cod bisque
Veal escalopes
Sauce aurore
Fluffy whipped potatoes
Petits pois

Pineapple creams
Brandy snaps

Veal escalopes and sauce aurore

A four-seasons menu—select different fresh vegetables to complement the veal escalopes and the special sauce. Pork fillet, beaten out by the butcher in the same way as veal is interchangeable—allow an extra 2–3 min. cooking time. Reserve a couple of tablespoonfuls of white wine for the soup—it makes all the difference to this bisque.

COUNTDOWN

THE DAY BEFORE: Take bisque from freezer and leave wrapped, but place in a bowl in the refrigerator. (In an emergency, heat it on the actual day, straight from the freezer.)

DURING THE MORNING: Take escalopes and sauce from freezer and place, still wrapped, in the refrigerator.

LATE AFTERNOON: Take pineapple creams from freezer, unwrap and leave in the refrigerator to thaw. Prepare vegetables of your choice. Set table, select wine. Place soup bowls, plates and vegetable dishes to warm. Whisk the sauce aurore, adding extra lemon juice to help thicken it; pour into serving dish. Decorate pineapple creams. Start cooking potatoes. Heat soup, add cream and garnishes. Cream potatoes, season and turn into warmed serving dish; cover with lid and keep warm. Start cooking the escalopes in melted butter; if necessary, arrange on a serving platter, cover with foil and keep warm whilst cooking the remainder. Set peas to cook while the soup is being eaten. Garnish the escalopes with lemon and take to the table, with the sauce in a separate dish. Serve

the pineapple creams accompanied by brandy snaps.

Prawn and cod bisque

4 oz. cod fillet, skinned
1 small onion, peeled and chopped
1 medium-size carrot, peeled and sliced
4 oz. button mushrooms, halved
2 oz. butter
2 pts. fish or chicken stock
juice and $\frac{1}{2}$ level tsp. grated rind from a
    small lemon
2 tbsps. white wine (optional)
seasoning

Makes $2\frac{3}{4}$ pts.

TO MAKE: Cut the cod into 1-in. cubes. Add the onion, carrot and mushrooms to the melted butter in a pan; sauté gently for 5 min. Add the cubes of cod and cook for a further 5 min. Purée in an electric blender with some of the stock, the lemon juice, lemon rind and wine; season to taste, then cool quickly.

TO PACK: Pour into a polythene bag placed in a pre-former.

TO FREEZE: Freeze until firm, remove from the pre-former and place inside another polythene bag. Seal and label.

TO THAW: Allow 24 hr. in the refrigerator.

TO SERVE: Pour the thawed soup into a saucepan and heat through very gently. Alternatively, unwrap the frozen soup and heat very slowly in a double saucepan. When the soup has just come to the boil, remove from the heat. Cool slightly, then stir in the 4 oz. prawns and ½ pt. cream, and adjust the seasoning. Add the drained canned sweet corn kernels or diced cucumber and some chopped parsley. Re-heat, but don't boil.

Breaded veal escalopes

(*see picture opposite*)

6 veal escalopes (4 oz. each)
2 oz. seasoned flour
2 eggs, beaten
6 oz. fresh breadcrumbs

TO MAKE: Ask your butcher to beat the escalopes thinly. Coat both sides with flour on a sheet of greaseproof paper. Dip each escalope in beaten egg and toss in breadcrumbs. Use the palm of the hand to pat the crumbs well onto the surface of the escalopes.

TO PACK: Place on a large sheet of foil with layers of freezer paper between so that they will separate easily. Wrap up securely in a parcel.

TO FREEZE: Overwrap using a polythene bag. Seal, label and freeze rapidly.

TO THAW: Allow 8 hr. in the refrigerator or cook from frozen.

TO COOK: Melt 2–3 oz. butter in a frying-pan. Cook the escalopes 2 at a time, allowing approx. 5 min. in all for thawed meat, or approx. 8–10 min. if cooking straight from

---

TO COMPLETE DISHES FROM THE FREEZER YOU WILL NEED

4 oz. fresh or frozen peeled prawns
½ pt. single cream
a 7-oz. can of sweet corn kernels *or*
2 oz. diced cucumber · parsley

For Escalopes and Sauce
butter for frying · lemon wedges · chives
lemon juice

For Pineapple Creams
¼ pt. double cream, whipped
crystallised violets
brandy snaps

---

the freezer. Add more butter as required.

TO SERVE: Garnish with lemon wedges.

Sauce aurore

2 5-fl.-oz. cartons of soured cream
1–2 tbsps. tomato ketchup
5 tbsps. lemon juice
chopped chives (optional)

Makes ½ pt.

TO MAKE: Combine soured cream with the ketchup. Finely grate a little rind from the lemon and add to the soured cream, with 4 tbsps. strained lemon juice.

TO PACK: Spoon into a ¾-pt. foil dish or plastic container.

TO FREEZE: Cover, label and freeze.

TO THAW: Allow 8 hr. in refrigerator or 3 hr. at room temperature.

TO SERVE: Whisk well, adding a further 1 tbsp. lemon juice. Sprinkle with chopped chives before serving.

Pineapple creams

a 15-oz. can of crushed pineapple
juice of 1 lemon
2 oz. caster sugar
½ pt. double cream, whipped
4 egg whites, stiffly whisked

TO MAKE: Drain off any free juice from the crushed pineapple, then purée the fruit in an electric blender to give ½ pt. purée. Add the lemon juice and sugar. Fold in the whipped cream, followed by the stiffly whisked egg whites.

TO PACK AND FREEZE: Turn the mixture into 6 small individual soufflé dishes. Freeze until firm, cover the tops with foil, then overwrap in a polythene bag, seal and label. Return them to the freezer.

TO THAW: Uncover, remove the foil and thaw in the refrigerator for 8 hr., or at room temperature for 3 hr. Don't worry if the texture is not very firm.

TO SERVE: Decorate with whipped cream and crystallised violets.

Menu for six

Kipper pâté   Melba toast
Coq au vin   Creamed potatoes   Broccoli spears or baby carrots
Orange sorbet

An excellent menu even for the inexperienced hostess, with only the vegetables to cook and toast to make after the guests have arrived. The kipper pâté—always a great success as a starter—allows for second helpings. A classic coq au vin mellows with re-heating and is therefore ideal for the freezer. The orange sorbet rounds off a memorable meal; it can, of course, be bought ready-prepared from many freezer food suppliers. Freeze the orange shells for this recipe when you have used the flesh for fruit salads, etc. The bought frozen orange juice ensures a consistently good flavour.

COUNTDOWN

FIRST THING IN THE MORNING: Take coq au vin from freezer, loosen seal, set on tray and leave at room temperature to thaw. Take out pâté, unwrap and transfer to serving dish; leave in lowest part of refrigerator.

EARLY EVENING: Lift pâté out of fridge. Set table, select wine. Prepare vegetables. Set plates to warm. Transfer coq au vin to casserole, plus thickened stock and mushrooms. Garnish pâté. Fill orange cups with sorbet and return them to freezer till required. Cook potatoes when guests arrive, and make toast as they are being seated at table.

Kipper pâté

a 12-oz. pkt. of frozen kipper fillets in butter
2 oz. butter
juice of $\frac{1}{2}$ a lemon
4 tbsps. double cream, lightly whipped
freshly ground black pepper

TO MAKE: Cook the kippers according to pkt. directions. Remove from the pkt., discard any dark skin, then flake fish and juices with a fork; allow to cool. Melt butter and beat into fish, with the lemon juice. (Use an electric blender for this if you have one.) Add cream and season with pepper.

TO PACK: Use a foil-lined or unlined 1-pt. serving dish or similar-sized foil container. Spread pâté evenly in container.

TO FREEZE: Freeze until firm, remove pâté from serving dish and overwrap; cover foil container or unlined serving dish with lid, or overwrap. Label.

TO THAW: Leave unlined serving dish and foil container wrapped in the refrigerator for 12 hr. or at room temperature for 6 hr., or peel away foil lining and return frozen pâté to serving dish, cover loosely and thaw as above.

TO SERVE: Garnish with wedges or twists of lemon and sprigs of parsley. Hand round freshly-made toast, wrapped in a napkin to keep it warm.

Coq au vin

6 fresh chicken quarters, cut in half
4 oz. butter
2 tbsps. cooking oil
$\frac{1}{4}$ lb. green streaky bacon rashers, rinded and quartered
12 shallots, peeled
2 oz. seasoned flour
4 tbsps. brandy
2 bay leaves
1 bottle of Burgundy

TO MAKE: Wipe the chicken joints. Heat half the butter and oil in a heavy-based frying pan. Gently cook the bacon and shallots for 4–5 min. without browning; remove them from pan with draining spoon and place in a large casserole. Toss the chicken joints in seasoned flour. Add the remaining butter and oil to the pan and fry the joints until brown all over—about 10 min. Warm brandy in a small pan, pour over chicken and set alight. When the flames have died down transfer the chicken to the casserole. Add bay leaves. Stir any remaining seasoned flour into the pan juices, then pour in wine. Bring to the boil, stirring, and pour over chicken. Cover the casserole and cook in the oven at 325°F (mark 3) for about 1 hr. Cool quickly.

TO PACK: Line a large shallow casserole with foil. Transfer coq au vin to the casserole. Cool.

TO FREEZE: Freeze until firm. Ease from the pre-former and overwrap with foil or plastic bag. Seal, label and return to freezer.

TO THAW: Unwrap coq au vin and return to casserole without foil. Cover and allow 16 hr. in refrigerator or 8 hr. at room temperature.

TO SERVE: Blend a little of the 1 pt. chicken stock with 1 oz. cornflour in a saucepan. Add the remaining stock and bring to boil; boil, stirring, for 2 min. Pour in the liquor strained from the coq au vin and cook for a few min., then pour back over the chicken in the serving casserole. Sauté the whole button mushrooms in butter and add with 2 cloves of garlic, skinned and crushed, to the casserole. Cover and re-heat in the oven at 375°F (mark 5) for $\frac{3}{4}$–1 hr. Adjust the seasoning, and sprinkle with chopped parsley before serving.

Orange sorbet

(*see picture on right*)

6 oz. sugar
$\frac{3}{4}$ pt. water
a 6$\frac{1}{2}$-fl.-oz. can of frozen orange juice (undiluted)
2 egg whites
6 orange shells (see below)

TO MAKE: Dissolve the sugar in the water, when dissolved bring to the boil and boil, uncovered, for 10 min. Turn the frozen orange juice into a bowl and pour on the sugar syrup. When cold, pour into a 1-pt. capacity ice-cube tray and freeze to a mushy consistency in the freezer. Whisk egg whites until thick and foamy but not dry; fold into the orange mush. Return the mixture to two

TO COMPLETE DISHES FROM THE FREEZER YOU WILL NEED
For Kipper Pâté
lemon · parsley
bread for melba toast

For Coq au Vin
1 pt. chicken stock · cornflour
6 oz. button mushrooms · parsley

For Sorbet
rose or other leaves to decorate

freezer trays or similar-sized foil containers and freeze until firm.

TO FREEZE: Overwrap with foil or plastic film, seal and label, then freeze until solid.

TO SERVE: Allow sorbet to thaw for 5 min. only. Spoon into 6 frozen orange shells, pack down firmly and replace lids on top. Place on a large serving dish and return to the freezer until required. Arrange a washed rose leaf or two round the base of each orange before taking to the table.

TO FREEZE ORANGE SHELLS: Scrub or wipe the oranges. Slice a lid from the stem end of each. Use a small sharp knife to loosen the flesh from the rind, then use a teaspoon to scoop out the fleshy centre (include in a fruit salad). Place cups and lid upside-down on absorbent paper to drain. Freeze on a flat surface until firm, then wrap in plastic film or plastic bags, seal, label and return to freezer.

Orange Sorbet

Menu for six

Coquilles St. Jacques
Noisettes of lamb
Buttered new potatoes
Tossed green salad
Pavlova with peaches

Coquilles St. Jacques

If there is time, allow the coquilles and the noisettes to thaw, but if unavoidable both may be cooked from frozen. The Pavlova case needs no thawing—just fill it with cream and fruit and leave it in the fridge until required.

COUNTDOWN

IN THE MORNING: Take the noisettes and the coquilles from the freezer and allow to thaw as directed below.

LATE AFTERNOON: Prepare the vegetables of your choice. Rinse the salad ingredients, drain thoroughly, then pop them into a large polythene bag in the refrigerator to crisp.

> **TO COMPLETE DISHES FROM THE FREEZER YOU WILL NEED**
>
> *For Coquilles*
> duchesse potato mixture (approx 1½ lb)
> if needed
> egg to glaze · lemon or parsley
>
> *For Noisettes*
> butter for grilling
> 4 oz. Maître d'hôtel butter (see page 161)
> 12 fried bread croûtes · parsley
>
> *For Pavlova*
> ½ pt. double cream, whipped
> a 16-oz. can of sliced peaches
> 2 oz. plain chocolate

Set the table and select the wine. Fry the croûtes. Whip the cream for the Pavlova and drain the sliced peaches. Fill the Pavlova case with cream and peaches and decorate with melted chocolate. Put the plates to warm. Arrange the salad and make up the dressing. Put the coquilles to cook. Put new potatoes on to cook. Set the noisettes to cook in the grill pan.

Coquilles St. Jacques

(*see picture above*)

½ lb. shelled fresh scallops
¼ pt. dry white wine
¼ of a small onion, peeled
a sprig of parsley
1 bay leaf
1 oz. butter
2 oz. button mushrooms, sliced
6 small natural scallop shells, washed
duchesse potato mix (optional—made with
   1½ lb. mashed potato)

For the sauce
2 oz. butter
2 oz. plain flour
¾ pt. milk
2 oz. grated cheese
seasoning

TO MAKE: Rinse, and slice the white parts of each scallop into 4; leave the coral whole. Place in a pan with the wine, onion, parsley and bay leaf. Bring to the boil and simmer for 5 min. Drain, keeping the strained liquor to one side. Melt the butter and sauté the mushrooms for 5 min. Prepare the sauce: melt the butter in a pan, add the flour and cook over a gentle heat without browning for 1 min.; stir in the strained liquor and the milk. Return the pan to the heat, bring to the boil, stirring till the sauce is smooth and thickens. Cool slightly, then stir in the sautéed mushrooms, cheese and scallops, with seasoning to taste.

TO PACK: Divide the mixture between the scallop shells (or 6 individual ovenproof dishes). Pipe duchesse potato mixture round the shells and brush with beaten egg (though this can be done when the scallops are taken from the freezer before cooking).

TO FREEZE: Freeze uncovered, so as not to damage the piped potato. Place inside 2 polythene bags.

TO THAW: Remove the seal and packaging, and if a potato border was not added before freezing, pipe it on now. Set the coquilles on a baking sheet, loosely covered so as not to damage the potato; leave in the refrigerator for about 8 hr.

TO SERVE: If taken straight from freezer, remove the outer wrapping; place the coquilles on a baking sheet. Cover loosely with foil and place in the oven at 425°F (mark 7). If thawed, re-heat for 15 min.; otherwise, allow 50–60 min. Uncover, brush with beaten egg and cook for a further 10–15 min., until golden. Garnish with a wedge of lemon or parsley sprigs.

Noisettes of lamb

2 best ends of neck of lamb (6 noisettes each)

TO MAKE: Ask your butcher to bone and roll the best ends. Wipe the meat with a clean, damp cloth, then cut each best end into 6 noisettes, cutting between the strings.

TO PACK: Place pieces of freezer paper between the noisettes so that they will separate easily before cooking. Cover in a double layer of foil.

TO FREEZE: Overwrap, using a polythene bag. Seal and label.

TO THAW: Place on a large plate and allow 12 hr. in the refrigerator, or for 5 hr. at room temperature (or cook from frozen).

TO COOK: Unwrap, then season to taste and dot with butter. Whether frozen or already thawed, brown them quickly on both sides under a hot grill, then reduce the heat and cook for a further 10–15 min. if thawed, or 30 min. if frozen; baste frequently. They should still be quite pink in the centre.

TO SERVE: Place some maître d'hôtel butter on each noisette and set on a croûte of fried bread. Garnish with sprigs of parsley.

Pavlova with peaches

3 egg whites
6 oz. caster sugar
$\frac{1}{2}$ tsp. vanilla essence
$\frac{1}{2}$ tsp. vinegar
2 level tsps. cornflour

TO MAKE: Draw an 8-in. circle in a sheet of non-stick paper and place the paper on a baking sheet. Beat the egg whites till very stiff, then beat in the sugar half at a time. Beat in the vanilla essence, vinegar and cornflour. Spread the meringue mixture on the paper over the circle, piling it up round the edges to form a case. Bake in the centre of the oven at 300°F (marks 1–2) for about 1 hr., till firm. Leave to cool, then carefully remove the paper.

TO PACK: Use a cardboard box or plastic box, or place on a cardboard base or baking sheet and overwrap in plastic film, or use a polythene bag. Seal and label.

TO FREEZE: Place in the freezer on top of other items, as a Pavlova is still quite fragile, even in the frozen state. Freeze until solid.

TO SERVE: The cake is ready to serve straight from the freezer. Unwrap and fill with the whipped cream and drained peaches. Melt the chocolate, spoon it into a forcing bag fitted with a No. 2 trellis pipe and run it over the peaches in petal shapes. Place the Pavlova in the refrigerator until required.

Menu for eight

Individual mixed fish pâtés   Hot toast fingers
Jugged hare with forcemeat balls and redcurrant jelly
Boiled potatoes   Buttered green or red cabbage
Oranges with caramel

This menu is not for friends on a reducing diet—though they might be tempted to forgo slimming just for one night! The jugged hare is rich but delicious, and when it comes from a freezer, avoids that tell-tale smell through the whole house, telling guests exactly what's for dinner. Ask the butcher for the hare already jointed, but plus the blood. (Even if you don't like the idea of the blood, remember it does make all the difference to the finished dish.) The orange sweet gives the perfect balance to this menu.

COUNTDOWN

THE NIGHT BEFORE: Take jugged hare from freezer, set on a plate, loosen the seal and leave in the refrigerator.

EARLY NEXT MORNING: Take individual pâtés, oranges in syrup and forcemeat balls from freezer. Loosen seals and leave in the refrigerator to thaw.

LATE AFTERNOON: Set table, select wines. Prepare vegetables of your choice. Make the caramel and leave to set; crush it just before using as the finish to the dessert. Turn the oranges into a serving bowl or individual dishes.

> **TO COMPLETE DISHES FROM THE FREEZER YOU WILL NEED**
> *For Fish Pâtés*
> **lemon · bread for toast**
>
> *For Jugged Hare*
> **parsley · red-currant jelly**
>
> *For Oranges with Caramel*
> **8 level tbsps. sugar · ½ pt. single cream**

EARLY EVENING: Put hare to re-heat in an ovenproof casserole. Place forcemeat balls on a baking sheet and heat through in the oven for ½ hr. before serving. Chop parsley for hare and potatoes. Garnish pâtés. Put cabbage on to cook. Set potatoes to cook when guests arrive. Make toast at the last minute, and wrap in napkin to keep warm.

Mixed fish pâtés

a 7½-oz. can of salmon
a 7-oz. can of tuna
4 oz. peeled prawns
6 oz. fresh white breadcrumbs
4 oz. butter, melted
juice and finely grated rind of 2 lemons
3 tsps. anchovy essence
½ pt. single cream
salt and freshly ground black pepper

Makes 8 individual pâtés and 1 large pâté for 4–6, for a future occasion

TO MAKE: Remove any dark skin from the salmon and flake the flesh with its juices, together with the tuna fish and its oil. Chop the prawns roughly. Place the breadcrumbs in a bowl with the melted butter, lemon juice and rind. Add the flaked fish and prawns; stir in the anchovy essence, then the cream, and season to taste.

TO PACK: Spoon fish mixture into 8 ramekins or individual soufflé dishes (4-fl.-oz. or 5-tbsps. capacity). Place the remaining mixture in a 1-pt. basin lined with foil.

TO FREEZE: Place the dishes on a baking sheet and freeze rapidly until firm. Overwrap each individual dish in a polythene bag or film; remove the large pâté from its basin, leave in the foil and overwrap. Seal, label and return the pâtés to the freezer.

TO THAW: Allow 6 hr. for small pâtés and 8–10 hr. for the large one in the refrigerator, plus 1 hr. at room temperature before serving. In each case, unwrap the pâtés.

TO SERVE: Garnish individual pâtés with a twist of lemon.

Jugged hare

1 hare, cut into pieces, with the blood
$\frac{1}{4}$ lb. bacon rashers, rinded
2 oz. lard
1 onion, peeled and quartered
2 carrots, peeled and sliced
2 sticks of celery, chopped
2 pts. stock
12 juniper berries
juice and thinly pared rind of 1 lemon
1 oz. butter
1 oz. plain flour
1 level tbsp. redcurrant jelly
1 tbsp. bottled Cumberland sauce
1 glass port or red wine

TO MAKE: Rinse and dry the hare joints. Keep the blood in a cool place until required. Cut the bacon into large pieces and place in a large frying pan with the lard. Add the joints of hare to the pan and fry for about 10 min., turning frequently until sealed all over. Turn into a deep casserole with the onion, carrots and celery. Pour in the stock and add the juniper berries, lemon juice and rind. Cover and cook in the centre of the oven at 325°F (mark 3) for about 3 hr. Strain the gravy from the casserole into a pan. Blend the softened butter and the flour to a paste, then stir, little by little, into the pan, to thicken the gravy. Bring to the boil, stirring. Cool, then stir in the redcurrant jelly, Cumberland sauce and port or red wine. After 5 min., stir in the blood.

TO PACK: Arrange the joints of hare in a large ovenproof serving dish or casserole lined with foil. Pour the gravy over and leave to cool. Cover with double foil or place a piece of foil over the dish, replace the lid and place in a polythene bag. Seal and label.

TO FREEZE: Freeze rapidly until solid.

TO THAW: Allow at least 12 hr., and if possible 15 hr., in the refrigerator overnight.

TO COOK: Unwrap and re-heat in the covered casserole in the oven at 350°F (mark 4) for 2–2½ hr., till bubbling.

TO SERVE: Sprinkle the hare with chopped parsley. Place the hot forcemeat balls in the gravy or pile into a small casserole. Serve redcurrant jelly separately.

Forcemeat balls

3 rashers of streaky bacon, rinded and chopped
$\frac{1}{2}$ oz. butter
4 oz. fresh white breadcrumbs
2 oz. shredded suet
2 tbsps. chopped parsley
1 tbsp. finely chopped onion
seasoning
beaten egg to bind
flour to coat

TO MAKE: Fry the bacon in the melted butter for 2–3 min. Add to the breadcrumbs, suet, parsley and onion in a bowl. Season, then bind with beaten egg. Form into 24 even-sized balls, using floured hands to shape them.

TO PACK AND FREEZE: Arrange the forcemeat balls in a plastic box, with freezer paper between the layers to prevent their sticking. Freeze rapidly until firm. Alternatively, freeze them individually on a baking tray, and when firm pack in a polythene bag and seal. Label, and store in the freezer.

TO COOK: Unwrap the forcemeat balls and place in a well-greased baking dish; cook in the oven at 350°F (mark 4) for about 30 min. Turn them over occasionally.

Oranges with caramel

8 oranges
$\frac{3}{4}$ pt. water
3 oz. granulated sugar

TO MAKE: Wipe oranges. Pare rind from 1 orange free of any trace of white pith. Place water and sugar in a heavy-based pan, stir until the sugar is dissolved, then allow to boil. Add the orange rind and simmer for a further

5 min. Remove from heat and allow to become cold. Meanwhile peel the oranges free of any white pith, and cut into thin slices, discarding the pips.

TO PACK: Arrange orange slices in a serving dish lined with foil or in a lidded foil container. Pour cold syrup over.

TO FREEZE: Overwrap the serving dish with double foil and then put in a polythene bag, or cover with lid if using a foil dish. Seal and label. Freeze until solid.

TO THAW: Allow 12 hr. in refrigerator or 6 hr. at room temperature.

TO SERVE: Make caramel by placing 8 level tbsps. granulated or caster sugar and 8 tbsps. water in a heavy-based pan. Over a low heat dissolve the sugar. Boil without stirring for about 7–10 min., until a pale caramel has formed. Pour onto a buttered or oiled baking sheet or marble slab, leave till set, then break into small pieces. Scatter over the oranges before serving, with $\frac{1}{2}$ pt. pouring cream.

Menu for four

Fresh tomato salad with French dressing
Chicken with curry and lemon   Freshly boiled rice
Cucumber slices with yoghurt dressing
Meringues Chantilly

An ideal menu for the cook who hates washing saucepans—just one for the whole of this dinner party! Choose this meal when tomatoes are sun-ripened and full-flavoured: slice them thickly and serve with wafer-thin rings of onion and a sharp-flavoured French dressing with or without herbs such as chervil. Creamy, lightly curried chicken with a subtle hint of lemon is an all-round winner. Meringue needs no thawing, but the time given is for the whipped cream filling.

COUNTDOWN

THE DAY BEFORE: Take chicken with curry and lemon from the freezer if it is to be thawed before cooking—the best method if forethought is used. It can, however, be cooked from frozen—see recipe.

DURING THE AFTERNOON: Take meringues from freezer and leave in fridge or in cool room, to allow the cream filling to thaw.

Set table, arrange flowers, set plates to warm and select wine. Toast flaked almonds; chop parsley. Put chicken to cook. Peel and slice tomatoes for salad, arrange on serving platter and scatter with finely chopped onion; pour French dressing over $\frac{1}{2}$ hr. before serving. Cook and drain rice and rinse in colander with hot water. Leave in the colander over gently steaming water, forking it through occasionally to keep the grains separate. Peel cucumber, slice thinly and place in a bowl with the yoghurt; chill well before serving with the chicken. Garnish the chicken with the toasted almonds and parsley before serving.

> **TO COMPLETE DISHES FROM THE FREEZER YOU WILL NEED**
> *For Chicken*
> 1–2 oz. flaked almonds · parsley

Chicken with curry and lemon

Chicken with curry and lemon

(*see picture above*)

a 3½–4 lb. oven-ready chicken cut into 8 joints
1½ oz. seasoned flour
2 level tsps. curry powder
2 oz. butter
1 tbsp. cooking oil
3 small onions
¾ pt. chicken stock
1 lemon, cut into thin slices
2 bay leaves

Makes 2 4-serving dishes

TO MAKE: Wipe chicken joints. Place seasoned flour and curry powder in a large polythene bag. Toss the chicken joints in the bag until they are well coated. Melt butter in a large frying pan, together with the oil. Fry chicken joints for 10–15 min., until really golden-brown on all sides; set to one side. Meanwhile, peel and chop onions. Add to the pan and cook for 5 min. Sprinkle any remaining flour into the pan and cook for a further 1 min., then stir in the stock, lemon slices and bay leaves. Bring to the boil, stirring.

TO PACK: Transfer chicken to 2 foil freezer trays, or freeze in 2 pre-formed casseroles (see page 182). Pour the contents of the pan over and leave until cold.

TO FREEZE: Cover with lid or overwrap with foil. Seal and label.

TO THAW: Thaw overnight in the refrigerator, and then cook in a covered casserole, or in the foil container with a foil cover, at 350°F (mark 4) for 1 hr. Alternatively, cook straight from the freezer, in the same way, at 400°F (mark 6) for 1½–2 hr., until the chicken is hot and bubbling.

TO SERVE: Leave in the casserole, or turn it into a hot serving dish; scatter with toasted almonds and freshly chopped parsley.

Meringues Chantilly

3 egg whites
6 oz. caster sugar

Filling
⅓ pt. double cream, whipped
1 small egg white
½ oz. icing sugar
a few drops of vanilla essence

Makes 8

TO MAKE: Line 2 baking sheets with non-stick paper. Whisk the egg whites in a deep basin until stiff and dry. Add half the sugar and whisk again until the mixture regains its former stiffness but is no longer opaque. Lastly, fold in the remainder of the caster sugar, using a metal spoon. Using 2 spoons or a large star vegetable nozzle and a forcing bag, shape meringue shells of even size. Dry off in a very cool oven at 250°F (mark ¼) for several hr., until dry, crisp and very slightly off-white. Cool on a wire rack. Whisk the double cream until it just holds its shape. Whisk the egg white until stiff, and fold into the cream with the icing sugar; stir in the essence lightly. When evenly blended, use to pair the meringue shells together.

TO FREEZE: Place on a flat tray and freeze until cream is firm. Place in a rigid container such as a cardboard box, separating each with crumpled paper. Overwrap with foil or plastic film. Remember that even when frozen, meringues are fragile.

TO THAW: Allow to thaw in the refrigerator for about 5 hr., or in a cool room for about 3½ hr.

Menu for six

Country-style pâté
Melba toast or French bread

Boeuf bourguignonne
Plain boiled potatoes
Leeks and carrot sticks

Melon, strawberry and almond
salad

Country-style Pâté

This country pâté is pleasantly moist, with a robust texture—a very practical item to have to hand in your freezer. This amount gives 6 generous servings. The rustic-style beef dish looks well in an oven-to-table flame-proof casserole which holds its heat for second helpings—but do use a thick heat-proof mat on the table. A light fruity dessert gives a happy balance to the menu.

COUNTDOWN

THE NIGHT BEFORE: Take pâté and boeuf bourguignonne from the freezer. Loosen wrappings and put in the refrigerator.

LATE AFTERNOON: Take sweet from freezer, loosen wrappings and leave in a warm place. Take the strawberries from freezer only 1 hr. before required. Toast the almonds in readiness for adding to the melon, with the

strawberries. Set table. Select wines. Prepare vegetables. Re-heat bourguignonne in an ovenproof casserole in the oven, or a flame-proof casserole on top of cooker. When pâté has been at room temperature for 2 hr., garnish it. Start cooking the potatoes when guests arrive, and the other vegetables as appropriate. Make toast at the last minute.

Country-style Pâté

(see picture above)

1 lb. lean veal
1 lb. lean belly of pork
$\frac{1}{2}$ lb. lamb's liver
1 small onion, peeled and chopped
2 tbsps. olive oil
2 tbsps. wine vinegar
1 tbsp. brandy or sherry
1 egg
salt and pepper
$\frac{1}{4}$ level tsp. dried sage
6–8 rashers of streaky bacon, rinded and
  stretched

Makes a 6-portion and a 2-portion pack.

TO MAKE: Cut the meats and liver into pieces and pass them through a coarse mincer. Add the onion, oil, vinegar and brandy to the meat mixture and blend well. Leave in a cool place for 2 hr. Add the beaten egg, seasoning and sage. Line an ovenproof 2-pt. dish (such as a casserole, terrine or soufflé dish), with the rinded and stretched bacon rashers. Spoon in the meat mixture, smooth the top and cover with foil. Set in a roasting tin, with water to come half way up the sides of the dish. Cook in the oven at 375°F (mark

---

TO COMPLETE DISHES FROM THE FREEZER YOU WILL NEED
For Country-style Pâté
tomato wedges and/or lettuce
bread for melba toast · butter

For Boeuf Bourguignonne
parsley

For Melon, Strawberry and Almond Salad
2 oz. flaked almonds
$\frac{3}{4}$ lb. fresh or frozen strawberries
$\frac{1}{2}$ pt. single or pouring cream

5) for about $2\frac{1}{2}$ hr. Remove from the water-bath, and leave to cool with a weight on top. Pour off any excess liquid, if not jellied.

TO PACK: Leave whole or cut into neat slices, stacking with pieces of freezer paper between the slices for easy separation and quicker thawing. Re-shape neatly and wrap in a double thickness of foil. Label, and overwrap with a polythene bag or film.

TO FREEZE: Freeze rapidly until solid. Store for up to 1 month.

TO THAW: Uncover, and loosely re-cover. Allow 16 hr. in refrigerator plus 2 hr. at room temperature.

TO SERVE: Either place in dish, upside-down and garnished with a bay leaf, as in picture, or serve in slices, garnished with tomato wedges and/or crisp lettuce leaves. Melba toast or French bread and butter make the classic accompaniment.

Boeuf bourguignonne

$2\frac{1}{2}$ lb. topside beef
4 tbsps. cooking oil
a 4-oz. piece of streaky bacon, rinded
2 level tbsps. flour
8 fl. oz. red wine
8 fl. oz. beef stock
2 bay leaves
1 clove of garlic, peeled and crushed
$\frac{1}{4}$ level tsp. 'pinch of herbs' mixture
3 tbsps. brandy
salt and pepper
12 very small onions or shallots, peeled
$\frac{1}{2}$ oz. lard or 1 tbsp. oil

TO MAKE: Cut the meat into chunky squares. Heat 3 tbsps. of the oil in a large pan and fry the meat until brown on all sides. Lift it out of the pan with a draining spoon and transfer to a large ovenproof casserole. Cut the bacon into chunky pieces and fry in the fat remaining in the pan. Stir in the flour and allow to brown, stirring occasionally. Stir in the wine, stock, bay leaves, garlic and herbs. Keep on a low heat. Warm the brandy in a small pan, ignite it and pour over the meat while it is still flaming. Pour the sauce over, then season to taste. Cover the casserole and cook in the oven at 325°F (mark 3) for $1\frac{1}{2}$ hr. Fry the whole onions or shallots in the lard or oil until brown; drain thoroughly and add to the

casserole. Reduce the oven heat to 300°F (mark 2) and cook for a further 1 hr. Remove from the oven and allow to become completely cold.

TO PACK AND FREEZE: Line an ovenproof serving casserole with a large piece of kitchen foil. Pour in the beef mixture, cover the top with foil and set in the freezer. Alternatively, the bourguignonne may be transferred to a rigid foil container. Freeze rapidly until solid. When quite frozen, remove from the casserole (if one is used), overwrap with foil or a heavy-duty polythene bag, seal and label. Store for a limited time only.

TO THAW: Allow 14 hr. in the refrigerator. Alternatively, the bourguignonne can be re-heated from frozen.

TO COOK: If thawed, re-heat on top of the cooker in a flameproof casserole for about $\frac{1}{2}$ hr., until bubbling. If cooking from frozen, unwrap and place in the original serving casserole (or leave in the rigid container), and put in the oven at 325°F (mark 3); allow 2 hr., or until bubbling.

TO SERVE: Discard the bay leaves, and garnish with chopped parsley.

Melon, strawberry and almond salad

6 oz. caster sugar
$\frac{1}{2}$ pt. water
$\frac{1}{4}$ pt. white wine
1 firm but ripe melon

TO MAKE: Dissolve sugar in water over the heat, stirring all the time. Cool, then add wine. Cut melon in half and scoop out seeds; peel, then cut into small dice.

TO PACK: Place fruit in foil container. Pour the syrup over.

TO FREEZE: When frozen, cover with lid or overwrap. Seal and label.

TO THAW: Thaw overnight (10–11 hr.) in refrigerator, or 5–6 hr. at room temperature.

TO SERVE: Add 2 oz. toasted flaked almonds and $\frac{3}{4}$ lb. fresh or almost-thawed frozen strawberries just before serving. Serve pouring cream or ice cream separately.

Menu for eight

Chilled watercress soup *French bread or croûtons*
Boeuf Stroganoff *Freshly boiled rice*
Sliced cucumber, tomato with chives *Red and green peppers*
Cheesecake topped with fruit

A quick, trouble-free menu—just perfect for the working wife-cum-hostess. Next to no preparation on the day, and little last-minute cooking, except for the rice, which can be cooked and drained before the guests arrive, then left over hot water to keep warm. The Stroganoff will be best dealt with while the guests are being seated at table.

COUNTDOWN

THE NIGHT BEFORE: Remove cheesecake from freezer, unwrap, coat with crumb mixture, then loosely cover with foil. Leave in refrigerator.

IN THE MORNING: Take Stroganoff from freezer, along with watercress soup. Loosen cover on Stroganoff, and transfer soup to a bowl. Leave both at room temperature.

EARLY EVENING: Set table, select wines. Prepare all the salad ingredients and the

---

TO COMPLETE DISHES FROM THE
FREEZER YOU WILL NEED
For Soup
Watercress leaves
French bread or croûtons

For Boeuf Stroganoff
5 fl. oz. soured cream

For Cheesecake
8 oz. digestive biscuits · 4 oz. butter
fresh fruit or canned apricots or
peach slices, with walnuts and
apricot glaze

---

dressing. Set plates to warm. Transfer Stroganoff to a saucepan or flameproof dish ready to re-heat. Invert cheesecake onto a serving plate and decorate with fruit. Cook rice, drain in colander and leave over gently steaming water until required; fork through occasionally. 'Refresh' frozen French bread or croûtons (see page 163). Leave the Stroganoff to heat through gently while the first course is being eaten.

Chilled watercress soup

(*see colour picture facing page 96*)

1 oz. butter
1 small onion, peeled and chopped
2 bunches watercress
$1\frac{1}{2}$ pt. chicken stock
1 pkt. (2–3 servings) instant potato
$1\frac{1}{2}$ pt. milk
seasoning

TO MAKE: Melt butter, sauté onion for 2–3 min. Meanwhile trim away two-thirds of the stem from the watercress. Wash, then dry and chop. Add to the pan and stir well. Cover, then cook over a gentle heat for a further 2–3 min. Add stock, simmer 15 min. Bring to the boil, remove from the heat, add instant potato, stir well before adding the milk. Return to a gentle heat for a few min. Adjust seasoning.

TO PACK: Allow to cool. Pour into a rigid plastic container, label and seal. Alternatively, pour into a polythene-lined pre-former and when frozen solid, remove the polythene bag from the pre-former, label and seal.

TO FREEZE: Freeze rapidly until solid.

TO USE: Defrost overnight in the refrigerator, or at room temperature for 8 hr. (A pre-formed package should be stood in a basin.) Stir well, and just before serving, garnish with watercress leaves. French bread or fried croûtons are a good accompaniment.

Boeuf Stroganoff

(see colour picture facing page 96)

3 lb. fillet of beef
8 oz. butter
2 medium-size onions, peeled and
    thinly sliced
½ lb. mushrooms, sliced
2 oz. flour
2 level tbsps. tomato paste
2 15-fl.-oz. cans of consommé
salt and freshly ground black pepper

TO MAKE: Wipe the meat, then cut it into strips approx. 3 in. by 1 in. Melt 2 oz. of the butter in a large pan, fry the onions for 3–4 min., and lift out on to a plate. Add a further 2 oz. butter, re-heat and fry the meat a little at a time, till sealed on all sides; add 2 more oz. butter during the cooking. Remove the meat from the pan with a draining spoon. Re-heat the remaining pan juices and add the remainder of the butter. Fry the mushrooms for 2–3 min. and add them to the meat and onions. Stir the flour into the pan juices, followed by the tomato paste. Continue to stir over a gentle heat for 1 min. Stir in the consommé, and cook quickly.

TO PACK: Pack the meat, onion and mushroom mixture separately from the sauce. Use 2 rigid foil containers for the meat, and 2 1-pt. polythene bags (pre-formed) for the sauce.

TO FREEZE: Freeze, uncovered, until firm, then cover the foil containers with lids. Seal and label all the packets.

TO THAW: Allow 16 hr. in the refrigerator.

TO SERVE: Add the meat, etc., to the sauce, then adjust the seasoning. Turn the mixture into a pan or flameproof casserole to re-heat on top of the stove. When it is thoroughly heated through but not boiling, turn it into the serving dish; keep warm, and just before serving, stir in the ¼ pt. soured cream.

Cheesecake topped with fruit

(see colour picture facing page 96)

3 oz. butter
4 oz. caster sugar
3 eggs, separated
2 oz. ground almonds
1½ oz. semolina
12 oz. full-fat cream cheese
3 oz. stoned raisins
grated rind and juice of 1 large lemon

TO MAKE: Cream the butter and sugar; add the egg yolks, almonds, semolina, cheese, raisins, lemon rind and juice. Mix well. Fold in the stiffly whisked egg whites.

Line the base of an 8½-in. (3-pt. capacity) cake tin with freezer paper and pour in the cheesecake mixture. Place on a baking sheet and bake in the centre of the oven at 350°F (mark 4) for about 50 min., until the filling is set, reducing the heat to 300°F (mark 2) if the filling is browning too quickly.

Note: This cake tends to sink on cooling.

TO PACK: Leave in the tin; when cold, cover with a lid or with kitchen foil. Overwrap, using a polythene bag, seal and label.

TO FREEZE: Freeze until solid.

TO THAW AND SERVE: Unwrap the cheesecake, but leave it in its container. Allow 24 hr. in the refrigerator, or 10 hr. at room temperature. Meanwhile, crush 8 oz. digestive biscuits in a bowl and add 4 oz. melted butter. Spoon this mixture on to the top of the thawing cheesecake and smooth with a knife. Leave until the cheesecake is fully thawed and the biscuit-crumb top is set. Ease around the edges with a round-bladed knife. Invert the cake, crumb side down, onto a serving dish and decorate with fresh fruit in season, or with canned apricot halves, plus shelled walnuts. Top with apricot glaze (see page 168).

BUFFET-STYLE MEALS FOR A DOZEN AND OVER

Catering for a crowd simply means that you've got to be that much better organised—but with a freezer, half the battle's won. Whether simple, like the quiche party for 25, or more elaborate, as in the wedding buffet for 35–40, these party ideas will take the sting out of entertaining on a larger scale, even for the inexperienced hostess.

Quiche party for 25

Allow one 8-in. flan for every three servings; for this party, two each of the flans listed—eight in all—will work out about right.

For the sweets, make double the amount of orange salad and caramel given on page 111, and make two vacherins as described on page 93. If you choose strawberries and cream, allow 3 lb. fruit.

Quiche lorraine

Quiche with prawn and spring onion filling

Quiche with bacon and sweet corn filling

Haddock and cheese quiche

Rice salad with lemon dressing

Green salad with French dressing

Tomato and onion salad with garlic dressing

French bread and butter

Orange salad and caramel

Strawberries and cream or

Vacherin with raspberries and cream

Quiche lorraine

(*see picture on page 124*)

6 oz. shortcrust pastry (6 oz. flour, etc.)

For the Filling
6 bacon rashers, rinded and chopped
2 medium-size onions, peeled and chopped
1 oz. butter
2 oz. Gruyère cheese, thinly sliced
equal quantities milk and single cream, to
   make $\frac{1}{4}$ pt.—4 tbsps. each
2 large eggs
seasoning

Serves 3 for buffet party (4–6 as a starter)

TO MAKE: Set an 8-in. flan ring on a baking sheet and line with the prepared pastry. Leave in the refrigerator to rest while you prepare the fillings. Fry the bacon and onion in the melted butter for a few min., till the onion is transparent and the bacon cooked through; allow to cool. Place the thinly sliced cheese in the base of the pastry-lined flan ring. Spoon the onion and bacon mixture over. Make a custard by whisking the milk, cream, eggs and seasoning together, and pour it over the filling in the flan case.

TO PACK AND FREEZE: Put in the freezer until firm. When frozen, cover the top of the flan with a round of non-stick or freezer paper. Remove the flan ring if you like, but don't forget to replace it before the flan is cooked! Lift the frozen flan from the baking sheet, using a palette knife or a fish slice. Wrap in foil to make a neat parcel. Several flans can be stacked on top of each other, of course, before being wrapped in foil. Over-wrap, seal and label.

TO COOK: Unwrap and place on a baking sheet. (Replace the flan ring if necessary.) Cover loosely with foil. Bake from frozen just above the oven centre, at 375°F (mark 5) for $\frac{3}{4}$ hr., then remove foil and cook for about 15 min. longer, until golden on top.

TO SERVE: Garnish with chopped parsley. Serve hot or cold.

For 6-in. Flan Cases
Use 10 oz. prepared shortcrust pastry (10 oz. flour, etc.) to line two 6-in. flan cases. Use double the amounts given for the basic fillings and for the custard, i.e., 4 eggs, etc.

For individual 4-in. Flan Cases
Use 6 oz. prepared shortcrust pastry (6 oz. flour, etc.) to line 4 individual rings, and make up a single quantity of filling.

Alternative quiche fillings

PRAWN AND SPRING ONION
Fry $\frac{1}{2}$ a bunch of washed, trimmed and chopped spring onions in 2 oz. butter for a few mins., then stir in 4–6 oz. peeled prawns. Cool, place over base of flan case and cover with the custard mixture.

BACON AND SWEET CORN
Trim and finely chop 6 rashers of bacon and fry in 2 oz. butter until just cooked. Drain a 7-oz. can of sweetcorn kernels, add to the pan and stir for 1 min. Cool, place over base of flan case and cover with the custard mixture.

HADDOCK CHEESE
Cook an 8-oz. packet of boil-in-the-bag frozen haddock as directed. Remove from the bag and discard the skin and any bones; flake with a fork and cool. Finely slice 2 oz. Gru-yère cheese, use to cover the base of the flan case, then top with the fish and the usual custard mixture.

Buffet menu for 15
Sweet-sour pork
Freshly boiled rice
Green salad

Oranges with caramel and cream
Profiteroles with chocolate rum sauce

Make up double the amounts given below for sweet-sour pork, and treble the amounts for the two sweets (pages 89 and 111).

Sweet-sour pork

2 lb. lean pork
deep fat for frying
8 oz. plain flour or equal quantities flour and cornflour
salt and pepper
4 eggs
3–4 tbsps. milk

For the Sauce
2 12-oz. cans of pineapple cubes
2 medium-size carrots, cut into matchstick pieces
1 green pepper, seeded and cut into strips
2 sticks of celery, scrubbed and finely sliced
2 tbsps. olive oil
$1\frac{1}{2}$ oz. cornflour
4 tsps. soy sauce
1 oz. brown sugar
3 tbsps. vinegar

Serves 8

TO MAKE: Trim the pork into neat chunky cubes, and set the fat to heat. Sift the flour (or flour and cornflour) into a bowl with the salt and pepper. Drop in the eggs, add the milk and beat to a smooth, thick batter. Coat the pork cubes in batter and fry for 15 min., or until the batter is golden and the pork cooked through. Set aside to cool quickly. Meanwhile prepare the sauce. Drain and re-move the juice from the cans of pineapple; make up to $1\frac{1}{2}$ pt. with water. Fry the carrots, pepper and celery in the hot oil for 2–3 min., stirring frequently. Blend the cornflour with a little of the pineapple liquid to a smooth paste, then stir in the remaining liquid. Add to the pan and bring to the boil, stirring, until the sauce is smooth and clear. Add the soy sauce, brown sugar, vinegar and pineapple cubes. Allow to cool quickly.

TO PACK: The pork cubes should be packed so that they are separated by freezer paper. Pour the sauce into a party-size foil, plastic or pre-formed container. Cover with lids or a double layer of foil, seal and label. Overwrap with a polythene bag if you wish.

TO FREEZE: Freeze rapidly until solid.

TO COOK: Thaw pork cubes overnight in the refrigerator. Remove the wrappings and place the sauce in a flameproof casserole or heavy-based pan over gentle heat. Break the sauce down with a wooden spoon as it begins to thaw (keeping it covered between times). Add 1 peeled, finely sliced and sautéed small onion and 1 oz. toasted almonds to the hot sauce just before serving. Set the pork balls on baking sheets in the oven at 425°F (mark 7) for about 15 min., until really hot.

TO SERVE: Place the pork balls on a serving dish and pour some of the sauce over them. Surround with freshly-boiled rice, or serve this separately, with a further bowl for the remaining sauce.

Informal menu for 12

Stuffed pancakes
Dressed salad of red and green peppers, chicory and watercress
Pavlova with peaches

Stuffed pancakes

½ pt. batter
lard for frying

filling
4 oz. onion, chopped
½ oz. butter
1 lb. minced beef
1 large carrot, grated
2 level tbsps. cornflour
a 14-fl.-oz. can of tomato juice
salt and freshly milled pepper
½ level tsp. each dried fine herbs and thyme
1 tsp. soy sauce

Serves 4

TO MAKE: Prepare 8 7-in. pancakes in the usual way, using ½ pt. batter. Sauté onion in butter without browning. Add mince, cook until sealed, add carrot and cook 5 min. Stir in cornflour, blended with tomato juice, seasoning, herbs and soy sauce. Bring to the boil, reduce heat and simmer, covered, for 10 min. When cold use to fill pancakes and roll them up.

TO PACK AND FREEZE: Arrange pancakes in a single layer in a baking dish, wrap in a polythene bag or overwrap in foil. Seal, label and freeze.

TO RE-HEAT: Unwrap the pancakes, return them to the original ovenproof dish and cover loosely with foil; place in the oven at 375°F (mark 5) and heat for about 50 min. Remove the foil cover and serve immediately, garnished with chopped parsley.

For 12 people, treble this quantity.

PAVLOVA: See page 109. Make 2 for 12 people.

Wedding buffet for 35–40

Baked salmon trout
Smoked trout and/or mackerel:
mustard cream

Boeuf en croûte with horseradish
cream
Boned turkey with apricot and
ginger stuffing
Coleslaw
Celery and potato mayonnaise
Chicory and orange salad with
French dressing
Garlic-dressed tomato and
onion salad
French bread and butter

Pavlova
Charlotte russe
Summer fruit salad with cream

Baked salmon trout

a 4–5 lb. salmon trout, cleaned but whole

TO PACK AND FREEZE: Coat the fish with layers of ice (see pages 89 and 206), wrap closely in kitchen foil, overwrap with a polythene bag, seal and label. Freeze until solid.

TO THAW: Allow 24–30 hr. in the refrigerator.

TO COOK: Unwrap, then wrap loosely in a sheet of well-buttered foil, adding 1–2 sprigs of parsley and 1–2 lemon slices, with a bay leaf if desired. Set on a baking sheet, and cook in the oven at 300°F (mark 2), allowing 30–35 min. per lb., or until the flesh is just beginning to show signs of coming away from the bone. Allow to cool in the foil.

TO COAT IN ASPIC
$\frac{3}{4}$ pt. aspic jelly
Radishes, cucumber, parsley, stuffed
   olives, tomato skin, shrimps, etc., to
   garnish

Remove the skin from the body of the fish, leaving on the head and tail. Make up the aspic jelly according to the packet instructions, and when it is just beginning to thicken, coat the fish thinly. Decorate the fish, using thin rounds of radish, strips of cucumber skin or thin cucumber slices, diamonds or strips of tomato skin, rounds of olive, sprigs of parsley, picked shrimps, etc., all dipped in aspic. Cover the decorated fish with further layers of aspic until the garnish is held in place. Leave to set. Serve with a mixed salad and mayonnaise, or as desired.
Note: The easiest way to carry out the glazing process is with the fish on a wire rack and with a large plate underneath to catch the drips. When the surplus aspic is set, chop it on damp greaseproof paper with a sharp knife, and use as an additional garnish.
BOEUF EN CROÛTE (see page 90); prepare double quantities.
Cook the beef on the day and allow to become cold. Serve in slices, garnished with plenty of fresh watercress and accompanied by horseradish cream (see page 163).
SMOKED TROUT AND MACKEREL (see page 92); allow 6 of each, and serve with the sauces suggested there.

Boned and stuffed turkey

a 10 lb. fresh oven-ready turkey, cleaned and
   boned—approx. 6 lb. meat
apricot and ginger stuffing (see page 86, but
   use treble quantities)
4 oz. softened butter
Seasoning

Serves 25–30

Ask your poulterer to clean and bone out the turkey for you. Stuff with the prepared mixture and tie or sew into shape.

TO COOK: Weigh, then put in a roasting tin and cover with 4 oz. softened butter and some seasoning. Cover with foil and cook in the oven at 325°F (mark 3), allowing 35–40 min. per lb. Half an hour before the end of the cooking time remove the foil, baste well, pour off the excess fat, then increase the oven temperature to 425°F (mark 7), so that the skin of the bird will brown. Lift on to a plate and allow to cool quickly.

TO PACK: Wrap in a double thickness of kitchen foil, overwrap with a polythene bag, seal and label.

TO FREEZE: Freeze rapidly until solid.

TO THAW: Allow about 2 days in refrigerator.

TO SERVE: Cut in neat slices; the platter may be garnished with apricots, if you wish.

Charlotte russe

¼ of a pkt. of lemon jelly
⅛ pt. boiling water
1½ pkts. of sponge fingers
½ pt. double cream, whipped
1 pt. cold custard (made with 2 level tbsps. custard powder and 1 level tbsp. caster sugar, with 1 pt. milk)
2–4 tbsps. Kirsch or Cointreau (optional)
1 level tbsp. powdered gelatine
3 tbsps. water

Serves 8

TO MAKE: Make up the jelly with the boiling water and set 4 tbsps. of it in the bottom of a straight-sided mould (2½–3 pt. capacity). Allow to set. If necessary, trim the sides of the sponge fingers, then brush the edges with the remaining liquid jelly. Line the sides of the mould with the fingers, pressing them closely together. Support the fingers with a ring of foil. Combine the whipped cream, custard and liqueur (if used). Dissolve the gelatine in the water in the usual way and add to the cream mixture. When this is on the point of setting, pour it into the centre of the mould, lifting the foil away, and allow to set, then trim off any surplus from the top of the sponge fingers.

As a variation, you can make a fruit-flavoured cream for the centre—use ½ pt. fruit purée to replace ½ pt. of the custard.

TO PACK AND FREEZE: Carefully envelop the whole dish in kitchen foil. When quite frozen, overwrap with a polythene bag, seal and label.

TO THAW: Unwrap, then stand the mould in very hot water for a minute or two to loosen the base. Cover with a plate and invert to un-mould the charlotte, but leave the mould over it to give it support. Leave it in the fridge for 14–16 hr. to thaw, or leave it at room temperature for approx. 8 hr. Meanwhile make up the remaining ¾ pkt. of lemon jelly and leave it in a shallow dish to set.

TO SERVE: Remove the mould. Chop the jelly and spoon two-thirds of it round the base of the sweet. Pipe extra whipped cream round the top edge and fill the centre with the remaining chopped jelly. Tie a ribbon round before serving.

PAVLOVA: See page 109; make two.

SUMMER FRUIT SALAD: See page 103; make double amount.

TEENAGE PARTIES

Three menus with a foreign flavour, based on hearty but interesting main dishes.

South American party for 12

Chilli con carne   Freshly boiled rice   Cucumber salad
Summer fruit salad with cream
Home-made ice cream and Melba sauce

Serve the meat dish straight from rustic-style ovenproof casseroles. Use bold coloured nap-kins in orange or red, and serve beer, cider or fruit cup in handsome goblets. Select some

South American music to set the scene, of course.

Make up double the quantity of chilli con carne given in the recipe, to allow really generous helpings for a dozen guests, and cook 2–3 oz. rice per person. Recipes for the sweets are on pages 103, 151 and 95.

Chilli con carne

3 lb. minced beef
3 tbsps. cooking oil
2 large onions, peeled and chopped
2 green peppers, seeded and chopped
2 15-oz. cans of tomatoes
salt and pepper
3 level tsps. chilli powder
1 tbsp. vinegar
1 level tbsp. sugar
a 2¼-oz. can of tomato paste

Serves 6–8

TO MAKE: Fry the beef in the hot oil until lightly browned; add the onion and peppers, then fry for further 5 min., until soft. Stir in the tomatoes, seasoning, chilli powder blended with the vinegar, sugar and tomato paste. Cover and simmer for 1 hr. Cool.

TO PACK: Spoon into a party-size foil dish.

TO FREEZE: Cover, label and seal. Overwrap with a polythene bag.

TO THAW: Allow to thaw overnight (or cook from frozen). Uncover and transfer to ovenproof casserole.

TO COOK: Add a 15¼-oz. can of red kidney beans or baked beans, if liked. Set in the oven at 400°F (mark 6) for about 1¼ hr until heated through.

TO SERVE: Serve with freshly boiled rice.

Greek party for 12

Taramasalata
Freshly made toast

Moussaka
Iced cucumber and mint salad

Ice cream
with honey and chopped nuts

Fresh fruit

An ideal menu for the young and hungry, which could be served equally well at the table or buffet style. Perhaps the Greeks would frown on cider to accompany the main course, but it combines well with the richness of the food. There are many records of Greek music to set the guests dancing after they've eaten so handsomely. Taramasalata is given on page 82; make up double quantities. For moussaka see page 102; make up double the amount given.

Italian party for 12

Iced cream of tomato soup
garnished with chives

Quick pizza
Watercress and chicory salad
French dressing
Iced zabaione or *Lemon sorbet*

Entertain Italian country style, and you'll have a tremendously inviting, colourful and liberal spread. A scone base is used for the pizzas instead of the more traditional yeast dough, as it takes less initial preparation time for this quantity. Make up three times the amount given here when you're catering for a dozen people. For sweets, see pages 25 and 91.

Quick pizza

12 oz. self-raising flour
1 level tsp. salt
10 tbsps. cooking oil
6–8 tbsps. water
2 small onions, peeled and chopped
2 14-oz. cans of tomatoes, drained
4 level tsps. mixed herbs
2 oz. butter
8 oz. cheese
20 olives (black or stuffed green)
2 2-oz. cans anchovies

Serves 8

TO MAKE: Mix the flour and salt, and stir in 2 tbsps. of the oil and enough water to mix to a fairly soft dough. Divide into eight. Roll out into 4-in. rounds and fry both sides in the remaining oil in a large frying pan (or see 'Variations'). Drain well. Make the topping by frying the onion, tomatoes and herbs in the butter. Spread a quarter of the grated cheese over the dough base, with the tomato mixture. Sprinkle the remaining cheese over. Slice the olives, wash and drain the anchovies, and arrange in a lattice design on top.

TO PACK: Place each pizza on a large square of foil.

TO FREEZE: Freeze rapidly, uncovered, until firm. When solid, wrap foil around pizza, secure and label. Overwrap in a polythene bag.

TO COOK: Remove the polythene bag, loosen the wrappings and leave lightly covered over with foil. Bake from frozen in a pre-heated oven at 350°F (mark 4) for about 45 min., until the cheese has melted; if necessary grill to brown the top for 1–2 min.

Variations

Roll out the pizza dough into an oblong to fit a well-oiled baking sheet measuring 10 in. by 8 in. Bake in the oven at 450°F (mark 8) for 15 min., until well risen and golden-brown.

Toppings:
(a) Cover with the tomato and onion topping,

For Pizza and Quiche parties: large and small pizzas made from the quick recipe on this page; quiche lorraine, prawn and spring onion quiche, bacon and sweet corn quiche and individual haddock cheese quiches

then arrange overlapping slices of salami (2 oz.) to cover the topping. Cut 4 oz. cooked ham into neat strips and use to make a lattice effect over the salami.

(b) Make up 4-in. rounds as in basic recipe. Cook and top with tomato mixture, arrange 2 sardines on each round and garnish with olives. Freeze and wrap in the same way.

TO PACK: Place on a sheet of foil.

TO FREEZE: Freeze quickly, uncovered, until firm. When quite firm, wrap foil round pizza to make a neat parcel. Overwrap with a polythene bag. Label and seal.

TO COOK: Unwrap. Cover loosely with foil. Bake from frozen in a pre-heated oven at 350°F (mark 4) for about 1 hr. Arrange half-slices of tomato in between the lattice to complete the decoration and sprinkle with a little grated cheese, if liked. Pop under a hot grill for 1–2 min. before serving.

HOT FORK SUPPERS

Curry, pasta and paella all lend themselves to making in large quantities, and serving fairly informally. Here are menus based on these three main dishes.

Curry party for 12

A curry party is always a popular way of entertaining. Perhaps the multitude of colourful side dishes you can offer has something to do with its appeal. We have listed our ideas below, along with the quantities of rice you'll require. Remember that even if you don't have the meats or fish for the curry prepared in advance and frozen, a curry sauce from the freezer tastes twice as good—it's so mellow and mature.

Beef, chicken and prawn curries
Freshly boiled rice   Side dishes
Fresh fruit salad or Orange salad or Strawberries and cream
or Lemon sorbet

BEEF CURRY: make up double the recipe quantities.

CHICKEN CURRY: make up double the recipe quantities.

PRAWN CURRY: make up double the recipe quantities.

RICE
Allow 2 oz. long-grain rice per head, and cook it according to the packet directions. Drain, and rinse with boiling water. When dry and fluffy, turn it onto a serving dish and sprinkle with paprika pepper.

SIDE DISHES
(a) Chop 3 large eating apples, sprinkle with lemon juice, then add raisins.
(b) Cut 4 bananas in slices, sprinkle with lemon juice and dust with paprika pepper.
(c) Peel and dice a cucumber. Mix with 2 5-fl.-oz. cartons of plain yoghurt.
(d) Bowl of 4–6 oz. salted peanuts.
(e) Bowl of mango chutney.
(f) 3 peeled and chopped tomatoes with 1 tbsp. finely chopped onion and a little parsley.

(g) Some freshly made poppadoms or chapattis to make the party authentic.

SWEET COURSE
Whether you choose a fresh fruit salad, orange salad, fresh strawberries and cream, lemon sorbet or some other sweet to follow, remember the point is that it must be something refreshing to the palate after the curry.

Basic curry sauce

2 Spanish onions
2 cooking apples
4 oz. butter
1 tbsp. cooking oil
3 oz. curry powder
2 level tsps. curry paste
2 oz. plain flour or cornflour
2 pt. prepared stock
3 tbsps. sweet chutney
2 level tbsps. tomato paste
juice of $\frac{1}{2}$ a lemon

Makes approx. 3 pts.

TO MAKE: Peel and chop the onions and

apples. Melt the butter and oil in a pan, add the onions and apples and cook gently without browning for 5–8 min. Stir in the curry powder and paste and cook for 5 min., stirring occasionally, to bring out the full flavour. Stir in the flour or cornflour and cook for 1 min., stirring all the time, before adding the stock. Bring to the boil, still stirring. Add the chutney, tomato paste and lemon juice, cover, and cook gently for about $\frac{3}{4}$ hr. Cool quickly.

TO PACK: Put in heavy polythene bags in plastic containers to shape up—1 pt. quantities are practical.

TO FREEZE: Freeze, then overwrap with foil or place in another polythene bag. Seal and label.

TO THAW: Turn the sauce into a double saucepan or in a heavy-based saucepan over gentle heat. Break up, using a wooden spoon, as the sauce thaws. Check the seasoning. Pour over thawed or freshly cooked chicken or beef or prawns (see next recipe) and place in a covered casserole in the oven at 375°F (mark 5) for $\frac{3}{4}$ hr., until hot and cooked through.

Chicken curry

a 4-lb. oven-ready fresh chicken (6 joints)
1–2 oz. seasoned flour
2 oz. butter
2 tbsps. cooking oil
1 oz. cornflour
2 pt. unseasoned chicken stock
2 level tsps. tomato paste
salt and pepper

Serves 4–6

TO MAKE: Wipe the chicken joints and toss them in seasoned flour. Fry in the hot butter and oil in a large frying pan until brown all over—about 10 min. Lift them into a large casserole. Blend the cornflour to a smooth paste with some of the stock, then add the remaining stock and pour into the juices in the pan; stir until the sauce thickens. Add tomato paste to improve the colour of the sauce, and stir in a little seasoning. Pour the sauce over the chicken, cover and cook in

the oven at 350°F (mark 4) for $\frac{3}{4}$ hr. Cool quickly.

TO PACK AND FREEZE: Line a roasting tin with heavy-duty foil, and pour in the mixture. Freeze until solid, then overwrap with foil or place in a large polythene bag. Seal and label. Replace in the freezer.

TO THAW AND SERVE: Allow 24 hr. in the refrigerator. Add to 1 pt. thawed curry sauce in a large casserole. Taste for seasoning, cover and heat through in the oven at 375°F (mark 5) for $1\frac{1}{2}$ hr., until bubbling. Pour off the curry sauce into a saucepan and boil to reduce it by half. Arrange the chicken in a serving dish and spoon the reduced sauce over it. Prepare side dishes—see page 125— and freshly boiled rice.

Beef curry

$1\frac{1}{2}$ lb. best stewing steak
1 oz. seasoned flour
2 oz. butter
$\frac{1}{2}$ pt. beef stock
1 level tsp. tomato paste
seasoning

Serves 4–6

TO MAKE: Wipe beef, trim and cut into neat pieces. Toss in seasoned flour, then fry in melted butter until brown on all sides. Stir in stock and tomato paste. Allow to come to the boil, then pour into a casserole. Cover and cook in the oven at 325°F (mark 3) for $1\frac{1}{2}$ hr., until fork-tender. Cool as quickly as possible.

TO PACK: Turn into two 2-portion foil dishes, or freeze in the casserole.

TO FREEZE: Overwrap or cover with lid. Label and freeze.

TO THAW: Allow 14 hr. in refrigerator. Add to 2 pt. thawed curry sauce and taste for seasoning.

TO COOK: Heat gently in a saucepan or place in covered casserole in the oven at 375°F (mark 5) for 1 hr., until bubbling.

TO SERVE: Make side dishes—see page 125 —and boil rice.

Prawn curry

For each 2–3 servings, add 4–6 oz. peeled prawns to 1 pt. thawed curry sauce. Heat through gently in a saucepan, or in a covered casserole in the oven at 375°F (mark 5) for $\frac{1}{2}$ hr., or until really hot.

TO SERVE: Make side dishes—see page 125 —and boil rice to serve as accompaniments.

Since no extra stock is added, this is a fairly hot curry; however, the flavour may be made more mellow by stirring in a little soured cream or natural yoghurt to taste.

Paella party for 12

To conjure up memories of a romantic evening in sunnier climes, try our paella party. Paella is a wonderful party idea— though basically quite simple, it can be decked out to suit the occasion and your pocket. We've used the traditional ingredients of chicken and shellfish, represented here by prawns and mussels; should you want to add a more luxurious touch, try adding some lobster or crayfish. Serve a plain green salad, if you prefer.

The gazpacho recipe is on page 88—make up double quantities.

For the sweets, see pages 105 and 93.

Gazpacho

Paella

Dressed mixed salad French bread

Pineapple creams

Vacherin with raspberries and cream

Paella

a 4 lb. oven-ready fresh chicken
$3\frac{1}{2}$ pts. stock from the chicken
1 lb. onions
3–4 tbsps. cooking oil
3 oz. butter
2 lb. American long-grain rice
2 pkts. of saffron powder
2 bay leaves
salt and freshly ground black pepper
a 7-oz. can of sweet red peppers, drained
    and chopped

Serves 12

Cook the chicken in 4 pts. water with a few flavouring vegetables for about 1–1$\frac{1}{2}$ hr. (or until tender). Lift it from the saucepan and allow to cool on a plate, then strip off the flesh and cut it into small pieces. Keep the stock. Peel, slice and chop onions and fry in the hot oil and butter for 4 min. Add the rice and cook over a gentle heat for 2–3 min.

stirring so that the rice absorbs the fat. Add the saffron powder, then half the stock, the bay leaves and some seasoning. Allow to bubble over a gentle heat for about 10 min., adding more stock as required to keep the rice from drying out. Stir in the chicken pieces. Remove from the heat and allow to become cold.

TO PACK: Spoon into 3 family or party size foil containers or foil-lined dishes. Divide the red peppers between the dishes, laying the pieces decoratively on top. Cover with the lid, seal and label. Overwrap with a polythene bag if you wish.

TO FREEZE: Freeze rapidly until solid.

TO THAW: Leave overnight in the refrigerator.

TO COOK: Peel and crush 2 cloves of garlic and fry in 2 oz. butter for 4 min. Line 1 or 2 large roasting tins with foil and divide the melted butter and garlic between them. Stir in the thawed rice and chicken mixture. Add 8 oz. peeled prawns. Cover loosely and put in the oven at 375°F (mark 5) for 15 min. Meanwhile cook a 8-oz. pkt. of frozen peas and a 4-oz. pkt. of sliced frozen beans in boiling water for 2 min. only; drain well. Add both to the paella in the tins, with the drained contents of a 10-oz. jar of mussels, and 1 tbsp. chopped parsley. Heat through for a further 15 min. Add a few tbsps. white wine if you feel the paella is a little dry.

TO SERVE: Garnish with lemon wedges, black olives and whole prawns. Serve at once, with a green salad and French bread.

Pasta party for 12

Sure-fire way to a successful evening; served with crisp salad and French bread, pasta specialities will delight the eye of the leanest and hungriest guest. When preparing for a party of this size, it's really a joy to be able to conjure the main course out of the freezer. Make up double the amounts in the recipes for lasagne and macaroni cheese

Chicken Tettrazini

Macaroni cheese   Lasagne

Dressed green salad   Tomato and onion salad
French bread and butter

Fresh pineapple slices
Fresh fruit—peaches or apricots, or as available

Cherries in wine

Chicken Tettrazini

1½ lb. cooked chicken flesh (from a 6-lb. boiling fowl)
12 oz. spaghetti
½ lb. button mushrooms
3 oz. butter
a 15-oz. can of plum tomatoes, drained, for garnish (optional)

For the sauce
3 oz. butter
3 oz. plain flour
1 pt. chicken stock
1 pt. milk
seasoning
¼ pt. white wine
4 oz. grated cheese

Serves 6

TO MAKE: Cut the chicken meat into pieces. Cook the spaghetti according to the packet directions and drain thoroughly. Pour boiling water over it to keep the strands separate. Rinse and drain the mushrooms and sauté them in the melted butter for 5 min. Prepare the sauce as follows. Melt the butter in a pan, stir in the flour and cook for 1 min. Remove from the heat and gradually stir in the stock and milk. Bring to the boil, stirring continuously, and cook for 2 min. Add seasoning and the wine, then cool slightly before stirring in the cheese. Add half the sauce to the chicken pieces and the remainder to the drained cooked spaghetti, with the mushrooms. Allow to cool.

TO PACK AND FREEZE: Line a large

Surprise Frozen Savouries and Sweets: see pages 61, 90, 101, 152, 154

ALCAN FOIL

shallow ovenproof dish with foil; spoon in the spaghetti mixture. Top with tomatoes (if used), then cover with chicken in sauce. Freeze until solid; remove from dish and wrap the foil over. Place in a large polythene bag, seal and label. Return it to the freezer.

TO COOK: Unwrap, then re-heat in the serving dish, with a light foil covering; allow about 1 hr. in the oven at 350°F (mark 4). Fork through a few times during the re-heating.

TO SERVE: Garnish with chopped parsley.

Lasagne

Bolognese sauce, made with 1 lb. minced
  beef (i.e. one-third the quantity in the
  next recipe)
4 oz. lasagne verdi
1 tsp. oil
¼ level tsp. salt
½ lb. cottage cheese
2 large eggs, beaten

Serves 6

TO MAKE: Have the bolognese sauce ready. Put the lasagne in a large pan half-filled with boiling water to which the oil and salt have been added; cook for 12 min., or until *al dente*. Drain in a colander and pour plenty of cold water on it. Dry on absorbent kitchen paper. Place the cottage cheese in a bowl with the beaten eggs.

TO PACK: Line a large shallow ovenproof dish with foil and oil this. Line the base with half the lasagne. Cover with all the bolognese sauce. Top with the remaining lasagne and the cottage cheese and egg mixture.

TO FREEZE: Freeze rapidly until set, remove from the dish, overwrap with foil, seal and label. Store in the freezer.

TO COOK: Remove the foil cover and replace the lasagne in the original ovenproof dish. Top with 1 pt. well-flavoured cheese sauce. Sprinkle with grated Parmesan cheese. Cook in the oven at 350°F (mark 4) for about 1 hr., or until cooked through.

TO SERVE: Garnish with more Parmesan cheese if you wish, and accompany by French bread and green and tomato salads.

Bolognese sauce

5 medium-size onions
8 oz. streaky bacon
4 oz. lard
3 lb. best lean minced beef
2 5-oz. cans of tomato paste
2 beef stock cubes
½ pt. water
¼ pt. red wine
salt and pepper

TO MAKE: Peel, slice and finely chop the onions. Rind the bacon and cut the rashers up finely. Fry the bacon in the lard, add the onion and cook for a further 5 min. Stir in the beef and cook until the meat begins to brown. Drain off the fat and reduce the heat. Stir in the tomato paste, crumbled stock cubes, water and wine. Add a little seasoning, cover and simmer for ¾–1 hr., stirring occasionally, until the meat is tender. Cool quickly. Use at once for lasagne or other pasta dishes, or freeze as follows:

TO PACK AND FREEZE: Put into 3 rigid plastic containers or lined pre-formers. Freeze rapidly until solid. Overwrap with foil or another polythene bag, seal and label.

TO THAW: Allow 3 hr. at room temperature or 6 hr. in the refrigerator, or re-heat gently in a saucepan, breaking the mixture up with a wooden spoon as it thaws. Add 1 clove of garlic, peeled and crushed, during the re-heating.

TO SERVE: Serve with freshly cooked pasta such as spaghetti or pasta shells.

Macaroni cheese

a 12-oz. pkt. of 'quick' macaroni
4 oz. mushrooms
a little butter

For the cheese sauce
4 oz. butter
4 oz. plain flour
2 pts. milk
½–1 level tsp. made mustard
8 oz. mature cheese, grated
seasoning
¼ pt. cider (optional)

Serves 6

Cooked Straight from the Freezer:
see pages 57, 59, 60

TO MAKE: Prepare the cheese sauce. Melt the butter in a pan, add the flour, stir well, then remove from the heat. Gradually add the milk, stirring all the time. Return the pan to the heat, and bring to the boil, stirring continuously until the sauce thickens. Cook for a further 2 min., remove from the heat and cool slightly. Stir in the mustard, cheese, seasoning and cider (if used). Cook the macaroni in boiling salted water as directed on the packet and drain thoroughly. Sauté the mushrooms in the butter. Stir the macaroni into the cheese sauce.

TO PACK AND FREEZE: Pour into 2 2-pt.

foil-lined dishes. Add the mushrooms, then cool quickly. Freeze rapidly until solid, then remove from the ovenproof dish. Overwrap with foil, label and place in a large polythene bag; seal.

TO RE-HEAT: Unwrap and return to the original ovenproof dish. Place in the oven at 350°F (mark 4), loosely covered with foil, for about $1\frac{1}{2}$ hr. Remove the cover, arrange slices from 4 fresh firm tomatoes on top, dot with butter and return to oven for 15–20 min.

TO SERVE: Serve hot, garnished with sprigs of parsley if liked.

THE WELL-ORDERED CHRISTMAS —AND OTHER OCCASIONS

There's planning ahead, ordinary style—and there's planning ahead in league with the freezer. And no doubt about it, the latter's the better bet, especially for Christmas catering.

There's no point in freezing Christmas pudding, the cake or the mincemeat, as these will all keep perfectly well. On the other hand, mince pies, breadcrumbs for stuffing, forcemeat balls and brandy butter can be dealt with bit by bit when you have a free half-hour. As to the turkey, when you come across a frozen bird at a competitive price, you can buy it well in advance and pop it in the freezer, rather than delay buying until the last minute, when prices often soar.

We've also given a lot of useful main courses and sweets, to make the entertaining days after Christmas carefree for you, too.

STARTER AND MAIN-COURSE IDEAS
These are good either during Christmas or afterwards. (See Index for pages)
Country-Style Pâté
Boeuf Bourguignonne
Steak, Kidney and Oyster Pie
Noisettes of Lamb
Veal Escalopes
Chicken Tettrazini (using leftover turkey instead of chicken)

Chicken with Curry and Lemon
Forcemeat Balls
Jugged Hare

Note re Breadcrumbs (which can be used straight from the freezer): weigh them up into portions of 2, 4 and 8 oz., for bread sauce and for stuffings—not only for the Christmas turkey, but also for perhaps a duck or goose for the New Year celebrations.

USEFUL CHRISTMAS SWEETS
WITH A LITTLE EXTRA SOMETHING:
Profiteroles
Baked Alaska
Vacherin filled with raspberries and cream
Pavlova
Crêpes Suzette

Mince pies

using Shortcrust Pastry

12 oz. shortcrust or flaky pastry
$\frac{3}{4}$–1 lb. mincemeat
milk or egg to glaze

Makes 16 or 20

Roll out the short pastry to about $\frac{1}{8}$ in. in thickness. Cut into about 20 rounds with a 3-in. fluted cutter, and 20 smaller rounds with a $2\frac{1}{4}$-in. fluted cutter. Line $2\frac{1}{2}$-in. patty tins with the larger rounds and fill with mincemeat. Damp the edges of the small rounds and place in position.

Mince pies

using Flaky Pastry

Roll out the flaky pastry to $\frac{1}{8}$ in. in thickness. Stamp out 16 rounds with a $2\frac{1}{2}$-in. plain cutter. Re-roll the scraps, cut another 16 rounds to use for the bases and place the bases on a baking sheet. Put a 1 heaped tsp. of mincemeat on each, damp the edges of the pastry, cover with the remaining pastry rounds and press the edges lightly together.

TO PACK: Leave the pies either in the patty tins or on baking sheets, unwrapped, until frozen firm.

TO FREEZE: Place in the freezer, and when quite firm, lift out from the tins or from the baking sheets; place in rigid containers with pieces of freezer paper between the layers and then overwrap, seal and label. Store in the freezer.

TO COOK: Take out the number of pies you need, return them to the original patty tins or baking sheet and cut a small slit in the top of each. Brush with a little water and sprinkle with caster sugar. Bake in the oven at 425°F (mark 7) for shortcrust pastry, or at 450°F (mark 8) if flaky pastry was used; cook for 20–30 min., or until golden-brown and cooked through.

TO SERVE: Sprinkle with more caster sugar, if you wish. Serve warm or cold.

Brandy butter

(hard sauce)

3 oz. butter
3 oz. caster or icing sugar
2–3 tbsps. brandy

TO MAKE: Cream the butter until pale and soft. Beat in the sugar gradually and add the brandy a few drops at a time, taking care not to allow the mixture to curdle. The finished sauce should be pale and frothy.

Rum butter

Make this as brandy butter, but use soft brown sugar, replace the brandy by 4 tbsps. rum and include the grated rind of $\frac{1}{2}$ a lemon and a squeeze of lemon juice. Use in the same way as brandy butter.

TO PACK: Turn the brandy or rum butter into the container in which it is to be served and cover with a double layer of foil, or turn it into a foil container.

TO FREEZE: Overwrap with a polythene bag. Label and seal.

TO THAW: Allow it 1 hr. to soften slightly at room temperature.

TO SERVE: Use to accompany Christmas pudding and mince pies.

The other occasions

Apart from a wedding, or an informal 21st birthday party at home, there are hosts of other times when you'll be called on to act as cook/hostess. Here are a few simple ideas to help you plan such an occasion.

Sit-down meal for 15 guests

Chilled watercress soup

Chicken Marengo

Saffron-flavoured rice

Cucumber salad

Pineapple creams

For the soup, follow the recipe on page 116, but make double the amount. The same goes for the Chicken Marengo, which follows, while for the pineapple creams (see page 105) you'll need treble the amounts given.

Chicken Marengo

a 4-lb. oven-ready fresh chicken, divided into 8 joints
3 tbsps. oil
1 oz. butter
2 onions, peeled and chopped
4 carrots, peeled and sliced
2 sticks of celery, scrubbed and chopped
4 oz. streaky bacon, rinded and chopped
3 level tbsps. flour
$\frac{1}{2}$ pt. chicken stock
2 15-oz. cans of plum tomatoes
6 tbsps. sherry
$\frac{1}{4}$ level tsp. salt
freshly ground black pepper
a bouquet garni
$\frac{1}{4}$ lb. button mushrooms, sliced

Serves 8

TO MAKE: Wipe the chicken joints, then fry in hot oil and butter for about 5 min., until golden-brown. Using a draining spoon, lift them from the pan into a casserole. Fry the vegetables and bacon in the fat until golden; lift onto a plate, using the draining spoon.

Stir the flour into the remaining fat in the pan and cook for 2–3 min. Gradually stir in the stock. Bring to the boil and continue to stir till the mixture thickens. Add the vegetables and bacon to the pan, with the tomatoes, sherry, seasoning, bouquet garni and mushrooms. Cover and cook in the centre of the oven at 350°F (mark 4) for 1$\frac{1}{4}$ hr., until the chicken joints are tender. Remove the bouquet garni and spoon off any excess fat on the surface. Allow to cool.

TO PACK AND FREEZE: Spoon the mixture into a family or party size foil dish. Freeze rapidly until solid. Cover with a lid, seal, overwrap with a polythene bag and label. Return the pack to the freezer.

TO THAW: Allow 17 hr. in the refrigerator, or cook from frozen.

TO COOK: Unwrap and transfer to a casserole, or leave in the foil dish. If thawed, allow 1 hr. to re-heat in the oven at 400°F (mark 6); if cooking from frozen, allow a further 1 hr. (2 hr. in all). Adjust the seasoning, and if you wish, thicken the juices with beurre manié (see page 167).

TO SERVE: Sprinkle with chopped parsley and serve with freshly boiled rice and seasonable vegetables.

TEA PARTIES

Once you have a freezer, the time-consuming 'fun' sandwiches can be made up in quantities when you're in the mood, then packaged into neat bundles for four, six or eight people. Innumerable cakes, large and small, can be stashed away in the freezer, too. Just remember that things like the devil's food cake frosting and the gâteau marguerite need care in storing, and so do meringues (see page 165), so it's best to use cake boxes.

Asparagus rolls   Stuffed olive pinwheels
Smoked salmon pinwheels   Chequerboard and ribbon sandwiches
Devil's food cake   Meringues   Gâteau marguerite

Asparagus rolls

3 1-lb. cans of green asparagus
4 small Hovis-type brown loaves
1½ lb. butter, softened

Makes 80 rolls

TO MAKE: Drain asparagus. Cut the crusts from the bread, butter the bread and slice thinly in the usual way. (Day-old bread is easier to handle with a knife.) Place an asparagus tip on each slice, then roll up carefully like a Swiss roll. Cut each roll in half crosswise, or leave whole.

TO PACK: Separate asparagus rolls by overwrapping in freezer paper. Pack tightly together in a rigid container.

TO FREEZE: Cover with a lid, seal, label and freeze till solid.

TO THAW: Loosen lid and leave overnight in the refrigerator, or thaw at room temperature for about 4 hr.

TO SERVE: Cut whole rolls in half diagonally. Arrange on plate. Garnish with parsley.

Stuffed olive pinwheels

(*see picture on page 136*)

1 large tin loaf (white)
8–12 oz. butter, softened
2–3 tbsps. chopped parsley
seasoning
lemon juice
30 stuffed green olives

Makes 40–50 pinwheels

TO MAKE: Cut the loaf lengthwise, then trim off the crusts. Blend the butter and chopped parsley together; add a little salt and pepper plus a squeeze of lemon juice. Spread on the bread slices. Place a row of stuffed olives near the edge of the bread, then roll up like a long sausage.

TO PACK: Wrap each roll in a sheet of silicone paper and place in a large foil container.

TO FREEZE: Cover with lid, label, seal and freeze till solid.

TO THAW: Loosen lid and thaw at room temperature for 4 hr. or overnight in the refrigerator.

TO SERVE: Slice, and serve immediately.

Smoked salmon and cream cheese pinwheels

(*see picture on page 136*)

1 large brown tin loaf
8 oz. butter, softened
3 3-oz. pkts. of cream cheese
1 lb. smoked salmon trimmings
freshly ground black pepper
lemon juice

Makes 9 uncut pinwheels; each cuts into 5 slices

TO MAKE: Trim crusts off loaf. Slice thinly in the usual way. Spread with butter and cream cheese, creamed together, and cover with pieces of smoked salmon. Season with freshly ground black pepper and a squeeze of lemon juice. Roll up each slice of bread like a Swiss roll.

TO PACK: Place in rigid containers, separated by strips of freezer or waxed paper.

TO FREEZE: Cover with lid. Seal, label and freeze till solid.

TO THAW: Loosen lid and allow to thaw at room temperature for about 5 hr., or leave overnight in the refrigerator. It is best to slice the pinwheels halfway through the thawing period, using a sharp knife.

TO SERVE: Garnish with lemon wedges.

Chequerboard and ribbon sandwiches

(*see picture on page 136*)

1 small white loaf
1 small brown loaf
4 oz. parsley butter (4 oz. softened butter creamed with 1½ tbsps. chopped parsley, plus seasoning and a squeeze of lemon juice)
3–3½ oz. cheese butter (1½–2 oz. cream cheese beaten into 1½ oz. butter)

TO MAKE THE CHEQUERBOARD: Remove the bread crusts, trimming the loaves to a similar size. Cut each loaf into 6 equal slices lengthwise. Liberally spread one side of all the brown slices with some of the parsley butter. Layer up the bread, starting with a brown slice, then a white slice, spread with cheese butter, then brown, then finally white —don't butter this slice. Make 3 stacks each consisting of 4 slices (2 brown and 2 white). Now slice lengthwise down through the 4 layers of bread. Lay this slice flat and spread with cheese butter. Cut another slice and lay on top so that the brown fingers lie on top of the white. Spread with parsley butter and continue to layer up. Repeat in the same way with each of the other 'stacks'.

TO MAKE THE RIBBONS: Cut each trimmed loaf into 4 long slices; spread half the slices with parsley butter and half with cheese butter. Cut each slice into 4 long ribbons, then arrange 4 brown strips on top of each other, butter the sides and place 4 white strips next to the brown. Repeat with brown strips, then white, so that the whole is square. Make up another loaf in the same way.

TO PACK AND FREEZE: Leave in whole loaves, not sliced, wrap in non-stick paper and overwrap in foil and a polythene bag. Seal, label and freeze till solid.

TO THAW: Loosen seal, then leave overnight in the refrigerator, or allow 6–7 hr. at room temperature.

TO SERVE: If liked, cover the ribbon loaves with more cheese butter and decorate as a savoury gâteau. Slice the chequerboard sandwiches just before the loaf is thoroughly thawed.

Devil's food cake

8 oz. plain flour
¼ level tsp. salt
½ level tsp. bicarbonate of soda
2 level tsps. baking powder
3 oz. plain or bitter chocolate, grated
8 fl. oz. milk (½ pt. less 3–4 tbsps.)
5 oz. butter or margarine
10 oz. caster or soft brown sugar
3 eggs, beaten
1 tsp. vanilla essence
butter cream made with 4 oz. butter and 8 oz. icing sugar (sifted) or 6 fl. oz. double cream, whipped
rum (optional)

TO MAKE: Line 2 9-in. sandwich cake tins. Sift the flour, salt, bicarbonate of soda and baking powder together. Warm the chocolate in the milk until it has dissolved. Cream the butter, adding the sugar gradually until the mixture is pale and fluffy. Add the eggs and vanilla essence gradually, beating well after each addition. Stir in the dry ingredients alternately with the chocolate milk. Divide the mixture evenly between the tins and bake in the centre of the oven at 350°F (mark 4) for 30–35 min. When the cakes are cooked, cool on a wire tray; sandwich together with butter cream or whipped cream. Before the cakes are sandwiched together they can if you wish each be sprinkled with 1 tbsp. rum.

Note: It is not possible to get exactly the same result as with a packet mix, since the American type of cake flour used is not on sale, but this recipe gives a very similar effect.

TO PACK: Place in a rigid box with two long strips of foil (double thickness) underneath the cake, so that it can be lifted without damage. Cover with the lid.

TO FREEZE: Set in freezer until quite solid, then place box inside a large polythene bag; label and seal.

TO THAW: Remove the wrapping. Allow about 4 hr. at room temperature.

TO SERVE: Place the cake on a silver cake-board or a flat plate. Make up seven-minute frosting (see below) and use to coat the cake. Swirl the frosting, and decorate with chocolate curls, vermicelli and crystallised violets.

Seven-minute frosting
2 egg whites
12 oz. caster sugar
a pinch of salt
4 tbsps. water
2 pinches of cream of tartar

This is an imitation American frosting that does not need a thermometer. Put all the ingredients into a bowl and whisk lightly. Place the bowl over hot water and continue whisking until the mixture thickens sufficiently to hold stiff 'peaks'.

Gâteau marguerite

(*see picture above*)

6 oz. butter
6 oz. caster sugar
3 large eggs
grated rind of 1 orange
6 oz. self-raising flour

For the rich orange cream
6 oz. butter
9 oz. icing sugar, sifted
1 egg yolk
3 tbsps. orange juice
2 tbsps. double cream (optional)

Serves 10

TO MAKE: Line the base of an 8¼-in. spring-release cake tin and place it on a baking sheet. Cream the butter, add the sugar and beat together until light and fluffy. Beat in the eggs one at a time. Lightly beat in the orange rind

Gâteau marguerite

and flour. Turn the mixture into the tin and level it. Bake in the centre of the oven at 350°F (mark 4) for about 45 min. Turn the cake out and cool on a wire rack. Cream the butter for the filling and add the icing sugar, alternately with egg yolk, orange juice and cream (if used), beating well after each addition. Split the cake into 2 layers, using a sharp knife, and sandwich together with some of the filling. Spread a layer of filling over the top. Use the remainder of the filling to coat the sides of the cake and smooth, using a palette knife. Use the blunt end of a knife blade to mark the top into spoke shapes as shown. Leave on a tray and set in freezer until firm.

TO PACK: Make 2 long strips of foil into a cross, then set the cake onto these and lift into a rigid container.

TO FREEZE: Overwrap in polythene, seal and label; freeze until solid.

TO THAW: Unwrap and thaw for about 4 hr. at room temperature.

TO SERVE: Set on cake-board and decorate with mimosa balls, dragees, flowers, etc.

TODDLERS' PARTIES

A birthday party with the main food straight from the freezer will appeal to many hostess/mothers, leaving as it does time to plan, organize, and keep an eye on the games and amusements.

Sandwich specials Crisps
Teddy bears cake
Milk shakes and fruit squashes

PINWHEEL SANDWICHES: see page 133, but instead of using smoked salmon, fill with thin slices of cooked ham in white or brown bread. Cut into slices when half-thawed, then cover with a polythene bag and leave till fully thawed.

ASPARAGUS ROLLS: some children like these, but if you're not sure of their tastes, try this combination. Spread slices of brown bread lightly with butter, then with cream cheese, and use drained canned pineapple fingers instead of asparagus; cut in the same way (see page 133).

CHEQUERBOARD SANDWICHES: see page 134 for making and for thawing times.

Teddy bears cake; pinwheel sandwiches; chequerboard sandwiches; potato crisps

Teddy bears cake

6 oz. butter or margarine
6 oz. caster sugar
3 eggs
1 oz. cocoa
2 tbsps. milk
5 oz. self-raising flour
6 oz. butter for icing
10 oz. icing sugar

Serves 10

TO MAKE: Grease and base-line an 8-in. round cake tin. Cream the fat and sugar until pale and fluffy. Add the eggs a little at a time, beating well after each addition. Blend the cocoa to a paste with the milk. Lightly beat into the creamed mixture, alternating with the flour. Turn the mixture into the prepared tin and level the surface. Bake in the centre of the oven at 375°F (mark 5) for about 45 min., until well risen and firm to the touch. Cool on a wire rack.

Make some butter cream by thoroughly creaming together the butter and sifted icing sugar. Coat the top and the sides with it. Mark grooves in the sides with an icing scraper. Mark the top of the cake with the blade of a knife.

TO PACK: Place the cake on 2 strips of foil set at right angles to each other on a baking sheet. Place in freezer until firm.

TO FREEZE: When quite firm, transfer on the foil strips to a cake box; overwrap, label and seal. Place near top of freezer, or somewhere where it won't be damaged.

TO THAW: Unwrap and place on a 10-in. cake board. Leave to thaw 4 hr. at room temperature.

TO SERVE: Tie a ribbon round the edge of the cake. Decorate the top with chocolate teddy bears and smarties.

6. So Good to Freeze

Some foods take to freezing like penguins to ice. Fortunately, they're the time-consuming ones, so in the lulls before the inevitable storms, get freezing the really worthwhile things like stews and casseroles, soups and sauces—and make yourself a supply of ice cream.

General note on Soups

When packing soups in $\frac{1}{2}$-pt. and 1-pt. lots, use rigid containers or pre-formed polythene bags. Always allow room for expansion and keep seasoning to a minimum—this can be adjusted during the re-heating. Milk, cream and garlic (crushed) are best added at point of serving unless otherwise directed. To use, release soup from container by running cold water over the surface, then turn it into a saucepan—preferably easy-clean. Heat very gently at first, stirring occasionally before bringing just to the boil. Alternatively, thaw before re-heating. Frozen soups do sometimes need diluting with extra stock before serving.

from the heat. Purée in a blender or put through a sieve. Season to taste.

TO PACK: Allow to cool. Pour into a rigid plastic container, label and seal. Alternatively, pour into a polythene-lined pre-former and when frozen solid, remove the polythene bag from the pre-former, label and seal.

TO FREEZE: Freeze rapidly until solid.

TO USE: Treat as in General Note. Add $\frac{1}{4}$ pt. milk at point of re-heating, and adjust the seasoning. Serve hot, accompanied by croûtons and garnished with wafer-thin slices of lemon arranged on the surface of the soup.

Cream of avocado soup

1½ oz. butter
4 oz. onion, peeled and chopped
1 large avocado
1 tbsp. lemon juice
1 level tbsp flour
1 pt. chicken stock
salt and freshly ground black pepper

Serves 4–5

TO MAKE: Melt the butter in a saucepan, add the onion and sauté until tender but not coloured. Halve the avocado along its length, twist the halves and separate; carefully bring a sharp, heavy knife down on to the stone, and lift it up to remove the stone. Peel away the tough skin of the avocado, roughly dice the flesh and toss in lemon juice. Add the flour to the onion, cook for a little longer, then add the stock and the avocado. Simmer covered for 10–15 min., remove

Cream of carrot soup

1 lb. carrots, peeled and chopped
1 stick of celery, scrubbed and chopped
$\frac{1}{4}$ of a small turnip, peeled and chopped
$\frac{1}{4}$ of an onion, peeled and chopped
1 oz. bacon, chopped
1 oz. butter
1½ pts. chicken stock
a bouquet garni
salt and pepper
3 level tbsps. flour
$\frac{1}{4}$ pt. milk

Serves 4

TO MAKE: Lightly fry the chopped vegetables and bacon in the butter for 5–7 min., until soft but not coloured. Add the stock, bouquet garni and seasoning, bring to the boil, cover and simmer for about 1 hr., until the vegetables are soft. Remove the bouquet garni and sieve the soup, or put it in an electric blender. Return it to the pan. Blend the flour and milk to a smooth cream; stir in a little of the hot liquid and pour into the soup in the pan. Bring to the boil and cook for 2–3 min., until the soup has thickened.

TO PACK: Allow to cool. Pour into a rigid plastic container, label and seal. Alternatively, pour into a polythene-lined pre-former and when frozen solid, remove the polythene bag from the pre-former, label and seal.

TO FREEZE: Freeze rapidly until solid.

TO USE: Treat as in General Note. Allow to cool slightly before adding 1–2 tbsps. cream. Garnish with chopped parsley.

Cream of cauliflower soup

½ lb. butter
1 lb. onions, peeled and finely sliced
3 lb. prepared cauliflower
1 level tbsp. curry powder
3 oz. plain flour
3 pts. stock, made with chicken stock cubes
3 pts. creamy milk
8 bay leaves
salt and freshly ground black pepper

Serves 20

TO MAKE: Melt the butter in a large saucepan, stir in the onion, cover and cook, stirring

Cream of celery soup

occasionally, until tender. Roughly chop the cauliflower and add to the pan, cover with a tightly fitting lid and cook for a further 15–20 min., stirring occasionally. Add the curry powder, return the pan to the heat and cook over a gentle heat for 2–3 min.; add the flour and cook for a few min. longer. Make up the stock and add to the pan, with the milk and the bay leaves. Bring to the boil, cover and simmer for about 45 min. Discard the bay leaves and adjust the seasoning. Purée the soup in an electric blender or pass it through a sieve.

TO PACK: Allow to cool. Pour into rigid plastic containers, label and seal. Alternatively, pour into polythene-lined pre-formers and when frozen solid, remove the polythene bags from the pre-formers, label and seal.

TO FREEZE: Freeze rapidly until solid.

TO USE: Treat as in General Note. You may need to add a little milk to regain the right consistency. Garnish with chopped parsley.

Cream of celery soup

(*see picture on left*)

1 oz. butter
1 head of celery, prepared and chopped
1 oz. plain flour
1 pt. chicken stock
a blade of mace
1 tsp. lemon juice
salt and freshly ground black pepper
2 oz. carrots, finely diced

Serves 4

TO MAKE: Melt the butter in a saucepan, add the celery and sauté for 5 min. Stir in the flour, cook for a few min., then gradually add the stock, stirring. Add the mace and lemon juice and season with salt and pepper; bring to the boil, cover and simmer for 20 min. Discard the mace. Blend or sieve the soup, return it to the pan, add the diced carrot and simmer until this is tender—about 15 min. Remove the pan from the heat, cool rapidly.

TO PACK: Allow to cool. Pour into a rigid plastic container, label and seal. Alternatively, pour it into a polythene-lined pre-former and when frozen solid, remove the polythene bag from the pre-former, label and seal.

TO FREEZE: Freeze rapidly until solid.

TO USE: Treat as in General Note. Add $\frac{1}{2}$ pt. milk at point of re-heating. Serve at once, garnished with celery leaves.

Cream of curry soup

2 level tbsps. ground almonds
2 level tbsps. desiccated coconut
$\frac{1}{4}$ pt. boiling water
1 medium-sized onion, chopped
1 oz. butter
1 oz. flour
1 level tbsp. curry paste
$1\frac{3}{4}$ pt. stock
2 oz. seedless raisins
a strip of lemon peel
1 bay leaf
1 level tbsp. cornflour

Serves 4–6

TO MAKE: Soak the ground almonds and coconut for 30 min. in the boiling water; drain, reserving the liquor. Lightly fry the onion in the butter until soft but not browned. Stir in the flour and curry paste and cook for 1 min. Stir in the stock, raisins, lemon peel and bay leaf, bring to the boil, cover and simmer for 20 min. Remove the bay leaf and lemon peel and stir in the liquor from the nuts, also the cornflour, blended with water to a cream. Bring to the boil and allow to thicken.

TO PACK: Allow to cool. Pour into a rigid plastic container, label and seal. Alternatively, pour into a polythene-lined pre-former and when frozen solid, remove the polythene bag from the pre-former, label and seal.

TO FREEZE: Freeze rapidly until solid.

TO USE: Treat as in General Note. (A little extra milk may be needed to thin the soup down). Cool slightly before adding 3 tbsps. double or single cream. Serve garnished with 1 small apple, peeled, sliced and lightly fried in a little butter.

Cream of mushroom soup

Cream of mushroom soup

(*see picture above*)

12 oz. onions, peeled and finely chopped
6 oz. butter
1 lb. button mushrooms, chopped
4 oz. plain flour
3 pt. chicken stock (made with 4 stock cubes)
salt and freshly ground black pepper

Serves 10

TO MAKE: Sauté the onions in the butter for 10 min., until soft but not coloured. Add the mushrooms and continue cooking for 5 min. Stir in the flour and cook for 3 min., then slowly add the stock, stirring all the time. Bring to the boil and simmer for 20 min. Add the seasonings.

TO PACK: Allow to cool. Pour into rigid plastic containers, label and seal. Alternatively, pour into polythene-lined pre-formers and when frozen solid, remove the polythene bags from the pre-formers, label and seal.

TO FREEZE: Freeze rapidly until solid.

TO USE: Treat as in General Note. Add 1 pt. milk at point of re-heating and simmer for 10 min. Adjust seasoning with garlic salt and lemon juice. Serve piping hot, garnished if you like with some freshly sautéed mushrooms.

Cream of vegetable soup

1 lb. vegetables
2 oz. butter
½ pt. white stock
salt and pepper
1 oz. flour
1 pt. milk

Serves 6

TO MAKE: Prepare whichever vegetables are chosen. Slice roughly (except peas). Melt half the butter in a saucepan, add the vegetables and fry gently for 5 min. without browning. Add the stock (this can be made from a chicken stock cube) and simmer with the lid on the pan for 10–15 min., until the vegetables are almost tender. Season. Meanwhile, make a white sauce, using 1 oz. butter, 1 oz. flour and 1 pt. milk in the usual way. Pour the cooked vegetables and sauce into the goblet of an electric blender. Switch to 'low' for a few seconds, then to 'high' until the soup is smooth and creamy—about 2–3 min. Check the seasoning.

Note: Suitable vegetables, in addition to those suggested in other recipes in these pages, are onions, leeks, tomatoes, broad beans, Brussels sprouts and green peas. With onion and tomato, use only ¼ pt. stock.

TO PACK: Allow to cool. Pour into a rigid plastic container, label and seal. Alternatively, pour into a polythene-lined pre-former and when frozen solid, remove the polythene bag from the pre-former, label and seal.

TO FREEZE: Freeze rapidly until solid.

TO USE: Treat as in General Note and serve at once, garnished with chopped parsley.

Broccoli soup

2 oz. butter
an 8-oz pkt. of frozen broccoli spears
1 level tbsp. flour
1½ pts. chicken stock
a pinch of nutmeg
salt and black pepper
1 oz. small pasta shapes

Serves 4

TO MAKE: Melt the butter, add the broccoli and sauté with the lid on the pan for 10 min. Stir in the flour, pour the stock over, bring to the boil and simmer for a further 10 min. Liquidise, or pass the soup through a sieve, add the nutmeg and adjust the seasoning. Drop in the pasta shapes and simmer until tender.

TO PACK: Allow to cool. Pour into a rigid plastic container, label and seal. Alternatively, pour into a polythene-lined pre-former and when frozen solid, remove the polythene bag from the pre-former, label and seal.

TO FREEZE: Freeze rapidly until solid.

TO USE: Treat as in General Note. Remove from the heat. Serve really hot.

Turkey broth

6 oz. carrot, peeled and coarsely grated
6 oz. onion, peeled and roughly chopped
1 oz. butter
1½ pts. strong turkey stock
1 bay leaf

Serves 6

TO MAKE: Sauté the vegetables in the butter until soft—about 10 min. Add the stock and bay leaf, bring to the boil, cover with a lid and simmer for 30 min. Discard the bay leaf.

TO PACK: Allow to cool quickly. Pour into a rigid plastic container, label and seal. Alternatively, pour into a polythene-lined pre-former and when frozen solid, remove the polythene bag from the pre-former, label and seal.

TO FREEZE: Freeze rapidly until solid.

TO USE: Treat as in General Note; when soup has thawed, add 2 oz. small pasta, adjust the seasoning, and cook gently until the pasta is fork-tender—about 15 min. Freshly chopped celery leaves, if available, make a good garnish.

Cream of chicken soup

(*see picture on right*)

1 oz. butter
2 level tbsps. plain flour
salt and pepper
1 pt. chicken stock
8 oz. cooked chicken pieces
Serves 4

Cream of chicken soup

TO MAKE: Melt the butter in a saucepan, add the flour and $\frac{1}{2}$ level tsp. salt; blend and cook for 1–2 min. Add the stock and chicken pieces and simmer gently for 10–15 min. Adjust the seasoning.

TO PACK: Allow to cool. Pour into a rigid plastic container, label and seal. Alternatively, pour into a polythene-lined pre-former and when frozen solid, remove the polythene bag from the pre-former, label and seal.

TO FREEZE: Freeze rapidly until solid.

TO USE: Treat as in General Note. Add about $\frac{1}{2}$ pt. milk and adjust the seasoning; don't boil. Serve at once, sprinkled with chopped parsley.

General note on Pâtés

Pâtés can be frozen in the container in which they have been made. All mixtures of this type should be cooled rapidly prior to freezing. The firmer type of pâté, when cold and after pressing, can be eased from the container (so that the container can be put into further use), then the pâté is wrapped in foil and overwrapped in a polythene bag ready for freezing. Thaw in the wrapping in the refrigerator overnight or for 5–8 hr., depending on size. Add any garnish—including melted butter—after freezing. Leave at room temperature for only a short time to 'come to' before serving.

Simple chicken liver pâté

2 oz. butter
2 bay leaves
a pinch of dried thyme
1 small onion, peeled and chopped
1 lb. chicken livers
salt and pepper
melted butter to cover

Serves 4–6

TO MAKE: Melt the butter in a pan, add the bay leaves, thyme and onion and cook gently for 2–3 min. Prepare the chicken livers and cut each into 2–3 pieces. Add to the pan and simmer gently for 5–7 min., until the livers are cooked. Remove the bay leaves. Mince the livers once or twice, using a fine grinder (the second mincing gives a smoother pâté). Season well and divide between 4–6 individual dishes, or place in one large one. Chill until set.

TO PACK: Stack the small dishes of pâté on top of each other, separated by greaseproof or non-stick paper. Wrap this pile, or the single large dish, in foil; seal and label.

TO FREEZE: Freeze rapidly until solid.

TO USE: Thaw the individual pâtés or the larger one in the refrigerator overnight. Cover with a thin layer of melted butter. Serve with fingers of hot buttered toast.

Pâté maison

1½ lb. lambs' liver
½ lb. chicken livers
½ lb. lean veal
1 lb. belly of pork, rinded and boned
4 oz. onion, peeled
1 clove garlic, peeled
2 level tsps. salt
½ level tsp. freshly ground black pepper
1 level tsp. dried basil
2 tbsps. brandy
½ lb. streaky bacon rashers, rinded

Serves 8–10

TO MAKE: Mince the lamb and chicken livers, veal, pork, onion and garlic once. Blend in the salt, pepper, basil and brandy. Stretch the bacon rashers by drawing the blade of a knife along the length of them. Use to line the base and sides of a 3½–4-pt. capacity loaf tin, or a similar-sized ovenproof dish or terrine. Spoon in the minced meats, and cover with more bacon. Place the pâté in a roasting tin with 1 in. water; lightly top with foil and cook in the oven at 350°F (mark 4) for 2½–3 hr. When cool, weight down and leave until cold in the refrigerator or other cold place.

TO PACK: Leave in the original container or turn out and wrap in foil; seal and label.

TO FREEZE: Freeze rapidly until solid. Store for up to 1 month.

TO USE: Thaw for 8 hr., or overnight, in the refrigerator. Serve with hot toast.

Farmhouse pâté

½ lb. belly pork
½ lb. lean veal
¼ lb. pigs' liver
¼ lb. fat bacon
3 peppercorns
1 level tsp. salt
a pinch of powdered mace
2 tbsps. dry white wine
1 tbsp. brandy
1 small clove garlic, peeled and crushed

Serves 4–6

TO MAKE: Finely mince the pork, veal and

liver 2 or 3 times. Cut 2 oz. of the bacon into small dice. Pound the peppercorns (or use coarse freshly ground pepper). To the minced ingredients add the prepared bacon, peppercorns or pepper, salt, mace, wine, brandy and garlic. Blend thoroughly and leave to stand for 2 hr. in a cool place. Stir again and turn the mixture into a 1-pt. ovenproof dish or 4–6 smaller ones. Cover the pâté with thin strips cut from the rest of the fat bacon. Stand the dish in a tin with 1 in. water and cook uncovered at 325°F (mark 3) until the contents show signs of shrinking—about 1¼–1½ hr. Some fat will have separated out, so use a fork to incorporate it back into the pâté. When the pâté is almost cold, cover with greaseproof paper, press with a weight and leave until completely cold.

TO PACK: Turn the pâté out, cut into portions, interleave with freezer paper and wrap in foil; seal and label.

TO FREEZE: Freeze rapidly until solid. Store for up to 1 month.

TO USE: Thaw in the refrigerator. Serve with fingers of hot buttered toast.

Note: This is a rough-textured pâté, with a full flavour.

Peter's pâté

1 lb. pigs' liver
2 oz. butter
1 onion, chopped
¼ lb. streaky bacon, rinded and diced
¼ lb. belly pork, diced
1 clove garlic skinned and crushed
1½ level tbsps. tomato paste
⅛ level tsp. black pepper
⅛ level tsp. garlic salt
⅛ level tsp. dried basil
⅛ level tsp. salt
4 tbsps. red wine
grated rind of ¼ of a lemon
2 bay leaves

Serves 8

TO MAKE: Remove the skin and any gristle from the liver. Melt the butter in a saucepan and fry the onion. Add all the other ingredients, cover and cook slowly for about 1½ hr.

Remove the bay leaves and drain the meat, retaining the liquor. Mince the meat finely and stir in the liquor. Press the mixture into a $1\frac{1}{4}$-pt. ovenproof dish. Cover and cook in the oven at 350°F (mark 4) for 30 min.; remove from the oven and allow to cool.

TO PACK: Leave in the original dish, or turn the pâté out and wrap in foil; seal and label.

TO FREEZE: Freeze rapidly until solid. Store for up to 1 month.

TO USE: Thaw overnight in the refrigerator. Just before serving, garnish with a new bay leaf. Serve with Melba toast.

Fresh salmon pâté

2 oz. butter
2 oz. flour
$\frac{3}{4}$ pt. milk
1 bay leaf
salt and pepper
$\frac{1}{4}$ level tsp. ground nutmeg
$\frac{1}{2}$ lb. fresh haddock fillet, skinned
1 lb. fresh salmon, skinned and boned
grated rind and juice of 1 lemon
1 tbsp. chopped parsley
2 eggs, beaten
melted butter

Serves 6–8

TO MAKE: Melt the butter in a pan, remove from the heat and stir in the flour. Cook for 2–3 min. Slowly add the milk, beating after each addition. Add the bay leaf, salt, pepper and nutmeg and boil gently for 2–3 min. Discard the bay leaf. Finely chop or mince the haddock and $\frac{3}{4}$ lb. of the salmon; add to the sauce. Stir in the lemon rind and juice, parsley and eggs. Divide the mixture between 6–8 buttered individual soufflé dishes (3-fl.-oz.). Brush the tops with melted butter. Slice the remainder of the salmon and decorate the tops. Place the dishes in a large roasting or similar tin, pour in enough water to come half-way up the soufflé dishes and cook in the oven at 300°F (mark 2) for about 40 min. Chill in the refrigerator.

TO PACK: Leave in the containers; wrap in foil, seal and label.

TO FREEZE: Freeze rapidly until solid. Store for up to 1 month.

TO USE: Thaw overnight in the refrigerator. Garnish with parsley sprigs and lemon slices. Serve with Melba toast.

Hunter's pâté

1 lb. fat streaky bacon rashers, rinded
1 lb. rabbit or hare flesh
1 lb. belly pork, trimmed
$\frac{1}{2}$ lb. pigs' liver
$\frac{1}{2}$ lb. pork sausage-meat
$\frac{1}{2}$ lb. garlic sausage
4 oz. onion, peeled
3 tbsps. sherry
2 tbsps. chopped parsley
2 level tbsps. dried sage
salt and freshly ground black pepper

Serves 10

TO MAKE: Grill or fry the bacon rashers until beginning to colour. Cut the rabbit or hare into small pieces. Put the pork, liver, sausage-meat, garlic sausage and onion through the mincer. Mix the rabbit or hare, sherry, parsley and sage, and season well with salt and pepper. Line a loaf tin measuring about $9\frac{1}{2}$ by $5\frac{1}{2}$ by $3\frac{1}{4}$ in. (top measurements) with the bacon. Turn the pâté mixture into the prepared tin. Fold the bacon ends over the mixture and cover with a lid of kitchen foil. Place the tin in a second tin containing $\frac{1}{2}$ in. water. Cook in the oven at 325°F (mark 3) for about 3 hr. Cool in the tin.

TO PACK: Unmould from the container; wrap in foil, seal and label.
TO FREEZE: Freeze rapidly until solid. Store for up to 1 month.
TO USE: Thaw overnight in the refrigerator. Serve cut in thick slices.

Pâté de Bruxelles

a 3-lb. oven-ready chicken
1 lb. pork, finely minced
a pinch of powdered allspice
a pinch of powdered cloves
a pinch of dried thyme
salt and freshly ground black pepper
2 tbsps. brandy or sherry
1 egg, beaten
$\frac{3}{4}$ lb. streaky bacon rashers

Serves 6–8

TO MAKE: Bone the chicken and cut the

flesh into fillets. Scrape the flesh from the bones and pound or mince it with the giblets. Mix the minced pork, allspice, cloves, thyme and seasoning with the pounded chicken. Add the brandy or sherry and sufficient beaten egg to form a soft forcemeat. Lightly grease a tin measuring 9 by 5 by 3 in. (2-pt. capacity) and line with bacon rashers. Add alternate layers of chicken and forcemeat, beginning and ending with forcemeat. Finish with more bacon and press the mixture well down. Cover with greaseproof paper and foil. Stand the tin in a baking tin containing about 1 in. of water. Bake at 300°F (marks 1–2) for 3 hrs. When the pâté is cooked, take off the foil, place a weight on top and leave in a cool place.

TO PACK: Leave in original dish or turn the pâté out and wrap in foil; seal and label.

TO FREEZE: Freeze rapidly until solid. Store for up to 1 month.

TO USE: Thaw overnight in the refrigerator. Serve cut in slices, with Melba toast or thinly cut brown bread and butter. This pâté may also be combined with other cold meats in a platter for a buffet meal.

Terrine of duck

a breast portion (about 1 lb. 12 oz.) of frozen
   duck, defrosted
salt
1 lb. belly pork
1 lb. pie veal
$\frac{1}{4}$ lb. back pork fat
$\frac{1}{4}$ pt. dry white wine
1 clove of garlic, peeled and crushed
freshly ground black pepper

Serves 8

TO MAKE: Place the duck portion in a roasting tin and sprinkle with salt. Cook in the oven at 325°F (mark 3) for 40 min. Meanwhile, trim the surplus fat from the belly pork and trim the pie veal. Cut 4–6 thin strips from the pork fat and reserve for garnish. Put the belly pork, veal and the rest of the pork fat twice through the mincer. Add the wine, garlic, $\frac{1}{2}$ level tbsp. salt and some pepper; mix thoroughly. Take the duck from the oven, remove the skin, cut the flesh from the bone and dice it. Add 1 tbsp. of the duck liquor to the minced ingredients. Put half this mixture in a 2–2$\frac{1}{2}$-pt. terrine or casserole, then add the duck meat and cover with the rest of the minced ingredients. Arrange the pork fat strips in a lattice on top and cover with a foil cap. Stand the terrine in 1 in. water in a roasting tin. Cook in the oven at 325°F (mark 3) for 1$\frac{1}{2}$–2 hr. Remove from the oven and take off the foil cap. Leave for 15 min. Cover with folded foil and press with a weight; chill.

TO PACK: Leave in the container; wrap in foil, seal and label.
TO FREEZE: Freeze rapidly until solid. Store for up to 1 month.
TO USE: Thaw overnight in the refrigerator. The terrine is served straight from the dish. When almost thawed, remove wrapping, slice 1 small orange and arrange on top of the terrine. Glaze with nearly set aspic jelly, and chill to firm up.

Hare terrine

1 hare
1 medium-sized carrot, peeled
1 medium-sized onion, peeled
1$\frac{1}{2}$ lb. pork sausage-meat
4 egg yolks
1 oz. seedless raisins
4 tbsps. stock
salt and freshly ground black pepper
$\frac{1}{2}$ lb. streaky bacon rashers, rinded

Serves 16

TO MAKE: Bone and fillet the hare; reserve the best pieces, and mince the remaining flesh twice. Grate the carrot and onion. Mix the minced hare, carrot, onion, sausage-meat, egg yolks, raisins and stock, and season well. Stretch the bacon rashers and use to line a terrine. Fill with alternate layers of hare fillets and sausage mixture. Flap the ends of the bacon rashers over. Cover and cook at 350°F (mark 4) for about 2$\frac{1}{2}$ hr. Pour off most of the fat and leave the terrine in a cool place until cold.

TO PACK: Leave in the original container, or remove and wrap in foil. Seal and label.
TO FREEZE: Freeze rapidly until solid. Store for up to 1 month.
TO USE: Thaw overnight in the refrigerator. Serve thickly sliced.

Cutlets en croûte

8 lamb cutlets, trimmed
salt and pepper
1 oz. butter
a 3-oz. can of pâté de foie
2 oz. fresh white breadcrumbs
1 clove garlic, peeled and crushed
1 large egg, beaten
8 oz. puff pastry (ready-made weight)

Makes 8

TO MAKE: Trim the cutlets sufficiently to expose 1 in. of tail bone; discard as much fat as practical. Season with salt and pepper. Melt the butter in a large pan and quickly brown the cutlets on both sides, then cool. Blend together the pâté, crumbs, garlic and 1 tbsp. beaten egg. Roll the pastry out to an oblong 20 by 18 in. Divide into 8 strips 18 in. long. Brush with egg. Spread the pâté mixture over one side of each cutlet. Wrap the pastry round the cutlets, egg side outside, overlapping each turn slightly over the previous one to enclose the cutlet, but leave the bone free.

TO PACK: Place in polythene bags or wrap in foil. Label and seal.

TO FREEZE: Freeze rapidly until solid.

TO USE: Allow the cutlets to thaw at room temperature for 4 hr. Place on a baking sheet and cook at 425°F (mark 7) for about 35 min.

Cherry-stuffed veal

7 lb. breast of veal, boned (approx. 5 lb. after
   boning)
$\frac{1}{2}$ lb. lean back bacon, in a piece
6 oz. glacé cherries
a little rosemary
oil
garlic salt (or 1 clove of garlic, peeled, and
   ordinary salt)

Serves 12

TO MAKE: Lay the veal on a chopping board. Cut into the meat where it tapers and pull back the flap to make an oblong shape. Rind the bacon and cut the piece in quarters along the length of the rinded fat, then in half at right angles to the first cut. Lay the strips of bacon at intervals along the meat,

parallel to the width. Position the cherries between the bacon, with the rosemary. Roll up the veal from the short side. Secure in position with skewers before tying neatly and firmly with string.

Place in a small roasting tin, brush with oil and dust with garlic salt (or halve the garlic clove and rub over the skin, then dust with salt). Roast at 400°F (mark 6) for $\frac{1}{2}$ hr.; reduce the temperature to 350°F (mark 4) and cook for about $2\frac{1}{2}$ hr. longer. If the meat is in danger of over-browning, cover with foil or with 2 layers of greaseproof paper, previously wetted.

TO PACK: Wrap in the piece; use foil, or wrap in plastic film and place in a polythene bag. Seal and label.

TO FREEZE: Freeze rapidly until solid. Store for up to 1 month.

TO USE: Thaw, wrapped, in the refrigerator for about 1 day.

Pork and ham galantine

1 lb. lean pork
1 lb. lean ham
1 level tbsp. finely chopped onion
$\frac{1}{4}$ pt. thick white sauce
$\frac{1}{8}$ level tsp. pepper
$\frac{1}{8}$ level tsp. salt
$\frac{1}{4}$ level tsp. dried rosemary
$\frac{1}{4}$ level tsp. dried summer savory (if available)
1 egg
thinly cut rashers of back bacon, rinded
prepared root vegetables, vinegar and salt to
   flavour cooking liquid

Serves 10–12

TO MAKE: Put the pork, ham and onion twice through the mincer. Blend with the white sauce, seasonings, herbs and egg. Shape the mixture into a roll about 3 in. in diameter. Flour a boiling cloth—a double thickness of old white sheet is suitable. Lay the rinded rashers overlapping each other over the cloth, spreading them so that they will cover the roll. Lay the roll on the rashers and fold the cloth over it, keeping the roll a good shape and overlapping the join in the cloth; tie the ends tightly.

Boil gently in water, with some flavouring root vegetables, a little vinegar and some salt for about $2\frac{1}{2}$ hr. (A saucer or similar utensil on the base of the pan prevents the roll coming directly in contact with the base of the saucepan.) Remove the roll and leave to cool under a board and weights; ensure that the most attractive part of the bacon covering is uppermost. Remove the cloth.

TO PACK: Pack in double foil or plastic film and place in a polythene bag. Seal and label.
TO FREEZE: Freeze rapidly until solid. Store for up to 1 month.
TO USE: Thaw, wrapped, in refrigerator for 1 day. Put galantine on a wire rack over a plate. Make up some aspic jelly, and when it is of the consistency of unbeaten egg white, spoon it over the galantine; repeat until it is well glazed. Garnish with sliced radishes, or as desired.

Marinaded venison

a piece of fresh venison weighing about 5 lb.

For the marinade
(Make about 24 hr. before the venison is to be served)
2 carrots, peeled and chopped
2 small onions, peeled and chopped
1 stick of celery, prepared
6 peppercorns
parsley stalks
a bay leaf
3 blades of mace
red wine as required

TO FREEZE: Place the venison, together with any blood, in a heavy-duty polythene bag. Secure, label and freeze rapidly until solid.

TO THAW: Place the venison, still in its bag, in a large bowl; loosen the top and leave in the refrigerator for at least 24 hr. Meanwhile make up the marinade by combining all the ingredients in a large container.

TO COOK: Place the venison in the marinade —there should be sufficient to half-cover the meat. Leave to soak for 12 hr., turning it over in the marinade 2–3 times. Remove the venison and cook as desired:
(a) Roasting by Simple Method: Brush the meat generously with melted fat or oil, wrap loosely in foil and roast in the centre of the oven at 325°F (mark 3), allowing 25 min. per lb. About 20 min. before the cooking is com-

pleted, remove the foil, dredge the joint with flour and return it to the oven to brown. Boil the marinade until reduced by half and use to make gravy.
(b) Roasting by Traditional Method (this gives a somewhat moister texture): Cover the joint with a paste made by mixing flour and water to a stiff dough, closely resembling a scone mixture; allow about 3 lb. flour for a saddle joint. Roll it out to $\frac{1}{2}$ in. in thickness and wrap round meat. Follow the roasting directions given above. About 20 min. before cooking is completed, remove the paste, dredge the joint with flour and return it to the oven to brown. Make gravy as above.

Serve hot, with redcurrant or cranberry jelly.

Raised pie

$\frac{3}{4}$ lb. lambs' liver
$\frac{3}{4}$ lb. lean pork
1 lb. pork sausage-meat
finely grated rind of 1 orange
2 tbsps. chopped parsley
$\frac{1}{8}$ level tsp. dried sage
2 level tsps. salt
freshly ground black pepper
jellied stock or aspic jelly
For the pastry
1 lb. plain flour
2 level tsps. salt
4 oz. lard
$\frac{1}{3}$ pt. water
beaten egg to glaze

Serves 8

TO MAKE: Mince the liver and pork and work into the sausage-meat, with the flavourings and seasonings. Sift the flour and salt into a bowl. Melt the lard slowly in the water in a saucepan, then bring to the boil, pour on to the flour and work to a dough; knead. Grease a long loaf tin measuring 13 by $4\frac{1}{2}$ in. by $2\frac{1}{4}$ in. deep ($3\frac{1}{2}$-pt. capacity), and line it with two-thirds of the pastry. Spoon the meat mixture into the centre. Brush the pastry rim with beaten egg. Roll out the remaining pastry to make a lid, put in place and seal the edges. Use any trimmings for decoration. Make a hole in the centre, and brush with egg. Bake at 400°F (mark 6) for 20 min., then reduce the heat to 350°F (mark 4) and bake for about 1 hr. 40 min. longer.

Allow to cool, then fill through the hole with well-seasoned jellied stock or aspic jelly. Leave until set.

Note: If wished, add jellied stock at the thawing stage. Adding warm stock to the half-thawed pie hastens thawing in the centre, and the stock sets on contacting the cold filling.

TO PACK: Double-wrap in foil, seal and label.

TO FREEZE: Freeze rapidly until solid.

TO USE: Thaw, wrapped, in the refrigerator for about 1 day.

Vol-au-vent and bouchée cases

For best results vol-au-vent cases should be freshly baked, but much of the meticulous preparation can be done in advance. Make up the puff pastry and cut out the cases in the usual way. From 1 lb. (ready-made weight) of puff pastry you can get about 1 dozen 3-in. vol-au-vent cases or 2 dozen 2-in. bouchée cases (see picture on right). Don't brush them with egg at this stage.

TO FREEZE: Place the cases on baking sheets and freeze until firm.

TO PACK: Stack with squares of non-stick or waxed paper between them, foil-wrap, then overwrap in polythene. Seal and label.

TO USE: Brush with egg and leave at room temperature for 15 min. Place in the centre of the oven at 450°F (mark 8) and bake until the pastry is well risen, golden and cooked through. If the pastry shows signs of becoming too brown, lower the oven temperature to 350°F (mark 4). Remove the pastry lids, and if necessary scoop out and discard any uncooked dough. Fill with hot filling and serve, or allow to cool and fill with a cold mixture.

Fillings

These may be frozen and re-heated, or they can be freshly made while the pastry cases are being baked. For this number of cases, you will need $\frac{1}{2}$ pt. basic sauce (such as Béchamel), with the addition of one of the

Mushroom bouchées

following: 6 oz. chopped cooked chicken or lean ham; 8 oz. flaked cooked salmon; 4 oz. shelled shrimps or prawns; 6 oz. chopped mushrooms, sautéed with butter and a dash of lemon juice.

Sausage rolls

(*see picture overleaf*)

12 oz. ready-made flaky pastry or shortcrust
1 lb. pork sausage-meat
egg to glaze

Makes about 18

TO MAKE: Roll the pastry out into an oblong approx. 14 by 10 in. Work the sausage-meat into 2 long 'ropes', each about 14 in. in length. Divide the pastry lengthwise into 2 strips and damp the long edges. Place each sausage 'rope' on a pastry strip, wrap the pastry over and seal the edges. Brush with egg, then cut into 2-in. lengths, approx. Place on baking sheets. Slash the top of each roll twice. If flaky pastry was used, bake at 450°F (mark 8) for 15 min., then reduce to 350°F (mark 4) and bake for a further 15 min. If shortcrust pastry was used, bake at 400°F (mark 6) for about 20 min. Cool quickly on a wire rack.

Sausage rolls

TO PACK: Place in rigid containers, as the pastry is fragile. Seal and label.

TO FREEZE: Freeze rapidly till solid.

TO USE: Thaw in the wrappings in the refrigerator for 6–8 hr., then, if the rolls are to be served warm, 'refresh' them in the oven at 375°F (mark 5).

TO FREEZE UNCOOKED SAUSAGE ROLLS: Divide up the sausage rolls, but don't brush them with egg. Put on trays in the freezer until firm, then pack, seal, label and return to the freezer. To use, brush with egg, place on baking sheets with raised sides and bake as above, but for a slightly longer time.

Sausage pielets

8 oz. shortcrust pastry (made with 8 oz. flour, etc.)
$\frac{1}{2}$ lb. bacon rashers, rinded
1 lb. pork sausage-meat
salt and freshly ground black pepper
1 egg, beaten
8 oz. puff pastry (ready-made weight)

Makes 15

TO MAKE: Roll out the shortcrust pastry thinly and use to line 15 deep patty pans. Finely dice the bacon, fry until the fat runs, then stir into the sausage-meat; season well. Spoon the mixture into the pastry cases and brush the edges with egg. Roll out the puff pastry and stamp out 15 lids. Keep the pastry trimmings to use for decoration. Place the lids over the sausage-meat and seal the edges.

Brush the lids with egg and add a pastry decoration. Bake at 450°F (mark 8) for about 30 min. Cool quickly on a wire rack.

TO PACK: Pack in foil or rigid containers; seal and label.

TO FREEZE: Freeze rapidly until solid.

TO USE: Thaw baked pies in the refrigerator for about 8 hr.; 'refresh' in a hot oven for 7–10 min. Unbaked pies should be returned to their patty pans, brushed over with egg and baked from frozen at 425°F. (mark 7) for about 40 min.

Note: Unbaked pielets may be frozen in the patty tins until firm, then removed from the tins and packed for storage.

Picnic pies

$\frac{1}{2}$ oz. butter
$\frac{3}{4}$ lb. streaky bacon, rinded and minced
$\frac{3}{4}$ lb. pie veal, minced
1 level tbsp. flour
$\frac{1}{4}$ pt. water
2 level tbsps. chopped parsley
freshly grated nutmeg
freshly ground black pepper
$\frac{1}{4}$ level tsp. dried thyme
salt
1 lb. plain flour for pastry
6 oz. hard margarine
6 oz. lard
beaten egg to glaze

Makes 24

TO MAKE: Melt the butter in a frying-pan, add the minced bacon and veal and fry gently until the fat begins to run—about 7 min. Stir in the flour and cook for a further 1 min. Stir in the water, with the parsley, nutmeg, pepper and thyme; add salt to taste. Leave to cool while making up pastry with the flour, fats, a pinch of salt and cold water. Lightly grease 24 patty tins (approx. capacity $2\frac{1}{2}$ tbsps. water); line with the pastry, reserving enough for lids and decoration. Brush beaten egg round the rims of the pastry cases and spoon in the meat. Cover with pastry and decorate with pastry leaves. (Freeze at this stage, or after baking.) Brush with beaten egg and bake at 400°F (mark 6) for about 30 min. Cool quickly on a rack.

To freeze unbaked, follow instructions above.

TO PACK: Pack in foil or rigid containers; seal and label.

TO FREEZE: Freeze rapidly until solid.

TO USE: Thaw baked pies in the refrigerator for about 8 hr., then 'refresh' in a hot oven for 7–10 min. Unbaked pies should be brushed with beaten egg and baked while still frozen at 400°F (mark 6) for about 35 min.

Chicken bake

2 4½-lb. oven-ready chickens
¼ lb. tomatoes, cut up
¾ lb. mushrooms, cut up
2 bay leaves
2 carrots, peeled and sliced
2 medium-sized onions, peeled and sliced
3 pts. water
4 oz. plain flour
1 level tsp. salt
½ level tsp. pepper
butter
4 tbsps. oil
¼ pt. dry sherry

Serves 12

TO MAKE: Skin the chickens, joint in the usual way, then cut the joints into small, easy-to-manage pieces. Reserve the trimmings and carcase frame for stock. Keep the chicken cool. To make stock, put the carcase, etc., giblets, tomatoes, mushrooms, bay leaves, carrots and onions in a pan with the water and simmer for about 3 hr., until well cooked. Strain and chill the stock.

Skim the fat from the chicken stock, which should measure 2 pts. Coat the chicken pieces in the flour seasoned with the salt and pepper. Melt 2 oz. butter with the oil, and brown the chicken a little at a time. Add any excess flour to the pan drippings. Slowly stir in the stock, bring to the boil, add the sherry and adjust the seasoning. Arrange the chicken in a large roasting tin and pour the sauce over. Cover tightly and bake at 350°F (mark 4) for about 1¼ hr., until the chicken is fork-tender. Reduce the juices if necessary to thicken to a glaze consistency. Allow to cool.

TO PACK: Pack the chicken and sauce in rigid plastic containers or suitable foil containers. Seal and label.

TO FREEZE: Freeze rapidly until solid.

TO USE: Thaw overnight in refrigerator. The next day, re-heat chicken at 350°F. (mark 4) for 40–45 min.; peel 3 lb. tomatoes, halve, and scoop out seeds; peel 1½ lb. mushrooms and remove the stalks, then slice the caps thickly. Remove the seeds from 3 green peppers and slice the flesh finely. Just cover the mushrooms with water, add 3 tbsps. lemon juice and 3 oz. butter and cook uncovered till the water evaporates—about 20 min. In a separate pan melt 3 oz. butter and lightly sauté the tomatoes; add the mushrooms and peppers, with seasoning to taste. Arrange the chicken round the edge of a large dish, with the tomato mixture in the centre. Garnish with chopped parsley.

Roast chicken galantine

a 3½-lb. oven-ready chicken, boned
½ lb. lean pork, minced
½ lb. lean veal, minced
½ lb. larding fat
2 level tsps. salt
½ level tsp. freshly ground black pepper
¼ oz. pistachio nuts, blanched and peeled
melted butter

Serves 6–8

TO MAKE: Alert your butcher in advance if you wish him to bone the bird for you; otherwise, tackle the job yourself. Mince the pork and veal and half the larding fat together and season well. Cut the remaining fat into long strips. Spread half the minced meats over the centre of the bird and lay the strips of fat along the length. Arrange the pistachio nuts in rows between the strips of fat. Force a little of the filling into each boned limb. Spread the remaining meat over the fat and nuts. Draw the sides together to envelop the meat, and sew up with trussing string, to re-shape the bird. Place in a small roasting tin. Brush with melted butter, season with more salt and pepper and cook at 375°F (mark 5) for about 1½ hr. Cool rapidly.

TO PACK: Pack in double foil, seal and label.

TO FREEZE: Freeze rapidly until solid.

TO USE: Thaw for 1 day in the refrigerator, unwrapped.

Cold cheese soufflés

$\frac{1}{8}$ level tsp. each of salt, pepper and Cayenne
  pepper
$\frac{1}{2}$ level tsp. French mustard
2 tsps. tarragon vinegar
$\frac{1}{2}$ pt. liquid aspic jelly
2 oz. Parmesan cheese, finely grated
2 oz. Gruyère cheese, finely grated
$\frac{1}{2}$ pt. double cream
$\frac{1}{4}$ pt. thick mayonnaise

Serves 6

TO MAKE: Tie a collar of greaseproof paper
round 6 individual soufflé dishes (2$\frac{3}{4}$-in. diameter), to extend 2 in. above the rim. Place
the salt, pepper, Cayenne and mustard in a
bowl, and add the vinegar and aspic, which
should be cold but not quite set. Beat until
frothy. Add the cheeses and mix well. Whip
the cream until almost stiff and fold in, with
the mayonnaise; blend thoroughly. Spoon
the mixture into the prepared dishes and
allow to set in a cool place.

TO PACK: Leave in the dishes, with the
paper collars still in place. Put on a baking tray.

TO FREEZE: Freeze until solid. Wrap in
double foil, seal and label. Return to the
freezer.

TO USE: Thaw at room temperature for about
3$\frac{1}{4}$–4 hr., with the paper collars still in place.
When thawed, remove papers and decorate
with 2 oz. toasted breadcrumbs. Serve with
warm buttered toast.

Sandwich layer gâteau

(*see coloured picture on back cover*)

1 large rectangular sandwich loaf, uncut
3 eggs, hard-boiled
2 tbsps. bottled mayonnaise
1 small red pepper
2–3 level tbsps. tomato paste
8 oz. full-fat cream cheese
2 oz. soft margarine
4 tbsps. chopped parsley
1–2 tbsps. lemon juice
1 oz. walnuts, finely chopped

Serves 8–10

TO MAKE: Remove all the crusts from round
the loaf. Using a sharp serrated knife, divide
the loaf lengthwise into 4 slices. Make up
the fillings as follows. Shell the eggs and chop
finely, then combine with the mayonnaise.
Carefully remove all seeds and traces of pith
from the red pepper; dice the flesh finely,
blanch, allow to cool and drain before mixing
with the tomato paste and 3 oz. of the cream
cheese. Put the margarine in a bowl and combine with 3 oz. cream cheese; add the parsley and lemon juice and mix well. Spread the
three fillings between the cut bread layers.
Spread the top surface with the remaining
2 oz. cream cheese, and sprinkle the walnuts
over.

TO PACK AND FREEZE: Place the sandwich
gâteau on some foil and partially freeze, uncovered, until almost solid before finally
covering the foil over to enclose it. Freeze
rapidly until solid; seal and label.

TO USE: Take out of the freezer overnight to
thaw in the refrigerator; loosen the wrappings, but leave covered at room temperature
until required, to 'come to'.

General note on Ice Cream

Home-made ice cream generally has a firmer
texture than the commercial ice cream, which
is more highly aerated. Home-made ice cream
can be left in freezing trays for storage in the
freezer, but this means that the trays are out
of use for other things. It is better to line the
ice trays with foil or waxed paper before the
ice cream is finally frozen; alternatively,
when the ice cream is almost frozen, but still
malleable, scoop it into rigid polythene
containers or clean, used bought ice cream
boxes. If using the first method, wrap the ice
cream in foil, overwrap, seal and label; for
the second method, simply overwrap it.

To use ice cream from the freezer it is
necessary to let it 'come to', i.e. to soften a
little, and timing is very much a question of
personal judgment. With some recipes, just
10 min. at room temperature is enough, but
to get even thawing, the ice-cube compartment of an ordinary refrigerator is the better
place, provided you know that it is set at
about 20°F (-7°C). Put the ice cream or
sorbet from the freezer into the compartment
and leave for up to 4–6 hr. Or, if this compartment proves too cold, then leave it in the
body of the refrigerator for about 2 hr.

Basic (vanilla) ice cream

½ pt. milk
1 vanilla pod
1 whole egg
2 egg yolks
3 oz. castor sugar
½ pt. double or whipping cream

Makes about 1 pt.: serves 4–6

TO MAKE: Bring the milk almost to the boil and infuse the vanilla pod for about 15 min.; remove the pod. Cream the whole egg, yolks and sugar together until pale. Stir in the flavoured milk and strain the mixture through a sieve back into the saucepan. Heat the custard very slowly, stirring all the time, until it just coats the back of a spoon. Pour it into a basin and leave to cool. Pour the cold custard into a shallow, rigid ice-cube tray or a shallow foil container and freeze until mushy. Remove from the tray and beat well. Fold the lightly whipped cream through it. Continue freezing until mushy; beat it a second time, and freeze again until firm.

TO FREEZE AND USE: See General Note.

VARIATIONS

Chocolate: Add 2 oz. plain chocolate and (optional) ½ oz. unsweetened chocolate, dissolved in the milk, to give a stronger flavour.
Praline: Add 2 oz. crushed praline, nut brittle or toasted hazelnuts at the end of the second beating.
Coffee: Add 2 tsps. coffee essence to the mixture when cold.
Pineapple: Drain a 15-oz. can of pineapple tidbits. Purée the pineapple in an electric blender, or crush it well. Beat it into the half-frozen ice cream.

COMMERCIAL ICE CREAM

Ice cream is best kept away from the coldest part of the freezer, so that it doesn't become excessively hard. When taking ice cream from a bulk container, a special scoop is very practical; using what is known as a 'size 16' scoop (giving a 3-fl.-oz. portion) you should get about 52 helpings from 1 gallon. Scoop evenly across the can, and replace the lid at once. It does help to warm the scoop before use, but don't make it too hot or you'll melt the surrounding ice cream.

Strawberry liqueur ice cream

¼ pt. double cream
8 oz. fresh strawberries, sieved to give ¼ pt. purée, or ¼ pt. frozen unsweetened strawberry purée
½ tsp. vanilla essence
1 tbsp. rum or Maraschino
2 oz. caster sugar

Serves 4–6

TO MAKE: Whip the cream in a deep bowl until it will hold its shape. Fold through it the purée, essence, rum or Maraschino and sugar. Turn the mixture into an ice-cube or similar shallow tray and freeze until half-frozen. Return it to the mixing bowl and whisk until smooth, then return it to the tray and put in the freezer until firm.

TO PACK AND FREEZE: Pack either in the freezing tray, with a double wrap of foil and an overwrap of polythene, or use rigid containers. Seal and label. Store in the freezer.

TO USE: Serve straight from the freezer.

VARIATIONS

1. Use raspberries instead of strawberries (the purée may need to be put through a very fine sieve to remove the pips).
2. Use a small can of crushed pineapple and adjust the amount of sugar to compensate for the sweet syrup.

Note: For a really light, smooth and 'ice-free' consistency, a rotating ice-cream maker should be used to freeze the mixture before it is stored in the freezer.

Grapefruit sorbet

6 oz. sugar
¾ pt. water
a 6½-fl.-oz. can of frozen grapefruit juice
2 egg whites

Serves 6

TO MAKE: Dissolve the sugar in the water. When dissolved, bring to the boil and boil, uncovered, for 10 min. Turn the frozen juice into a bowl and pour on the sugar syrup. When cold, pour into a 1-pt. ice-cube tray and freeze to a mushy consistency. Whisk the egg whites until thick and foamy but not dry. Fold into the grapefruit mush, return the mixture to the freezer tray and freeze until firm.

TO PACK AND FREEZE: See General Note.

TO USE: Allow to soften slightly in the refrigerator before scooping into glasses. Decorate each glass with a mint sprig and serve with fan wafers.

Peach sorbet

3 oz. sugar
½ pt. water
a few strips of lemon rind, free of pith
2 yellow peaches
1 tbsp. lemon juice
1 egg white

Serves 4

TO MAKE: Put the sugar and water in a saucepan and dissolve the sugar over a moderate heat. Add the lemon rind, bring to the boil and boil gently for 10 min. Blanch the peaches, peel, and discard the stones. Dice the flesh, add the strained syrup and purée in an electric blender, or pass the mixture through a sieve. Stir in the lemon juice and leave to cool. Turn the mixture into an ice-cube tray, and freeze until mushy, then fold in the egg white, whisked until stiff but not dry. (This is best done in a bowl.) Return the mixture to the tray and freeze until firm.

TO PACK AND FREEZE: See General Note.

TO USE: Allow to soften slightly in the refrigerator before scooping out into glasses. Decorate each glass with a slice of fresh peach and a mint sprig.

Ice cream gâteau

(*see colour picture facing page 128*)

1 recipe quantity of vanilla ice cream (see page 151)
2 15-oz. cans of sliced peaches, drained
4 tbsps. brandy
2 8-in. fatless sponge cake layers

Serves 8–10

TO MAKE: Soften the ice cream until of a stiff spreading consistency. Line an 8-in. cake tin with non-stick paper and spoon in half the ice cream. Allow to harden in the freezer. Meanwhile soak the drained peaches in 2 tbsps. peach juice and the brandy. Arrange the peach slices over the ice cream layer, spoon the juice over and chill until firm. Cover with the remaining ice cream and re-freeze. Take the ice cream and fruit layer from the freezer and sandwich it between the sponge cakes.

TO PACK: Place the gâteau on a large sheet of foil and wrap round to enfold completely. Seal and label.

TO FREEZE: Freeze rapidly until firm.

TO USE: Remove the gâteau from the freezer and thaw in the refrigerator for at least 6–8 hr. Before serving, lightly whip ¼ pt. double cream until it holds its shape. Pile on top of the gâteau, decorate with a few peach slices, if available, and add some ratafias, over which you can 'drizzle' some melted chocolate.

Rum parfait

1½ oz. blanched almonds
4 eggs, separated
3 oz. caster sugar
2 tbsps. rum
a 6-oz. can of Danish cream

Serves 6

TO MAKE: Slice the almonds into fine shreds and lightly grill until golden. Whisk the egg yolks with the sugar until thick and fluffy. Whisk in the rum and add the toasted nuts. Fold in the cream. Whisk the egg whites and fold into the mixture. Rinse a 2-pt. ring mould out with cold water, and sprinkle the inside with sugar. Pour in the egg mixture and cover with foil. Freeze until firm.

TO PACK: Leave in the mould, covered with foil and wrapped in more foil; seal and label.

TO FREEZE: Freeze rapidly until solid.

TO USE: Loosen the parfait round the edges, dip the mould into hot water for a few seconds, and invert on to a serving dish. Decorate with glacé cherries and angelica, and serve at once.

Apricot bombe

1 recipe quantity of vanilla ice cream (see page 151)
2 oz. blanched almonds, finely chopped
a 15-oz. can of apricots
4 tbsps. brandy

Serves 6

TO MAKE: Allow the ice cream to soften a little and stir in the almonds. Spoon two-thirds of it into a chilled 1-pt. pudding basin and press it against the sides to form a shell. Drain the apricots. Pile the fruit, with 2 tbsps. of the juice and the brandy, into the centre; top with a 'lid' of the remaining ice cream. Cover with foil, and freeze until firm.

TO PACK AND FREEZE: Overwrap with foil, seal and label. Freeze rapidly.

TO USE: To unmould the bombe, dip the basin in warm water for a few seconds and invert on to a chilled serving plate.

Ice cream with chocolate sauce

TO USE: Before serving, unmould, softening slightly by dipping the mould into hot water for a few seconds.

Honey bombe

2 fl. oz. (3 tbsps.) water
$\frac{1}{2}$ lb. clear honey
6 egg yolks
$\frac{3}{4}$ pt. double cream, whipped

Serves 10–12

TO MAKE: Put the water and honey into a small pan and bring to the boil; cool for 10 min. Put the honey and egg yolks into a basin, place over a pan of hot water and whisk for up to 20 min., until thick and creamy (the time will be shorter if you use an electric mixer). Remove from the heat and whisk from time to time until cold. Fold in the whipped cream. Turn the mixture into a 3-pt. pudding basin or bombe mould, previously chilled. Freeze until firm—3–4 hr.

TO PACK: Cover with foil, overwrap, label and seal. Return it to the freezer.

Sauces for ice cream

(*see picture above*)

Ice creams are often greatly improved by the addition of a well-flavoured sauce. It is not worth-while to freeze such a sauce, because of the time needed to re-heat and then cool it before serving, so make the sauce shortly before the meal. The amounts given make enough sauce for 6–8 servings. Fruit sauces require a basic syrup, made as follows: Dissolve 1 lb. caster sugar in 1 pt. water; bring to the boil and boil until it reaches 220°F. (If you have no sugar-boiling thermometer for testing, this means boiling in a 4-pt. saucepan for about 12 min.) Cool.

Lemon Cream Sauce: Melt 1 oz. butter, stir in 2 tbsps. lemon juice, the finely shredded rind of $\frac{1}{2}$ a lemon, 4 tbsps. double cream, $\frac{1}{4}$ pt. basic syrup and 2 level tsps. arrowroot blended with $\frac{1}{4}$ pt. water. Bring to the boil and cook until thick. Drizzle the hot sauce over the ice cream and serve immediately.

Cherry Sauce: Drain a can of pitted black cherries (reserving the juice) and stir the fruit into $\frac{1}{4}$ pt. basic syrup. Blend 3 level tsps. arrowroot with just $\frac{1}{4}$ pt. of the cherry juice; bring to the boil, add the cherries and syrup, and flame with 2 tbsps. brandy.

Blackberry Sauce: Make as for Cherry Sauce, using blackberries, with rum instead of brandy.

Rich Chocolate Sauce: Melt 4 oz. plain chocolate with 2 level tbsps. golden syrup and 4 tbsps. evaporated milk over a low heat —don't boil. When smooth, increase the heat to the desired serving temperature.

Coffee-Caramel Sauce: Dissolve 8 oz. caster sugar in a thick pan over a moderate heat. Increase the heat to brown the mixture a little. Slowly add $\frac{1}{2}$ pt. boiling coffee and boil for 6 min. Cool slightly, but serve while still warm.

Honey Sauce: Melt 2 oz. butter, stir in $1\frac{1}{2}$ level tsps. cornflour and gradually add 4–6 oz. thin honey. Bring to the boil and cook for 1–2 min.

Melba Sauce: See page 95.

Apricot mousse

(*See colour picture on front cover*)

2 1-pt. tangerine jelly tablets
boiling water
a 29-oz. can of apricot halves
a small can of evaporated milk
2 tbsps. apricot brandy (optional)

Serves 6–8

TO MAKE: Place the jelly tablets in a measure and make up to 1 pt. with boiling water; stir to dissolve and leave until beginning to set. Drain the apricots and pass them through a sieve (or use an electric blender) to give $\frac{1}{2}$ pt. purée. Whisk the purée into the jelly until frothy, then fold in the evaporated milk until evenly blended. Add liqueur to taste. Turn the mixture into a $2\frac{1}{2}$-pt. fancy ring mould. Leave in the refrigerator to set. Unmould on to non-stick paper placed on a baking sheet.

TO PACK: Place the uncovered mousse in the freezer and leave until firm, then double-wrap in foil, seal, label and return it to the freezer.

TO FREEZE: Freeze rapidly until solid.

TO USE: Remove wrapping, place on serving plate, cover lightly and thaw at room temperature for 5 hr. Fill the centre with thawed frozen fruit salad (see page 159) or with fresh salad.

Strawberry soufflé

(*See colour picture facing page 128*)

3 eggs, separated
3 oz. caster sugar
Water
3 level tsps. powdered gelatine
2 tbsps. brandy (optional)
$\frac{1}{4}$ pt. strawberry purée
$\frac{1}{4}$ pt. double cream

Serves 4–6

TO MAKE: Prepare a 5-in. soufflé dish with a band of double greaseproof paper or foil forming a collar 2 in. above the rim. Whisk the egg yolks, sugar and 2 tbsps. water in a bowl over hot water until thick and creamy. Remove from the heat and continue to whisk until the mixture is cool. Place the gelatine, 2 tbsps. water and brandy in a basin over hot water and stir until dissolved; allow to cool. Add a little egg mixture and fold it through before adding to remainder. Fold the strawberry purée through, blending fully together before adding the whipped cream. Stiffly whisk the egg whites and gently fold into the mixture until evenly blended. Pour into the prepared soufflé dish.

TO PACK AND FREEZE: Leave the collar of paper or foil round the soufflé; freeze until firm on a flat tray. Remove from tray, overwrap, seal and label. Return soufflé to freezer.

TO USE: Remove wrappings, but cover loosely with a polythene bag, thaw overnight in the refrigerator, or at room temperature for about 4 hr. When thawed, carefully remove the collar. Decorate the sides of the soufflé with grated chocolate and top with small strawberries, as shown in the photograph. Chocolate-coated rose leaves make a pretty finishing touch for special occasions— see page 165.

Lemon soufflé

3 egg yolks
2 oz. caster sugar
grated rind and juice (4 tbsps.) of 2 lemons
½ pkt. lemon jelly
2 tbsps. water
¼ pt. double cream
3 egg whites

Serves 4

TO MAKE: Prepare a 5-in. soufflé dish as in previous recipe. Whisk together the egg yolks, sugar, lemon rind and juice in a deep bowl over hot water until really thick. Dissolve the jelly in the water: either place both in a small pan over a low heat, or put them in a basin over hot water: stir well. When luke-warm, whisk into the egg yolk mixture. Leave in a cool place; when half-set, fold in the whipped cream. Lastly fold into the stiffly whisked egg whites. Turn the mixture into the prepared soufflé dish placed on a flat baking sheet.

TO PACK AND FREEZE: Freeze until firm. Leave the collar in place. Wrap in foil and overwrap. Seal and label. Return it to the freezer.

TO USE: Remove wrappings but cover loosely with a polythene bag. Thaw at room temperature for about 4 hr. or in the refrigerator overnight. Remove the collar, and decorate the soufflé with crystallised lemon slices, mimosa balls and strips of angelica.

Apricot chiffon

½ pkt. orange jelly
2 tbsps. water
a 21-oz. can of apricot halves
2 tbsps. lemon juice
¼ pt. double cream
2 egg whites

Serves 6

TO MAKE: Dissolve the jelly in the water (either put both in a small pan over a low heat, or put in a basin over hot water); stir well. Sieve or blend the apricots, together with the syrup. Stir in the lemon juice and dissolved jelly. Put in a cool place; when beginning to set, fold in the unwhipped cream

and stiffly whisked egg whites. Pour into 6 small containers and chill until set.

TO PACK: Cover with foil and overwrap; seal and label.

TO FREEZE: Freeze rapidly until solid.

TO USE: Thaw unwrapped, but loosely covered, at room temperature for about 4 hr. Decorate with a sprig of mint.

Blackcurrant snow

1 lb. cooking apples
a 1-pt. pkt. of blackcurrant jelly
1 egg white
1 oz. caster sugar

Serves 4–5

TO MAKE: Peel and core the apples, slice and cook in the minimum of water until a thick pulp is obtained. Blend or sieve and then cool. Place the jelly cubes in a measure and make up to ½ pt. with boiling water. Stir to dissolve; cool in a bowl until half-set. Whisk to a froth, then whisk in the apple purée. Whisk the egg white until stiff, add the sugar and whisk again until stiff. Fold in the blackcurrant mixture and turn it into a serving dish.

TO PACK: Pack in the dish, cover with foil and overwrap with foil. Chill.

TO FREEZE: Freeze rapidly until solid.

TO USE: Thaw unwrapped, but loosely covered with a polythene bag, for about 4 hr. at room temperature. Before serving, halve 1 green-skinned eating apple, core and slice thinly. Dip each slice in lemon juice to prevent discoloration and arrange the pieces neatly in a circle on top of the sweet, slightly overlapping each other.

Chocolate cups

a 1-pt. pkt. of lime jelly
8 oz. plain chocolate
8 tbsps. sherry
4 tbsps. orange juice
2 tbsps. apricot jam, sieved
8 oz. sponge cake crumbs
2 tbsps. milk
¼ pt. double cream

Serves 16

TO MAKE: Make the jelly up as directed on the packet; pour ½ pt. of it into a shallow tin and leave in a cool place to set. Melt the broken chocolate in a bowl standing over warm water. Set out some paper bun cases, using two together; carefully and evenly coat the inside of each with melted chocolate. Allow to harden in a cool place, and re-coat if necessary.

Blend together the sherry, orange juice and apricot jam and stir in the sponge cake crumbs. Carefully ease the paper cases from the chocolate shells. Divide the cake crumb mixture between the chocolate cups. Whisk the half-set jelly in a measure until frothy, and divide between the cups. Whisk the milk and cream together until the mixture will hold its shape. Pipe round the edge of each cup. Dice the remaining jelly and spoon it into the centre of the cream ring.

TO PACK: Pack in a single layer in rigid plastic containers, seal and label.

TO FREEZE: Freeze rapidly until solid.

TO USE: Thaw overnight in the refrigerator, or at room temperature for about 4 hr.

Orange creams

grated rind of 1 orange and juice of 2 oranges
a little lemon juice
a 1-pt. pkt. of lemon jelly
2 tbsps. water
2 eggs, separated
4 tbsps. double cream

Serves 4

TO MAKE: Measure the orange juice and if necessary make up to ¼ pt. with lemon juice. Dissolve the jelly in the water (either place both in a small pan over a low heat, or put in a basin over hot water); stir well. Beat in the egg yolks. Add the orange juice and grated rind and leave in a cool place. When almost set, fold in the lightly whipped cream and stiffly whisked egg whites. Spoon the mixture into 4 individual containers and chill.

TO PACK: Cover with foil, overwrap, seal and label.

TO FREEZE: Freeze rapidly until solid.

TO USE: Thaw unwrapped, but loosely covered with a polythene bag, at room temperature for about 4 hr.

Marmalade cream

a 1-pt. pkt. of lemon jelly
2 tbsps. lemon juice
4 tbsps Chivers Olde English Marmalade
¼ pt. single cream
¼ pt. double cream

Serves 4–6

TO MAKE: Place the jelly cubes in a measure and make up to ½ pt. with boiling water; stir to dissolve. Take out 4 tbsps. of the jelly and mix with 2 tbsps. cold water. Spoon into a 1½-pt. jelly mould and leave to set. Add the lemon juice to the remainder of the jelly and chill until half-set. Fold in the marmalade until well blended. Whisk the creams together until the mixture will hold its shape. Fold evenly into the half-set jelly. Turn the mixture into the mould and leave to set.

TO PACK: Leave in the mould, cover and overwrap. Seal and label.

TO FREEZE: Freeze rapidly until solid.

TO USE: Transfer to the refrigerator and thaw overnight in the mould. Before serving, unmould and decorate with blanched pistachio nuts.

Pineapple chiffon flan

8 oz. sweetmeal biscuits
4 oz. butter, melted
1 oz. caster sugar
For the filling
4 tbsps. water
2 level tsps. powdered gelatine
3 large eggs, separated
6 oz. caster sugar
a 15-oz. can of crushed pineapple, drained
grated rind and juice of 1 lemon
8 oz. full-fat soft cream cheese

Serves 6–8

TO MAKE: Crush the biscuits and blend the crumbs with the butter and sugar. Use to make a case in a 10-in. loose-bottomed French fluted flan tin.

Pour the water for the filling into a cup and sprinkle the gelatine over. Beat the egg yolks and 2 oz. of the sugar until pale; add the pineapple, lemon rind and juice. Turn the mixture into a saucepan and cook, without boiling, until thick. Blend in the soaked gelatine and then the cream cheese. Cool until on the point of setting. Whisk the egg whites stiffly and gradually whisk in 3 oz. sugar. When at the 'peak' stage, fold in the remaining 1 oz. sugar and the pineapple cheese. Turn the filling into the biscuit case and chill. Remove the flan tin.

TO PACK: Carefully place the flan on a foil-lined baking sheet. Put into the freezer unwrapped until firm. Wrap in foil, or put in a suitable-sized rigid container, seal and label.

TO FREEZE: Freeze rapidly until solid.

TO USE: Slightly loosen the wrappings and thaw at room temperature for about 4 hr. Pipe a whirl of freshly whipped cream on each portion.

Pineapple chocolate velvet

a 1-pt. pkt. of orange jelly
4 oz. plain chocolate
a 15-oz. can of pineapple pieces
$\frac{1}{4}$ pt. double cream
$\frac{1}{4}$ pt. single cream

Serves 4–6

TO MAKE: Put half the jelly cubes in a measure and add $\frac{1}{4}$ pt. boiling water; stir to dissolve. Add the chocolate, broken into pieces, and stir to melt. Cool, but don't allow to set. Pour the mixture into a 7-in. (1$\frac{1}{2}$-pt.) plain ring mould, tilting the mould to line it evenly with chocolate. Chill.

Melt the remaining jelly in $\frac{1}{4}$ pt. heated pineapple juice and leave until half-set. Whip the creams together until the mixture will hold its shape. Fold in the jelly and the drained pineapple. Turn the mixture into the lined mould and chill.

TO PACK: Leave in the mould, cover, overwrap, seal and label.

TO FREEZE: Freeze rapidly until solid.

TO USE: Thaw overnight in the refrigerator. Before serving, unmould, and add some fresh whipped cream and fruit, if you wish.

Lemon cheesecake

2 1-pt. pkts. of lemon jelly
4 tbsps. water
2 eggs, separated
$\frac{1}{2}$ pt. milk
grated rind of 2 lemons
6 tbsps. lemon juice
1 lb. 4 oz. plain cottage cheese
$\frac{1}{2}$ oz. caster sugar
$\frac{1}{4}$ pt. double cream, whipped
For the crumb base
4 oz. digestive biscuits
2 oz. caster sugar
2 oz. butter, melted

Serves 8

TO MAKE: Dissolve the jelly in the water in a small pan over a low heat—don't boil. Beat together the egg yolks and milk, pour on to the jelly, stirring, and return the mixture to the saucepan; heat for a few min., without boiling. Remove from the heat and add the lemon rind and juice. Cool until beginning to set. Stir in the sieved cottage cheese, or blend the jelly mixture and unsieved cheese in an electric blender. Whisk the egg whites stiffly, add $\frac{1}{2}$ oz. caster sugar and whisk again until stiff. Fold quickly into the cheese mixture, followed by the whipped cream. Turn the mixture into an 8-in. spring-release cake tin fitted with a tubular base.

Crush the digestive biscuits and stir in the sugar and melted butter. Use to cover the cheese mixture, pressing lightly down. Chill.

TO PACK: Turn out carefully on to a piece of foil laid on a baking tray.

TO FREEZE: Freeze rapidly until firm. Wrap carefully, seal and label, and return the cheesecake to the freezer.

TO USE: Unwrap, place on a serving plate and cover loosely with a polythene bag; thaw at room temperature for 6–8 hr. Decorate with glacé cherries and a mint sprig.

Lemon freeze

2 oz. cornflakes, crumbled
2 level tbsps. caster sugar
1 oz. butter, melted
For the lemon layer
2 eggs, separated
a small can of sweetened condensed milk
4 tbsps. lemon juice
3 level tbsps. caster sugar

Serves 8

TO MAKE: In a bowl blend together the cornflake crumbs, sugar and butter until well mixed. Press all but 4 tbsps. into the base of a 1½-pt. ice-cube or other suitable shallow dish. Beat the egg yolks in a deep bowl until really thick and creamy. Combine with the condensed milk. Add the lemon juice and stir until thickened. Beat the egg whites until stiff but not dry. Gradually beat in the 3 tbsps. caster sugar; fold through the lemon mixture. Spoon into the ice tray and sprinkle with the remaining cornflake crumbs.

TO PACK: Leave in the ice tray; cover, over-wrap, seal and label.

TO FREEZE: Freeze rapidly until solid.

TO USE: Leave for a short time at room temperature to soften slightly. Serve cut into 8 bars.

Strawberry galette

6 oz. butter
3 oz. caster sugar
9 oz. plain flour
For the filling
a 1-pt. pkt. of strawberry jelly
a 5-fl.-oz. carton of soured cream
1 lb. fresh strawberries, hulled
juice of 1 orange

Serves 8

TO MAKE: Cream together the butter and sugar. Beat in half the flour, then work in the rest. Knead lightly. Press into the base and up the sides of a 9-in. loose-bottomed fluted flan tin. Prick the base. Bake at 350°F (mark 4) for about 30 min. Cool.
    Make up the jelly to ¾ pt. with hot water;

cool. To ¼ pt. cool jelly add the soured cream, and when nearly set pour into the flan case. Cover with sliced strawberries. Add the orange juice to the rest of the jelly; when on the point of setting, use to glaze the fruit. Leave to set.

TO PACK: Remove from the flan tin and put on a flat surface in the freezer. When firm, wrap carefully, seal, label and return to the freezer.

TO FREEZE: Freeze rapidly until solid.

TO USE: Unwrap and thaw at room temperature for about 4 hr. Decorate with whirls of freshly whipped cream.

Baked apple flambée

6 large cooking apples
4 oz. butter
4 oz. soft brown sugar
1 lemon
6 oz. glacé cherries, halved
1 tbsp. brandy

Serves 6

TO MAKE: Wipe and core the apples and make a cut in the skin round the middle of each. Place in an ovenproof dish. Fill the centre of each with a little of the sugar and a small knob of butter. Bake at 350°F (mark 4) for about 30–35 min., basting occasionally. Meanwhile melt the remaining 4 oz. butter and the sugar in a pan; boil gently for about 4 min., until a rich caramel sauce is obtained. Remove the rind of the lemon free of any white pith; cut into very fine shreds. Add the lemon juice and rind, the halved cherries and the brandy to the pan. Blend thoroughly and simmer for 1–2 min. Fill each baked apple with the mixture. Allow to cool.

TO PACK: Use one large or 6 individual ovenproof containers; pour the sauce around the apples. Cover with double foil or heavy-duty polythene, seal and label.

TO FREEZE: Freeze rapidly until solid.

TO USE: Take off the wrappings and re-heat straight from the freezer at 425°F (mark 7) for about 40 min.

Redcurrant sponge flan

(*See colour picture facing page 97*)

a 1-pt. pkt. of strawberry jelly
½ lb. frozen redcurrants (see page 216)
apricot glaze (see page 168)
an 8½-in. sponge flan case
2 oz. flaked almonds, browned
¼ pt. double cream, whipped
1 tbsp. milk
whole sprigs of redcurrants to decorate
  (optional)

Serves 6–8

TO MAKE: Make the jelly up to ¾ pt., following the directions on the packet. Allow to set until of the consistency of egg white. Leave the redcurrants to thaw at room temperature —usually about 1½ hr. Meanwhile heat up a little apricot glaze and brush it round the sides of the sponge flan. Roll the sides of the flan in the browned almonds. Place the flan on a serving dish; sprinkle the redcurrants over the base. When the jelly is of the right consistency, spoon it over the fruit. Chill until set. Whip the cream with the milk, then, using a serving spoon, arrange spoonfuls of cream round the top of the flan. Decorate with whole sprigs of frozen redcurrants, if available.

Note: This recipe, using previously frozen fruit, makes a quick but very effective party dessert. For extra-rapid setting, add the frozen currants to the jelly—this thaws the currants and chills the jelly; then spoon the mixture into the flan case.

Mixed fruit salad

2 15-oz. cans of sliced peaches
a 16-oz. can of pineapple cubes
4 green-skinned eating apples
2 dessert pears
4 oranges
4 tbsps. orange liqueur (optional)
lemon juice to taste—about 4 tbsps.
4 bananas (or add these before serving)
½ lb. black grapes, peeled and seeded (or add
  these before serving)
1 can of frozen orange juice

Serves 24

TO MAKE: Turn the contents of the cans into a large bowl. Core the apples, and peel if preferred; slice thinly and add to the bowl, turning the slices in the syrup. Peel, core and chop the pears and add, turning them also in the syrup. Peel the oranges, removing all white pith, and divide into segments, free of membranes. (Do this over the bowl, to catch the juice.) Add the orange segments to the salad. Stir in the liqueur and lemon juice, mixing well. Either add the bananas and grapes before freezing or, if you prefer, after thawing. Make up the frozen orange juice to half the normal strength and add.

TO PACK: Divide the salad among some rigid plastic or foil containers. To prevent discoloration, cover the surface of the salad with waxed or freezer paper, crumpled and then laid entirely over the fruit surface. Add no extra covering until after freezing.

TO FREEZE: Freeze rapidly until solid. Put on the lids, seal, label and return the salad to the freezer.

TO USE: Either thaw overnight in the refrigerator, or at room temperature for about 4 hr. Add the bananas and grapes, if not already included.

Berry brûlée

(*See colour picture facing page 97*)

½ lb. frozen (stemmed) blackcurrants
4 tbsps. water
3 oz. Demerara sugar
1½ level tsps. arrowroot
¼ pt. soured cream
light soft brown sugar
powdered cinnamon

Serves 4

TO MAKE: Blackcurrants which have been frozen by the dry pack method (see page 216). are best for this purpose, though not essential. Cook from frozen in about 3 tbsps. water. Simmer until almost tender, add the Demerara sugar, return to the boil and cook for a few min. longer. Blend the arrowroot with 1 tbsp. water, stir into the fruit and boil gently, stirring, for 1–2 min. Cool, then spoon the mixture into ovenproof individual dishes. Top with the soured cream and cover with a layer of soft brown sugar mixed with a pinch of cinnamon. 'Flash' under a hot grill until bubbling. Serve with sponge fingers.

Raspberries and poached peaches

(*See colour picture facing page 97*)

5 whole peaches frozen in syrup (see page 218)
2–3 tbsps. apricot brandy (optional)
½ lb. frozen whole raspberries (see page 216)

Serves 5

TO MAKE: Allow the peaches to thaw overnight in the refrigerator. Remove the fruit and place on one side while you boil the syrup to reduce it to a glazing consistency. Add the brandy and blend well before removing the pan from the heat to cool. Allow the raspberries to thaw at room temperature —usually about 1½ hr. Arrange the peaches on a flat serving dish or glass, pour the syrup over and decorate with the raspberries.

Lattice jam tart

(*see picture on right*)

4 oz. shortcrust pastry (made with 4 oz. flour)

Serves 4–6

TO MAKE: Roll out the pastry to fit a foil-lined 10-in. ovenproof plate. Trim round the edges, mark with a fork, and re-roll the

Lattice jam tart

trimmings into a rough oblong; from this cut strips for the lattice, using a pastry wheel. Lay a round of greaseproof paper over the pastry base before placing the strips across in a lattice pattern.

TO PACK: Leave on the plate, but uncovered, until frozen.

TO FREEZE: Freeze rapidly until solid. Wrap in foil, place in a polythene bag, seal and label. Alternatively, if you wish to free the plate, simply slide off the frozen pastry on to the foil lining, wrap and store in the freezer.

TO USE: When required, slip the pastry base back on to the plate. Spread with 6 level tbsps. jam, arrange the lattice on top and bake at 400°F (mark 6) for about 25 min., until the pastry is golden-brown.

Prime Vegetables for the Freezer: see pages 212–215

7. Cook's Aids

The trouble with the last-minute trimmings is that there's so much else to do in that last minute. If *you* turn into a dervish at dishing-up time, think of the joy of having the trimmings ready-prepared—and read all about it. It's equally blissful to have a squirrel's horde of those less glamorous standbys like breadcrumbs and seasoned flour, baker's yeast and well-flavoured stock. (See the colour picture facing page 176).

MAÎTRE D'HÔTEL AND GARLIC BUTTERS: Ideal for topping steaks, chops and other grills such as fish. Cream 1 lb. unsalted butter until smooth. Beat in the grated rind of 2 lemons, 4 tbsps. lemon juice, 8 level tbsps. chopped parsley and a little seasoning. Divide into two, and add 4 skinned and crushed cloves of garlic to one portion. Chill both portions slightly in the freezer or refrigerator until of a manageable consistency. Form each piece into a long sausage shape between sheets of waxed or non-stick paper. Re-firm in the fridge or freezer, and cut into 2 oz. portions. Wrap each in foil. (Alternatively, freeze the butter roll whole and cut off slices as required—see colour picture

Useful standbys that keep well in the freezer. Breadcrumbs, egg yolks and whites (separated), lemon and orange peel (grated or slivers), herbs and white sauce—all packed in suitable-sized containers and labelled.

Fresh Fruits for the Freezer: see pages 215–218

facing page 176). Make a neat parcel, seal and label. Pack the firm labelled parcels together in one polythene bag. Use straight from the freezer. (Store for up to 3 months for maître d'hôtel butter, 1 month for garlic.)

MINT BUTTER: Weigh out 1½ oz. mint leaves and ½ oz. parsley heads; wash and drain. Put in a pan with 4 tbsps. water and cook uncovered for 5 min., by which time most of the water will have evaporated. Pass the mixture through a sieve. Cream 4 oz. unsalted butter and work in the mint purée, a good squeeze of lemon juice and a pinch of salt. Form into a long sausage shape, and finish as above. (Store for up to 3 months.)

BUTTER BALLS take time to make when needed, but a few stored in the freezer—even those left over from a party—are handy for almost instant use. (Store for up to 3 months.)

STOCK: Particularly if you use a pressure cooker, the making of good-quality home-made stock is a simple affair. Even chicken

Mint, chives, parsley, sage and rosemary can all be frozen on the stalk or chopped and frozen in ice-cube trays. Concentrated mint sauce will also freeze well

bones, with skin, giblets, etc., are well worth converting into a jellied stock; cooked meat bones, browned carrot, onion and celery, bacon rinds and mushroom peelings make a very useful concentrated stock. Or you can start from scratch with raw beef and veal bones. When the stock is ready, pour some of it into ice cube trays—useful when only a few tablespoonfuls are needed—or use preformers. Freeze. (Store for up to 2 months as cubes, 3 months for larger amounts.)

Incidentally, the freezer is the ideal place to store a few odd trimmings and bones left when you have prepared or carved a bird, to wait till you have enough accumulated, or enough time, to turn them into stock.

PARSLEY and other fresh herbs may be frozen unblanched. Freeze clean parsley heads (pack the stalks separately—these are often required as a flavouring in recipes) and crumble whilst still frozen—to 'chop' the parsley. Alternatively, chop large amounts of crisp fresh parsley, or other herbs, divide between small containers (e.g., ice-cube trays) and freeze until firm. Leave in the small containers or take from the ice-cube trays and pack carefully in rigid containers. Use straight from the freezer as an addition to stews, casseroles, sauces, etc. (Store for up to 6 months.)

SAUCE CUBES: So convenient when only a small amount of sauce is needed at any one time. Make up a well-flavoured curry, tomato, Espagnole or other sauce, using for preference a home-made stock base rather than instant cubes. Cool, and pour into ice cube trays. Freeze unwrapped, divide into cubes and freeze in polythene bags. To use, select the number of cubes required and reheat slowly, preferably in an easy-clean pan. (Store for up to 2–3 months.)

DUXELLES: This paste or mince, made of mushrooms, or mushroom peelings and stalks, is used for flavouring sauces, soups, ragoûts, stuffings, stews and so forth. Chop very finely ½ lb. mushrooms or stalks and peelings; chopped herbs may also be added. Melt 1 oz. butter in a pan and add the mushrooms and a light seasoning of salt and pepper. Cook gently until the mixture is dry, stirring often to prevent burning. Turn it into a small container and when cold, seal, label and freeze. (Store for up to 3 months.)

HORSERADISH CREAM: Whip $\frac{1}{4}$ pt. double cream and fold into it 1 tbsp. bottled creamed horseradish. Add a good squeeze of lemon juice and turn the mixture into a small serving dish or rigid foil container. Cover with double foil and overwrap with a polythene bag. Seal and label. To use, unwrap, but leave the top loosely covered, and allow to thaw for 6 hr. in the refrigerator. Dust with paprika pepper before serving. (Store for up to 2 months.)

MINT SAUCE: The leaves may be frozen whole, or chopped as for other herbs, and used to make up the sauce at the point of serving. However, for an almost instant sauce, you can chop enough mint to give $\frac{1}{2}$ lb., moisten with a little vinegar and add 1–2 oz. caster sugar. Freeze in small amounts—ice-cube trays make ideal containers. When the mixture is frozen, pack the cubes in polythene bags or wrap individually in foil and then mass together in an overwrap; seal and label. To use, add more vinegar, or one-third water and two-thirds vinegar, and leave to thaw. For a brighter colour, moisten before freezing with boiling water instead of cold vinegar, and proceed as above, adding undiluted vinegar to thaw. (Store for up to 6 months.)

CRANBERRY SAUCE: Simmer 6 oz. sugar and $\frac{1}{4}$ pt. water in a pan until the sugar dissolves. Add $\frac{1}{2}$ lb. fresh or thawed frozen cranberries and cook over a medium heat for about 10 min., until the fruit has broken up; cool. Pot, leaving a small head-space, cover with foil and freeze. (Store for up to 2–3 months.)

CRANBERRY RELISH: Traditionally belongs to the turkey, but also complements pork and gammon. Into the goblet of a powerful electric blender put $\frac{1}{2}$ lb. fresh cranberries and 1 apple, cored and finely chopped, but not peeled. Remove the pips from 1 orange and 1 lemon; mince the flesh finely and stir into the cranberry mixture, together with $\frac{1}{2}$ lb. granulated sugar. Pot, leaving a small head-space, cover with foil and freeze. (Store for up to 2–3 months.)

BREADCRUMBS: To prepare fresh breadcrumbs in quantity, especially with the aid of an electric blender, is a real time-saver. When frozen the crumbs remain separate, and the required amounts can be easily removed. Pack in polythene bags, sealed containers, or even screw-topped jars. (Store for up to 3 months.)

There is no need to thaw crumbs to be used for stuffings, pudding and sauces, but for coating fried foods leave them at room temperature for 30 min.

BUTTERED CRUMBS: A delicious crisp savoury topping for sauce-coated au gratin dishes, or for sweet dishes if sugar is added. Melt 1 oz. butter in a frying pan, stir in 4 oz. fresh white breadcrumbs, until blended, then fry slowly until evenly browned and golden. When cold, pack in polythene bags; freeze. (Store for up to 1 month.)

FRIED BREAD CROÛTONS and fried bread shapes for canapés and party snacks freeze well and can be prepared in quantity for up to 1 month's supply. When frozen, they remain separate for easy handling.

Cut slices of white bread $\frac{1}{4}$–$\frac{1}{2}$ in. thick, remove the crusts and cut into $\frac{1}{4}$–$\frac{1}{2}$ in. cubes, or into fancy shapes, e.g. stars. Fry in shallow or deep fat until crisp and golden; drain well. Pack as for breadcrumbs and freeze. To thaw and 'refresh', place uncovered but still frozen, in the oven at 400°F (mark 6) for 5 min. (Store for up to 3 months.)

GARLIC AND OTHER SAVOURY BREADS: These go down so well when served with soups on a buffet occasion that it's worth stocking up before a party. Make 1-in. cuts along French or Vienna loaves to within $\frac{1}{2}$ in. of the base, open up and spread generously with creamed butter flavoured with garlic, cheese or herbs. Wrap the loaves tightly in foil, then freeze. Store for up to 1 week—the crust begins to shell off after this time. To thaw and 'refresh', place the frozen, foil-wrapped loaf in the oven at 400°F (mark 6); a French stick takes about 30 min., and a Vienna loaf about 40 min.

A little soda water in the polythene bag, shaken well, will prevent ice cubes sticking together in the freezer

tops with a little milk and if desired sprinkle with poppy seeds. Bake at 400°F (mark 6) until golden-brown. Pack and freeze as usual. (Store for up to 3 months.)

FRUIT ICE CUBES: Fresh-fruit-flavoured cubes are invaluable at party times for chilling a drink or for adding, say, the orange, lemon or grapefruit flavour without unduly diluting a drink. Try also tomato cubes (made by chilling a tomato cocktail mixture), or experiment with fresh orange juice cubes added to tomato juice. To prevent cubes sticking together during storage, when you pack them in a polythene bag, place them in the bag, pour over them a little soda water and shake bag well, to coat each cube; seal and label.

To make decorated ice cubes, add the juice of 1 lemon to $\frac{1}{2}$ pt. water and pour into ice-cube trays. Slice the remaining lemon, then cut the slices into quarters and pop a small piece into each section. Freeze in the usual way, turn out and pack. The same treatment can be given to oranges or limes.

Another pleasant trick is to pop a Maraschino cherry into each section of the ice-cube tray, then fill up with soda water—good for punches and apéritifs.

CITRUS FRUIT RIND: When only the juice of the fruit or just the flesh is needed for a recipe, the rind is often wasted. Freezer-owners should thinly pare the rind free of pith, or grate the rind before squeezing the juice out or using the flesh (it's easier to do it first rather than afterwards). Pack the rind by itself, closely wrapped in foil or packed in small containers, or in a jar with sugar, to give lemon or orange sugar—a natural flavouring for cakes, biscuits, breads and so on. The strips of rind can be popped—still frozen—into cold drinks.

CHEESE TITBITS: When making cheese pastry for savouries or flans, roll out any leftover trimmings and cut into fancy shapes to make these titbits, which are useful for decorating soups or to serve separately; if topped with a little pâté they can accompany an apéritif. If you are making the pastry specially for this purpose you will need:

4 oz. plain flour
a pinch of salt
2 oz. butter or margarine
2 oz. Cheddar cheese, finely grated
a little beaten egg or water to mix
milk to glaze
poppy seeds to decorate (optional)

Mix the flour and salt together and rub in the fat as for shortcrust pastry, until the mixture resembles fine breadcrumbs. Mix in the cheese and add the egg or water, stirring until the ingredients begin to stick together. Then with one hand collect the dough together and knead very lightly to give a smooth dough. Roll out as for shortcrust pastry and cut into fancy shapes. Brush the

PRALINE: Keeps surprisingly well, and gives an interesting topping for ice cream or a flavourful addition to soufflés, mousses, butter creams and so on. In a pan heat together 6 oz. unblanched almonds and 7 oz. caster sugar, until the sugar melts; shake the pan from time to time. When the mixture is beginning to turn a pale straw colour, stir it lightly with a metal spoon and continue to cook until deep gold. Turn it out on to an oiled slab or metal tray and crush when hard. Pack in a polythene bag, freeze and store.

NOUGATINE: Put 5½ oz. caster sugar in a heavy-based pan and dissolve over a very low heat. When it is caramel-coloured, add 4 oz. finely chopped blanched almonds a little at a time, stirring gently with a metal spoon. Turn the mixture out quickly on to an oiled surface, then, using a whole (washed) lemon, roll out and pat the nougat till it is quite thin. Using a warmed cutter, stamp out 12–14 'leaf' shapes; leave the remainder of the nougat to set, then roughly crush it. (Should the nougatine become too set before all the leaves are cut out, pop it into a warm oven for a few minutes to soften.) When it is quite cold, pack into jars. (Store for up to 2 months.)

Use to decorate cold sweets, etc.

CHOCOLATE SHAPES AND CARAQUE: These very delicate decorations will freeze quite well, so it's worth keeping a few in a rigid box in the freezer for special occasions; store for up to 2 months.

Squares: Melt some cooking chocolate. Using a palette knife, spread it in a thin, even layer over a sheet of non-stick parchment paper, but don't take it quite to the edges. When firm, but not brittle, cut squares of the required size, using a sharp knife, with a ruler as guide. When it is firm, place the paper over the edge of a table, pull it down, and ease the squares off one at a time.

Leaves: Melt the chocolate. Collect some small rose leaves, preferably with the stem attached. Spread a little of the chocolate over the *under*side of each leaf, using a teaspoon. Place on non-stick paper and leave to set. When hard, pull the leaves away, starting from the stem. Work gently but quickly, to avoid the chocolate melting.

These leaves are good for decorating soufflés, mousses and gâteaux.

Caraque: Melt the chocolate in the usual way and spread it thinly on a marble slab. When it is just on the point of setting, shave it off in curls with a thin, sharp knife. Some of the softer blocks of chocolate or special chocolate covering can be 'curled' by using a potato peeler on the flat side of the block.

WHIPPED CREAM ROSETTES OR WHIRLS: These make an easy-to-handle decoration for all varieties of sweet dishes.

Whip fresh double cream until just stiff enough to hold its shape—don't overwhip, as piping tends to thicken up the cream, and it will become unmanageable. Pipe rosettes or shell shapes on to waxed or non-stick paper placed on a flat baking sheet. Freeze unwrapped until firm; remove the shapes from the paper and pack carefully into rigid containers, with waxed or non-stick paper between the layers; seal, label and return them to the freezer. (Store for up to 9 months.)

To use, place in position on the dish to be decorated and allow ample time to thaw—preferably in the refrigerator for 1–2 hr.

MERINGUE SHELLS: Line a baking sheet with a sheet of greaseproof or non-stick paper. Whisk 2 egg whites until very stiff, add 2 oz. granulated sugar and whisk again until the mixture regains its former stiffness. Lastly fold in 2 oz. caster sugar very lightly, using a metal spoon. Put into a forcing bag fitted with a large fluted star nozzle. Pipe 'shell' shapes on to the lined baking sheet and bake in a very cool oven, at 250°F (mark ¼), until the meringues are firm and crisp, but still white. (If they begin to brown, prop the oven door open a little.) Allow to cool before packaging in rigid plastic containers for freezing. Can be used straight from the freezer for decorating vacherins, etc. (Store for up to 3 months.)

MOCHA SAUCE: To serve with ice cream, profiteroles, chilled pears, bananas, filled meringues, etc. Melt 8 oz. plain dark chocolate; add 2 oz. butter and 3 level tbsps. instant coffee blended with 6 tbsps. milk. Heat in a double pan, or in a bowl over hot water, until smooth—stir constantly. Pour into a ¾-pt. rigid container. When cold, cover, overwrap, seal and label, then freeze. To use, reheat in a double pan or over hot water. (Store for up to 6 months.)

LEMON CURD: Freezing extends the life of a curd up to 3 months. To make about 2 lb. curd you need the grated rind and the juice of 4 lemons, 4 eggs, beaten, 4 oz. butter and 1 lb. sugar. Put them all in the top of a double saucepan or in a basin standing over a pan of simmering water. Stir until the sugar has dissolved. Continue heating, stirring from time to time, until the curd thickens—about 20–25 min. Strain the mixture into small dry pots or rigid plastic containers, leaving a little headspace. Cover with double foil, secure and label. Freeze in the usual way.

UNCOOKED JAM: In preserves made without cooking, the fresh fruit flavour is superb and the set is more like that of a conserve, not firm like boiled jam. Crush $1\frac{1}{4}$ lb. raspberries or strawberries with 2 lb. caster sugar. Leave to stand for about 1 hr. in a warm kitchen, stirring occasionally. All the sugar should be dissolved. Now add $\frac{1}{2}$ bottle liquid pectin, such as Certo, and 2 tbsps. lemon juice. Stir for a further 2 min. Pour into small dry jars, leaving $\frac{1}{2}$ in. headspace, and cover with foil. Leave in the warm kitchen for a further 48 hr., then freeze. (Makes about $3\frac{1}{2}$ lb.; store for up to 6 months.)

8. Cook's Know-how

The only snag with having a freezer is that it leaves you with no excuses. People are going to expect the best from the new super-capable you—so here are some perfection-ensuring reminders to keep you up to scratch.

TO BAKE BLIND: Short pastries are frequently baked 'blind' to make flan cases. Line the flan tin or ring with the pastry, easing this well into the corners; press lightly to remove all traces of air. Neaten the edges by trimming with a knife, or roll the rolling pin over the top. Neaten the edges again with the fingers. Put a piece of greased greaseproof paper into the flan and cover with dried beans, crusts or pasta, or use kitchen foil by itself instead of paper. Bake in the centre of the oven at 400°F (mark 6) for 15 min., until the pastry is set. Remove the beans and paper, then reduce the heat to 350°F (mark 4), return the flan to the oven and bake for 5–10 min., to dry out.

TO REFRESH: When food needs to be cooled quickly after cooking or blanching, rinse it under cold water.

The term also means to crisp up baked pastry, etc.

TO MARINADE: To impregnate meat, fish, poultry, etc., before it is cooked, in order to flavour it and make it more tender. A marinade may be cooked or uncooked, and the food may be left in it for just an hour or so, or for several days. The amount of liquid used is usually hardly enough to cover the food, so marinading is best done in a polythene bag, placed in a basin or jug and turned over from time to time. Sometimes the marinade, or a portion of it, is used in the actual cooking.

TO WHIP CREAM: Use double or whipping cream and chill it beforehand; place it in a chilled deep bowl and whisk with a cold rotary beater until it is fluffy and can just hold its shape. (For less than $\frac{1}{4}$ pt., use a large fork.)

TO DISSOLVE POWDERED GELATINE: Place the measured amount of liquid in a small bowl or cup and sprinkle over it the measured amount of gelatine. Place the container in a saucepan, with water halfway up, and heat until the gelatine has dissolved. Alternatively, sprinkle the gelatine over the cold measured liquid and leave to soak for a few minutes, then add to the hot liquid, stirring until dissolved.

TO MELT CHOCOLATE: Break the chocolate into small pieces, put into a bowl and stand this over hot (not boiling) water. See that no water gets into the bowl and that the temperature of the chocolate does not become too high—chocolate melts at about 104°F. Remove the chocolate from the bowl with a scraper. Alternatively, place the chocolate in a bowl and leave in a *cool* oven until melted.

TO BLANCH NUTS: Put almonds into boiling water and soak for 2–3 min. Soak pistachio nuts for 5 min. with a pinch of bicarbonate of soda to accentuate their green colour; pour off the hot water and add cold. Ease off the skins by pinching each nut between the thumb and forefinger. Dry before using.

A ROUX: Used for thickening which is carried out at the beginning of the cooking period. Generally equal amounts of fat and flour (or cornflour) are used, though sometimes slightly more fat is included. The fat is just melted, but not made hot, and the flour is added while the pan is off the heat. The mixture is stirred, then returned to the heat and cooked for 1–2 min. Add the warm (not hot) liquid all at once, stir well, then bring to the boil, beating, and simmer for about 5 min.

BEURRE MANIÉ: This offers a very practical way of thickening for use when a sauce is re-heated from frozen. Often a slightly thinner sauce is recommended for freezing, and

167

the extra thickening is added during re-heating. Butter and flour—it is usually better to have slightly more fat than flour—are creamed together; the resulting paste is then added in pieces and by degrees to the warm liquid and gently stirred or shaken. Cooking is then continued for about 5 min. longer.

SEASONED FLOUR I: The amounts of seasoning to use vary, depending on the quantity of flour incorporated, but for a light dusting the following proportions may be used as a guide: $\frac{1}{2}$ lb. plain flour, 1 oz. salt and $1\frac{1}{2}$–2 level tsps. pepper.

SEASONED FLOUR II: This flavoured flour is invaluable for preparing meat to be used in casseroles or for flouring meats, poultry and vegetables before frying; it keeps well. Mix 1 lb. plain flour, 2 oz. salt, $\frac{1}{2}$ oz. pepper, $\frac{1}{2}$ oz. dry mustard, and if you wish some freshly chopped or dried herbs—a good mixture is 2 rounded tsps. each of thyme and parsley and 1 rounded tsp. of sage or tarragon.

EGG GLAZE: Use either straightforward beaten egg, beaten with a little water, or, for an extra glossy brown, add a pinch of salt to plain beaten egg. Brush over the pastry top of pies, etc.

APRICOT GLAZE: Place $\frac{1}{2}$ lb. apricot jam and 2 tbsps. water in a saucepan over a low heat and stir until the jam softens. Sieve the mixture, return it to the pan, bring to the boil, and boil gently until the glaze is of suitable consistency. Use warm or cold on sweet pastries, or for attaching for instance almond paste to the surface of a fruit cake.

VANILLA SUGAR: Vanilla essence can cause an unpleasant flavour when used in a frozen dish; it is therefore better to use vanilla sugar, which can either be bought in a concentrated form, or made at home by keeping a vanilla pod in a jar of caster sugar (mark the container clearly).

French dressing

8 tbsps. oil—corn or olive
2 tbsps. wine or garlic vinegar
$\frac{1}{2}$ level tsp. dry mustard
2 level tsps. caster sugar
freshly ground black pepper to taste
salt or garlic salt to taste

Measure all ingredients into a screw-top jar. Shake up just before using.

This and that

Always put foil dishes on a baking sheet to re-heat.

Never put anything into the oven covered with a plastic or polythene wrapping. Always use kitchen foil as a freezer wrap if you want to be able to put the dish straight from the freezer into the oven.

Foil-line a loose-bottomed flan tin, so that when frozen the food can be lifted out easily, ready to return to the original tin for re-heating after freezing.

Remember that bags full of frozen liquid collapse when thawed—so put them whilst thawing in a cup/jug/bowl or other type of deep container.

To thicken pie juices as the fruit cooks, add 1 level tbsp. cornflour to the sugar used for each 1–$1\frac{1}{2}$ lb. fruit; toss the fruit in the mixture before turning it into the pie dish.

To help to prevent soggy-bottomed pastry cases, brush the surface with melted butter or margarine before freezing and filling. Put the pie plate on a hot baking sheet.

Whenever stock is needed, commercial stock cubes can be used, but remember that *no* further seasoning should be added before freezing. Adjust the seasoning at point of re-heating or serving.

THE METRIC SYSTEM

Comparative ounce/gram weights.
(All weights to nearest whole figure)

0·035 oz.	= 1 gram		$8\frac{3}{4}$ oz.	= 250 grams
1 oz.	= 28 grams		9 oz.	= 255 grams
2 oz.	= 57 grams		10 oz.	= 284 grams
3 oz.	= 85 grams		11 oz.	= 312 grams
$3\frac{1}{2}$ oz.	= 100 grams		12 oz.	= 340 grams
4 oz.	= 113 grams		13 oz.	= 369 grams
5 oz.	= 142 grams		14 oz.	= 397 grams
6 oz.	= 170 grams		15 oz.	= 425 grams
7 oz.	= 198 grams		16 oz.	= 454 grams
8 oz.	= 227 grams			(0·454 kilograms)
			$17\frac{1}{2}$ oz.	= 500 grams

Note: 1 kilogram = 2·2 lb.

Comparative British Imperial pint/litre capacity.

$\frac{1}{2}$ pint	= 0·28 litre 284 ml		$\frac{1}{2}$ litre	= 0·88 pint (generous $\frac{3}{4}$ pint)
$\frac{3}{4}$ pint	= 0·43 litre 420 ml		$\frac{3}{4}$ litre	= 1·32 pints
1 pint	= 0·57 litre 568 ml		1 litre	= 1·76 pints
$1\frac{1}{4}$ pints	= 0·71 litre		$1\frac{1}{4}$ litres	= 2·20 pints
$1\frac{1}{2}$ pints	= 0·85 litre		$1\frac{1}{2}$ litres	= 2·64 pints
$1\frac{3}{4}$ pints	= 0·99 litre		$1\frac{3}{4}$ litres	= 3·08 pints
2 pints	= 1·14 litres		2 litres	= 3·52 pints
$2\frac{1}{2}$ pints	= 1·42 litres		$2\frac{1}{2}$ litres	= 4·40 pints
3 pints	= 1·70 litres		3 litres	= 5·28 pints
$3\frac{1}{2}$ pints	= 1·99 litres		$3\frac{1}{2}$ litres	= 6·16 pints

Note: 1 gallon (8 pints) = 4·55 litres.

1 litre	= 0·22 gallon
10 litres	= 2·2 gallons

1 decilitre	= $3\frac{1}{2}$ fl. oz.
5·6 decilitres	= 20 fl. oz. (1 pint)
1·8 centilitres	= 1 tablespoonful
0·6 centilitre	= 1 teaspoonful

HANDY MEASURES

Almonds, ground	1 oz. =	$3\frac{3}{4}$
Breadcrumbs, fresh	1 oz. =	7
Breadcrumbs, dried	1 oz. =	$3\frac{1}{4}$
Butter, lard, etc.	1 oz. =	2
Cheese, Cheddar, grated	1 oz. =	3
Chocolate, grated	1 oz. =	$3\frac{1}{4}$
Cocoa	1 oz. =	$2\frac{3}{4}$
Coconut, desiccated	1 oz. =	5
Coffee, instant	1 oz. =	$6\frac{1}{2}$
Coffee, ground	1 oz. =	4
Cornflour, custard powder	1 oz. =	$2\frac{1}{2}$
Curry powder	1 oz. =	$3\frac{1}{2}$
Flour, unsifted	1 oz. =	3
Gelatine, powdered	1 oz. =	$2\frac{1}{2}$
Ginger, ground	1 oz. =	$3\frac{1}{2}$
Mustard, dry	1 oz. =	$3\frac{1}{2}$
Rice, uncooked	1 oz. =	$1\frac{1}{2}$
Semolina, ground rice	1 oz. =	3
Sugar, granulated, caster	1 oz. =	2
Sugar, icing	1 oz. =	$2\frac{1}{2}$
Syrup, unheated	1 oz. =	1
Yeast, granulated	1 oz. =	$1\frac{1}{2}$

} level tablespoonfuls approx.

Liquid ingredients—water, milk, cooking oil

2 tablespoonfuls $= 1\frac{1}{4}$ fl. oz. $= \frac{1}{16}$ pint
4 tablespoonfuls $= 2\frac{1}{2}$ fl. oz. $= \frac{1}{8}$ pint
6 tablespoonfuls $= 3\frac{3}{4}$ fl. oz. $= \frac{3}{16}$ pint
8 tablespoonfuls $= 5$ fl. oz. $= \frac{1}{4}$ pint

COOKING TEMPERATURES

Oven Temperatures: The ovens of most modern electric and gas cookers are thermo-statically controlled; once the thermostat has been set, the oven heat will not rise above the selected temperature.

In the case of thermostatically controlled electric ovens, it is usually found that the thermostat scale is marked either in degrees Fahrenheit, or in serial numbers (1, 2, 3, etc.), corresponding with 100°F, 200°F, 300°F (38°C, 93°C, 149°C) and so on.

Oven heats in the recipes in this book are indicated by the temperatures, and the oven settings used in most modern cookers; the table below shows the various equivalents, plus a verbal description. If in doubt about settings for your own cooker you can ask advice from your electricity or gas showrooms.

Approx. temp. and elec. oven setting	Standard gas thermostat	Oven Description
250°F (121°C)	$\frac{1}{4}$	Very cool
275°F (135°C)	$\frac{1}{2}$	Very cool
300°F (149°C)	1, 2	Cool
325°F (163°C)	3	Warm
350°F (177°C)	4	Moderate
375°F (191°C)	5	Fairly hot
400°F (204°C)	6	Fairly hot
425°F (218°C)	7	Hot
450°F (232°C)	8	Very hot
475°F (246°C)	9	Very hot

Liquids

Boiling	212°F (100°C)
Simmering	approx. 205°F (96°C)
Blood heat (also called tepid and luke-warm)	approx. 98°F (37°C)
Freezing point	32°F (0°C)

CALORIES AND CARBOHYDRATE COUNTING

The chart below gives figures for the number of grams of carbohydrate per oz. of various foods, and the calorific values. In many instances the calorific values are high, although the carbohydrate value is low, and *vice versa*. Because one may not be eating a total of too many calories, but taking more calories in carbohydrate form than the body can burn up, some people may find it easier to concentrate on controlling the carbohydrates rather than to count up the calories. Try to limit the daily intake of carbohydrate to 60 grams.

	Grams of carbohydrate per oz.	Calories		Grams of carbohydrate per oz.	Calories
FRUIT					
Apples	3·5	13	Blackcurrants	1·9	8
Apricots, raw	1·9	8	Cherries	3·4	13
dried	12·3	52	Gooseberries,		
Avocados	0·7	25	green	1·0	5
Bananas	5·5	22	ripe	2·6	10
Blackberries	1·8	8	Grapes, black	4·4	17
			white	4·6	18

	Grams of carbo-hydrate per oz.	Calories		Grams of carbo-hydrate per oz.	Calories
Grapefruit	1·5	6	Chicory	0·4	3
Lemons	0·9	4	Cucumber	0·5	3
Melons	1·5	7	Leeks, raw	1·7	9
Olives in brine	trace only	30	cooked	1·3	7
Oranges	2·4	10	Lentils	5·2	27
Peaches	2·6	11	Lettuce	0·5	3
Pears	3·1	12	Marrow	0·4	2
Plums, Damsons	2·7	11	Mushrooms	0·0	2
Prunes	11·4	46	Onions	0·8	4
Raisins	18·3	70	Parsley	trace	6
Raspberries	1·6	7	Parsnips	3·8	16
Rhubarb	0·2	1	Peas, raw	3·0	18
Strawberries	1·8	7	boiled	2·2	14
Sultanas	18·4	71	dried,		
Tangerines	2·3	10	cooked	5·4	28
Tomatoes	0·8	4	Potatoes, old	5·6	23
			new	5·2	21
NUTS			chips	10·6	68
Almonds	1·2	170	crisps	14·0	159
Brazils	1·2	183	Pumpkin	1·0	4
Chestnuts	10·4	49	Radishes	0·8	4
Coconut,			Seakale	0·2	2
desiccated	1·8	178	Spinach	0·4	7
Peanuts	2·4	171	Spring greens	0·3	3
Walnuts	1·4	156	Swedes	1·1	5
			Turnips	0·7	3
VEGETABLES			Watercress	0·2	4
Artichokes	0·8	4			
Asparagus	0·3	5	**MEAT, POULTRY**		
Beans, broad	2·0	12	Bacon, back		
butter	4·9	26	(fried)	0·0	169
French	0·3	2	Beef (lean and fat)		
haricot	4·7	25	Topside,		
runner	0·3	2	roast	0·0	91
Beetroot	2·8	13	sirloin, roast	0·0	109
Broccoli	0·1	4	silverside	0·0	86
Brussels sprouts	0·5	5	corned	0·0	66
Cabbage, raw	1·1	7	Chicken, roast	0·0	54
cooked	0·2	2	Duck, roast	0·0	89
Carrots, raw	1·5	6	Ham, boiled	0·0	123
cooked	1·2	5	Heart	0·0	68
Cauliflower	0·3	3	Kidney	0·0	45
Celery, raw	0·4	3	Liver, ox (fried)	1·1	81
cooked	0·2	1			

	Grams of carbo-hydrate per oz.	Calories
Luncheon meat		
(canned)	1·4	95
Mutton, chop	0·0	36
leg, roast	0·0	83
Pork, leg, roast	0·0	90
Rabbit, stewed	0·0	51
Sausages, fried	4·5	81
black	4·2	81
Tongue, sheeps',		
stewed	0·0	84
Tripe	0·0	29
Turkey, roast	0·0	56
Veal, roast	0·0	66

FISH

	Grams of carbo-hydrate per oz.	Calories
Cod (steamed)	0·0	23
Crab	0·0	36
Haddock	0·0	28
Hake	0·0	30
Halibut	0·0	37
Herring	0·0	54
Kippers	0·0	57
Lemon Sole	0·0	26
Lobster	0·0	34
Mackerel	0·0	53
Oysters	trace	14
Plaice	0·0	26
Prawns	0·0	30
Salmon, canned	0·0	39
fresh	0·0	57
Sardines, canned	0·0	84
Shrimps	0·0	32
Sole	0·0	24

SUGARS, PRESERVES, ETC

	Grams of carbo-hydrate per oz.	Calories
Chocolate, milk	15·5	167
plain	14·9	155
Chutney, tomato	11·0	43
Glacé cherries	15·8	137
Honey	21·7	87
Ice cream	5·6	56
Jam	19·7	74
Jelly, packet	17·7	73
Lemon curd	12·0	86

	Grams of carbo-hydrate per oz.	Calories
Marmalade	19·8	74
Mars Bar	18·9	127
Sugar, Demerara	29·6	112
white	29·7	112
Syrup, golden	22·4	84
Treacle	19·1	73

MILK AND MILK PRODUCTS

	Grams of carbo-hydrate per oz.	Calories
Cheese, Cheddar	trace	120
Edam	trace	88
Blue	trace	103
Gruyère	trace	132
Cottage	0·65	30
Cream, double	0·6	131
single	0·9	62
Milk, whole	1·4	19
skimmed	1·4	10
Yoghurt, low-fat	1·4	15
Eggs	trace	46
Butter	trace	226
Margarine	0·0	226
Lard	0·0	262
Oil	0·0	264

CEREALS AND CEREAL PRODUCTS

	Grams of carbo-hydrate per oz.	Calories
All-Bran	16·5	88
Arrowroot	26·7	101
Pearl barley,		
cooked	7·8	34
Bemax	12·7	105
Bread, Hovis	13·5	67
large white	14·9	69
malt	14·0	71
Procea	14·3	72
Cornflakes	25·2	104
Cornflour	26·2	100
Energen rolls	13·0	111
Flour 100%	20·8	95
85%	22·5	98
80%	22·9	99
75%	23·2	99
Macaroni, spaghetti,		
cooked	7·5	32

	Grams of carbo-hydrate per oz.	Calories		Grams of carbo-hydrate per oz.	Calories
Oatmeal porridge	2·3	13	Vinegar	0·2	1
Puffed wheat	21·4	102	**DRINKS**		
Rice, polished	8·4	35	Bournvita	19·2	105
Ryvita	21·9	98	Bovril	0·0	23
Sago	26·7	101	Cocoa	9·9	128
Semolina	22·0	100	Coffee with chicory		
Shredded Wheat	22·4	103	essence	16·1	63
Tapioca	27	102	Lemonade	1·6	6
Weetabix	21·9	100	Lucozade	5·1	19
MISCELLANEOUS			Marmite	0·0	2
Salt	0·0	0	Tea (Infusion)	0·0	1
Pepper	19·3	88	Coffee (Infusion)	0·1	1

Note: 'Trace' indicates that traces of carbohydrate are known to be present; an estimation may or may not have been carried out, but in any case the amount in question is of no quantitative dietetic significance.

PART 2

What You Need to Know about Freezing

BLANCHING—*most vegetables need blanching before you put them into the freezer, so a basket like those shown is a practical buy. The collapsible type takes up less space during storage*

Food values and what you lose

If you read your science-fiction, you'll know that tomorrow's spacemen are going to travel in deep-freeze, so that they can thaw out at the end of their 1000-year journeys as fresh as the day they left Mother Earth. All this is a long way from science-fact, but the theory's good, because the marvellous thing about freezing is that it simply makes time stand still. It doesn't change or kill anything (like canning and bottling, for instance, which only manage to preserve food by heating to death the things that make it decompose). It merely inactivates those things (enzymes and micro-organisms, if you really want to know), so that once the food is thawed out, they can whizz back into action again. In fact, they whizz back quicker than ever, so that frozen food, particularly fruit and vegetables, deteriorates more rapidly than fresh once thawed. But to sum up—freezing means the natural cycle of life can take up exactly where it left off —something to remember when people curl a lip and dismiss frozen food as 'unnatural'.

Vegetables prove a partial exception. Unless some of the enzymes are killed off prior to freezing, they discolour and develop 'off-flavours'—which is why it's necessary to blanch them first (see 'Basic Know-How'). Blanching involves boiling them in water, and since vitamin B and C are water-soluble and unstable at high temperatures, the process results in losses of about 20% of the former

Some home-freezing truths about Alcan.

To many housewives the name Alcan brings to mind kitchen foil for wrapping and cooking the turkey. But foil has many uses, as does the whole Alcan range. In home-freezing for example, Alcan products can be used successfully in any number of ways.

FOIL. Standard and Extra-Wide in both normal or double-length rolls. Plus a special extra-long, extra-wide, mini-catering roll of special interest for the deep-freeze user. Because it moulds to fit any shape, you can wrap practically any food in foil before placing in a deep-freeze.

FOIL DISHES. Alcan have a range of 14 foil dishes including 5 with lids especially for the freezer. They are designed for storing and freezing individual food items or even whole meals, cooked in advance and frozen until needed. One great advantage with Alcan Freezer Dishes is that you can take them from a deep-freeze and put them *directly* in the oven.

WRAP. A tight-cling, transparent-film food wrap. When pressed to itself or to the surface of a container WRAP 'clings' forming a virtually air-tight seal. And

 being transparent you can see at a glance what's inside.

BIG BAGS. 25 large polythene bags-on-a-roll with extra-deep gussets that expand as you fill the bag. Big Bags come with re-usable wire twists for sealing them tight.

Next time you think of home freezing, think of Alcan. We can help in quite a few ways.

ALCAN FOIL, CHESHAM, BUCKS.

and 30% of the latter. It sounds disastrous, but before you throw your hands up in horror, remember fresh vegetables are going to lose just as many vitamins when you cook them. And while you're at it, remember that with freezing, you can catch vegetables at the very peak of their condition. Commercially frozen vegetables, for instance, really *are* frozen straight from the fields, whereas 'fresh' vegetables may have taken days getting to the shops, losing up to 50% of their vitamin C on the journey. What you lose on the swings you gain on the roundabouts, and all you can do is minimise the loss. This is why it's vital to carry out blanching as quickly as possible, and not try to cope with vast quantities at a time.

Preparing food for freezing

Whether you're about to prepare vegetables, fruit, meat or fish, remember that food can only come out of the freezer as good as you put it in. Freezing doesn't *improve* quality, so don't waste valuable freezer-space on anything less than the best. With vegetables this means freezing them just as they reach maturity; the carbohydrate content of peas and beans, for instance, changes from starch to sugar at this point.

With fruits, this means freezing them just as they become ready for eating, but if you haven't managed to get around to them in time, slightly over-ripe fruits can still be used for purées. (These take up less room in the freezer, and they're a marvellous stand-by for sauces, desserts and baby foods.) You'll be relieved to hear that tough-skinned fruits like redcurrants, blackcurrants and gooseberries can be frozen just as they come. Even juicy ones like strawberries and raspberries only need sprinkling with sugar, or freezing free-flow fashion without sugar (see picture below), though firm-textured fruits like peaches and

FREE-FLOW PACK—*this is a particularly good method for fruit that is going to be used for decoration, especially for strawberries. Place the fruit on a tray, freeze until firm, then pack in a rigid foil container*

apricots prefer freezing in a syrup for best results. If they're not to discolour (and this goes for apples and pears, too), they also like the addition of ascorbic acid—vitamin C to the uninitiated—or soaking in a solution of lemon juice. Either way, this increases the food value, and even though fruits may leak some natural sugar and vitamins during thawing, you can make sure none of them get wasted by eating the fruits in their own syrup.

Already-butchered meat demands next to no preparation. Excess fat should always be removed, because it tends to go rancid before the flesh during storage, and whenever possible, it makes sense to remove any bones as well. These only take up freezer space without giving any return for your money, and you can always use them for making much-more-economical-to-store soups and stocks. As for ready-prepared poultry, it's almost impossible to go wrong, provided you remember that giblets won't keep as long as the rest of the bird, and package them separately. Similarly, don't stuff a bird, then freeze it raw, because this slows up the freezing and thawing times to such an extent that trouble can arise through growth of micro-organisms.

The unfreezables

Some foods don't take kindly to freezing, though they usually tolerate it with special preparation. Eggs are the most notorious example. Freeze them in their shells and they'll crack their way out; freeze them hard-boiled and the result will be nearly rubbery enough to bound across the kitchen floor. What's the solution? Separating the yolks from the whites before freezing—a simple method that's completely successful. A little persuasion often works wonders. Some kinds of potato, for instance, which go leathery in pre-cooked dishes, behave perfectly well if you mash them first. But salad ingredients stay thoroughly obstinate. Lettuce, watercress, celery and chicory go limp and mushy—and there's no way of getting their crispness back. Single cream (i.e., with less than 40% butter fat) separates on thawing, and you have to whip it into a frenzy to get it back to normal—if it ever agrees to go back to normal. Other dubious areas: anything with garlic tends to develop a musty flavour within a short time, which is a bit of a blow if you can't imagine your favourite terrine without it. Custards separate out, so freeze them before cooking (see Bulk Cookery); mayonnaise curdles, and it's wise to keep the thickening of sauces to a minimum and use beurre manié at the point of re-heating. Don't freeze dishes containing a very high proportion of gelatine, especially anything depending entirely on it as the stabilising agent, e.g., a moulded jelly. These are the worst awkward customers; others may be a bit niggly, but the 'Basic Know-How' section tells you how to deal with them tactfully.

Wrapping everything up

The trouble with freezing is that you have to do what you're told. There isn't much scope for bending the rules, and this applies particularly to packaging. Freezing converts water to ice within the cell structure of the food, and this is a state that *must* be maintained. If careless packaging allows further moisture to be withdrawn from other foods, or from the interior of the freezer, then frosting will appear on the exterior of the food. And if it's allowed to continue, moisture will eventually be withdrawn from the food itself, causing dehydration and loss of nutrients. At its drastic worst, the food could become so dried out and desiccated that there wouldn't be any liquid left for it to re-absorb at the thawing stage. We're not suggesting that anyone might fling the food in the freezer unwrapped (if one did, it would come out shrivelled and a fraction of its former weight), but one might get a bit slapdash with the sealing—and this is enough to do plenty of damage. With meat and poultry, for instance, exposed areas would develop 'freezer burn'. This is the name given when tissues go tough and spongy—so tough and spongy, in fact, that no amount of clever cooking can put it right. And with any kind of food, strong smells might travel from one faulty package to another, so that a delicate lemon ice cream could come out reeking of curried beef. The longer you intend to store the food, the more important it is that you should package it properly. For short-term storage—3–4 weeks—you might get away with cutting the corners, but the effects will show themselves as time passes. Now you know the reasoning behind it (it's not just a conspiracy on the part of the wrapping manufacturers), here's how you can make sure your food stays intact throughout freezing.

REMOVAL OF AIR—*a very important step in the freezing of all food. Extract air by either placing the polythene bag in water to displace the air, or by sucking the air out with a straw*

First thing is to package solids tightly, so that you expel as much air as possible. This is easy if you're wrapping something in aluminium foil, which fits where it touches, but it's not so simple if you're filling a rigid container, and run out of food halfway up. You can't squeeze the surplus air out, but you can fill up the vacant space with some crumpled non-stick, waxed or freezer paper. (This last is an attempt to combine overwrapping and underwrapping material, and can be a rather unnecessary expense.) It's even more difficult to expel air from a polythene bag, especially when the contents are awkwardly shaped or easily broken. If you're getting desperate you should lower the full bag into a bowl of water, so that the water-pressure can force the air up and out (remember to dry the bag before freezing, so you don't find yourself having to chip it out when you need it). Alternatively, pinch one of the children's drinking straws and suck the surplus air out.

Liquids are a very different proposition, because instead of squeezing air out, it's essential to leave at least $\frac{1}{2}$ in. of 'headspace' in—up to 1 in. for 1 pt. This is because water expands one-tenth on freezing—something you won't need telling if you had burst pipes last winter. Unless you leave room for expansion, soups, sauces, fruits packed in syrup, etc., will push off their lids; worse still, if you've used a screw-top jar (difficult to remove food from, and unless the glass is specially toughened, frighteningly fragile), food could shatter its way out. (Bear this in mind if you're ever tempted to chill a bottle of wine in an emergency, because if you leave it too long, it will be splattered around the freezer by the time you get to it.) If you do use a glass container, make sure it has straight sides—which make it easier to get the contents out again—and leave 1–2 in. headspace.

Solids-plus-liquids, like stews and casseroles, or fruit in syrup, need to have a layer of liquid on the top, with no boulders of food sticking out picturesquely. Remember to leave $\frac{1}{2}$ in. headspace. See the top right-hand picture opposite for treatment of part-filled containers.

HEADSPACE—*allow about $\frac{1}{2}$ in. space for solids in thickened liquids, about 1 in. for 1 pt. liquid, and a little more for larger amounts. Don't forget that when a lid is to be fitted onto, say, a rigid foil container, the contents should be below the line where the lid is to be put in position*

To remove an obstinate frozen 'parcel' from a rigid container or bag, dip it in warm water for just a few minutes to loosen; this is a good way to extract apple purée which is to be reheated straight from the frozen state

CONTAINERS *which are only part-filled or whose contents rise above the surface of the liquid, such as fruit salad, should be given an inner cover of crumpled greaseproof or waxed paper before being wrapped*

There are masses of packaging materials on the market, but many do the same job. You'll only need a few of them, so it shouldn't prove expensive, especially as many of them can be used again and again. Heavy-duty (250-gauge) polythene bags, for instance, can be washed, dried and used *ad infinitum*—though do check them thoroughly in case they've become punctured during use; thinner ones can be used for overwrapping. These bags are so versatile (gussetted versions are good for large quantities), that some people practically manage with them alone. They use them for wrapping bread and cakes, fruit and vegetables, meat, fish and poultry—though in this latter food group, they usually add an overwrapping of mutton cloth or stockinette for extra protection. When using polythene bags for liquids, it's a good idea to fit the bag into a

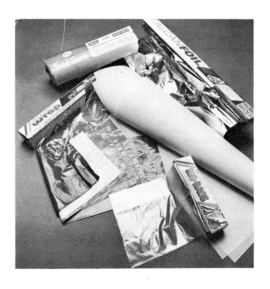

PLIABLE WRAPS—*for short-term storage (up to 1 month), you can use materials such as waxed paper (in which sliced bread is sold), or single household foil, but for longer storage it is worthwhile to take more care with the packing. Self-cling polythene film and generous amounts of foil used double are particularly suited to the close moulding needed to exclude air. Overwrapping in mutton cloth or polythene bags prevents piercing of the surface. Different coloured polythene bags are ideal for quick identification. Non-stick or waxed paper is useful for separate cutlets, cake portions, etc.*

OVERWRAPS—*a protection against damage to the foil or polythene underwrap when frozen items are moved about in the freezer. A roll of mutton cloth (stockinette) is best. Simply insert the package in a length of the cloth and tie off the ends securely*

PRE-FORMERS—*use a heavy-gauge polythene bag, or 2 thinner ones, one inside the other. Slip the bags inside a rigid container and fill with the contents, remembering to leave a headspace. Freeze until solid. Remove the pre-former, then seal, label and overwrap*

regular-shaped container before filling and freezing it, so you can slip it out when it's solid, neatly-shaped and ready for stacking. This is known as 'pre-forming', and any clean straight-sided container, like an empty sugar carton, or of course a plastic box, will do the job efficiently. If the filled polythene bag sticks—see first picture on previous page.

Just as some people swear by polythene bags, others find aluminium foil the mainstay of their packaging. Ordinary weight kitchen foil must be used double, and wrapped fairly generously, but the heavy-duty quality (aluminium of 0.025 mm) may be used singly. Any foil-wrapped packages are best overwrapped in thin polythene bags or mutton cloth, as foil punctures relatively easily. Heavy-duty foil is tough enough for re-use, too (soak it well, brush the food from the creases, and dry thoroughly), but you'd be well advised to keep it for short-term use only, once it's 'second-hand'. Foil is ideal for moulding round awkward shapes like joints of meat, fish and poultry, but add a polythene bag for extra security—or an overwrapping of mutton cloth or stockinette, if there's any danger of sharp bones piercing through. It's a good idea, too, to overwrap items intended for longer-term storage. Foil is also ideal if you want to end up with a neatly-shaped casserole instead of a space-wasting lumpy bundle. Of course, you *can* freeze food in its casserole dish (remembering that china and pottery slow the rate of freezing, and that the pack will need a lot of space), but if you want to keep the casserole itself in circulation, line it with foil first, leaving a good margin for wrapping over; spoon in the contents, and once they've frozen

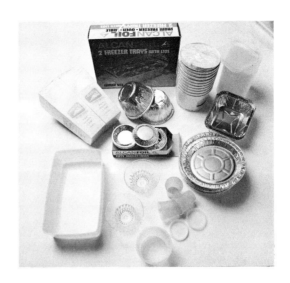

RIGID CONTAINERS—*everything that goes into the freezer should be well packed in moisture-and-vapour-proof containers. The longer the food is to be stored, the more important this becomes. This selection meets all eventualities. Rigid foil containers are a very practical buy; self-sealing plastic boxes (such as Tupperware) have a very long life; waxed containers, if treated with care, can be used a second time; specially toughened glass dishes are handy for mousses and other desserts which don't take kindly to being spooned out for serving*

solid, slip out the package and fold the foil over, then overwrap before freezing. Slip the unwrapped package back into the original casserole dish for re-heating. (If the foil tends to stick, dip the package for just a minute or two into warm water.) Only proviso: unless the casserole dish is straight-sided and lipless, the contents may not 'slip out' as obligingly as we're suggesting. An alternative method is to cook the food in the casserole without foil, freeze it, then dip the casserole in warm water just long enough to loosen the contents, which are then removed and wrapped in the usual way.

Although foil can, as we've said, be re-used for freezing, in many cases (poultry, for instance), it makes sense to keep it on and use it for cooking the frozen food. This freezer-to-oven possibility explains why rigid aluminium foil dishes are so popular. You can cook, freeze and re-heat in the same container, wash it up (soaking well, and brushing any food out from the angles), and start all over again for short-term usage. Before freezing, the dishes can be over-wrapped with a double layer of foil, or placed in a polythene bag as an added protection.

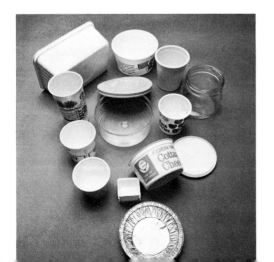

SECOND USERS—*collect an assortment of containers for re-use; if these have already been used for commercially frozen products they are, of course, low-temperature-tested. Otherwise, make sure that the material is non-toxic at freezer temperature-as a safeguard you can line them with thin polythene. Some plastics become brittle at low temperatures, so need handling with care*

PAD *bones on cutlets and other cuts of meat or poultry with a cap of foil, to prevent damaging the outer wrap at a later stage. Use a 'concertina' style of wrapping to separate cutlets with non-stick or freezer paper*

PORTIONING—*for more rapid thawing, portion cake slices, meat, sandwiches etc, before freezing; use non-stick or waxed paper or Cellophane. Pack either side by side or stacked*

Waxed containers are less essential than polythene bags and foil—but they're very handy to have around. If treated gently, it's possible to use them several times, but unless they're already specially-lined, line them with polythene bags for the second, third and fourth times round. Tub shapes are usually recommended for soups and sauces, but they waste freezer-space, which is why some people stick to the squares and oblongs. A few words of warning: never fill them with anything hot, because the wax will melt and leave the container porous. And be cautious about using empty waxed cream containers, etc., instead of the real thing. These are only very lightly waxed, and frozen food can start deteriorating inside them after a week or two. If box lids don't have an adequate seal, put a turn of special freezer tape round the join.

You'll have no such worries with plastic containers. These are almost indestructible (Tupperware, for instance, carries a 10-year guarantee), and because they have snap-on lids, they're completely airtight. (When you reach the 'Sealing' section below, you'll realise just how much of an advantage this is.) Rigidity means you can safely store fragile foods like vol-au-vents, cream-filled meringues and gâteaux in them—and though they may seem expensive at the time of buying, they'll more than earn their keep over the following years. Commercial ice cream often comes in a plastic container; if you want to keep it in the freezer for longer than 3 weeks, however, this needs to be overwrapped.

P.S. on packaging

To some extent, packaging of cooked or partly-cooked dishes is dictated by how you want to serve them. The family won't mind if you plonk the food down on the table in its aluminium foil container, and of course if you're dishing out individual portions in the kitchen, the problem won't arise at all. With informal guests, you can always pretty the container by adding a paper ruff (like the one shown on page 29), or simply by sitting it inside a good-looking serving dish. But for formal occasions, it's much better to freeze the food in a 'presentable' container in the first place, if it's something that doesn't like being transferred. (There are some super freezer-to-oven-to-table dishes appearing on the market.) Don't risk transferring a steak-and-kidney pie, for instance. It's almost bound to collapse, leaving you with a mangled mess instead of the show-stopper you'd intended. For other foods, the pre-formed method is ideal.

P.P.S. on packaging

The biggest mistake beginners make is that they forget to freeze food in meal-size portions. It's all very well meticulously packaging 12 lamb chops, but if you only need 4 for dinner, you'll find yourself desperately trying to hack them off. It isn't funny when you're in a hurry—especially as you can't re-freeze meat once it's thawed out completely. And it's not much better when you've cooked enough liver pâté to last you for months—and want one solitary portion in the middle of the day. You *can* try sawing off chunks with a special freezer knife, but life would have been a lot simpler if you'd frozen it into manageable portions in the first place. And just imagine trying to saw off a 'piece' of Bolognese sauce or beef casserole! How can you avoid it? Separate chops, steaks, pâté-portions, sliced cake, etc., with double sheets of waxed or non-stick paper, Cellophane or polythene film, prior to freezing. And package casseroles, etc., in the quantities you'll want to eat them in—not more than 2 pts. is a useful rough guide—even if it does mean using several containers. Sauces should be in still smaller quantities, preferably no more than $\frac{1}{2}$-pt. size. Small units are always preferable to large, and shallow packs to deep—as they freeze quicker and better and thaw and re-heat quicker, too.

Sealing

Most people use plastic-covered wire twist-ties for sealing polythene bags, but if you're afraid they may wriggle loose during long-term storage, you can heat-seal the polythene bags instead. This sounds very complicated—but all it entails is placing a strip of brown paper over the two open ends and running a warm iron over it; or you can use a special sealing iron. All kinds of parcels (whether they're wrapped in foil, non-stick or waxed paper, Cellophane or polythene film) need sealing with freezer tape. This has a special adhesive (as opposed to something like Sellotape, that would come sadly unstuck at sub-zero temperatures) —and be generous with it. Use it for your waxed containers, too, unless they

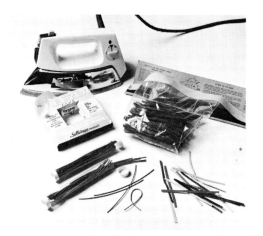
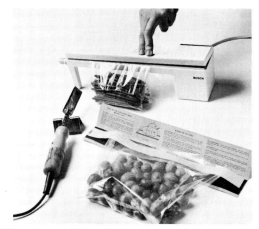

SEALING—*a special sealing iron or press completes this job neatly and efficiently when you use heavy-gauge polythene bags. Bags can also be heat-sealed by putting a piece of paper or tape over the polythene and pressing with a warm iron. Or seal by twisting the top of the bag into a bunch and securing with a 'twist-tie'— a piece of plastic-coated wire or a pipe cleaner. Special sealing tapes which withstand freezer temperatures are handy to use on box lids and fold-in parcels and for fixing labels*

have screw-top lids which are air-tight. As we've already mentioned, all Tupperware-type plastic containers have air-tight lids, so presuming you put them on correctly, frozen food inside can come to no harm.

Labelling

Last but not least comes labelling, and it's almost as important as packaging if you're not to serve up apple pie instead of the chicken and ham you'd been meaning to. It's easy to think you'll remember what's what, especially when you can still see the contents clearly through polythene, but polythene soon frosts over and leaves you with a guessing game. Tie clearly marked labels onto your polythene bags, giving the date of freezing, the contents, the number of portions and—if you're feeling super-efficient—the re-heating time. Stick

LABELLING—*clearly label all items for the freezer. Special self-adhesive labels are suited to low temperatures. (If they are placed under thin film there is no danger of finding a collection of labels at the bottom of the freezer when it comes to defrosting time; if the wrap frosts over, the warmth from your finger will reveal the writing.) To write on a tie-on label or straight on the package, use special freezer non-smear 'felt' (or wax) pencils or crayons; a ball-point pen is suitable for writing either on a label which is then covered with polytape, or on paper tape itself, or on non-waxed wrapping paper*

special waterproof labels on your packages (underneath the polythene over-wrapping, if you're using one). Write on your tubs and cartons with a water-proof felt pen, a chinagraph pencil—or even lipstick if you've run out of every-thing else. And to save yourself groping around in a chest-type freezer with icy hands, group foods-of-a-kind together in different coloured string bags.

How to freeze

Eager to freeze as you may be, please bear with us while we give a brief des-cription of how freezing works. Mistakes rarely make the food inedible, but they may affect its taste, texture and—most vital of all if you're feeding a young growing family—its food value.

Most foods are largely made up of water, and even something as seemingly solid as lean meat contains about 70% of it. All freezing does is convert this water to ice crystals. Quick freezing results in tiny ice crystals, retained within the cell structure, so that on thawing, the structure is undamaged and the food value unchanged. But slow freezing results in the formation of large ice crystals, which damage the cell structure and cause loss of nutrients. As this damage is irreversible (slow-frozen food shows loss of texture, colour and flavour when thawed), you'll see why it's vital to follow the manufacturer's instructions.

First essential is never to freeze more than one-tenth of your freezer's capacity in any 24 hours. If for instance you have a 120 lb. freezer (approximately 6 cubic feet), you should only ever freeze about 12 lb. of food at a time. It's *possible* to freeze more, of course, but because the addition of the unfrozen food pushes up freezer-temperature, the results are going to be *slow-frozen—* the very thing you want to avoid. Second essential is to freeze the food in precisely the way the manufacturer tells you to. Forget what you've seen other people do, because what's right for their freezer could be wrong for yours. Many freezers have a 'fast' or 'super' freeze switch and this should be turned on an hour or so before you freeze any quantity of food. Don't forget to turn the switch back to normal after the fresh food is frozen hard otherwise you'll use more electricity than necessary. If you're going to freeze only a small casserole, a loaf of bread or a similar small quantity of food, there's no need to use the fast freeze switch. Other freezers have a special rapid freezing compartment, and once the food's frozen, it has to be transferred to the rest of the freezer; with some, it's necessary to freeze the food against the base or sides, or on whichever shelf carries the evaporator coils. Beyond checking the temperature setting (it's worth investing in a small thermometer), there's nothing more to it.

Storage

Once the food's in the freezer, how long can you leave it there? As far as safety goes, practically for ever as long as you maintain a constant temperature of

−18°C (or 0°F if you're still thinking that way). But as far as food value, taste, colour and texture go, different foods have different storage times.

Maximum recommended storage time for most vegetables is 10–12 months (only 6–8 for vegetable purées); vegetables sautéed in butter have a reduced storage life; for most fruits packed in syrup or sugar, 9–12 months (but only 6–8 for fruits packed alone or as purées—and only 4–6 months for fruit juices). Meats like beef and lamb can be stored for up to 8 months, but fattier meats like pork should only be kept for 6 months. This is because the fat tends to oxidise and go rancid, something that destroys fat-soluble vitamins like vitamin A, as well as spoiling flavour. Oxidation can take place in oily fish like mackerel, too, which is why they can only be kept for 3–4 months, as opposed to 6 months for white fish.

All these estimates (and 'Basic Know-how' provides more specific information) are on the conservative side, because although the ideal is to store food at a *constant* temperature of −18°C (0°F), this is a counsel of perfection. Every time you take something out of the freezer, the temperature's going to rise, and it's going to take some time for the thermostat-controlled compressor to bring it back to normal. Similarly, every time you add an unfrozen product, you're going to create a small temperature gradient—though you can keep it to the minimum by chilling packages in the refrigerator first.

These small fluctuations of temperature are fairly harmless. Big swings aren't, however, because even if you've quick-frozen your food to make sure only small ice crystals form, any pronounced fluctuation is still going to affect ice-crystal formation—with possible loss of quality.

Really drastic rises in temperature excluded and presuming your food's been efficiently packaged, it shouldn't come to any real harm through faulty storage. Even if a temperature gradient has been set up, causing air to circulate and draw out more moisture than usual, your food won't be able to suffer desiccation or freezer burn if none of the air can reach it. In fact, the only scope for damage inside an air-tight package is if you didn't manage to squeeze out all the air to begin with. Then, it's possible for air to circulate *within* the package, drying out the food and depositing the moisture on the insides of the pack as cavity ice—a process that can't be put completely right at the thawing stage. All of which underlines just how vital the packaging stage is.

Thawing

If your memory's not all it should be, you'll be pleased to hear that there are quite a few foods that need no thawing when they come out of the freezer. Stews, pre-cooked pies and casseroles are quite happy to go into the oven still frozen, but unless you freeze them in fairly shallow dishes to begin with, there's always the danger they won't have cooked right through. Small fish, and small cuts of meat like chops and steaks, are equally happy to be cooked straight from frozen, and so are whole joints of meat (see the Meat section), provided you can be sure the inside cooks before the outside overcooks. Vegetables, of course, not only needn't be thawed but *shouldn't* be thawed (and if you're a real nutrition-fiend, why not try slow-cooking them in a heavy saucepan with a knob of butter instead of water, so that you can make the most of every vitamin going). As for bread and rolls, thawing them in a warm oven crisps them up, and makes them as fragrant as if you'd just baked them. By the way, if a foil wrapping tends to stick, dip the package into warm water for a minute or two.

Just for once, salesmen are reasonably accurate when they enthuse about 'instant' meals, but there are exceptions. Poultry absolutely *has* to be completely thawed out prior to cooking, and whole fish prefer being thawed out as slowly as possible if they're to retain their juiciness and texture. Fruit that's to be eaten without any further preparation likes the gentlest possible thawing, too. This minimises the amount of leak (not that this will bother you in terms of food value if you're eating it in its own syrup), and prevents it from going too soft and mushy. Even with the most considerate thawing, though (in the refrigerator, as we're about to find out) fruit tends to 'fall', which is why many people eat it while there's still a little ice in it.

The slowest and best way of thawing is in the refrigerator. Always leave food in its original wrapping, because otherwise meat will bleed and lose some of its quality and colour; fruit will lose its juice and suffer in texture; fish will dry out and generally coarsen. And always leave yourself plenty of time. One humble pound of food can take anything up to *6 hours* to thaw, which means a 4 lb. salmon trout could keep you waiting for 24 hours.

This probably explains why many people sacrifice a little in the way of quality for quicker results. Food thawed at room temperature only takes up about half the time—and in real emergencies, you can submerge the package in a bowl of water or hold it under a running tap. But however you thaw the food, don't leave it lying around at room temperature for longer than necessary. Although freezing brings micro-organisms to a grinding halt, remember that they try to make up for lost time as soon as thawing sets them free. This means that food becomes extra-perishable once it's thawed—so pop it into the fridge, or preferably, eat it right away.

Finally, just to set your mind at rest, partly-thawed food—provided that the packet hasn't been opened—may be refrozen without danger to health, but the actual quality of the food deteriorates, so it's not a practice to be recommended, though it's allowable to avoid undue wastage.

Re-heating

In general, frozen foods you want to serve hot should be heated as rapidly as possible, as this preserves the flavour and texture. Whenever practical, heat from frozen. If you're using the oven, you'll find that a temperature of about 400°F (mark 6) will be fine for combined thawing and re-heating from frozen. As a guide, a shallow 2-pt. pack will take about 1 hr. (The advantage of freezing in smallish packs is obvious when it comes to heating up.) You can speed up the process a little by leaving the casserole or what-have-you unlidded. As the food thaws, fork it over gently to separate the pieces. A sauce, once thawed, should be vigorously whisked to restore its smoothness, unless this would break down any firm pieces.

If you have only a small amount of food to re-heat, you can do it very satisfactorily in a double boiler; if you are in a hurry, a mixture that includes some sauce or liquid can be put into a saucepan and placed directly over a low heat, but watch it, and beware of sticking.

Meat

Tackling a Carcase: If you've ever watched someone inexperienced trying to chop an onion with a sharp kitchen knife, multiply the anxiety ten-fold, and you'll have some idea of what you'd be like if you tried to tackle a meat carcase with a cleaver. When salesmen wax eloquent about how much you can save this way, they forget to mention that butchers take years to learn their trade.

There are a few other things they forget to mention, too. Like the fact that you'll need an enormous freezer. A mere hind or forequarter of beef, for instance, is going to weigh about 150 lb.—enough to half-fill a 12 cubic-foot-freezer. And as your family's going to get heartily sick of beef unless you've frozen some pork, lamb, veal and poultry as well, there'll be precious little room left for equally important fruit, vegetables, pre-cooked dishes, etc. Like the fact that that same 150-lb. hind of beef, a marvellous bargain at 25p a lb., isn't going to be quite such a bargain when you've had to throw away (or process) 30 to 40 lb. of it in bones, fat and waste. And when you've realised that it isn't all steaks and succulent joints, but things like shin and flank as well. Like the fact that if your carcase is freshly slaughtered, you're going to have to chill it, in the case of pork and veal; also hang it, in the case of beef and lamb—a tedious and long-drawn-out process. Like the fact that once you've chilled pork or veal, it has to be frozen *immediately* if it's to have a long storage life. And as you can only freeze one-tenth of your freezer's capacity in any 24 hours, you're going to have to do some quick mental menu-making, so you can freeze the cuts you want to eat last, first, and the cuts you want to eat first, last.

Probably the biggest amount of carcase-meat within the average person's freezing scope is a forequarter of lamb. If it's freshly slaughtered, first chill it in the refrigerator at 40°F (5°C) as quickly as possible, something that will take between 1 and 2 days. Then hang it, something that will take between 6 and 12 days. Good hanging—always important for flavour and texture—is especially vital when meat is to be frozen, as it reduces the amount of drip when the meat is thawed. Next, invest in a tiny saw and a really sharp boning knife. Finally, get down to the meaty bit (a) by removing the shoulder (b) by removing the breast (c) by removing the middle and best end—these should give you 5 prime cutlets and 3 middle neck, but switch from your knife to your saw and chine them before freezing in total; saw right through them for freezing cutlets separately; (d) by trimming off the neck tendon from the stewing end and (e) by boning the breast. Run up either side of the cartilage to remove cartilage bone, having taken the flap back, and remove the bones, firm skin and excess fat before freezing.

That's enough to prove it's a skilled job, and if you do get access to larger amounts of carcase going cheap, it's usually worth spending a little of what you're saving on a butcher's services. You may have to ask around until you find one who's willing, but it's far more satisfactory to get him to chill or/and hang it, joint it and even freeze it for you if he has commercial blast-freezing facilities, which do produce the best results for meat. This is because meat needs to be quick-frozen, and unless you have a 'fast' freeze dial that can get your freezer temperature down to $-24°C$ ($-11°F$) or below and keep it there, you might only be capable of producing slow-frozen results.

Of course, if you're offered sound-quality meat at a *very* low price, it may be worth while buying it to freeze at home, even though the end result won't be quite so excellent as the blast-frozen product. *If* you're freezing your own meat, remember that very lean meats tend to dry out. A thin layer of fat and good 'marbling' help to prevent this; however, too much fat tends to become rancid. This is why excess fat is best removed wherever practical and—as the speed at which fat goes rancid depends on the amount of pre-freezing oxygen present—removal of air and good packaging are vital. This is not so vital when considering short-term storage: just use good-quality meat for freezing. Another hint—a freezer thermometer is a worthwhile investment.

Buying from Frozen-Meat Specialists: It's sad to dampen people's do-it-yourself enthusiasm, but not *too* sad, because you can still make enormous savings on meat if you buy bulk-purchase packs of ready-frozen joints. Meat prepared and packed by frozen-meat specialists is available by direct supply; through frozen food wholesalers; or from cash-and-carry outlets. But if you buy it, do go by recommendation—and see that the order form states exactly what cuts are on offer. Overall prices can be misleading, especially when a selection pack holds a very high percentage of economy cuts (cuts that you may not even like or know how to cope with), or the meat turns out to be imported, instead of the British you'd perhaps expected. Another point worth checking is that the meat you're buying has been frozen fairly recently. You don't want to buy meat that's been hanging around in a commercial freezer, so that by the time you transfer it to your own, its recommended storage life is nearly up.

What's in a Pack: As a rough guide, here's what you could expect to find in a few 'typical' packs.

BEEF: Hindquarter (approx. 150 lb.): sirloin, fillet, T-bone steak, rump, top-side, silverside, thick flank (top rump or bed steak), leg of beef, flank, ox-kidney, skirt.

Forequarter (approx. 150 lb.): back, top and forerib, leg of mutton cut (shoulder), chuck and bladebone, flank and brisket, clod and sticking, shin, ovenbuster (Jacob's ladder).

Fore roast pack: top rib, back and forerib, leg of mutton cut and rolled brisket.

Hind roast pack: sirloin, topside, silverside, thick flank (top rump).

Braising pack: chuck, bladebone, leg of mutton cut (shoulder).

Stewing pack: clod and sticking, shin of beef, pot roast, brisket.

PORK: Side of pork: one leg, one hand and spring, one belly, one loin, one spare rib and one blade bone.

LAMB: Hindquarter: one leg, one loin.

Forequarter: one shoulder, one breast, middle and best end, scrag.

Buying from the Butcher: Many butchers offer generous discounts if you buy from them in bulk at regular intervals. This is probably the best way of ensuring that the meat is precisely what you need— and of the same quality that you would usually buy. And if the butcher is really geared up to the situation, he'll tailor the meat to your requirements, pack it, blast-freeze it, and even deliver it to your door. This way, you can order just enough meat to last you three months (of course it will happily keep much longer, but it gets more expensive in terms of freezer-running-costs the longer you keep it), and make sure that you don't end up with all one type of meat, so that you have to pay full retail prices to break the monotony with an alternative type. The other advantage of buying from a butcher is that you can make use of seasonal bargains. Buy your forequarter of pork in August/September or your leg of pork for Christmas in September/October; buy oxtails in midsummer when nobody fancies a winter dish. And although frozen meat that's been allowed to thaw is quite unsuitable for re-freezing, you can safely buy chilled boneless beef from the Argentine if the price looks right. Equally, frozen Spring New Zealand lamb (with no sign of thawing, of course), is worth snapping up around December. Take your butcher's advice, and to help you with what he's talking about, here's a guide to the various cuts, and what they are good for.

Beef

1. LEG OF BEEF: excellent gravy or stewing beef.
2. (a) TOPSIDE: no bone, very good quality meat: can be slow-roasted or braised, and is fine for pot-roasting.
   (b) SILVERSIDE: no bone; favourite joint for salting, but can be used fresh, when it is boiled or braised.
3. TOP RUMP (*thick flank*): can be slow-roasted, casseroled or braised, whole or cut in thick steaks.
4. RUMP: full of flavour but not as soft-textured as fillet: grill or fry; can also be roasted.
5. SIRLOIN: with or without fillet. Wing rib is a sirloin cut without the fillet. Steaks from upper part are known as entrecôte and porterhouse: roast sirloin whole, on the bone or with fillet removed, also boned and rolled; grill or fry fillet.
6. RIBS: top, fore and back: roast on the bone, or boned and rolled; can also be pot-roasted and braised.
7. CHUCK AND BLADE (*shoulder cuts*): stew, braise or casserole; leg of mutton cut needs long, slow cooking or slow roasting.

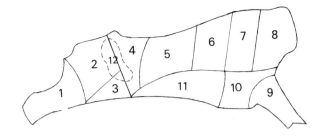

8. CLOD AND STICKING (*neck cuts*): use for stewing.
9. SHIN: is excellent gravy beef.
10. BRISKET: has a fair amount of bone and fat: can be cooked as for silverside.
11. FLANK (*the belly*): can be thick or thin: needs slow, moist cooking; thick flank can be slow-roasted.
12. AITCHBONE: a large joint, often boned or partially boned for convenience when carving: generally roasted, but sometimes salted and boiled.

SKIRT (not shown): thin, lean steak from the inside of the animal—has a good flavour and makes good gravy if used as part of the meat for pies and puddings.

Veal

1. KNUCKLE: braise or stew (especially for osso bucco).
1 with 2. LEG OF VEAL: roast (frequently boned and stuffed).
2. FILLET: roast (add extra fat), grill, or fry (as for escalopes and schnitzels).
3. CHUMP LOIN: use as for 2.
4. LOIN: roasts, sautés and braises; chops can be grilled or fried.
5. BEST END OF NECK: roast or braise; cutlets are often fried or sautéed.
6. SCRAG OR MIDDLE NECK: braise or stew.
7. SHOULDER, EXCLUDING KNUCKLE: roast, on the bone or stuffed and rolled.

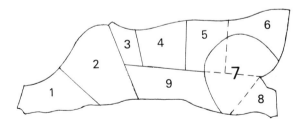

8. KNUCKLE: braise or stew; use in ragoûts and blanquettes.
9. BREAST: makes a flavoursome roast when stuffed; must be cooked slowly.

Pork

1. HEAD: use for brawns, etc.
2. SPARE RIB: as a joint, roast; as chops, grill or fry.
2 with 3. NECK END: roast.
2 with 3, 4, 5 and 6. LONG LOIN: roast.
3. BLADE BONE: roast
4. FORE LOIN: roast.
4 with 5 and 6. SHORT LOIN: roast.
5. MIDDLE AND KIDNEY LOIN: roast, or—if cut as chops—grill or fry.
6. CHUMP END LOIN: roast, or—if cut as chops—grill or fry.
7. FILLET END OF PORK: roast; grill or fry when cut up.
7 with 8 and 9. LEG OF PORK: roast.
8. KNUCKLE END OF PORK: roast
9. TROTTER: boil or braise.

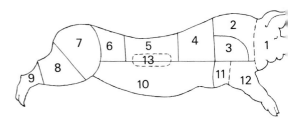

10. BELLY (*streaky pork*): boil (usually salted) or roast; cut in strips and fry; mince or cut up finely and include in pâtés and terrines.
11. THICK END OF BELLY: roast.
11 with 12. HAND AND SPRING: less expensive roasting joint.
12. HAND OF PORK: roast; if salted, boil.
13. AMERICAN SPARE-RIB CUT: use for barbecues.

Lamb

1. KNUCKLE (*shank*) END OF LEG: roast.
1 with 2. LEG OF LAMB: roast.
2. FILLET END OF LEG: roast (suitable for kebabs).
3. CHUMP LOIN (*as chops*): fry or grill.
4. LOIN AND LOIN CHOPS: in the piece, roast; as chops, fry or grill.
5. BEST END NECK: in the piece, roast; as chops or cutlets, fry or grill.
6. MIDDLE NECK (shaded in diagram): cut up for braising, casseroling and stewing.
7. SCRAG: cut up for stewing.
8. SHOULDER: roast.

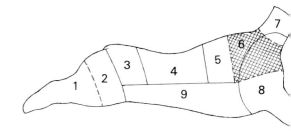

9. BREAST: roast (when boned, rolled and stuffed), braise or stew.

Packing Meat for the Freezer: Make sure that joints are of manageable size and pack them—preferably without bone—in a parcel-type wrap, using freezer paper or foil (the latter is sometimes difficult to remove from a frozen surface, but perfectly all right when the meat is thawed).

Steaks, chops, escalopes, etc., which can be cooked from frozen, should be interleaved with double Cellophane or polythene film, for easy separation.

If you're freezing meat for stews, etc., bone it, cut into pieces of the required size and pack tightly in a polythene bag or rigid container, excluding as much air as possible.

Keep offal in small units for quick thawing, likewise mince—which *must* be absolutely fresh.

Overwrap all meat, to protect it against puncturing and freezer burn, then seal well. Freeze as soon as possible after purchase.

Storage Times

Beef	—	8 months	Mince	—	3 months
Lamb	—	6 months	Offal	—	3 months
Pork and veal	—	6 months	Sausages	—	3 months

Cooking Frozen Meat: To thaw or not to thaw—that is the question—and in recent Good Housekeeping Institute tests, the guinea-pig guests answered overwhelmingly in favour of not thawing. Overall, they found that joints cooked from frozen had a very much better flavour (regardless of whether they'd been blast-frozen or quick home-frozen) than those that had been thawed, although they had to admit that the thawed counterparts were rather more tender.

The only snag about cooking straight from frozen, of course, is the difficulty of cooking the inside without over-cooking the outside. This isn't a problem with steaks, chops and other cuts that are 1 in. or less in depth—but obviously as the cuts of meat get bigger, the difficulty increases.

When cooking joints from frozen it is essential that the internal temperature is checked with a meat thermometer which has a special spiked end so that it can pierce the meat. About 30 min. before the end of cooking time insert the thermometer into the centre of the joint, taking care that it does not touch the bone. Cooking time may vary according to the shape and composition of the joint, and individual preferences.

Beef—seal the joint in hot fat in a pre-heated oven at 450°F (mark 8) uncovered, for 20 min., turning once. Reduce the oven temperature to 350°F (mark 4), cover the meat and cook 50 min. per lb., basting frequently.

Temperature of medium cooked meat using a meat thermometer—160°F.

Lamb—seal the joint in hot fat in a pre-heated oven at 450°F (mark 8) uncovered, for 20 min. turning once. Reduce the oven temperature to 350°F (mark 4), cover the meat and cook 60 min. per lb. basting frequently.

Temperature of meat using a meat thermometer—180°F.

Pork—place the joint into a cold oven set at 425°F (mark 7) and allow 25 min. per lb. plus 25 min. over from the time the oven reaches the set temperature.

Temperature of meat using a meat thermometer—190°F.

When cooking small meat cuts from frozen, the general rule is to start cooking over a high heat to brown both sides and seal in the juices and then to lower the heat and cook right through.

Large sausages
baked   1–1¼ hr. 350°F (mark 4)
grilled   10 min. starting at a low temperature
(These are best baked or grilled as in frying they tend to split; turn occasionally during cooking.)

Small chipolata sausages		Cooking sliced liver from frozen	
baked	45 min. at 375°F (mark 5)	fried	20 min.
grilled	12–15 min.	baked in sauce	1 hr. at 350°F
fried	12–15 min.		(mark 4)

When should you Thaw it? Obviously for very large or solid joints, thawing before cooking is the safest bet. As a rough guide, allow 6 hr. per lb. in the refrigerator, or 3 hr. per lb. at average room temperature; slow thawing results in less drip, so it's best done in the refrigerator. Mince and stewing or braising meats are also best thawed, though in an emergency you can get by without.

Once thawed, the meat should be cooked at once. If for some reason it has to wait even a short time, be sure to keep it in the fridge.

Cooking Thawed Meat: Completely thawed frozen meats are cooked in exactly the same way as their fresh meat counterparts.

Note: It's perfectly in order to use frozen meat in making up and cooking a dish, and then to freeze this dish in the usual way.

Poultry
Freezing Chickens (including Capons and Poussins): It's not worth spending your efforts on anything other than young, plump, tender birds. Commercial quick-frozen raw poultry is so readily available it's only an advantage to freeze it at home when the price is very favourable. If the birds are your own (and presuming you haven't grown too fond of them), starve them for 24 hr. before killing, and if possible set to and pluck out the feathers while the corpse is still warm—they come out much easier that way. Hang the chicken for a day before drawing, and be sure to freeze at the lowest possible temperature for your freezer (ideally, −32°C or −25°F) because higher temperatures can give disappointing results. And remember to turn the temperature control down low

at least 24 hr. before you're planning to freeze a bird—this will give it a chance to get really cold. Once frozen, maintain at the normal freeze temperature.

How you freeze your birds depends on how you're going to cook them. Obviously if you're going to make a chicken casserole, you'll be wasting freezer space if you freeze a chicken whole, instead of cutting it up into more convenient pieces. And talking of wastage, remember that chicken fat is excellent rendered down for cooking chips in, and that any odd scraps and bones can make fabulous concentrated stocks for using in soups and sauces. More sizeable remnants of cold roast chicken (carved or not) and poached chicken may be satisfactorily frozen too.

For freezing *whole*, wipe and dry the bird after plucking and drawing it. Pack the giblets separately instead of inside, because they'll only keep for a quarter of the time the chicken can be stored.

Now amass your trussing equipment (just a trussing needle and a piece of thin, fine string), and place the bird on the table with the breast uppermost and the legs on the right-hand side. Insert the threaded trussing needle through the top joint of one leg, through the body and out through the other leg, leaving an end of string. Catch in the wing, then pass the needle through the body and catch in the bottom of the opposite leg. Again, insert the needle through the bottom end of the leg, pass the needle through the body and through the bottom of the opposite leg. Finally, pass the needle diagonally through the body and catch in the remaining wing. Tie string tightly. Don't stuff the chicken, as it takes too long to freeze and thaw. If you wish, package any stuffing separately.

For freezing chicken *portions*, divide small birds (around 2–2$\frac{1}{2}$ lb.) into quarters. With young birds, this can be done quite painlessly with poultry secateurs or a sharp knife. Cut the bird in half, through and along the breastbone. Open the bird out, and then cut along the length of the backbone. If you want to remove the backbone entirely, cut along either side of it, then lift it out—and don't forget to use it for making stock. If you're using a knife, you'll have to tap the back sharply with a heavy weight to cut through the bony sections. Either way, once the bird is in two halves, lay these skin side up. Divide each in half again by cutting diagonally across between wing and thigh —allocating more breast meat to the wing than to the thigh, to even out the amount of meat per portion.

For freezing smaller chicken *joints*, to be used in casseroles, etc., cut the thigh loose along the rounded edge and pull the leg away from the body to isolate the joint. Break the thigh backwards so that the knife can cut through the socket of each thigh joint, and loosen the wings from the breast meat in the same way. Divide the legs into two pieces in the centre of the joint. Lastly, turn over the body of the bird onto its back and carve the breast meat from the breastbone. Both breast portions may be halved, and the back is divided into two–three pieces.

Packing for the Freezer: Before packing whole birds in heavy-duty polythene bags, first pad the legs with foil so that they can't spike their way through the wrapping. Exclude as much air as possible before sealing the bag (this is a good opportunity for using the lowering-into-water trick or the drinking straw that we suggested in the packaging section). With chicken quarters, pack individually in foil or polythene bags, and then combine into a larger package to save space. Similarly, freeze chicken joints all together in a polythene bag—but first, divide them up with Cellophane, or waxed or freezer paper.

Cold roast or poached chicken should be cooled as rapidly as possible after cooking. Pack in double foil, with any stuffing parcelled separately, and freeze at once.

Thawing and Cooking Chickens: Unlike frozen meat, frozen whole chickens *must* be thawed completely before cooking, so remember to leave plenty of time. A 3-lb. bird is going to take 8–10 hr. to thaw out at room temperature or at least 15 hr. in a refrigerator; chicken joints (portions) need 3 hr. and 6 hr. respectively and, of course, to keep all its juices, you must thaw chicken while it's still in its packaging material. If it hasn't thawed completely and you can't possibly wait any longer, at least take the precaution of prolonging the cooking time. Don't be alarmed, by the way, if the poultry bones have turned a sinister darkish-red. It's all to do with oxidation of haemoglobin, and is nothing to worry about. The only thing you really have to be careful about is in the cooking. Heat won't have an internal sterilising effect until a temperature of 91°C (195°F) has been reached—which is another good reason for investing in a meat thermometer.

To thaw frozen roast or poached chicken, remove the foil and place the chicken in a polythene bag; leave at room temperature for about 9 hr., or in the refrigerator for about 20 hr. Previously carved meat will thaw more quickly, but may be a little dried in texture.

Storage Times
Chicken   —   12 months   Giblets   —   2–3 months

Turkeys: In general, these are treated like chickens. But remember that because they are so bulky, they take up a lot of valuable freezer space, so it's not good planning to store them for too long. The maximum storage time is 6 months.

Turkeys need a considerable time for thawing and the refrigerator is the best place for the operation. Small birds take about 2 days, larger ones 3–4 days.

Leftover roast turkey may be frozen as for chicken. It's best cut off the bone, and any fat should be discarded, while stuffing should be packed separately. To avoid excessive drying, freeze it with gravy or stock, unless it's only to be stored for a very short time.

Ducklings and Geese: Choose young birds without too much fat, which can cause rancidity—though on the other hand, excessively lean birds may be dry. Dress in the usual way, and pack the giblets separately, as their storage time is limited compared with that of the bird, e.g. Duckling (Duck), and Goose 4–5 months, but giblets 2–3 months.

Pack and freeze as for chicken.

To thaw in the refrigerator, allow 24–36 hr., or at room temperature, about 12 hr. In either case, leave in the wrapping. Cook at once after thawing.

Freezing Game: Venison, like ordinary meats, requires some skill in the art of butchery, so it's best to ask the butcher to deal with it, if you're ever confronted with a carcase. Briefly, it needs to be chilled, hung for up to 6 days, then jointed and frozen, packed and thawed like other meats. Cook as for fresh venison. It has a storage life of up to 12 months.

Hares are game, rabbits aren't—but it's convenient to bracket them together here. Prepare them as for cooking fresh. If you like the gamey flavour, hang a hare for 7–10 days before freezing it, but rabbits are not treated in this way.

Since most recipes call for portioned hare or rabbit, it's sensible to pack them this way, discarding the more bony parts (which can be used for casseroles, pâté and stock). Pack, freeze and thaw as for meat, and cook as usual.

The recommended storage time is 6 months.

Game birds are actually supposed to improve with freezing. Bleed the bird as soon as possible after shooting. Hang, undrawn, until sufficiently 'high' for your personal taste. If necessary, a bird can be frozen for a *short* time with its feathers on, and plucked after thawing. Pluck, removing the feathers in the direction in which they grow. Draw, wash, drain and thoroughly dry. Pack, removing as much air as possible, in a really heavy-gauge foil or polythene bag before freezing in the usual way.

When required, thaw thoroughly, preferably in the refrigerator, and cook immediately.

Water birds should be plucked, drawn and frozen quickly after killing. (Remove the oil sac from the base of the tail.)

Storage time 6–8 months.

Bacon

On occasions bacon could be a useful freezer item, but it is very important to follow directions carefully and not to exceed the recommended storage times, otherwise both texture and flavour may be disappointing. *It is most important to freeze only bacon which is perfectly fresh*, so when you want to buy bacon for freezing it is advisable to inform the supplier of your intention, so that he can meet this requirement. If possible, the bacon should be frozen on the day it is supplied to the retailer—the longer the bacon has been cut or kept in the shop, the shorter its storage life in the freezer. Smoked bacon can be stored for longer periods than unsmoked before any risk of rancidity arises.

To Pack and Freeze: Commercial vacuum-packing is generally accepted as the most suitable wrapping, since the maximum amount of air is extracted, so if possible buy bacon for freezing ready-packed in this way. Again, the bacon should be frozen on or very near the day when it was vacuum-packed. However, quite acceptable results have been achieved in our own kitchens when top-quality bacon has been closely wrapped in kitchen foil or plastic film and overwrapped in polythene bags. Don't have more than $\frac{1}{2}$ lb. rashers in a package. If you wish, they can be interleaved for easier separation—use waxed or non-stick paper—but this is not necessary if the packs are made up to suit individual cooking needs. Wrap bacon chops individually. Joints (up to 3–4 lb.) should be overwrapped in a polythene bag. It is also wise to overwrap vacuum-packed bacon, and to check each one carefully to make sure the vacuum is intact and that the bacon does not move about within the pack.

Freeze as quickly as possible.

To Thaw and Cook: Thaw either overnight in the refrigerator, or at room temperature. For rashers, chops and steaks allow about 3 hr. at room temperature, or overnight in the refrigerator—loosely wrapped, with overwrap removed. For joints, leave overnight at room temperature, or allow 1 day in the refrigerator. Vacuum-packed joints and rashers should be thawed in the bag. To thaw rashers rapidly, leave in the wrap and place in hot water for 5 min.; dry well on kitchen paper before cooking. To remove any excess salt from thawed joints, cover with cold water, bring to the boil, then pour off the water. Refill the pan with fresh cold water; bring to the boil again, reduce heat to simmering point and finish cooking, allowing 20 min. per lb. and 20 min. over.

Storage Times

RASHERS:	smoked up to 7 weeks
	unsmoked up to 5 weeks
CHOPS AND STEAKS:	smoked up to 7 weeks
	unsmoked up to 5 weeks
BACON JOINTS:	smoked up to 8 weeks
	unsmoked up to 6 weeks

Note: After the periods stated a definite change of flavour is noticed in some cases, so it is not recommended to keep bacon beyond these limits.

Planned shopping

After years of planning ahead for all of one week, a freezer takes some getting used to, because suddenly you're expected to plan ahead for months. Plan is too precise a word, though. It's more a matter of seizing opportunities as they come, so you can make use of them later. Seasonal fruits and vegetables provide obvious examples, because you can buy things like asparagus and strawberries at glut-prices and eat them when they're a luxury. So do buy bargain offers. If your supermarket's selling butter at 2 pence off per lb., instead of buying a hesitant 2 lb. and hoping you can eat it up before it goes off, you can buy 10, and live off it till the next bargain offer comes round.

Plenty of bargains aren't so obvious. Meat and poultry prices fluctuate so eccentrically that it's difficult to keep up with them; study the form for a while, then buy enough to see you through the next price rise. (Only condition: make sure meat or poultry is fresh—you can't re-freeze what's already been frozen and thawed. Alternatively, ask to be served straight from the freezer, and rush the food home before it can start thawing.)

You'll be surprised how much food your family gets through in a couple of months. In fact, it's worth keeping a record of just how much in the first year of freezer-ownership, so you can bulk-buy with absolute confidence. A family of four, for instance, could easily demolish a dozen chickens in three months, and provided you'd planned your cooking as well as your shopping, they'd run no risk of monotony. Suppose you got the butcher to joint 9 of them and kept the other 3 for roasting. You could use the legs for making coq au vin, chicken à la king, poule au pot, curried chicken; the wings for portions of chicken fricassee; the livers for making a fabulous pâté; the breasts for freezing raw, so that they could form the basis of several speedy meals; the odds and ends for boiling up to make concentrated stock for soups and sauces.

This kind of thinking big can be very rewarding—provided you manage to ring the changes. The most luxurious food can bore people to tears, and they'll start groaning 'Oh no! Not scampi again'. Buying in quantity only makes sense where the food's going to get eaten up regularly and willingly, and as you'll find out in Part 3, the way to plan shopping is so that the freezer trebles its capacity during each year. For example, with a freezer of 240 lb. capacity (about 12 cubic feet), you should aim at freezing about 300 lb. of fruit and vegetables; 200 lb. of meat and poultry; 120 lb. of baked and prepared foods; and buying 100 lb. of commercially frozen food. Remember, the freezer costs the same to operate half-full as when it's packed to capacity.

Freezing services

Although your local butcher and greengrocer will probably be quite happy to sell food in bulk at reduced prices, the simplest way of stocking your freezer is to buy already frozen food from the many frozen food distributors. These people have depots all over the country (you really would have to live in the back of the beyond to be outside their reach), and you can either collect your food from them or have it delivered. Collecting the food (once you're an old hand you'll call it 'cash and carry') has the advantage that you can buy just as much as you like. Food usually comes supplied in bags or wrappings that keep it insulated for at least 3 hours, so you don't have to break any speed limits rushing it home; alternatively, you can always buy a portable insulated container from a firm like The Insulated Container Company, Deepfreeze Centre, High Street, Chobham, Surrey.

If you prefer to have the food delivered, you may find yourself up against a minimum delivery order, usually in the region of £5 to £10 worth of food. In other words, you're better off shopping at your local supermarket if all you've run out of is a packet of peas. Most of the delivery services are well geared up to their customers' needs. Unlike gas and electricity men, who keep you trapped indoors all day for a visit that never materialises, they tell you when to expect them (not to the exact hour perhaps, but at least they manage to say which morning or afternoon)—and they keep to it. Some even ring the day beforehand to check that you haven't changed your plans, and they're not making a fuss about nothing. Frozen food can't sit waiting in the porch like a loaf of bread or a bottle of milk: if you have to go out, arrange for a neighbour to pop it into your freezer for you, or store it in her own until you can collect it.

Newcomers to freezing may feel apprehensive about buying in bulk, especially if they've heard tales of people struggling to cut lumps off massive slabs of cod. In the bad old days of freezing, bulk-buying did mean solid catering-pack blocks: perfect for a school or hospital, but quite overpowering for the average household. Now however, all it means is buying food in big enough I.Q.F. (individually quick frozen) quantities to save up to one-third on it. If you buy

BULK BUYING in lots of 2½ lb. and more is an economy. It's often more practical to portion off into family-sized packs—do this quickly so that the food remains frozen throughout

40 plaice fillets, for instance, they'll come separated by sheets of a special polythene-type film, so that you can peel off as many as you need. Vegetables are just as easy to manage, because with the exception of spinach and broccoli (these still come *en masse*, but you won't have any trouble cutting off a meal-size portion if you buy a proper frozen food knife), they remain free-flow when they're frozen. This means you can simply tip out as many peas (savings of up to 30p on a 5-lb. pack), sliced green beans (savings of up to 50p), Brussels sprouts (savings of up to 50p) and mixed vegetables (savings of up to 60p) as you need, re-sealing the pack and popping it back into the freezer until next time. As for meat, buying it ready-jointed saves a lot of trouble. It comes packed into appropriate family-sized portions, and a 20-lb. quantity of quality steaks and beef joints bearing the Fribo trademark, for instance, would only cost just over £7·80.

Frozen food depots began with the basics, but some of them soon caught onto the demand for luxuries, so that you can buy game as well as chicken, salmon as well as haddock, artichokes as well as broad beans. From there, it was only a short step to supplying complete gourmet meals, and a firm like Kitchen Range, for example, can take all the slog out of a dinner party by delivering taramasalata, boeuf marseillaise and a superb Windsor cheese flavoured with mulberry wine.

We've rounded off this section with a far-flung selection of depot addresses. If you can't find yourself on the freezer map, however, send 12p plus a large S.A.E. to The Good Housekeeping Institute, Chestergate House, Vauxhall Bridge Road, London SW1V 1HF—and we'll be only too glad to send you a more comprehensive list.

The Anglian Tendabeef Company Ltd., Llay Industrial Estate, Llay, Wrexham, Denbighshire, supplies top quality meat. It's distributed by various good wholesalers throughout the country, so you shouldn't have much trouble tracking it down. *Alveston Kitchens*, Timothy's Bridge Road, Stratford-on-Avon, Warwickshire, make ready-cooked speciality dishes, including a superb pâté, in one- or two-portion packs. Their catering packs are available through distributors, too, if you want to take the easy way out when you're entertaining. *Bejam Bulk Buying Ltd.*, 1 Garland Road, Honeypot Lane, Stanmore, Middx., HA7 1LE, have numerous depots. You name it and they're almost sure to supply it—including a range of kosher foods. *Birds Eye Ltd.*, Station Avenue, Walton-on-Thames, Surrey, boast a number of depots, stocking all the famous Birds Eye foods, as expected. *Bertorelli's Ice Cream Ltd.*, Barnet Bypass, Boreham Wood, Herts, supplies delicious water ices with flavours ranging from obvious strawberry to delicate melon. *W. Brooks & Son*, Hatcham Road, London, SE15 1TX, serve the Greater London area with a wide range of frozen foods. *Cordon Bleu Freezer Food Centres Ltd.*, Cordon Bleu House, Cromwell Road, Bredbury Industrial Estate, Ashton Road, Bredbury, Cheshire, SK6 2SL, produce the kind of quality their name has become famous for. *Everest Refrigeration Company Ltd.*, Westmorland Road, London NW9 9RS, confines itself to London and the Home Counties again. *Kitchen Range Ltd.*, 88 Queen's Gate, London SW7 5AY have a good range of gourmet menus, which vary with the months to make the most of the best ingredients going: not cheap—but the food is top quality. *Leytons (Foods) Ltd.*, Priddy Wells, Somerset, BA5 3DB, send gourmet dishes through the post only. There's a £16 deposit on insulated containers. *Associated Fisheries and Foods Ltd.*, PO Box 96, Brighton Street, Hull, Yorks., specialise in meat, instead of the fish you might suppose. *Ross Foods Ltd.*, Rye Lane, Dunton Green, Sevenoaks, Kent, carry their own Ross products—minimum £10 order, free of delivery charge. *The Lord Fisher*, Kilverstone, Thetford, Norfolk, specialises in lamb. Postal service only (minimum order 18 lb.). Wednesday's despatch day, so watch for the postman on Thursday. *W. West*, 165 Hertford Road, Enfield, Middx., supplies the North London area with individually tailored quality produce, especially meat: £10 minimum order—and a handy 24-hour telephone service. To make sure you give your custom to the right firm, send for price lists and full details, and then you can compare one with the other in the comfort of your armchair. But don't go by the price lists alone: cost isn't the criterion—and quality is something you can only find out about by trying.

BASIC KNOW-HOW

FOOD AND STORAGE TIME	PREPARATION	FREEZING	THAWING AND SERVING
MEAT, RAW (leave unstuffed) Beef: 8 months Lamb: 6 months Veal: 6 months Pork: 6 months Freshly minced meat: 3 months Offal: 3 months Cured and smoked meats: 1–2 months Sausages: 3 months	Use good quality, well-hung fresh meat. Removing bones will save space. Butcher in suitable quantities. Place polythene sheets between individual chops or steaks	Package carefully in heavy-quality polythene bags. Group in similar types, and overwrap with mutton cloth, stockinette, thin polythene or newspaper, to protect against puncturing and loss of quality	All meats may be cooked from frozen (see page 195), but with large joints avoid over-cooking meat on outside and leaving it raw at centre. When thawing, use the refrigerator; keeping wrappings on, allow about 6 hr. per lb. Small items like chops, steaks, can be cooked frozen, but use gentle heat. Partial thawing is necessary before egg-and-crumb coating, etc.
MEAT, COOKED DISHES Casseroles, stews, curries, etc.: 2 months	Prepare as desired, see that the meat is cooked but not over-cooked, to allow for re-heating. Do not season too heavily—check this at point of serving. Have enough liquid or sauce to immerse solid meat completely. Potato, rice or spaghetti, unless otherwise stated, are best added at point of serving; same applies to garlic and celery	When mixture is quite cold, transfer to rigid cartons; for dishes with a strong smell or colour, inner-line cartons with polythene bags, use foil dishes or freeze in foil-lined cook-ware. See pre-formers	Re-heat food from cartons or polythene bags in a saucepan or casserole dish. Pre-shaped foil-wrapped mixtures can be re-heated in the original dish. When re-heating in a casserole, allow at least 1 hr. for heating through in the oven at 400°F (mark 6) then if necessary reduce heat to 350°F (mark 4) for 40 min. and leave until really hot. Alternatively, heat gently in a pan, simmering until thoroughly heated
MEAT, ROAST 2–4 weeks	Joints can be roasted and frozen for serving cold—don't over-cook. Re-heated whole joints are not very satisfactory. Sliced and frozen cooked meat tends to be dry when re-heated	Best results are achieved by freezing whole joint, thawing, then slicing prior to serving. But small pieces can be sliced and packed in polythene if required to serve cold, or put in foil containers and covered with gravy, if to be served hot	Allow plenty of time for thawing-out—about 4 hr. per lb. at room temperature, or double that time in the refrigerator, in the wrapping. Sliced meat requires less time

FOOD AND STORAGE TIME	PREPARATION	FREEZING	THAWING AND SERVING
MEAT LOAVES, PÂTÉS 1 month	Follow regular recipe. Package in the usual way, after cooling rapidly. Keep for minimum time	When quite cold, remove from tin, wrap and freeze	Thaw preferably overnight or for at least 6–8 hr. in the refrigerator
POULTRY AND GAME Chicken: 12 months Duck: 4–6 months Goose: 4–6 months Turkey: 6 months Giblets: 3 months Game birds: 6–8 months Venison: 12 months	Use fresh birds only: prepare and draw in the usual way. Do not stuff before freezing. Cover protruding bones with grease-proof paper or foil. Hang game desired time before freezing	Pack trussed bird inside polythene bag and exclude as much air as possible before sealing. Freeze giblets separately. If wished, freeze in joints, wrap individually, and then overwrap	Thaw in wrapping, preferably in refrigerator. Thaw a small bird overnight; birds up to 4 lb. up to 12 hr.; 4–12 lb. up to 24 hr.; over 12 lb. 48–72 hr. Joints 6 hr.
FISH, UNCOOKED Whole (Salmon, fresh-water fish)	Must be really fresh—within 12 hr. of the catch. Wash and remove scales by scraping tail-to-head with back of knife. Gut. Wash thoroughly under running water. Drain and dry on a clean cloth	For best results, place whole fish unwrapped in freezer until solid. Remove, dip in cold water. This forms thin ice over fish. Return to freezer; repeat process until ice glaze is $\frac{1}{4}$ in. thick. Wrap in heavy-duty polythene; support with a thin board.	Allow to thaw for 24 hr. in a cool place before cooking. Once thawed, use promptly
Fish steaks	Prepare in the usual way	Separate steaks with double layer of Saran; wrap in heavy polythene	May be cooked from the frozen state
Oily fish: 2 months Salmon: 2 months White fish: 3 months Smoked salmon: 3 months			
SHELL FISH 1 month	Advisable only if you can freeze the fish within 12 hr. of being caught		
FISH, COOKED Pies, fish cakes, croquettes, kedgeree, mousse, paellas: 2 months	Prepare according to recipe, but be sure fish is absolutely fresh. Hard-boiled eggs should be added to kedgeree before re-heating	Freeze in foil-lined containers, remove when hard, then pack in sealed bags	Either slow-thaw in refrigerator or put straight into the oven at 350°F (mark 4) to heat, depending on the type of recipe
SAUCES, SOUPS, STOCKS 2–3 months: if highly seasoned 2 weeks	All are very useful as stand-bys in the freezer	When cold, pour into rigid containers, seal well and freeze	Either thaw for 1–2 hr. at room temperature, or heat immediately until boiling point is reached
PIZZA, UNBAKED	Prepare traditional yeast mixture	Freeze flat until solid, then	Remove packaging and place

PASTRY, UNCOOKED Shortcrust: 3 months Flaky and puff: 3–4 months	Roll out to size required (or shape into vol-au-vent cases). Freeze pie shells unwrapped until hard, to avoid damage. Use foil plates or take frozen shell out of dish after freezing but before wrapping. Discs of pastry can be stacked with waxed paper between for pie bases or tops *Note*: there is little advantage in bulk-freezing unshaped short-crust pastry, as it takes about 3 hr. to thaw before it can be rolled out. Bulk flaky and puff—prepare up to the last rolling; pack in polythene bags or heavy-duty foil and overwrap. To use, leave for 3–4 hr. at room temperature, or overnight in refrigerator	Stack pastry shapes with 2 pieces of Saran or waxed paper between layers, so that if needed, one piece can be removed without thawing the whole batch. Place the stack on a piece of card-board, wrap and seal	Thaw flat discs at room temperature, fit into pie plate and proceed with recipe. Unbaked pie shells or flat cases should be returned to their original container before cooking: they can go into oven from the freezer (ovenproof glass should first stand for 10 min. at room temperature); add about 5 min. to normal baking time
PASTRY, COOKED Pastry cases: 6 months Meat pies: 3–4 months Fruit pies: 6 months	Prepare as usual. Empty cases freeze satisfactorily, but with some change in texture. Prepare pies as directed (using an aluminium foil dish). Brush pastry cases with egg white before filling. Cool completely before freezing	Wrap carefully—very fragile. Protect the tops of pies with an inverted paper or aluminium pie plate, then wrap and seal	Leave pies at room temperature for 2–4 hr., depending on size. If required hot, re-heat in the oven. Flan cases should be thawed at room temperature for about 1 hr.; refresh if wished
PASTRY PIES, UNCOOKED Double crust: 3 months	Prepare pastry and filling as required. Make large pies in a foil dish or plate, or line an ordinary dish or plate with foil and use as a pre-former. Make small pies in patty tins or foil cases. Do not slit top crust of fruit pies before freezing	Freeze uncovered. When frozen, remove small or pre-formed pies from containers and pack all pies in foil or polythene bags	Unwrap unbaked fruit pies and place still frozen in the oven at 425°F (mark 7) for 40–60 min., according to type and size. Slit tops of double crusts when beginning to thaw. (Ovenproof glass should first stand for 10 min. at room temperature.) Add a little to usual cooking time

At the top of the first thaw/cook column (partially cut off):

400°F (mark 6) for about 20 min., or leave in packaging at room temperature for 2 hr. before re-heating as above for 10–15 min.

FOOD AND STORAGE TIME	PREPARATION	FREEZING	THAWING AND SERVING
Top crust: 3 months	Prepare pie in usual way; cut fruit into fairly small pieces and blanch if necessary; toss with sugar; or use cold cooked savoury filling. Cover with pastry. Do not slit crust	Use ovenproof glass or foil dishes. Wrap in foil or plastic film, protecting as for cooked pies	Unwrap, place in a pre-heated oven and bake, allowing extra time. Cut a vent in the pastry when it begins to thaw
Biscuit Pie Crust: 2 months	Not easy to handle unfilled unless the crust is pre-baked. Shape in a sandwich tin or pie plate, lined with foil or waxed paper. Add filling if suitable	Freeze until firm, then remove from tin in the foil wrapping and pack in a rigid container	Filled: serve cold; thaw at room temperature for 6 hr.
PANCAKES, UNFILLED 2 months	Add 1 tbsp. corn oil to a basic 4 oz. flour recipe. Make pancakes, and cool quickly on a wire rack. Interleave them with lightly oiled greaseproof paper or polythene film. Seal in polythene bags or foil	Freeze quickly	To thaw: leave in packaging at at room temperature for 2–3 hr., or overnight in the refrigerator. For quick thawing, unwrap, spread out separately and leave at room temperature for about 20 min. To re-heat, place stack of pancakes wrapped in foil in the oven at 375°F (mark 5) for 20–30 min. Alternatively, separate pancakes and place in a lightly greased heated frying pan, allowing $\frac{1}{2}$ min. for each side
PANCAKES, FILLED 1–2 months	Only choose fillings suitable for freezing. Don't over-season	Place filled pancakes in a foil dish, seal and overwrap	Place frozen in packaging in oven at 400°F (mark 6) for about 30 min.
SPONGE PUDDINGS, UNCOOKED 2 months	Make in the usual way. Use foil or polythene basins, or line ordinary basins with greased foil	Seal basins tightly with foil, overwrap and freeze at once. To freeze pudding mixture in pre-formed foil, remove from basins when frozen, then overwrap Note: allow room at this stage for later rising	Remove packaging, cover top with greased foil and place, frozen, to steam—$1\frac{1}{2}$-pt. size takes about $2\frac{1}{4}$ hr. Don't forget to return a pre-formed pudding mixture to its original basin
SPONGE PUDDINGS, COOKED	Prepare and cook in the usual	Freeze quickly	As above—a $1\frac{1}{4}$-pt. pudding takes

Food	Preparation	Packing	Thawing
Mousses, creams, etc. 2–3 months	frozen in new toughened tableware glasses by Duralex	container until firm, then remove container, place sweet in polythene bag, seal and return to freezer	for about 6 hr., or at room temperature for about 2 hr.
ICE CREAM 3 months Commercially made: 1 month	Either home-made or bought ice creams and sorbets can be stored in the freezer	Bought ice creams should be re-wrapped in moisture-proof bags before storing. Home-made ones should be frozen in moulds or waxed containers and over-wrapped	Put in freezing compartment of the refrigerator for 6–8 hr., to soften a little. Some 'soft' bought ice cream can be used from freezer, provided it is not kept in the coldest part
CREAM Whipped: 3 months Commercially frozen: up to 1 year	Use only pasteurised, with a 40% butter-fat content, or more (i.e. double cream). Whipped cream may be piped into rosettes on waxed paper	Transfer cream to suitable container, e.g. waxed carton, leaving space for expansion. Freeze rosettes unwrapped; when firm, pack in a single layer in foil	Thaw in refrigerator, allowing 8 hr., or 1–2 hr. at room temperature. Put rosettes in position as decoration before thawing, or they cannot be handled
CAKES, COOKED Including sponge flans, Swiss rolls and layer cakes: 6 months (Frosted cakes lose quality after 2 months; since aging improves fruit cakes, they may be kept longer)	Bake in usual way. Leave until cold on a wire rack. Swiss rolls are best rolled up in cornflour, not sugar, if to be frozen without a filling. Do not spread or layer with jam before freezing. Keep essences to a minimum and go lightly with spices	Wrap plain cake layers separately, or together with Saran or waxed paper between layers. Freeze frosted cakes (whole or cut) unwrapped until frosting has set, then wrap, seal and pack in boxes to protect icing	Iced cakes: unwrap before thawing, then the wrapping will not stick to the frosting when thawing. Cream cakes: may be sliced while frozen, for a better shape and quick thawing. Plain cakes: leave in package and thaw at room temperature. Un-iced layer cakes and small cakes thaw in about 1–2 hr. at room temperature: frosted layer cakes take up to 4 hr.
CAKE MIXTURES, UNCOOKED 2 months	Whisked sponge mixtures do not freeze well uncooked. Put rich creamed mixtures into containers, or line the tin to be used later with greased foil, add cake mixture and freeze uncovered. When frozen, remove from tin, package in foil and overwrap	Return to freezer	To thaw, leave at room temperature for 2–3 hr., then fill tins to bake. Pre-formed cake mixtures can be returned to the original tin, without wrapping. Place frozen in pre-heated oven and bake in usual way, but allow longer cooking time

FOOD AND STORAGE TIME	PREPARATION	FREEZING	THAWING AND SERVING
SCONES AND TEABREADS 6 months	Bake in usual way	Freeze in polythene bag in convenient units for serving	Thaw teabreads in wrapping at room temperature for 2–3 hr. Tea scones: cook from frozen, wrapped in foil, at 400°F (mark 6) for 10 min. Girdle scones: thaw 1 hr. Drop scones: thaw 30 min. or cover and bake for 10 min.
CROISSANTS AND DANISH PASTRIES Unbaked, in bulk: 6 weeks Baked: 4 weeks	Unbaked: Prepare to the stage when all the fat has been absorbed, but don't give the final rolling. *Baked, see page 75*	Unbaked: Wrap in airtight polythene bags and freeze at once	Leave in polythene bag, but unseal and re-tie loosely, allowing space for dough to rise. Preferably thaw overnight in a refrigerator, or leave for 5 hr. at room temperature. Complete the final rolling and shaping, and bake
BISCUITS BAKED AND UNBAKED 6 months	Prepare in the usual way. Rich mixtures—i.e. with more than ¼ lb. fat to 1 lb. flour—are the most satisfactory	Either baked or unbaked, pack carefully. Wrap rolls of un-cooked dough, or pipe soft mixtures into shapes, freeze and pack when firm. Allow cooked biscuits to cool before packing	Thaw uncooked rolls of dough slightly; slice off required number of biscuits and bake. Shaped biscuits can be cooked direct from frozen state: allow 7–10 min. extra cooking time. Cooked biscuits may require crisping in warm oven
BREAD 4 weeks	Freshly-baked bread, both bought and home-made, can be frozen. Crisp, crusty bread stores well up to 1 week, then the crust begins to 'shell off'	Bought bread may be frozen in original wrapper for up to 1 week; for longer periods, seal in foil or polythene. Home-made bread: freeze in foil or polythene bags	Leave to thaw in the sealed polythene bag or wrapper at room temperature 3–6 hr, or overnight in the refrigerator, or leave foil-wrapped and crisp in oven at 400°F (mark 6) for about 45 min. Sliced bought bread can be toasted from frozen state
BOUGHT PART-BAKED BREAD AND ROLLS 4 months	Freeze immediately after purchase	Leave loaf in the bag. Pack rolls in heavy-duty polythene bags and seal	To use, place frozen unwrapped loaf in oven at 425°F (mark 7) for about 40 min. Cool for 1–2 hr before cutting. Rolls: place

SANDWICHES 1–2 months	Most types may be frozen, but those filled with hard-boiled eggs, tomatoes, cucumber or bananas tend to go tasteless and soggy	Wrap in foil, then in polythene bag	Thaw unwrapped at room temperature or in the refrigerator. Times vary according to size of pack. Cut pinwheels, sandwich loaves, etc., in portions when half-thawed
TOASTED SANDWICHES Up to 2 months	Use white or brown bread—cheese, ham, fish are all suitable, but avoid salad foods; season lightly	Interleave for easy separation. Wrap in foil or polythene bags	Place frozen unwrapped sandwiches under a hot grill; thawing will take place during toasting
MARMALADE 6 months; useful if it's not convenient to make marmalade when Seville oranges are in season	Wash, dry and freeze Seville oranges whole, or prepare marmalade to cooked pulp stage—i.e. before addition of sugar	Pack whole oranges in polythene bags; pulp in suitable containers	Thaw, still wrapped, in fridge, allowing 6–8 hr. per lb. for whole fruit and 9–12 hr. per lb. for pulped, then finish cooking
BUTTER Salted: 3 months Unsalted: 6 months	Always buy fresh stock (farmhouse butter must be made from pasteurised cream)	Overwrap in foil in $\frac{1}{2}$–1-lb. quantities	Allow to thaw in refrigerator
COMMERCIALLY FROZEN FOODS Up to 3 months as a rule *Note*: The times quoted by the manufacturers are often less than those given for home-frozen foods, because of the handling in distribution, before the foods can reach your own freezer	No further preparation, etc., needed, except for ice cream, which should be overwrapped if it is to be kept for longer than 3 weeks	Follow directions on packet	
HERBS Up to 6 months	Wash and trim if necessary. Dry thoroughly	Freeze in small bunches in a rigid foil container or polythene bag. Alternatively, herbs, especially parsley, can be chopped before freezing	Can be used immediately. Crumble whilst still frozen
EGGS separated 8–10 months	Freeze only fresh eggs—yolks and whites separately	Pack in waxed or rigid containers. Yolks—to every 6 yolks add 1 tsp. salt or 2 tsps. sugar, to single yolks add $\frac{1}{4}$ tsp. salt or sugar;	Thaw in refrigerator or rapidly thaw at room temperature for about $1\frac{1}{2}$ hr.

Vegetables

Blanching (scalding) is essential when dealing with vegetables; its purpose is to destroy the enzymes present, preserve the colour, flavour and texture, and, to a certain extent, to reduce the micro-organisms present; it also helps to retain Vitamin C. The blanching water can be used 6 or 7 times, thus achieving less loss of minerals and a Vitamin C build-up in the blanching water. After this time, replace by fresh water. The vegetables should be prepared and then blanched in not less than 6 pts. boiling water to each 1lb., and the water must return to the boil in 1 min. after the vegetables are added. Don't attempt to blanch more than 1 lb. at a time. Follow the times in the chart below. A blanching basket makes life easier.

After blanching, remove vegetables at once and plunge them into *ice-cold* water (add ice cubes to the water) to prevent over-cooking and to cool as quickly as possible. Cooling time is usually the same as the scalding time.

Careful timing ensures the best results, so a 'pinger' or a watch with a minute hand is really the only answer. Read 'Golden Rules before Freezing', page 10.

Notes: In an emergency—when for example you are dealing with a glut crop—vegetables can be frozen unblanched and stored for not more than 2 months, but this method is not to be generally recommended.

For the sake of convenience we have included avocados, tomatoes and chestnuts under the heading of Vegetables, since they are mostly used as savoury items. The same applies also to the Calendar of Freezing beginning on page 218.

VEGETABLE	PREPARATION	BLANCHING TIME
Asparagus	Grade into thick and thin stems but don't tie into bunches yet. Wash in cold water, blanch, cool and drain. Tie into *small* bundles, packed tips to stalks, separated by non-stick paper	Thin stem—2 min. Thick stems—4 min.
Artichokes Globe	Remove all outer coarse leaves and stalks, and trim tops and stems. Wash well in cold water, add a little lemon juice to the blanching water. Cool, and drain upside-down on absorbent paper. Pack in rigid boxes	Blanch a few at a time, in a large container for 7–10 min.
Aubergines (Egg plant)	Peel and cut roughly into 1-in. slices. Blanch, chill and dry on absorbent paper. Pack in layers, separated by non-stick paper	4 min.
Avocados	Prepare in pulp form. Peel and mash, allowing 1 tbsp. lemon juice to each avocado. Pack in small containers. Also good frozen with cream cheese to use as a party dip	
Beans—French, Runner, Broad	Select young, tender beans; wash thoroughly French—trim ends and blanch Runner—slice thickly and blanch Broad—shell and blanch In each case, cool, drain and pack	3 min. 2 min. 3 min.

VEGETABLE	PREPARATION	BLANCHING TIME
Beetroot	Choose small beets. Wash well and rub skin off after scalding. Beetroot under 1 in. in diameter may be frozen whole; large ones should be sliced or diced. Pack in cartons *Note*: Short blanching and long storage can make beetroot rubbery	Small whole—5–10 min. Large—cook until tender—45–50 min.
Broccoli	Trim off any woody parts and large leaves. Wash in salted water, and cut into small sprigs. Blanch, cool and drain well. Pack in boxes in 1–2 layers, tips to stalks	Thin stems—3 min. Medium stems—4 min. Thick stems—5 min.
Brussels sprouts	Use small compact heads. Remove outer leaves and wash thoroughly. Blanch, cool and drain well before packing	Small—3 min. Medium—4 min.
Cabbage Green & red	Use only young, crisp cabbage. Wash thoroughly, shred finely. Blanch, cool and drain. Pack in small quantities in polythene bags	$1\frac{1}{2}$ min.
Carrots	Scrape, then cut into small dice. Blanch, cool, drain and pack	3–5 min.
Cauliflower	Heads should be firm, compact and white. Wash, break into small sprigs, of about 2 in. in diameter. Add the juice of a lemon to the blanching water to keep them white; blanch, cool, drain and pack	3 min.
Celery	Trim, removing any strings, and scrub well. Cut into 1-in. lengths. Suitable only for cooked dishes	3 min.
Celeriac (Celery root)	Wash and trim. Cook until almost tender, peel and slice	—
Chestnuts	Wash nuts, cover with water, bring to the boil, drain and peel. Pack in rigid containers. Can be used to supplement raw chestnuts in recipe, can be cooked and frozen as purée for soups and sweets	1–2 min.
Chillies	Remove stalks and scoop out the seeds and pithy part. Blanch, cool, drain and pack	
Corn on the Cob	Select young yellow kernels, not starchy, over-ripe or shrunken. Remove husks and 'silks'. Blanch, cool and dry. Pack individually in freezer paper or foil *Note*: There may be loss of flavour and tenderness after freezing	Small—4 min. Medium—6 min. Large—8 min.

VEGETABLE	PREPARATION	BLANCHING TIME
Courgettes	Choose young ones. Wash and cut into $\frac{1}{2}$ in. slices. Either blanch, or sauté in a little butter	1 min.
Fennel	Trim and cut into short lengths. Blanch, cool, drain and pack	3 min.
Kohlrabi	Use small roots, 2–3 in. in diameter. Cut off tops, peel and dice. Blanch, cool, drain and pack	$1\frac{1}{2}$ min.
Leeks	Cut off tops and roots; remove coarse outside leaves. Slice into $\frac{1}{2}$-in. slices and wash well. Sauté in butter or oil, drain, cool, pack and freeze. Only suitable for casseroles or as base to Vichyssoise	Sauté 4 min.
Marrow	Young marrows can be peeled, cut into $\frac{1}{2}$–1 in. slices and blanched before packing—leave $\frac{1}{2}$ in. headspace	3 min.
Mushrooms	Freeze as Duxelles (see page 162) or choose small button mushrooms and leave whole, wipe clean but don't peel. Sauté in butter. Mushrooms larger than 1 in. in diameter: suitable only for slicing and using in cooked dishes	Sauté in butter 1 min.
Onions	Can be peeled, finely chopped and packed in small plastic containers for cooking later; packages should be over-wrapped, to prevent the smell filtering out *Note:* Small onions may be blanched whole and used later in casseroles	2 min. Small whole—4 min.
Parsnips	Trim and peel young parsnips and cut into narrow strips. Blanch, cool and dry	2 min.
Peas, Green	Use young, sweet green peas, not old or starchy. Shell and blanch, then shake the blanching basket from time to time to distribute the heat evenly. Cool, drain and pack in polythene bags or rigid containers	1 min.
Mange-tout (Sugar Peas)	Trim the ends. Blanch, cool, drain and pack	2–3 min.
Peppers, Sweet	Freeze red and green peppers separately. Wash well, remove stems and all traces of seeds and membranes. Can be blanched as halves for stuffed peppers, or in thin slices for stews and casseroles	3 min.

VEGETABLE	PREPARATION	BLANCHING TIME
Potatoes	Best frozen in the cooked form, as partially-cooked chips (fully-cooked ones are not satisfactory), croquettes or duchesse potatoes (see page 49) New: choose small even-sized potatoes. Scrape, cook fully with mint and cool. (Appearance similar to that of canned potatoes.) Chipped: Part-fry in deep fat for 2 min., cool and freeze for final frying	3 min.
Spinach	Select young leaves. Wash very thoroughly under running water; drain. Blanch in small quantities, cool quickly and press out excess moisture. Pack in rigid containers or polythene bags, leaving $\frac{1}{2}$-in. headspace	2 min.
Tomatoes—	Tomatoes are most useful if frozen as purée or as juice.	
Purée	Skin and core tomatoes, simmer in their own juice for 5 min. until soft. Pass them through a nylon sieve or liquidise, cool and pack in small containers.	—
Juice	Trim, quarter and simmer for 5–10 min. Press through a nylon sieve and season with salt—1 level tsp. salt to every 2 pts. Cool, and pack in small containers.	
Turnips	Use small, young turnips. Trim and peel. Cut into small dice, about $\frac{1}{2}$ in. Blanch, cool, drain and pack in rigid containers *Note*: Turnips may be fully cooked and mashed before freezing—leave $\frac{1}{2}$ in. headspace	$2\frac{1}{2}$ min.

Unsuitable for freezing: Chicory, endive, kale, lettuce, radishes, Jerusalem artichokes (suitable only as soups and purées).

Fruit

THE SYRUP

When preparing fruits for the freezer, make sure you have sufficient syrup available. This should be made in advance, and the best plan is to make it a day ahead and allow it to chill overnight in the refrigerator, since it has to be used cold. As a rough guide, for every 1 lb. fruit you need $\frac{1}{2}$ pt. syrup (made according to the individual directions). Dissolve the sugar in the water, bring to the boil, remove from the heat, strain if necessary and leave to cool, lightly covered. Pour the syrup over the fruit or place the fruit in a container with the syrup. Light-weight fruits which tend to rise in liquids can be held below the surface by means of a damped and crumpled piece of non-absorbent paper.

Incidentally, when you come to serve fruit frozen in syrup, open it only just before serving; keep stone fruit submerged in the syrup as long as possible.

FRUIT	PREPARATION
Apples, sliced	Peel, core and drop into cold water. Cut into approx. $\frac{1}{4}$-in. slices. Blanch for 2–3 min. and cool in ice-cold water before packing. Useful for pies and flans.
Purée	Peel, core and stew in the minimum amount of water—sweetened or un-sweetened. Sieve or liquidise. Leave to cool before packing.
Apricots	Plunge them into boiling water for 30 sec. to loosen the skins, then peel. Either (a) cut in half or slice into syrup made with 1 lb. sugar to 2 pts. water, with some ascorbic acid (vitamin C) added to prevent browning; for each 1 lb. pack allow 200–300 mg. ascorbic acid. Immerse the apricots by placing a piece of clean, crumpled, non-absorbent paper on the fruit, under the lid. (b) Leave whole, and freeze in cold syrup. After long storage, an almond flavour may develop round the stone.
Berries, etc. (including currants and cherries)	All may be frozen by the dry pack method, but the dry sugar pack method is suitable for soft fruits e.g. raspberries. *Dry Pack:* Sort the fruit; some whole berries may be left on their sprigs or stems for use as decoration. Spread the fruit on paper-lined trays or baking sheets, put into the freezer until frozen, then pack. *Dry Sugar Pack:* Pack dried whole fruit with the stated quantity of sugar (4–6 oz. to 1 lb. fruit), mix together and seal.
Blackberries	Dry sugar pack—allow 8 oz. sugar to 2 lb. fruit. Leave a headspace, and pack in rigid containers.
Blueberries	Wash in chilled water and drain thoroughly. Can be (a) dry packed (b) dry sugar-packed—about 4 oz. sugar to 1–$1\frac{1}{2}$ lb. fruit. Slightly crush berries, mix with sugar until dissolved and then pack in rigid containers; (c) frozen in cold syrup—2 lb. sugar dissolved in 2 pt. water.
Gooseberries	Wash and thoroughly dry fruit. Pack (a) by dry method in polythene bags, without sugar; use for pie fillings; (b) in cold syrup using 2 lb. sugar to 2 pt. water; (c) as purée—stew fruit in a very little water, press through a nylon sieve and sweeten to taste; useful for fools and mousses.
Loganberries	Choose firm, clean fruit. Remove stalks and dry-pack in rigid containers. Dry-sugar-pack—see Blackberries
Strawberries and Raspberries	Choose firm, clean, dry fruit; remove stalks. Pack (a) by dry method; (b) by dry sugar method—4 oz. sugar to each 1 lb. fruit; (c) as purée—pass through a nylon sieve or liquidise clean berries; sweeten to taste—about 2 oz. sugar per $\frac{1}{2}$ lb.—and freeze in small containers, useful for ice creams, sorbets, sauces or mousses.
Blackcurrants	Wash, top and tail. (a) Dry and use dry pack method for whole fruit. (b) Purée—cook to a purée with very little water and brown sugar, according to taste.
Redcurrants	Wash and dry the whole fruit, then freeze on a paper-lined tray in a single layer until frozen. Pack

FRUIT	PREPARATION
Cherries	Remove the stalks. Wash and dry. Use any of these methods: (a) dry pack method: place whole fruit on a paper-lined baking sheet, freeze until firm, then pack. (b) Dry sugar pack (8 oz. sugar to 2 lb. stoned cherries), pack in containers cooked or uncooked, best used stewed for pie fillings. (c) Cover with cold syrup (1 lb. sugar to 2 pts. water, mixed with $\frac{1}{2}$ tsp. ascorbic acid per 2 pts. syrup); leave headspace. Take care not to open packet until required, as fruit loses colour rapidly on exposure to the air.
Damsons	Wash in cold water. The skins are inclined to toughen during freezing. Best packing methods are: (a) in a purée, to be used later in pies; (b) halve, remove the stones and pack in cold syrup (1 lb. sugar to 2 pts. water); they will need cooking after freezing—can be used as stewed fruit.
Figs	Wash gently to avoid bruising. Remove stems, then use one of the following methods: (a) freeze unsweetened, either whole or peeled, in polythene bags; (b) peel and pack in cold syrup (1 lb. sugar to 2 pts. water) (c) leave whole and wrap in foil—suitable for dessert figs.
Grapefruit	Peel fruit, removing all pith; segment and pack (a) in cold syrup (equal quantities of sugar and water—use any juice from the fruit to make up the syrup). (b) In dry sugar pack—allowing 8 oz. sugar to 1 lb. fruit, sprinkled over fruit; when juices start to run, pack in rigid containers.
Grapes	The seedless variety can be packed whole; others should be skinned, pipped and halved. Pack in cold syrup—1 lb. sugar to 2 pts. water.
Greengages	Wash in cold water, halve, remove stones and pack in syrup—1 lb. sugar to 2 pts. water, with ascorbic acid added (see Apricots). Place in rigid containers. Do not open pack until required, as fruit loses colour rapidly. Skins tend to toughen during freezing.
Lemons and Limes	There are various methods. (a) Squeeze out juice and freeze it in ice-cube trays; remove frozen cubes to polythene bags for storage. (b) Leave whole; slice or segment before freezing. (c) Remove all pith from the peel, cut into julienne strips, blanch for 1 min., cool and pack; use for garnishing dishes. (d) Mix grated lemon peel and a little sugar to serve alongside pancakes. (e) Remove slivers of peel, free of pith, and freeze in foil packs to add to drinks.
Mangoes	Peel and slice ripe fruit into cold syrup—1 lb. sugar to 2 pts. water; add 2 tbsps. lemon juice to each 2 pts. syrup. Serve with additional lemon juice.
Melons	Cantaloup and honeydew melons freeze quite well (though they lose their crispness when thawed), but the seeds of watermelon make it more difficult to prepare. Cut in half and seed, then cut flesh into balls, cubes or slices and put straight into cold syrup—1 lb. sugar to 2 pts. water. Alternatively, use dry pack method, with a little sugar sprinkled over. Pack in polythene bags.
Oranges	Prepare and pack as for grapefruit or squeeze out and freeze the juice; add sugar if desired and freeze in small quantities in containers or as frozen orange cubes. Grate peel for orange sugar as for lemon sugar.

Peaches	Really ripe peaches are best skinned and stoned under running water, as scalding them to ease skinning will soften and slightly discolour the flesh. Firm peaches are treated in the usual way. Brush over with lemon juice. (a) Pack halves or slices in cold syrup—1 lb. sugar to 2 pts. water, with ascorbic acid added (see Apricots); pack in rigid containers, leaving $\frac{1}{2}$ in. headspace. (b) Purée peeled and stoned peaches by using a nylon sieve or liquidiser; mix in 1 tbsp. lemon juice and 4 oz. sugar to each 1 lb. fruit—suitable for sorbets and soufflé-type desserts.
Pears	It is really only worthwhile freezing pears if you have a big crop from your garden, as they discolour rapidly, and the texture of thawed pears can be unattractively soft. Peel, quarter, remove core and dip in lemon juice immediately. Poach in syrup—1 lb. sugar to 2 pts. water—for $1\frac{1}{2}$ min. Drain, cool and pack in the cold syrup.
Pineapple	Peel and core, then slice, dice, crush or cut into wedges. (a) Pack unsweetened in boxes, separated by non-stick paper. (b) Pack in syrup—1 lb. sugar to 2 pts. water—in rigid containers; include any pineapple juice from the preparation. (c) Pack the crushed pineapple in rigid containers, allowing 4 oz. sugar to about $\frac{3}{4}$ lb. fruit.
Plums	Wash, halve and discard stones. Freeze in syrup with ascorbic acid (see Apricots; use 1 lb. sugar to 2 pts. water). Pack in rigid containers. Do not open packet until required, as the fruit loses colour rapidly.
Rhubarb	Wash, trim and cut into $\frac{1}{2}$–1 in. lengths. Heat in boiling water for 1 min. and cool quickly. Pack in cold syrup, using equal quantities sugar and water, or dry-pack, to be used later for pies and crumbles.

Fruits not suitable for freezing: Bananas, pomegranates.

What to do when— a calendar of freezing

Fresh foods which are available all the year round don't of course justify freezer space, except for the sake of convenience.

With the wide choice of imported fruit and vegetables, and the extended periods when we can buy our own home-grown vegetables, seasons are to a certain extent disappearing, but we do still get gluts for a number of reasons, and that's where the freezer can really help make the most of a bargain (though never forget that quality is of prime importance).

We list here monthly reminders of items which may be good buys and are then worth considering for the freezer. Obviously, even from year to year, fluctuations do occur, and therefore the seasons may vary; in the main our lists cover the peak buying or cropping times.

All the year round

Mushrooms, potatoes, cabbages, sweet peppers (look out for good buys and freeze them down for soups, dips, etc.), carrots, cauliflower, tomatoes, onions, grapes, oranges, lemons (it's worth freezing citrus juice and rind when the price is good and the fruit thin-skinned and full of juice), grapefruit (here again you can find better quality fruit at certain times—look for a fruit that is heavy for its size, and freeze in segments; September/November is a good time). Chicken, capons, ducklings, turkey and rabbit are other good standbys.

JANUARY

FRUIT	VEGETABLES	FISH	GAME	POULTRY
apples, cooking	aubergines	halibut: good	partridge	capons
apricots	broccoli	for freezing	pheasant	chickens
cranberries	celery, home-	salmon: cheap-	(not Scotland)	goose
oranges, Seville	grown	est to buy	plover	guinea fowl
peaches, imported	baby onions	and use just	snipe	pigeon: freezes
pineapple	seakale	now	teal	well
	horseradish		hare	turkey: sometimes
			venison	cheap after
			woodcock	Christmas
			mallard	rabbit
			capercaillie	quail

Notes
1. Citrus fruits with a limited season (Sevilles, tangerines, limes) can be scrubbed, packed in suitable quantities and frozen whole until required. To make marmalade the frozen fruit is cooked by the 'whole' method; alternatively, it may be cut up and cooked first.
2. Make up pastry lids, flan rings, etc., from any remaining pastry left over from Christmas.
3. Now the children are back at school, stock up your freezer. Have you a supply of casseroles so that you can produce a meal straight from the freezer for unexpected guests? If not, prepare now!

FEBRUARY

FRUIT	VEGETABLES	FISH	GAME	POULTRY
apples; cooking	Jerusalem arti-	mackerel: first	plover	capon
and eating	chokes	of its two	hare	chicken
apricots	aubergines	seasons,	venison	goose
grapes	avocados	second being		rabbit
grapefruit	beetroot	Sept./Oct.		quail
oranges, Seville	broccoli	salmon: Feb./		
peaches, imported	cabbage	Sept.		
pineapple, im-	celery, home-	shrimps		
ported	grown			
	horseradish			
	mushrooms			
	onions			
	parsnips			
	old potatoes			
	peppers, green			
	savoy			
	seakale			
	spring greens			
	swedes			
	tomatoes			
	turnips			

Notes
1. During a quiet moment this month, make a few Easter biscuits, and perhaps an egg-shaped sponge coated in chocolate, ready for Easter.
2. Make a few family favourite dishes for the children to enjoy while home at half-term.
3. It could be worthwhile freezing some leeks for Vichyssoise before the season wanes.

MARCH

FRUIT	VEGETABLES	FISH	GAME	POULTRY
pineapple	aubergines	mackerel	plover	capon
	horseradish	salmon: Feb./		chicken
	parsnips	Sept.		duck, duckling
	seakale	scallops: Sept./		pigeon
		Apr.		turkey
				rabbit
				quail

Note

Now's the time when eggs may be cheaper, so make lemon curd. What about making and freezing one or two Pavlovas topped with an orange curd filling for a simple dessert?

APRIL

FRUIT	VEGETABLES	FISH	POULTRY
rhubarb	aubergines	lobster: Apr./Sept.,	capon
	carrots	but best to freeze	chicken
	cauliflower	June/Aug. Freeze whole,	duck, duckling
	spinach	cooked. Allow to cool,	guinea fowl
	seakale	wrap in foil and place	pigeon
		in freezer bag	rabbit
		halibut	quail
		mackerel: Apr. is end	
		of first mackerel	
		season	
		plaice or dab: Apr./Oct.	
		Best to buy and	
		freeze end of Apr.	
		beginning May	
		salmon: Feb./Sept.	

Note

With summer fast approaching, prepare in advance flans, pasties, mousses and a good supply of cakes and biscuits to be taken away on holiday or on picnics.

MAY

FRUIT	VEGETABLES	FISH	POULTRY
apricots	asparagus	haddock: May/July	capon
pineapple	aubergines	halibut: Nov./June	chicken
rhubarb	broccoli	plaice or dab: see notes	duck, duckling
	carrots	for Apr.	pigeon
	cauliflower	lobster: Apr./Sept.	rabbit
	courgettes	prawns, shrimps: May/	quail
	new potatoes	Dec. Can be left whole	
	peppers, green	and frozen; use later	
	spinach	in dishes or for garnishing.	
	tomatoes	If you have plenty of	
		time, shell prawns or	
		shrimps before freezing	

1. Salmon will be plentiful this month for making mousses, pâtés or cocktail sandwiches and for freezing as cutlets.
2. Looking towards the days of packed meals for outdoor eating, prepare a quantity of individual frozen sandwiches, small pies and cakes—especially good for children on holiday outings. Wrap individually in foil or polythene bags for freezing. To thaw for lunch-time, remove from freezer early in morning, leave in wrapping and pack for carrying. Add fresh salad and fruit, to round off the meal.

JUNE

FRUIT	VEGETABLES	FISH	POULTRY
apples (windfalls)	asparagus	haddock: best to	capon
apricots	aubergines	freeze this month	chicken
cherries	broccoli	halibut: end of its	duck, duckling
mangoes	carrots	season	guinea fowl
peaches, English	cauliflower	plaice or dab	pigeon
pineapple	courgettes	trout, sea and river	rabbit
raspberries	garden peas	crab: best to freeze	quail
rhubarb	new potatoes	in summer—June/Aug.	
strawberries	peppers, green	(a) whole, cooked	
	and red	and frozen; prepared	
	spinach	afterwards—though	
	tomatoes	this method is not	
		recommended	
		(b) dressed and flesh	
		piled into shell.	
		Just needs defrosting	
		before use	
		crayfish: June/Aug.	
		Freeze:	
		(a) whole, cooked	
		(b) tails—freeze	
		raw for use later—	
		poached or baked	
		lobster: best to	
		freeze now—whole	
		and cooked	
		prawns, shrimps: freeze	
		shelled and cooked	

Notes
1. June and July are the time to freeze soft fruits, for winter use in sauces, sorbets, ice creams.
2. Make freezer jam with raspberries and cherries.
3. Prepare a 'nest egg' of parsley and mint from the garden for winter use.
4. The new variety of small one-person cauliflower is ideal for the freezer.

JULY

FRUIT	VEGETABLES	FISH	POULTRY
apricots	artichokes, globe	haddock: last month this	capon
blackcurrants	aubergines	is good for freezing	chicken

JULY (contd)

FRUIT	VEGETABLES	FISH	POULTRY
cherries	beans, French	plaice or dab: see	duck, duckling
fresh figs	broad	previous notes	guinea fowl
gooseberries	beetroot	trout, river and sea	pigeon
seedless grapes	broccoli	crab, crayfish: see	rabbit
limes	cauliflower	previous notes	quail
loganberries	courgettes	lobster: see previous	
mangoes	garden peas	notes	
nectarines	peppers, green	prawns, shrimps	
yellow peaches	and red		
(imported) or	new potatoes		
English	spinach		
raspberries	tomatoes		
strawberries			

Notes
1. Track down limes about now and freeze whole, or pack juice and peel separately for round-the-year Daiquiris.
2. Take advantage of summer fruits to make fruit salad.
3. It would be worthwhile about now to prepare a macédoine of diced root vegetables—with or without peas

AUGUST

FRUIT	VEGETABLES	FISH	GAME	POULTRY
apricots	artichokes, globe	plaice or dab	black grouse	capon
blackberries,	aubergines	trout	grouse	chicken
cultivated	beans, French,	crab	venison: Aug/	duck, duckling
blackcurrants and	broad, runner	crayfish	Feb.	guinea fowl
redcurrants	beetroot	lobster	snipe	pigeon
cherries	horseradish	prawns	hare	rabbit
figs, fresh	marrow	shrimps	ptarmigan	quail
gooseberries	peppers, green			
seedless grapes	and red			
greengages	peas, home-grown			
limes	red cabbage			
loganberries	spinach			
peaches, yellow	tomatoes			
and English				
plums				
raspberries (on				
the wane)				
strawberries (on				
the wane)				

Notes
1. There may be some late apple windfalls now; though under-ripe, they purée quite satisfactorily.
2. Now is the time to think about making jugged hare, or to marinade or stew venison—see recipes in 'So Good to Freeze'.

SEPTEMBER

FRUIT	VEGETABLES	FISH	GAME	POULTRY
apples, cooking	artichokes, globe	mackerel: second	black grouse	capon
bilberries	aubergines	of its two	grouse	chicken
blackberries	beans, runner	seasons	hare	duck
damsons	beetroot	trout, sea and	venison	goose
fresh figs	broccoli	river	snipe	guinea fowl
greengages	courgettes	lobster: see	teal	pigeon
melons	leeks	previous notes	mallard	turkey
yellow peaches	marrow	prawns	partridge	quail
(on the wane)	baby onions	shrimps	ptarmigan	rabbit
pears	peppers, green			
plums	and red			
	red cabbage			
	spinach			
	swedes			
	tomatoes			

Notes
1. Buy freshly-killed game from your butcher now, to enjoy it when out of season, but make sure it really is freshly-killed.
2. Late raspberries and strawberries are sometimes available, and are worth catching if you missed the main crop.
3. A good month for making ratatouille.
4. Now is the time to start looking out for economical bulk buys in cooking apples, to freeze down as purée or slices for pies, etc.
5. Fresh grated coconut freezes quite well and is useful for making coconut milk to use in curries or as flavouring for glacé icing.

OCTOBER

FRUIT	VEGETABLES	FISH	GAME	POULTRY
apples, cooking	aubergines	mackerel: Sept./	black grouse	capon
damsons	beetroot	Oct.	grouse	chicken
melons	Brussels sprouts	salmon, Scottish	partridge	duck, duckling
plums	celery, home-	(at cheapest	pheasant	goose
pumpkins	grown	around end of	plover	guinea fowl
nectarines	horseradish	Oct./Jan.)	snipe	pigeon
peaches	leeks	prawns	teal	turkey
pears	marrows	shrimps	hare	rabbit
quinces	baby onions		venison	quail
	parsnips		capercaillie	
	peppers, green		woodcock	
	spinach		mallard	
	swedes		ptarmigan	
	tomatoes			
	chestnuts			

Notes
1. Buy fresh turkeys now, while they are cheap, and prepare for the freezer, ready for Christmas.
2. Make simple cocktail nibblers: they'll just need re-heating for entertaining guests and/or for drinks parties.
3. Chestnuts can be prepared ahead for Christmas.

NOVEMBER

FRUIT	VEGETABLES	FISH	GAME	POULTRY
apples, cooking	aubergines	halibut: Nov./	black grouse	capon
cranberries	broccoli	June	grouse	chicken
pears	Brussels sprouts	salmon: Scottish	partridge	goose
mandarins	celery, home-	cheapest now	pheasant	guinea fowl
tangerines	grown		plover	pigeon
	horseradish		snipe	turkey
	leeks		teal	rabbit
	baby onions		hare	quail
	peppers, green		venison	
	red cabbage		capercaillie	
	swedes		ptarmigan	
			mallard	
			woodcock	
			wild goose	

Notes

1. Make various finishing touches and garnishing ideas, as shown in the colour picture facing page 176, ready for Christmas.
2. You might like to preserve some of the more seasonal citrus fruits, like mandarins and tangerines, while they're available.

DECEMBER

FRUIT	VEGETABLES	FISH	GAME	POULTRY
apples, cooking	artichokes,	halibut: Nov./	black grouse	capon
apricots	Jerusalem	June	grouse	chicken
cranberries	aubergines	prawns	partridge	goose
grapes	avocados	shrimps	pheasant	pigeon
pineapple	broccoli		plover	turkey
	Brussels sprouts		snipe	rabbit
	celery, home-		teal	quail
	grown		hare	
	baby onions		venison	
	parsnips		capercaillie	
	peppers, green		ptarmigan	
	red cabbage		mallard	
	swedes		woodcock	
	tomatoes		wild goose	

Notes

1. At the beginning of the month, ready for Christmas, make cranberry jelly, mince pies, stuffings, breadcrumbs for sauce; blanch Brussels sprouts and broccoli.
2. Make sure you have supplies of double cream for serving with desserts.

PART 3

What You Need to Know about Freezers

Choose a home freezer

Even if the mouth-watering recipes in Part I have got you raring to go, don't rush out to the shops and buy the first likely-looking freezer within your price range. You're going to be living with it for a long time (15 years is the average freezer life expectancy), so it's worth while making sure you suit each other.

As soon as you start your hunt, you'll realise that freezers fall into two main categories: upright models and chest models. And as soon as you start asking advice from your freezer-owning friends, you'll realise that each type has adherents as fierce as any political party. In a way this is reassuring. If people with uprights insist they're best, and people with chests insist *they're* best, you can't go far wrong whichever you choose. But so you can join in the battle fully armed with information, here are the essential differences.

Which type?

Upright freezers are very like refrigerators in appearance. They stack their storage upwards and have front-opening doors, whereas chest freezers stack their storage sideways and have top-opening lids. This means uprights take up far less floor space—sometimes as little as 2 square feet for a big 12 cubic foot model—which gives them a marked advantage if you're trying to fit your freezer into a tiny kitchen. (Not that freezers *have* to fit into the kitchen, but that's something we'll tell you more about later.) As well as looking like refrigerators, upright freezers are just as easy to load and unload, too. They come generously fitted with shelves and/or pull-out baskets, so everything's within easy reach, and you can see what you're after as soon as you open the door. This gives them another marked advantage, if organisation isn't your strong point. With chest freezers, even though models come with one or two baskets (and if there's room it's always possible to add more), there's far less guidance about how you store your food. The internal fittings don't dictate what you can and can't do, so the muddle-minded could find themselves rummaging through parcels like a Post Office sorter at Christmas. And what's more (people with weak backs please note) they'd find themselves doing the sorting in a very uncomfortable position, because they'd have to reach down as much as 30 in. to pick up packets that happened to be on the bottom.

All this seems to be swinging the decision in favour of uprights, but of course freedom to store food how you like it can be a positive advantage to anyone clear-minded, particularly if awkward-shaped items are to be frozen. Joints of meat, for instance, fit together quite happily in the wide-open-spaces of a chest, but just one fair-sized joint might take up almost a whole shelf in an upright and waste the space around it. And chest freezers have one advantage that will always ensure them a big following: they're generally cheaper to buy.

One final variation on the theme: it's possible to buy combined refrigerator/ freezers, which in effect, consist of a conventional fridge up above with an upright freezer down below—or *vice versa*. These obviously save floor space in a tiny kitchen, and as most offer a 6 cubic foot freezing capacity, they only make sense for people with small-to-medium freezing ambitions.

How big?

It's difficult to tell in advance how big a freezer anyone's going to need, and the following is only a rough rule of thumb. Each cubic foot of storage space is reckoned to house between 20 and 25 lb. of food, so if you allow 2 cubic feet of space per member of the family, plus 2 for luck, you won't be far out in your calculations. Like all rules of thumb, however, this is an over-simplification. One cubic foot *may* store 25 lb. of obligingly neat things like packets of frozen spinach and cod steaks, but the 25 lb. shrinks rapidly when you think in terms of angular legs of lamb and knobbly chickens. And obviously a housewife living in the country, frantically trying to keep up with her bean-stalks and apple trees, is going to need far more freezing space than a town housewife dependent on her local greengrocer. But despite all these variables, there does seem to be one constant: almost all freezer-owners wish they'd bought a bigger one. Apparently once they've got the hang of freezing they want to freeze more and more, and—provided they can keep pace with the eating—this is the most economical way of going about it.

How much?

Now comes the crunch. How much do freezers cost? Well, both upright and chest freezers get proportionately cheaper as they get bigger, which is one good reason for buying the biggest you can afford.

Even the smallest freezer will set you back at least £85. The average purchase price now (i.e., 1976) is around £170–£270, for a 12–14 cubic foot freezer, but you can pay about £400 for a very large one or a sophisticated frost-free model.

FREEZER BUYING POINTS—*Look for a 'fast freeze' switch that lowers the temperature enough to freeze newly added items quickly; an alarm light that goes on when freezer temperature rises above normal; easily accessible controls; well-designed shelves and storage baskets; special compartments for newly-added items to be frozen; a light to make it easier to find things*

Enough to make a major hole in anyone's bank balance, but—apart from hire-purchase or credit-sales, etc.—there's no way round it. Second-hand freezers are only worth considering if the seller can guarantee servicing facilities. And often, what's offered as a second-hand freezer isn't a freezer at all: it's a conservator, meant for storing *already* frozen food, but incapable of satisfactorily freezing *fresh* food from scratch. To make sure that you are getting a true food freezer look for the four star symbol which is a sign that the appliance is designed to freeze fresh food as well as to store frozen food. Incidentally frozen food compartments in domestic refrigerators are only intended for storing frozen foods. With one star they can store already frozen food for up to one week and with two stars up to one month. Three-star compartments can store already frozen food for three months and some will freeze small quantities of fresh food. But small really *means* small—about 3 lb. in any one 24-hr. period. Buying a freezer does involve finding a big lump of money, especially as you have to find another big lump to fill it with food, but a glance at 'Long-term Running Costs', below, should convince you you're doing the right thing.

Where to put the freezer

Obviously the ideal home for a freezer (provided it doesn't have to go bang up against a cooker or central heating boiler—both situations that would work the compressor to death), is the kitchen. If you've plumped for a chest model, anything up to about 8 cubic feet will probably come in a convenient work-top height of between 33 and 36 in. This not only provides a handy extra work surface, but means the freezer can fit snugly in with your existing kitchen units. (Unfortunately it will probably stick out at the front, but perfectionists can always bring the other units forward by adding a false back for 100% alignment.) It's difficult to make larger chest-types, particularly the 12 cubic foot-plus ones, look an integral part of the kitchen. They may be too high to fit in, and all you can do is make sure you situate yours at the *end* of a row of kitchen units—so you can lift the lid without banging into a top cupboard!

Wherever possible, uprights, too, prefer being placed at the end of a row of units, so that there's a handy loading and unloading surface nearby. At first glance, it looks a good idea to tuck them away in a corner, but this doesn't turn out too well in practice. Some uprights have doors that need opening through an angle greater than 90°, which means that if in a corner you wouldn't be able to open them wide enough to pull out a shelf or basket. And even if the door does open within its own width, you'd still be hemmed in by the wall as you attempted to load and unload.

No room in the kitchen

All this presumes there's room in your kitchen for a freezer, but what happens if you've already squeezed a quart into a pint pot and can't manage any more? You just have to find a home for it somewhere else. Fortunately the somewhere else can be anywhere that's cool, dry and allows air to circulate freely around the freezer. For tight fits where air can't circulate, it's possible to buy a freezer with a fan-cooled condensor: see 'How It Works'. It could be the old walk-in larder; the new utility room; the space under the stairs; even up in the landing alcove (hang a pretty roller blind in front and no-one will be any the wiser). The spare bedroom's an equally good place—provided you realise the freezer's going to give off unwanted heat in the summer, and provided you warn guests: otherwise they're likely to jump out of their skins when the thermostat-controlled compressor starts up in the middle of the night. Freezers with a skin-type condenser (see p. 232) are the quietest.

Again though, all this presumes there's room in your house for a freezer, and if there isn't, you just have to find a home for it outside. Here, the biggest problem is damp, so the potting shed's right out if the mushrooms grow through the floor and the rain leaks in through the roof. Any *slight* rising dampness can be counteracted by standing it on wooden blocks, raising the freezer about 2 in. off the ground to allow for air circulation all round, but probably the best protection you can give the cabinet is a regular going-over with a silicone polish. This applies particularly if you put your freezer in the garage (one of the most popular places, because it's likely to be near at hand, soundly built and ready-wired for electricity). However dry it is, the minute someone drives in a wet car, the wet's going to make a beeline for the freezer's warm surface, where it will condense and rust the metal.

What other drawbacks are there? Well, the thought of burglars is worrying (remember there'll probably be about £100 worth of food ready for the taking), but you can easily reduce the chances of theft by buying a freezer with a lock in the first place. Similarly, if the thought of the freezer quietly breaking down

FREEZER PACKING—*To get the maximum use from the freezer space, pack it neatly; with a certain amount of organisation things are much more quickly found. An upright freezer with two compartments lends itself to the type of system shown in our photograph—the top is reserved for more regular use, and labelled to cover complete meals, while the lower cabinet holds straightforward butchers' meat, fish, garden produce and bulk cookery. Do remember that the door temperature is slightly higher than that of the body of the freezer, so this is the place to keep short-term storage items*

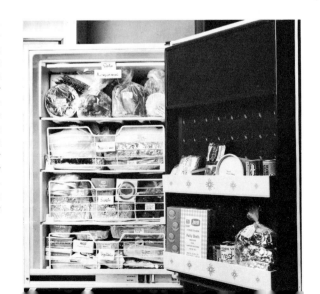

at the bottom of the garden and not getting discovered for a week makes you anxious, all you have to do is get an alarm bell fitted, and it will ring inside the house if the temperature ever rises to danger level. (From time to time you'll have to check that the batteries haven't gone flat.) A final word of warning: don't take 'the bottom of the garden' too literally. It won't be much fun staggering through the snow with the Boeuf Bourguignonne. If there's absolutely no alternative and the freezer has to live a long way from the house, try to squeeze a small freezer indoors somewhere, or plan to replace your existing refrigerator with a fridge/freezer, so you only need stock up from Big Brother about once a month.

The price of installation

If you're lucky enough to have a spare three-pin socket outlet conveniently near where you want to run your freezer, installation isn't going to cost you anything. But if it isn't *really* near, make sure any connecting flex is fixed securely to the wall, because people who trip over trailing flexes only pause to curse: they don't stop to check whether they've jerked out the plug. Ideally, the socket should be independent (as opposed to being part of a twin or used with an adaptor), because it's all too easy to switch off the wrong appliance by mistake. And if your children are still at the itchy-fingered stage, invest in a piece of adhesive tape, so you can stick the switch securely down.

Where there isn't a spare three-pin socket outlet (perhaps the freezer's going in the garage, where the wiring's very basic), resist the temptation to connect it to an ordinary electric light point 'for the time being'. Using an unearthed light circuit isn't just dangerous—it's expensive too, if a fuse blows and leaves £s worth of food thawing out unnoticed. An electrician is going to charge £20–£30 for installing a three-pin socket outlet (safely earthed, and intended for the amount of current you'll be putting through it), in the house or a garage which is adjacent to the house (if the garage is not near the house it'll cost quite a bit more).

Running costs

On average, a freezer costs slightly more to run than a refrigerator. Obviously, small ones cost less than large ones—but not proportionately less. Freezers use up about $1\frac{1}{2}$–2 units of electricity per cubic foot per week. The amount of electricity used depends on the amount of food in the freezer and how frequently you open the door. It's most economical to have the freezer as full as possible and to open the door as little as possible.

These are only rough estimates, of course. Someone who keeps the freezer in a cool garage and only opens it twice a week is going to get a smaller electricity bill than someone who keeps it in a warm kitchen, and has several children helping themselves to ice cream twice a day. This is why, if your freezer's going to be surrounded by warm air and is going to be opened frequently, it's worth considering a chest freezer in preference to an upright. Chest freezers are slightly cheaper to run because of that familiar law of nature: warm air rises. With a top-opening chest, cold air stays sluggishly on the bottom and only a little manages to escape, whereas with a top-to-bottom-opening upright, much more air manages a getaway, and the compressor has to set to work to get the temperature back down where it should be. Alternatively, consider a two-door upright, which is virtually two freezers in one. Then you can use the top for short-term storage, the bottom for long-term storage.

Long-term running costs

Salesmen are very fond of saying that a freezer pays for itself in the first year of operation, but even taking into account savings of up to one-third with bulk buying, they're being optimistic. The benefits are much longer-term, especially if you are honest enough to admit that savings on bulk buying can get cancelled out by improved standards of eating. If you really want to know how much a freezer is going to cost you, take a do-it-yourself accountancy approach.

Let's suppose, for instance, that you're a family of four. Allowing 2 cubic feet per person, plus 2 for luck, this brings you up to a 10 cubic foot freezer, so you may well have added an extra 2 and bought a 12 cubic foot freezer. This will have cost you between £170–£270, but we'll say £200 for the sake of argument. Installation will have cost about £20, and filling it up with food another £60–£100 (a frightening amount to find, but it only happens once, and from then onwards you can 'top up' fairly painlessly). Now let's suppose that instead of spending your £300 in this way, you'd invested your money at 5% per annum. This would bring in about £15 a year, which means your freezer's costing you £15 a year before you even switch it on. What's more, as it's only going to live about 15 years, it's going to be depreciating at the rate of about £13 a year. Now add on a generous £25 a year for electricity and £10 a year for insurance (see 'Help!' below), and owning a freezer turns out to be costing you about £48 a year. In other words, this is the minimum amount of money you've got to be able to save on food each year—just to break even, let alone make a profit.

It's quite easy to find out whether you're managing it or not. A 12 cubic foot freezer stores a maximum of 300 lb. of food. If your family eats its way through almost this amount three times a year (at the rate of 4 lb. per person per week), at the most it's going to cost 5 pence to store each 1 lb.—an amount you should easily be able to save by buying in bulk instead of at normal retail prices. (And obviously, if you freeze a lot of your own produce, you're going to be saving a great deal more.) So how can you lose? A freezer begins to *cost* money instead of *saving* when you use it as a long-term store instead of keeping the contents regularly turning over. If you keep a packet of fish fingers hanging about for a year, it's going to have cost you 15 pence a pound to store, and the chances of having bought it at such a big reduction in the first place are practically nil. The moral of the story: only out-of-season foods should be stored for longer than three months. Keep the rest turning over, and you'll save all the way.

How it works

The crucial operating parts of a freezer are the compressor, the condenser and the evaporator, and the magic ingredient is refrigerant vapour. When the motor is started, refrigerant vapour is drawn from the evaporator by the compressor and is forced under pressure into the condenser. Here the heat absorbed in the evaporator, together with that generated in the compressor, is given off, and as the vapour cools it condenses into a liquid. The liquid refrigerant is then forced into the evaporator at high pressure through a fine-bore capillary tube or expansion valve, and the sudden fall in pressure as it passes into the evaporator causes the refrigerant to boil fiercely, and to change back to vapour (a process that absorbs heat). *This* is what freezes the food and keeps it frozen. The vapour then passes on to the compressor, so that the whole cycle can start again.

In most freezers the compressor is sealed in a self-contained unit. It doesn't need any attention—which is why most manufacturers feel safe in giving it a 5-year guarantee.

The condenser is a system of tubes that transfers the heat to the outside air. There are three main types. The static plate condenser has a kind of radiator at the back of the cabinet which dissipates the heat; the fan-cooled condenser has a fan that forces the heated air through a grille in the front of the cabinet; and the skin-type condenser transfers the heat directly through the walls of the cabinet. If you have to fit your freezer into a confined space, make sure you buy one with a fan-cooled condenser—check this point when you buy (you can usually see the grille at the front). A freezer with a static plate condenser can also be fitted into a line of equipment but you must leave space at the back for air circulation. A freezer with a skin-type condenser must be placed so that air can circulate freely around it to carry the warm air away.

The evaporator is the system of coils that absorbs the heat from the frozen food. In chest freezers, the coils are attached to the inner lining of the cabinet, which explains why food has to be frozen against the walls, if there isn't a freezing compartment. In upright freezers, it's often possible to see the evaporator coils snaking their way underneath the special freezing shelves.

Cleaning and caring

As you'll discover when you come to 'Help!', freezers rarely break down, and if they do, there's nothing you can do about it beyond screaming for an expert. But what you can do is look after your freezer properly, and this starts as soon as it gets delivered. First move is to give it a quick wipe round inside with a cloth or sponge soaked in a solution of bicarbonate of soda. (This consists of 1 tbsp. of bicarbonate of soda to a quart of warm water.) Make sure the freezer is thoroughly dry before plugging in, wait two or three hours for the temperature to drop, and you're all systems go for the inaugural bout of freezing.

As soon as the freezer is in use, frost will start building up on all the interior surfaces. This is quite normal, and you don't have to worry about it until it becomes about $\frac{1}{4}$ in. thick. At this point, there's nothing for it but to get down to defrosting operations. How often you have to tackle this minor chore depends on your type of freezer, where you keep it, and how often you use it. A frequently-opened upright in a warm room could need defrosting three times a year. A seldom-opened chest, in a morgue-like cellar, might need only an annual attack.

Either way, the main thing is not to put off the evil day. If you do, packages of food will start sticking together; you won't be able to read the labels; and you won't be able to pull out shelves and baskets without practically dislocating a shoulder blade. In addition, the ice will be filling up valuable storage space—and it may even rim the lid or door until it's impossible to shut the freezer properly. It's obviously best to fall into a natural defrosting rhythm, picking the times when your freezer's at its emptiest. This could be in the New Year, when all the Christmas food has been demolished. It could be in the summer, leaving you ready and prepared for the gluts of autumn fruit. You'll soon learn which times suit you best and realise that whenever they arise, they present a good opportunity to do some serious stocktaking.

A few hours before you start defrosting, 'freeze' plenty of newspapers or a clean old sheet to provide chilled wrappings. Switch off the current, and remove the frozen food, wrapping it in the newspapers, or in the special sacks you get for bulk purchases at freezer centres, and placing it somewhere cool. The fridge is the perfect place, but if there isn't enough room, remember to stack the wrapped food as closely together as possible; the more compactly it's stacked the colder it will stay, and it's not a bad idea to minimise air-circulation by covering the pile with a rug or blanket.

Leave the freezer open meantime, and to speed up the melting rate, place bowls of hot water inside. (If you're in a desperate hurry, you *can* use a hand-held hair drier on the ice-covered walls, but keep it constantly on the move, and don't concentrate on just one area.) Rather than wait for the ice to melt, start scraping down the sides and shelves as soon as it's loosened, because it's much easier clearing out ice chippings than mopping up water. However, never *ever*, use anything metal. The ideal weapon is a wooden or plastic spatula, and if you spread a towel on the bottom of the freezer to catch the pieces, it will be far easier to lift out than having to fish out fragments of ice individually.

Finally, wipe round the freezer with the same solution of bicarbonate of soda as above, make sure it's thoroughly dry, and switch on the current again. The whole performance should only take an hour (perhaps two for a big freezer), though it's best to wait another hour before actually replacing the food.

You ought to remove the dust from the fan of a fan assisted freezer about twice a year. To clean the fan, switch the freezer off at the mains, unscrew the inlet grille and remove the dust carefully with the dusting attachment of a vacuum cleaner or a soft brush. Replace the grille and switch on again. Keep the grille round the condenser on a static plate model dust free too.

Help!

Nothing strikes panic into the freezer-owner's breast as quickly as a power cut, but panic is the one thing you musn't do when the dreaded event occurs. However much you may long for action, just sit tight, and resist the temptation to rush over and see what's happening to your lovingly frozen food. Provided your freezer has a fairly full load—and you haven't let any warm air in by peeping at the contents—food should stay frozen for at least 12 hours. Even with a lesser load you're safe for at least 6 hours.

Much the same rules apply if the freezer breaks down. This hardly ever happens, so check that wiring, plugs and fuses are in order before you go to the expense of a service call. If the check proves negative, phone the freezer manufacturer's local agent for service. You'll find the address and telephone number on the instruction leaflet or guarantee card, and you'll find the instruction leaflet or guarantee card taped to the side of the freezer—won't you? Not many manufacturers operate an all-night telephone answering system (this is something you should check on when you buy your freezer in the first place).

Emergency measures

If mending the freezer is going to prove a long job, the service depot should be able to lend a replacement freezer, or store your frozen food for you in one of their freezers. Alternatively, see if your friends have any spare room in their freezers, so that you can divide your frozen load between them. If none of these alternatives is open to you (and it's very unlikely that none of them would be, so don't let what's about to follow daunt you), ring your nearest supplier of dry ice. *His* number should be taped on the side of the freezer, too, of course, but if it isn't, your local freezer depot might be able to help with the information. Dry ice comes in large 25 lb. pieces, and as it's extremely dangerous to handle, keep the children well out of the way, and wear a very thick pair of gloves for protection. Chop it up into small pieces, place layers of cardboard over the frozen food for protection, and pack the dry ice tightly on top of the cardboard. This should keep the food safely frozen for at least another day.

Rescue operations

Even if food has started thawing out, it's quite safe to re-freeze it provided ice-crystals are still present. Once the ice-crystals have melted, however, the situation changes. Provided the food still feels firm and cold, it *is* possible to re-freeze fruit, bread and some baked goods, but the only way to retrieve still-cold raw meat, fish and poultry is to cook it promptly and thoroughly—and then re-freeze it. As for pre-cooked meat, fish and poultry, there's nothing for it but to heat it thoroughly—and eat as much as you possibly can. Unfortunately, any food that's thawed out completely enough to cease feeling cold will have to be thrown away. This applies whether it's raw or pre-cooked, though you can make an exception if you're absolutely sure it's only been in a thawed state as long as you would normally leave it to thaw before cooking or re-heating. Remember how the enzymes and micro-organisms probably work extra-fast to make up for lost time, and you'll find it much easier to be safe rather than sorry. Another exception may be fruit. If it looks and tastes all right, you'll still be able to use it in purées, sauces and jams.

Insurance

Throwing away food is always a painful business, but it's not quite so painful if you've had the sense to get your freezer's contents insured. Several companies handle this kind of insurance and you may even be able to get them included in your household insurance policy. Some freezer centres offer a special insurance to cover service and contents, provided of course you buy from them in the first place. If you're having trouble finding freezer insurance, consult a specialist like Ernest Linsdell Ltd., 419 Oxford Street, London, W1. Premiums cost about £2·75 for every £200 worth of food, and are well worth the money if you're a compulsive worrier. Always check exactly what a policy covers. Insurance brokers get plenty of claims—but not always because the freezer broke down or because the power supply was cut off. Often someone 'borrowed' the freezer socket for the electric mower and simply forgot to plug in again—and this is a disaster most insurance companies take care *not* to cover.

Index